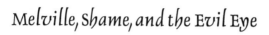
Melville, Shame, and the Evil Eye

SUNY Series in Psychoanalysis and Culture
Henry Sussman, Editor

Melville, Shame, and the Evil Eye

A PSYCHOANALYTIC

READING

Joseph Adamson

State University of
New York Press

Published by
State University of New York Press

© 1997   State University of New York

For information, address the State University of New York Press,
State University Plaza, Albany, NY 12246

Production by Bernadine Dawes • Marketing by Dana Yanulavich

Library of Congress Cataloging-in-Publication Data

Adamson, Joseph, 1950–
    Melville, shame, and the evil eye : a psychoanalytic reading /
Joseph Adamson.
        p.   cm. — (SUNY series in psychoanalysis and culture)
    Includes bibliographical references and index.
    ISBN 0-7914-3279-3 (HC : alk. paper). — ISBN 0-7914-3280-7 (PB :
alk. paper)
    1. Melville, Herman, 1819–1891—Knowledge—Psychology.
2. Psychoanalysis and literature—United States—History—19th
century. 3. Novelists, American—19th century—Psychology.
4. Melville, Herman, 1819–1891—Psychology. 5. Evil eye in
literature. 6. Shame in literature. I. Title. II. Series.
PS2388.P8A63   1997
813'.3—dc20   96-8837
                                                              CIP

1 2 3 4 5 6 7 8 9 10

To the memory of my father,
Robert Townsend Adamson
(1922–1995),
from whom I first heard of Herman Melville
and of "deep, earnest thinking"

CONTENTS

ACKNOWLEDGMENTS

I would like to thank a number of people for their encouragement and help. Philip Collington offered invaluable feedback in the early stages. Anna Sonser and Joe Sigman were kind enough to be my first readers, and to offer their critical perceptions. Jean Wilson, as always, provided indispensable support and impeccable advice.

Many thanks to Benjamin Kilborne for his enthusiasm and for his constructive suggestions. Henry Sussman was a warm and heartening voice at a critical point in the completion of this work, and I would like to express my appreciation here.

Finally, I would like to offer my deeply felt thanks to Léon Wurmser. His support has been crucial, and I greatly value his generosity of spirit.

Abbreviations used in the text for citation of works by Melville are as follows: *BB = Billy Budd; CM = The Confidence-Man; Corr. = Correspondence; IP = Israel Potter; MD = Moby-Dick; PT = Piazza Tales; P = Pierre; R = Redburn; WJ = White-Jacket.* The editions used are those cited in the Melville entry in the bibliography.

Citations of secondary works in the text and notes use the author-date system, which is keyed to the bibliography.

And Saul eyed David from that day on.
—1 Sam. 18:9

the arch interferer, the envious marplot of Eden.
—Melville, *Billy Budd*

Melville and Shame

Be sure of this, O young ambition, all mortal greatness is but disease.
—Melville, *Moby-Dick*

I

Over the last two decades in North America we have witnessed the emergence of two broadly related psychoanalytic currents that are of particular relevance to the study of literature: self-psychology, inspired by Heinz Kohut's analysis of narcissistic personality disorders; and what might be roughly called *shame psychology*, the variety of theories that focus on the importance of shame in psychological development. It is fair to say, given their exceptional explanatory power, that neither of these advancements has commanded the interest from literary critics and scholars that one might expect. Psychoanalytic models of a Lacanian and a poststructuralist provenance have been invaluable in stimulating a renewed activity in psychological approaches to literature. But they have also had the effect of discouraging any widespread curiosity about approaches that lie outside the routine of their particular theoretical framework. There have been, of course, significant exceptions (though their exceptional nature continues to prove the rule). Impressive books by Barbara Ann Schapiro (*The Romantic Mother*, 1983), J. Brooks Bouson (*The Empathic Reader*, 1989), Jeffrey Berman (*Narcissism and the Novel*, 1990), and Henry Sussman (*Psyche and Text*, 1993), as well as an important collection of essays edited by Lynne Layton and Schapiro (*Narcissism and the Text*, 1986), have shown the enormous value of Kohut's contribution to the psychoanalytic understanding of literature and culture. More recently, Eve Sedgwick and Adam Frank, with the publication of *Shame and its Sisters* (1995), have provoked interest among literary theorists in the role of affect and shame.

Sussman in particular has argued persuasively for a theoretical shift in the psychoanalytic models that we employ in the study of literature, recognizing that, in recent years, in "the literatures of psychoanalysis and psychology an attempt had become necessary to postulate and explore a model of subjectivity no longer within the confines of the Freudian model" (1993, x). The by now almost predictable emphasis on, as he puts it, "the schematic trajectories of the signifier as they illuminate the History of the post-Cartesian subject" (159) needs to be reconsidered in the light of new psychoanalytic discoveries. Gordon Hirsch, in an intriguing essay on shame in Jane Austen's *Pride and Prejudice*, has come to similar conclusions: "One reason for the importance of studies of shame in contemporary psychological research is the emphasis on observed, primary affect, and on a response to this affect which is also frequently evident on an emotional level, without an inordinate reliance on abstract psychological metatheory" (1992, 65). In general, it is fair to say that in Western culture the world of emotion or feeling has been dangerously neglected. It has been associated with the "irrational" side of human beings and has been denigrated as a negative or atavistic feature that impedes higher human development. Silvan Tomkins in particular has condemned this dismissive understanding of emotional life. His research on affect has demonstrated that the affective complexity of human beings is one of the most distinctive features of their success as a species. Since the perception of affect has been ignored and left undeveloped in favor of more formal languages of communication, one of the most important functions of literature has been to provide a privileged place of redress, a sphere of language where emotional life can be explored and refined in ways that are discouraged elsewhere. As Tomkins points out, "In poetry, drama and the novel, language is the primary vehicle for the expression, clarification and deepening of feelings, but this role has in part been made necessary by the reduction in visibility of affects, effected by language which embeds, distorts or is irrelevant to affects, and which thereby impoverishes the affective life of man" (1962, 219). In literature, the writer uses language to undo the concealment and distortion brought about by those many formal and abstract languages that tend to treat emotional life as insignificant and essentially without value.

Melville's work is a particularly fruitful place to explore this new emphasis in contemporary psychoanalysis. Doubtless, the affect that one is most likely to think of in relation to his work is anger. More specifically, it is what Kohut calls narcissistic rage, the anger that results from narcissistic injury, an emotional reaction that any student of shame would explain as a response to searing shame or humiliation. Kohut himself has cited *Moby-Dick*, along with Kleist's *Michael Kohlhaas*, as a supreme example of "interminable narcissistic rage" (1978, 617), of how "endless hate and lust for revenge—without regard even for one's own survival—can result from wounded self-esteem" (531).

The concepts of narcissistic injury and narcissistic rage involve, of course, an entire theory of the development of the self. Michael Franz Basch says Kohut "distilled three basic needs from early development: (1) to have one's competent performance validated and approved; (2) to be protected and supported at times of stress or tension" and "(3) to be acknowledged by one's kin as a fellow being" (1989, 14).[1] These needs are the basis of three forms of transference: the mirror transference, the idealizing transference, and the alter-ego transference. The first two would seem to have the most theoretical importance (the alter ego transference seems to be some kind of hybrid of the other two), and are correlated to what Kohut conceives of as a bipolar self consisting of the two poles of the *grandiose self* and the *idealized selfobject*. The former corresponds to the part of the self that grows and develops as the child's grandiosity (its imaginary feelings of power and of control over its environment) and exhibitionism (its pure pleasure in showing itself and in being seen and admired by others) are consistently confirmed by a responsive caregiver (i.e., the child feels it is responded to and properly seen and heard); the latter corresponds to the part of the self that develops through identification—usually of a visual and imitative nature—with an apparently all-powerful caregiver (i.e., the child is allowed to feel it is at one with the all-powerful other).

In the early stages of its development the child does not recognize clearly demarcated personal boundaries between itself and the caregiver, and thus Kohut coined the term *selfobject* to refer to the way that the child perceives significant others: the maternal object, for example, is perceived to some degree as a part of the self. Gross empathic failure by the so-called selfobject—a severe lack of proper cooperativeness and responsiveness, for whatever reason—makes the child feel as though it has lost control of a part of itself, and overwhelming feelings of betrayal, helplessness, and powerlessness pervade the self and cause intense humiliation and rage. The individual is thus unable to internalize structures provided by a healthy interaction with others and fails to develop a strong sense of self; consequently, it never entirely grows out of this imaginary perception of significant others as part of the self. In adult life the ego remains under the control of repressed components of an *archaic* self, and it finds itself at the mercy of archaic emotional reactions, not having outgrown what are essentially infantile relations with the world. The ego is either unduly subject to the claims of what Kohut calls the grandiose-exhibitionistic self, and repeatedly and obsessively seeks to be affirmed and admired by cooperative selfobjects, or it is controlled by the "unrequited longing to be strengthened and protected when necessary by an alliance with an admired, powerful figure" (Basch 1989, 15). These are the mirror and the idealizing transferences, respectively.

In the case of Melville we can see how severe disappointment in both the mirroring and idealized selfobject results in the insistence of both the grandiose and the idealizing poles. These two poles play a determining role in the depiction of personality in his work, and the forms of behavior associated with them—the tendencies to inappropriate grandiosity, exhibitionism, or excessive idealization that can be observed in so many of the characters in his novels—represent various manifestations of traumatic narcissistic injury.

One obvious manifestation in Melville's work of the pole of the grandiose self is Ahab's need to vindicate, in what is clearly a defensive reaction to acute feelings of shame, his sense of unconquerable power, the feeling that he is omnipotent and infallible; indeed, it is the need for vindication in this area that confers on him an aura of charisma and allows him to induce a state of fascination in the crew of the *Pequod*. Another manifestation, however different in kind—it has all the elements of a full-blown fantasy—is the successful exhibitionistic display of Billy Budd, who, without any special effort of his own, is lovingly mirrored by all around him. At the same time, Billy's docile dependency on Captain Vere throughout his trial and sentencing suggests—ironically enough, since it is the latter who condemns him to death—the infantile identification with an omnipotent protector figure, and is a perfect illustration of the idealizing transference. The basis of the idealizing pole of the personality is, as Basch describes it, the "contentment, safety, and reassurance conveyed to the infant and small child when he is tenderly but firmly enveloped by or carried in his parents' arms" (1989, 15). The action of being held and protected plays an important part in Melville's work, as in the portrayal of Ishmael awakening in the bridegroom clasp of the uninhibited Queequeg, a character depicted throughout the novel as a great deliverer who plucks the helpless from the jaws of death. Ishmael recalls his awestruck emotion later on as he watches his friend rescue a man from drowning, and remarks: "[F]rom that hour, I clove to Queequeg like a barnacle" (*MD*, 157). The relationship between Ishmael and Queequeg also partakes of what Kohut calls "the alter ego transference," a variant of the mirror transference that answers "the need to have one's humanness, one's kinship or sameness with others of the species, quietly acknowledged," to have one's "belonging to the group affirmed," to be "quietly sustained by another in whose presence one feels accepted" (Basch 1989, 15).

As the grandiose self provides the basis for healthy ambition and goals, so the idealized selfobject is the basis of internalized ideals and values in later life. Ideals and ambition are, as we shall see in the course of this study, the two focal points that help to align Melville's characters on a psychological plane, although any literary character, like any personality, is defined to some extent by both poles. Captain Vere, for example, is a character whose personality seems largely based on a transmuting internalization of idealized objects into the form of values and ideals; conversely, as the narrator comments concerning him at the end of the story: "The spirit that 'spite its philosophic austerity may yet have indulged in the most secret of all passions, ambition, never attained to the fulness of fame" (129). Like envy—"did ever anybody seriously confess to envy?" (77)—ambition is a secret passion, and like envy it is intimately related to narcissism, shame, and the claims of the grandiose self.

These two poles, of the grandiose self and the idealized selfobject, seem to have played a decisive role in Melville's vocation as a writer. If the grandiose-exhibitionistic pole provides the ambition and wish for successful display necessary to the creative writer, it is the idealizing pole that is able to channel that ambition into the creative process. Kohut claims that idealization, as "one of the two main roads of the development of narcissism," is "the main source of libidinal fuel for some of the socioculturally important activities which are subsumed under the term creativity" (1971, 40). In the same way, Léon Wurmser sees idealization and creativity as functioning "very prominently as a powerful counterpoise to, and 'healing' of, the core of unlovability" or "primary woundedness" (1981, 295–96). Indeed, if there is a precedent for the following study in literary criticism, at least in terms of its overall thesis, it would be something like Christopher Ricks's *Keats and Embarrassment*. Ricks views embarrassment—a potentially crippling or paralyzing emotional reaction—not as something simply negative, but as an integral part of Keats's creativity, as something the English poet frankly exploited in his art and poetry and was thus able to transform and transcend (at least in his work). I believe that something similar can be argued regarding the sources of Melville's creative power.

Kohut's conception of a bipolar self also helps to illuminate three other important aspects of Melville's work and life.

First of all, the central roles of mirroring and idealized selfobjects can be linked to the theme of archaic (often visual) merger in Melville. If the wish to be recognized and admired involves a sense of at-oneness with the other that stems from being seen and heard, the wish to be supported by an omnipotent protector figure often involves union through an intense visualization of the object. Kohut's idea of archaic merger with selfobjects—the feeling of being at one with the other—helps to explain the prevalent imagery of fusion or merger in Melville's work, which can be understood as an expression of the longing to return to an archaic homeostatic state. This fascinatory longing for narcissistic merger may take the form of a kind of metaphysical idealism, or pantheism, as depicted in the chapter in *Moby-Dick* entitled "The Mast-Head." But it is also often expressed as an archaic desire to fuse with another person or persons. As Sharon Cameron puts it: "The fantasy in *Moby-Dick* is that all human identities might be joined by Siamese ligature, following which all men, fused, will be squeezed into 'each other'" (1991, 2). This "desperate longing for binding ties and fusion, or a mirror relationship" (Wurmser 1981, 20) is given what is perhaps its most plaintive expression in the poem "After the Pleasure Party," where it is conceived of as a yearned-for union with one's other half: "And such the dicing of blind fate / Few matching halves here meet and mate."

Secondly, related to this intense wish for merger, and to what Kohut sees as the archaic demands of the grandiose self, is the theme of charisma. In his essay "Creativeness, Charisma, Group Psychology," Kohut explains the charismatic and messianic personality structures as expressions of the grandiose-exhibitionistic self on the one hand (the charismatic figure evokes a sense of unconquerable power that strikes a deep chord in the group) and the idealizing pole of the self on the other (the messianic figure inspires others through a fervent attachment to transcendent ideals and values). In some sense, this is the distinction between Ahab and Pierre: Ahab is driven by the all-consuming need to overpower and defeat his enemy no matter what the cost, while Pierre, like Kleist's Michael Kohlhaas, is motivated by an intense identification of his personal integrity with unattainable ideals; the one redresses a slight to the self, the other defends the right. It is important to remember, however, that in Pierre's case (as in Kohlhaas's) the injustice in question also involves a series of outrageous humiliations, and that, even in upholding a principle, he reacts throughout like someone in a state of interminable narcissistic rage.

Thirdly, linked to the theme of charisma in Melville is what Kohut calls the transference of creativity. In the same essay, Kohut examines how an individual engaged in an intense creative task, the pursuit of which requires a temporary withdrawal of libidinal energy from the self, must look outside himself for someone to serve selfobject functions, either the idealizing ones of carrying or protecting, or those validating and approving ones of mirroring and admiring. Kohut's central example is the relationship between Freud and Fliess. An equally dramatic instance of this phenomenon, and one that we will have occasion to explore in some detail, is the much-discussed relationship between Melville and Hawthorne.

II

The gradual turning, since Freud, of psychoanalytic attention to the neglected area of the role of the emotions or of affect in psychic development does not necessarily entail a wholesale rejection of Freud's basic discoveries and insights. But it certainly requires a thoroughgoing reevaluation of a theory that placed too much importance on the drives at the cost of neglecting the vital part played by the emotions. According to Freud, fear or anxiety, for example, is to be interpreted in light of a primarily sexual conflict (the fear of castration, for example, in light of forbidden libidinal desires or wishes). Similarly, interest, curiosity, and excitement, no matter what the apparent object, would be seen as having a sexual origin. In the famous "Counterpane" chapter in *Moby-Dick*, Ishmael is punished by his stepmother for the "caper" of trying to climb up the chimney. Traditionally minded Freudian critics have interpreted this episode as the expression of an oedipal sexual wish and the ensuing penalty of isolation as a displaced form of castration, the punishment being imposed by a maternal figure allied with the paternal law.[2] It is a matter of observation, however, that the excited exploratory impulse of the curious child is as natural an impulse as sexual curiosity or wishes, and is often just as subject to prohibition and shaming. The severe restriction and inhibition of what Wurmser calls *theatophilic* wishes—active curiosity, the desire to see and to explore the world—can be as psychically damaging as any undue repression associated with sexual wishes. Destructive feelings of shame are often induced by—and induce—such inhibition, and Ishmael's traumatic reaction to the confinement and isolation that is imposed on him by his stepmother ("Nay, to this very hour, I often puzzle myself with it" [*MD*, 26]) suggests a particularly destructive environment in this regard.

Another example, almost a commonplace now of Melville criticism, is the interpretation of the passage in *Billy Budd* in which Claggart, offended when Billy accidentally spills his soup as he is walking past, quickly suppresses his angry retort ("he was about to ejaculate something hasty at the sailor") on recognizing the young sailor. The image of "greasy liquid" and the word "ejaculate" are typically seen as a displaced symbolism that points to Claggart's repressed homosexual desire for Billy. While the sexual element here is doubtless important, what is perhaps more decisive is the nature of the affect involved: in this case, Claggart's checking of his anger or rage, which consequently seeks an indirect and vindictive channel of expression. The devious concealment of shame-anger at an envied object who has triggered deep-seated feelings of inferiority, shame, and resentment is perhaps just as significant as the fact that this aggressiveness and wish to humiliate on Claggart's part is also highly sexualized.

The most cogent critique of the Freudian model in terms of its neglect of the role of emotion has been offered by Silvan Tomkins in the opening parts of his monumental four-part study of affect, *Affect, Imagery, Consciousness*, in which he examines in great detail the differences between, and the relationships among, drives and affects.[3] For Tomkins, affects, like drives, are part of the innate biological apparatus of human beings and have served an essential function in the evolution of the human species. A human being is unique in that he or she is *affectively* equipped, as he puts it in the simplest terms, "to want to remain alive and to resist death, to want to experience novelty and to resist boredom, to want to communicate, to be close to and in contact with others of his species, to experience sexual excitement and to resist the experience of head and face lowered in shame" (1962, 170). Part of the problem with Freud's model was that, in a historical period in which both instinctual and affective life were subject, at least among a certain social class, to a high degree of denial and repression, the complex emotional coloring of sexual experience made Freud lose sight of the significance of affective life and led him to confuse the role of drives—hunger, thirst, elimination, sex, pain, breathing—with the very distinct role of affects:

> Thus, in the concept of orality, the hunger drive mechanism was confused with the dependency-communion complex, which from the beginning is more general than the need for food and the situation of being fed. In the concept of anality, the elimination drive mechanism has been confused with the contempt-shame humiliation complex, which not only is more general than the need to eliminate but also has earlier environmental roots than the toilet training situation. In the concept of the Oedipus complex, the sex drive mechanism, admittedly more plastic than a drive such as the need for air, was confused with the family romance, which involves the far more general wishes to *be* both parents and to *possess* both parents. (Tomkins 1962, 109)

Tomkins isolates nine basic affects. The positive ones are interest-excitement and enjoyment-joy. (The hyphenation of the terms is meant to show the range of affect, from mild to extreme.) The negative affects, greater in number, serve to disrupt states of positive affect and to impel the organism to respond in defensive or aggressive ways: fear-terror, distress-anguish, anger-rage, shame-humiliation, dissmell, and disgust. There is, finally, the neutral, so-called resetting affect of surprise-startle. Tomkins explores the nature of these affects in minute detail, and shows how what we call emotions are, in fact, complex amalgams of affects, which are combined in different ways according to the strategies adopted by the individual. For example, what some shame analysts call humiliated fury or shame-anger, or what Kohut calls narcissistic rage, Tomkins would understand as a shame affect that reaches such a painful point of overload that it triggers anger, an affect distinct from but often accompanying shame. The particular power of shame to combine with other affects—anguish, contempt, rage, fear—is one of the things that make it such a crucial element in the emotional life of human beings.

Tomkins postulates that "The innate activator of shame is the incomplete reduction of interest or joy. Hence any barrier to further exploration which partially reduces interest or the smile of enjoyment will activate the lowering of the head and eyes in shame and reduce further exploration or self-exposure powered by enjoyment or joy" (1963, 123). As Charles Darwin, Tomkins's precursor in the scientific exploration of the emotions, describes the same reaction: "Under a keen sense of shame there is a strong desire for concealment. We turn away the whole body, more especially the face, which we endeavour in some manner to hide. An ashamed person can hardly endure to meet the gaze of those present, so that he almost invariably casts down his eyes or looks askant" (1901, 340). We are all familiar with the experience of mistaking from a distance a stranger for a close acquaintance, and after having hailed the person with signs of affection and mutuality, realizing one's error; embarrassment ensues—one looks away, one feels "stupid," confused, and disoriented—and any further interaction is immediately broken off. As Donald Nathanson points out, the reaction is not something that we can consciously control: "As soon as we have seen the face of the other person our own head droops, our eyes are cast down, and, blushing, we become briefly incapable of speech" (1992, 135). Shame affect has thus performed its function: it has reduced interest in the object by limiting positive affect and temporarily discouraged any further attempts at communion. Tomkins suggests that the power of shame has something to do with human physical survival, and one can think of any number of situations where the state of being unduly fascinated in an object would be life-threatening. "Shame affect," as Nathanson summarizes Tomkins's findings, "is a highly painful mechanism that operates to pull the organism away from whatever might interest it or make it content," and thus it is "painful in direct proportion to the degree of positive affect it limits" (138).

It is important to note that for Tomkins shame affect does not require the presence of another person to be activated, though it is an affect that is absolutely crucial in its social manifestations and in the development of a sense of self and of self-image. The reduction of positive affect is incomplete, Tomkins emphasizes, in the sense that shame does not force the subject to utterly abandon the goal of regaining the prior state of positive feeling once shame has dissipated. Thus, shame is an affect or emotion that is particularly instrumental as a protective mechanism regulating human beings in their eagerness for communal life, in their expressiveness, in perception, and in interaction with others and with their environment. Human beings are particularly social and curious creatures, and shame functions as a negative affect that serves to reduce the positive affects of interest and enjoyment that govern curiosity and communality, whenever these activities are perceived as frustrated, undesirable, or dangerous in some way.

An immediate example in *Moby-Dick* of Melville's sensitivity to the various manifestations of shame may serve to illustrate some of the issues just raised. In the opening passages of the novel there is a humorous description of Ishmael, seated at breakfast with a group of whalers, confronting a rather heavy atmosphere of bashfulness, timidity, and embarrassment:

> I was preparing to hear some good stories about whaling; to my no small surprise, nearly every man maintained a profound silence. And not only that, but they looked embarrassed. Yes, here were a set of sea-dogs, many of whom without the slightest bashfulness had boarded great whales on the high seas—entire strangers to them—and duelled them dead without winking; and yet, here they sat at a social breakfast table—all of the same calling, all of kindred tastes—looking round as sheepishly at each other as though they had never been out of sight of some sheepfold among the Green Mountains. A curious sight; these bashful bears, these timid warrior whalemen! (30)

These shame variants—bashfulness, shyness, embarrassment—have a bearing on the important theme of sociability in Melville's work. Later in the novel, for example, in commenting on the significance of the custom of sociable "Gams" or "gamming"—the communing of vessels on the high seas—the narrator opines that, on the analogy of two strangers naturally saluting one another if "casually encountering each other" in the "inhospitable wilds," it is all the "more natural that upon the illimitable Pine Barrens and Salisbury Plains of the sea, two whaling vessels descrying each other at the ends of the earth . . . should not only interchange hails, but come into still closer, more friendly and sociable contact" (238–39). The motif of painful shyness or reserve then appears: when English and American whalers do exchange salutations and meet, the narrator notes, "there is too apt to be a sort of shyness between them; for your Englishman is rather reserved, and your Yankee, he does not fancy that sort of thing in anybody but himself" (239).

The description of the hulking whalers whom Ishmael joins for breakfast—"all of the same calling, all of kindred tastes—looking round as sheepishly at each other as though they had never been out of sight of some sheepfold"—is a perfect depiction of the shame naturally felt in the presence of strangers. Shame involves both the fear of rejection and the wish to affiliate, illustrating Tomkins's view that it is triggered by the incomplete reduction of positive affect (interest-excitement or enjoyment-joy, to use his terminology). The feeling of shame, as Tomkins puts it, is a case of "I want to, but," and, unless it is of a particularly searing quality, it leaves the door open for a resumption of communion with the object. These "warrior whalemen," as Melville's narrator ironically observes, feel no timidity whatsoever in the presence of the whales they hunt; doubtless there is fear, but no shame. This is because there is no possibility of an interpersonal bridge, of being affiliated or in communion; one cannot, of course, feel shame in the presence of another species. Without this possibility there can be no shame, for to feel shame in the presence of another implies that a potential attachment is involved. The same logic can be found in Starbuck's insistence, in "The Quarter-Deck" chapter, that Ahab should not take vengeance on a "dumb brute," should not be "enraged with a dumb thing" (163–64). To feel embarrassed in front of a whale is as irrational as feeling that to be defeated by one is a horrible humiliation. As Nathanson puts it: "If I have been defeated by another person, I have been ranked among humans and therefore experience shame; if I am ruined by an earthquake, there is no implication that I am better or worse than any other human, consequently there is no shame (1987a, 194).

The central role that Freud ascribed to the guilt and fear of punishment associated with drive conflicts led him to ignore the importance and complexity of emotional life; instead, he linked shame almost exclusively to matters of sexual knowledge and exposure. He regarded shame as an affective mechanism inhibiting inappropriate scopophilic and exhibitionistic drives or wishes—wishes to see and to know, to show and display oneself, in a sexually intrusive manner.[4] Again, Freud tended to narrow the field of explanation to the area of drives—oral, anal, genital—whereas, along with Tomkins and Nathanson, Wurmser has come to understand shame as closely linked to wishes to see or to show (oneself) that are not sexually specific, though they may certainly become so in the course of development. Wurmser sees these wishes as innate and having to do with the desire to explore the surrounding world. Shame is a necessary check on such wishes, but in traumatic situations—in which shame becomes a chronic experience for the infant—it has a toxic effect on the development of healthy desires to know and discover the world and commune with others, and on the development of a confident and trusting ego or "self." What Wurmser describes as *theatophilic* and *delophilic* wishes and fears, Tomkins describes in terms of modes of interaction based on the two positive affects—excitement-interest and enjoyment-joy—and shows the way this interaction may be seriously impeded by negative affect. But the conclusions drawn by these two seminal thinkers, however much their terminology may differ, affirm essentially the same thing: that high levels of negative affect are poisonous in their influence on the human being's ability to engage fully in perceptual and expressive interaction with the human and physical environment, and thus may lead to extremely destructive psychological conflicts. "The modes of attentive, curious grasping and of expressing oneself in nonverbal as well as verbal communication are the arena where in love and hatred, in mastery and defeat our self is forged and moulded. If this interchange is blocked and warped, the core of the self-concept is severely disturbed and becomes permanently twisted and deformed" (Wurmser 1987, 83).

Wurmser has explored in great depth the conflicts in which shame plays a predominant part and in which perception and expression become too exclusively bound up with the management of negative affect, to the point where looking and showing are experienced almost exclusively as expressions of wishes for union, power, and destruction. As Wurmser defines shame, it is "a basic protection mechanism in the areas of perception and expression, a protection in the sense of preventing overstimulation in these two areas, as well as 'drive restraint' in the form of preventing dangerous impulses of curiosity and self-exposure" (80–81). These impulses or "drives" are: "(1) the urges for active, magical exhibition—the wishes to fascinate; 2) their reverse: the fear to be passively exposed and stared at; 3) the urges for active curiosity; and 4) their reverse: the fear of being fascinated and overwhelmed by the spectacles offered by others" (81). The first two drives, in other words, are, very roughly, exhibitionistic; the last two, voyeuristic, if you like, or scopophilic. This very adaptable scheme is also consistent with Kohut's essential insights. Wurmser himself has correlated what he calls the delophilic (exhibitionistic) drive to the pole of the grandiose-exhibitionistic self and the theatophilic (scopophilic) drive to the pole of the idealized selfobject. This expressive-perceptual framework, together with the Kohutian hypothesis of a bipolar self, is thus an especially illuminating instrument of analysis when applied to the theme of fascination, passive and active, a theme that is intimately linked to the role of the "evil eye" in Melville's work.

It is clear that, though Kohut himself uses the word sparingly, the most significant element in the profile of the narcissistically damaged personality is the experience of shame. Narcissistic injury—the root cause of narcissistic personality disorder—is more or less synonymous with mortification or humiliation. As Howard Bacal points out,

> [W]hile Kohut had indicated that narcissistic rage is associated with a sense of shame (Kohut 1977: 77), Morrison (1989) underscores shame as the central affect associated with "narcissistic rage." He regards shame, along with its more extreme counterpart, humilia- tion, as the quintessential reaction to the sense of helplessness in the face of the experience of selfobject failure. However, since these affects are so intolerable, they are quickly erased from conscious- ness and, at the same time, trigger the expression of narcissistic rage at the offending object. (1990, 236)

What Kohut calls empathic failure on the part of the selfobject refers, quite simply, then, to the inducing of a feeling of shame—a humiliating or mor- tifying feeling of powerlessness and helplessness—in the emerging self. For example, an inconsistent display of interest by the parent, a pattern of ex- cessive attention followed by prolonged apparent indifference, brings about a feeling of shame in the child, as does, of course, in a much less subtle way, continual subjection to explicit forms of abuse and humiliation (verbal, physical, sexual). Shame draws attention to the self in a particularly painful manner, and as a chronic affective experience makes the subject feel some- how defective or flawed; it consequently has a profound impact on self- estimation and self-image.

Selfobject failure, or gross empathic failure, which triggers shame in the child, also affects one's trust in the world. It is interesting to compare Kohut's understanding of such empathic failure and its psychological con- sequences with Helen Merrell Lynd's description of the effects of shame:

> Sudden experience of a violation of expectation, of incongru- ity between expectation and outcome, results in a shattering of

trust in oneself, even in one's body and skill and identity, and in the trusted boundaries or framework of the society and the world one has known. As trust in oneself and in the outer world develop together, so doubt of oneself and of the world are also intermeshed.

The rejected gift, the joke or the phrase that does not come off, the misunderstood gesture, the falling short of our own ideals, the expectation of response violated—such experiences mean that we have trusted ourselves to a situation that is not there. We have relied on the assumption of one perspective or *Gestalt* and found a totally different one. (1958, 46)

Ultimately, this "shattering of trust" can lead to an all-pervasive feeling of self-estrangement and meaninglessness, both of oneself and of one's environment. This is an experience that a passage from Melville's *Pierre* depicts in a particularly evocative way. The protagonist's search for the soul's ultimate meaning is expressed through the metaphor of an archaeological dig:

Ten million things were as yet uncovered to Pierre. The old mummy lies buried in cloth on cloth; it takes time to unwrap this Egyptian king. Yet now, forsooth, because Pierre began to see through the first superficiality of the world, he fondly weens he has come to the unlayered substance. But, far as any geologist has yet gone into the world, it is found to consist of nothing but surface stratified on surface. To its axis, the world being nothing but superinduced superficies. By vast pains we mine into the pyramid; by horrible gropings we come to the central room; with joy we espy the sarcophagus; but we lift the lid—and no body is there!—appallingly vacant as vast is the soul of a man! (*P*, 284–85)

This idea that there is nothing but an appalling vacancy at the heart of life is a reflection of the devastating effects of a loss of trust in the world, and points to the paralyzing sense of estrangement and alienation that is one of the legacies of traumatic shame.

In Lynd's insightful description of the way in which shame destroys self-trust and trust in the world lies, one could say without exaggeration, all of self-psychology. Thus it is no surprise that Kohutians such as Andrew

Morrison should show a special interest in shame, or that psychoanalysts such as Wurmser should indicate a deep respect for the work of Kohut. Objective self-awareness—that is, the very experience of something we can call a self—would, indeed, seem to be intimately connected to shame. This can be seen particularly well in the case of embarrassment. Brought on by an unwished-for attention to the self, it has the effect of making one confused, incoherent, and red in the face, and thus succeeds only in drawing further attention to the self and causing more embarrassment. This uncontrollable spiral effect clearly illustrates the important link between shame and objective self-awareness, and is of particular relevance to the understanding of certain aspects of personality that appear in Melville's work. The adolescent Redburn, for example, suffers from an acute form of self-consciousness that expresses itself, among other things, in a proneness to blushing. Billy Budd's "emotional difficulty of utterance" (*BB*, 106) would seem to be the symptom of an analogous disorder. There was, the narrator observes of Billy at the beginning of the story, "just one thing amiss in him. No visible blemish indeed . . . but an occasional liability to a vocal defect. . . . under sudden provocation of strong heart-feeling his voice, otherwise singularly musical, as if expressive of the harmony within, was apt to develop an organic hesitancy, in fact more or less of a stutter or even worse" (53). The emphasis on something "amiss," a "blemish," a "defect," suggests the feelings of embarrassed self-consciousness and shameful exposure that victimize the one who stutters, stuttering itself being brought on by intense shame affect or, as the narrator puts it, "strong heart-feeling."

The pivotal role of shame in the development of human personality has been examined in a fascinating and extremely diversified body of research. In developing my approach to the specific questions posed by Melville's works I have tried to take full advantage of the great variety of perspectives offered in studies by Helen Merrell Lynd, Silvan Tomkins, Helen Block Lewis, Donald Nathanson, Carl Schneider, Leon Wurmser, and others. The sophistication of the available literature has allowed me to explore in great detail the extent to which Melville's writings are attuned to the various modes of shame (such as feelings of embarrassment, humiliation, mortification, disgrace, or dishonor) and the reactions to shame (narcissism, excessive idealization, destructive feelings of rage, resentment, and envy, turning the tables, scorn, contempt, and defiance). The experience of searing shame or humiliation may cause the developing self to respond in a variety of ways, depending on the circumstances. One may isolate oneself from others, fall into a state of depression, suppress and build up violent feelings of shame until they express themselves in envy, hatred, and resentment, avoid feelings of shame through an overvaluation of oneself or of others, or find ways of overcoming such feelings of shame. This might be through the illusion of pride, as Nathanson calls it—that is, excelling or outshining others in a social context—or (since not all responses need be negative and destructive) through creative activities and imaginative self-expression. Nathanson has proposed a compass of shame, which consists of four cardinal points representing different possible responses to shame affect. It is a dramatic indication of the importance of understanding the role of shame in Melville's work that all four cardinal points—withdrawal, avoidance, attack self, and attack other—are amply and variously represented in his writings.

It is worth nothing here that, if the contemporary psychoanalytic interest in shame has been delayed in the impact it has had on literary criticism, the same, fortunately, need not be said for many of the shame theorists mentioned in this study, attuned as they are in the most sophisticated way to the world of literature and culture and to the insight it has to offer about shame and its effects on inner life. In particular, Lynd, Tomkins, Kohut, and Wurmser have shown a keen and profound interest in the interpenetration of psychoanalytic theory and literature. Wurmser's own penetrating discussion of writers such Dickens, Ibsen, Kafka, Nietzsche, Lagerkvist, and others is a model of what a criticism richly informed by a psychoanalytic understanding of the role of shame has to offer. In terms of literary form, Kohut and Wurmser have demonstrated a deep interest in tragedy and the tragic character, and have shown how tragic works are capable of shedding light on conflicts rooted in narcissism, shame, and the defenses against shame.[5] The corollary, perhaps of more interest to the literary critic, is just as true: the psychoanalytic understanding of these conflicts can help us to a fuller understanding of the deeper import of tragedy as a literary form. This is of particular relevance to the study of Melville's work, which is so deeply informed by tragic conflicts, an aspect that, in *Moby-Dick* in particular, is consistently played off against the comic perspective provided by Ishmael. The comic view, in turn, can be clarified by the relationship between shame and laughter as it has been explored by Nathanson and others.[6]

III

Before we look at aspects of Melville's life and personality that are particularly illuminated by an understanding of the psychodynamics of shame, it might be useful to offer a brief biographical sketch of his career as a writer.

Melville was born in 1819, the third child of Allan and Maria (née Gansevoort) Melvill (the *e* was added after his father's death). At the age of twelve, his life changed dramatically upon the sudden death of his father, whose business and reputation were left in ruins. Given the family's financial straits, Herman was forced to try out various occupations, but was unable to find permanent employment. At the age of nineteen, he voyaged to Liverpool as a sailor on a merchant ship, an adventure described in detail in the novel *Redburn*. Back home, it was not long before he was at loose ends again. He set out on a voyage along the Erie Canal with a friend, and then drifted down the Mississippi on the riverboats. At the age of twenty-one, with little to look forward to at home, he joined the crew of a whaling vessel that was on its way around the world. He jumped ship at the Marquesas Islands, where he spent a month-long sojourn among the "cannibals." He then joined the crew of another vessel and ended up leading a mutiny against an apparently high-handed captain. Arrested, he was for a brief time confined on Tahiti. Out of these adventures came Melville's first two books, *Typee* and *Omoo*. He arrived in the Hawaiian islands in 1843. After several months of vagabonding, he signed on the frigate the *United States* in August and made his way back home, a fourteen-month voyage.

When he returned home, after almost three years abroad, he was twenty-four years old, with a good deal of life experience under his belt but no great prospects. At the suggestion that he publish an account of his adventures, he wrote his first book, *Typee*, a fictionalized account of his stay on the Marquesas islands. The novel was published in 1846, and enjoyed remarkable success, giving Melville a celebrity of sorts. Four more books followed before *Moby-Dick*. *Omoo* was a continuation of the adventures recounted in *Typee*, and was also relatively successful. But his next book, *Mardi*, a highly ambitious work of great literary complexity and originality, was not well received. He was now married—his wife Elizabeth was the daughter of Lemuel Shaw, chief justice of the Supreme Court of Massachusetts and an old friend of his father—and with a growing family to support he felt the urgency of establishing himself once and for all as a professional writer. Feeling personally injured and somewhat resentful at the failure of *Mardi*, he wrote very quickly two books designed more deliberately for public consumption. In 1849 *Redburn* and *White-Jacket* appeared, the one a fictionalized account of his trip to Liverpool and the other one an account of his experience aboard the ship the *United States*—"The World in a Man-of-War," as it is subtitled.

In the summer of 1850, Melville met Hawthorne in the Berkshires in Massachusetts, where both men had established their residence for a time. Hawthorne, who was fifteen years older than Melville, had just gained a name as the author of *The Scarlet Letter*. The two quickly became friends and enjoyed, for a brief period, a congenial and even intense relationship based, among other things, on their common creative interests. It was during this period that Melville, at the height of his creativity, wrote *Moby-Dick* (1851) and *Pierre* (1852). The response to both books was deeply disappointing. *Moby-Dick*, though met with praise, sold very few copies and attracted a number of extremely ungenerous and contemptuous reviews, including a particularly wounding one by Evert Duyckinck, an ostensible friend of Melville's and the publisher of the influential literary magazine *The Literary World*. *Pierre*, vilified by the critics, fared even worse. This was beginning of the end for Melville as a professional writer. He continued to write, but with no commercial or even critical success, and eventually ended up earning his living as a customs inspector in the Port of New York.

The last half of Melville's life was marred by a growing and debilitating sense of failure and, it seems, severe bouts of depression and anger. Melville seems to have had an extremely unhappy family life, deeply troubled and weighed down as it was by his dark moods and his erratic and conflicted state of mind. He seems to have inflicted abuse on his children and wife, and both his sons were to die prematurely, one a suicide. His writing took on an extremely compulsive quality, and he imposed on his wife and his relatives to sustain him in his creative endeavors. In the decades that followed *Moby-Dick* and *Pierre*, in spite of his lack of popular success as a writer, he was, nonetheless, able to produce a substantial body of work of great artistic merit: several stories (two of which, "Benito Cereno" and "Bartleby, the Scrivener," are of particular value), *Israel Potter*, *The Confidence-Man*, an important collection of poems, and *Clarel*, an extremely ambitious, full-length verse epic. At the end of his life he wrote *Billy Budd;* though it was not discovered for decades after his death and remained unpublished until

1924, it is now recognized as one of his finest achievements. Melville died in 1891.

Not only Melville's work but what we know of his life points, at every turn, to the significance of the experience of shame. The Indo-European origins of the word *shame* have to do with hiding and covering; the Germanic root *skam/skem*, as Wurmser notes, can be "traced back to the Indo-European root *kam/kem*: 'to cover, to veil, to hide'" (1981, 29). In their fascinating study *Herman Melville's Malcolm Letter*, Hennig Cohen and Donald Yannella have explored the complex shame-driven strategies of conceal- ment and covering up that played such an important part in the Melvill- Gansevoort family. An exaggerated sense of family honor, the source of a good deal of mythmaking and fictionalizing, and an obsession with public reputation made the threat of shame and disgrace particularly acute. Family secrets played an important part, and collusion in covering them up seems even to have included not only Melville's family and descendants but crit- ics and biographers. Allan Melvill's fathering of a child out of wedlock (he was only fourteen at the time) was covered up by his family and remained hidden for years, and the same is probably true, as Elizabeth Renker has carefully detailed, of Herman's emotional and physical abuse of his wife.[7] The former embarrassing little secret, of course, makes its way into *Pierre* in association with a father whose disturbing last days recall the unpleasant and awkward circumstances surrounding Allan Melvill's death. Later, in fear again of public exposure, the Melville family covered up through silence and euphemism the circumstances and truth of Malcolm's mysterious death by his own hand. "When there was danger that the family name might be sullied, then the family would close ranks and pretend that nothing un- seemly had occurred" (Cohen and Yannella 1992, 56). This reflex was typi- cal and characterized the way other "painful and some disgraceful episodes in the family story were treated" (69). In *Pierre* the theme of a destructive family policy of secrecy and concealment, denial and covering up, is promi- nent. Shame-driven secrecy and hiding are often associated with cryptic pyramid-like structures in Melville, as, for example, in the comic story "I and My Chimney." "Infinite sad mischief," the narrator opines about his wife's plans to break into the chimney wall in search of a rumored "secret closet," "has resulted from the profane bursting open of secret recesses" (*PT*,

376). Cohen and Yannella quite appropriately cite the following passage from *Billy Budd* as an analogy to the way the public relations were handled in the Melville family polity:

> Like so many other events in every age befalling states everywhere, including America, the Great Mutiny was of such character that national pride along with view of policy would fain shade it off into the historical background. Such events cannot be ignored, but there is a considerate way of historically treating them. If a well-constituted individual refrains from blazoning aught amiss or calamitous in his family, a nation in the like circumstance may without reproach be equally discreet. (1992, 55)

The "private Melville," to use Philip Young's phrase, was someone whose personal destiny remained tied in so many ways to a shame-bound family. The process of such a family, as Marilyn J. Mason describes it, "is severely galvanized against honest human disclosures. Family members obey these rules unconsciously and learn not to ask, not to comment. In this way, information that is 'owed' to the family becomes a shameful secret. . . . These rules organize a family's dynamics" (1993, 37–38).

The most traumatic *public* event in Melville's young life was the death of his father in 1830 when Herman was twelve, an event whose significance has by now become an autobiographical commonplace in Melville studies. As Richard Chase observed over forty years ago: "To anyone studying Melville's work as a meaningful totality, the death of Melville's father will gradually appear to be the event with which one must begin" (1949, 2). The point is debatable perhaps, given the complex nature of Melville's family environment which more recently acquired documents have done much to clarify; however, the repercussions of his father's death are undeniable. Newton Arwin describes the trauma in the following way: "In the midst of a general insecurity, the most vital embodiment of security, the security of fatherhood, was forcibly wrested from him, and the frightening sense of abandonment, the reproachful sense of desertion, must equally have been intense and overwhelming" (1957, 23). Indeed, the circumstances of Allan Melvill's death would have represented a particularly crushing and shameful defeat, not just for the deceased, but for his family. Not only did he die a bankrupt, thus leaving his family in an awkward and anxious situation of helpless dependency on charity, but he lingered for some days in a state of mental derangement, a haunting event that is alluded to more than once in Melville's works. Allen Melvill's son may well have read with a particularly painful understanding the confession by Thomas Browne, an author from whom he absorbed so much:

> I am naturally bashful, nor hath conversation, age, or travell, beene able to effront, or enharden me, yet I have one part of modesty, which I have seldome discovered in another, that is (to speake truly) I am not so much afraid of death, as ashamed thereof; tis the very disgrace and ignominy of our natures, that in a moment can so disfigure us that our nearest friends, wife and children stand afraid and start at us. (1977, 111)

This passage from *Religio Medici* is quoted by Schneider in his study of shame to illustrate "two elements in which shame is consistently present—the sense of stigma, blemish, and defilement, and the sense of loss of control" (1977, 81–82).

To make a bad situation worse, especially for a man who had such an exceptional reputation for probity, Allan Melvill's financial collapse was further tainted by the suggestion of dishonorable business practices.[8] In 1827, after entering into an illegal secret partnership in order to secure a loan, and unable to pay off his debts, he begged his brother-in-law, Peter Gansevoort, to help him financially. He expressed fear that the project would "explode to my utter disgrace" and that "My honour, dearer than life itself, [would] be forfeited" (quoted in Rogin 1983, 251). The disgraceful circumstances surrounding his death, combined with his delirious mental state at the time, must have been traumatic enough to leave the family in a conflictual state of mourning, as Neal Tolchin has cogently argued.[9] I would like to argue, however, that this conflicted mourning is itself a symptom of a more deep-rooted problem that is better approached in terms of traumatic narcissistic injury and shame. This would have been all the more the case given the particular narcissistic sensitivity of the family to any blemish to the family name and reputation.

Herman must have suffered greatly from the failure by his family to mark and confirm, in any honest or wholehearted way, the meaning of his father's life. Such a failure, according to Schneider, "is in some degree to diminish that life and its humanity. Thus, we can perceive the importance of appropriate funeral ritual and memorialization, and grasp the shame of a death not appropriately honored" (1977, 82). Moreover, the inherent threat in shame of abandonment would have been amplified by Maria Melville's feeling that she and her children had been deserted in their destitution and disgrace by friends and family. She complained of her family's cruel desertion by Allan Melvill's family and, in the same way, "reproached her brothers for leaving her family in poverty. She begged them for the meagre sums necessary to pay her rent, her servant, and to save her furniture from a debtor's sale. She accused Peter of having lost his feeling for her" (Rogin 1983, 31). The shame implicitly felt by the family was, in fact, commemorated by a single letter: an *e* was subsequently added to the family name to ward off creditors and the disgrace and dishonor that come with them.

With *Redburn*, a novel that begins with the central character in a state of bitter "disappointment" and humiliation caused by his father's death, we can begin to chart, in Michael Rogin's words, "the collapse of Melville's idealization of his father. The defences which Melville had erected to protect himself from seeing that father . . . have all come tumbling down" (1983, 249). By the time we get to *Pierre*, the process is complete and the theme of disgrace or dishonor surrounding a mourned father is fully dramatized. Indeed, in her pioneering work on shame Lynd cites the latter novel as a particularly good illustration of "the special character of shame felt by children for their parents," a feeling that can "pierce deeper than shame for oneself. . . . No matter how disgusted I am with myself, in some respects I can perhaps change. But the fact that these are my parents, that I am the fruit of their loins, is unchangeable" (1958, 53–54). Turning to Melville's novel, she observes that "Pierre's whole life and self were uprooted when he discovered that he had all his life been cherishing a false image of the integrity of his father" (54). She then quotes the following passage:

He looked up, and found himself fronted by the no longer wholly enigmatical, but still ambiguously smiling picture of his father . . . endure the smiling portrait he could not; and obeying an irresistible nameless impulse, he rose, and without unhanging it, reversed the picture on the wall. (*P*, 87)

The gesture depicted here is especially significant in terms of the gaze aversion characteristic of shame, the extreme social form of which is ostracism: Pierre turns his back on his father by turning his father's "face"—in a literal "loss of face"—against the wall so he cannot be seen.

As we have already suggested, this particular crisis in Melville's early life points to a more deep-rooted problem. Melville grew up in a familial environment that in many ways resembles those described by Kohut in his analysis of narcissistic personality disorders. By all accounts, the personalities of both parents displayed signs of grandiosity and rage. Allan Melvill was an ambitious but unsuccessful man given to unrealistic dreams, with a propensity to excessive idealizations and hero worship.[10] The latter tendency is reflected in his intense interest in family genealogy and in the vigor with which he "sought to enhance the reputation of the forefathers, both Melvill and Gansevoort," as reflected, for example, in "the family penchant for composing tendentious biographical sketches" (Cohen and Yannella 1992, 32) of its members.[11] He was also a man prone to fits of anger, and appears to have been a severe disciplinarian—"a sanctimonious child-beater and scoundrel" (Metcalf 1991, 70), as Clare Spark puts it. This abusive behavior seems to have been passed on to Herman. According to Edwin S. Schneidman, a clinical psychologist, Herman Melville "had been a psychologically 'battered child' and, in a way typical for battered children, psychologically battered his own children when it came to be his turn to be a parent" (quoted in Cohen and Yannella 1992, 111). Humorous comments that Melville makes in a letter to his brother Thomas (25 May 1862), then captain of a vessel sailing for Hong Kong, suggest as well, perhaps, a sanctioning of humiliating physical punishment that he may have learned from his own father; with reference to the younger members of the crew, he advises:

> As for your treatment of those young ones, there I entirely commend you. Strap them, I beseech you. You remember what the Bible says:—
>> "Oh ye who teach the children of the nations,
>>> Holland, France, England, Germany or Spain,
>> I pray ye *strap* them upon all occasions,
>>> It mends their morals—never mind the pain"
> In another place the Bible says, you know, something about spareing the strap & spoiling the child. (*Corr.*, 377)

In conversation with Schneidman Henry Murray "talked about Melville's children's terror of their father and the apparent absence of love in the home" (quoted in Cohen and Yannella 1992, 111). There is evidence that "Herman was a heavy drinker and that he was verbally abusive toward Elizabeth and the children with the intention to humiliate," and that Malcolm's suicide may well have been "an act of hostility toward his father for a lack of attention and affection" (Renker 1994, 129). Shortly before Malcolm's suicide, things seem to have gotten out of hand, and Elizabeth came very close to deserting her husband for his harsh treatment.[12]

For her part, Maria Melville, Herman's mother, appears to have been very much a narcissistic personality, "no monster," in Edwin Haviland Miller's words, though "imprisoned in her egomaniacal world" (1975, 77). Especially after his death, Melville's mother "usurped Allan Melvill's role in the family. *She* was the voice of authority, *she* held the rod, *she* relentlessly criticized her children, instead of providing the uncritical support Melville imagined in Ruth and Agar" (Clare Spark, quoted in Metcalf 1991, 58).[13] Paul McCarthy's rendition is particularly evocative:

> Maria, apparently stronger than her husband, was quietly aggressive and purposeful. . . . Raised in a patrician family in Albany, Maria expected to advance socially in New York City and eventually become a member of what she regarded as the "fashionables." Despite occasional family successes through the years, Maria never realized her ambition. Her disappointments must have been felt and shared by all others in the family. As a mother, Maria was devoted and caring, but she was also strict and sometimes coercive, as shown in her requirement that the children sit quietly around her bed during her afternoon naps. As the maid could have cared for the children during those periods, the practice appears inconsiderate and selfish. During family crises Maria become prone to periods of depression, which would affect the children. As regular summer retreats to Albany suggest, Maria was overly dependent upon Albany relatives. Allan occasionally pointed out, perhaps with some justification, that his wife loved her brother, businessman Peter Gansevoort, more than she loved him. . . . In managing the family, Maria served as both mother and father and in the process may have loved some children too much and others too little. (1990, 5)

Melville's "misogyny" has been much commented on; but it is important to recognize that much of it may have its roots in the sort of narcissistic domination and control to which his mother subjected her children. The depiction of the cold and imperious Mrs. Glendinning in *Pierre* appears to be, to a very large extent, a depiction of Melville's own mother, while the portrait of the manipulative wife and mother Goneril in *The Confidence-Man* is a sign of Melville's acute insight into the personal costs of severe narcissistic disturbance. The fact that women are quite markedly absent from Melville's work is even more telling. It is worth quoting Alice Miller's observations concerning the even more misogynistic Nietzsche: "As a child Nietzsche was surrounded by women intent on bringing him up correctly, and he had to use all his energies to endure this situation. . . . If he had been able to see *the way the women in his childhood really were*, then it would not have been necessary for him to generalize by making all women into witches and serpents and to hate them all" (1990, 98–99).

In light of the upbringing that two such personalities must have provided, it is no accident that the image of what Alice Miller has called "poisonous pedagogy" haunts Melville's work, from the disciplining of Ishmael by his stepmother to the legally justified cruelty of the fatherly Captain Vere.[14] According to Kohut, "Under optimal circumstances the child's evaluation of the idealized object becomes increasingly realistic" and leads "to the acquisition of permanent psychological structures. . . . If the child suffers the traumatic loss of the idealized object, however, or a traumatic (severe and sudden, or not phase-appropriate) disappointment in it, then optimal internalization does not take place" (Kohut 1971, 45). In such a situation, "the psyche remains fixated on an archaic selfobject, and the personality will throughout life be dependent on certain objects in what seems to be an intense form of object hunger" (45). The traumatic event of his father's death, given the particularly mortifying circumstances that attended it, when Herman was twelve and entering adolescence—a particularly vulnerable period in the development of a cohesive sense of self—would have reactivated and reinforced Melville's earlier sense of rejection and disappointment in his narcissistically disturbed parents. Kohut describes the consequences of such severe loss and disappointment: "Unconsciously fixated on an idealized selfobject for which they continue to yearn, and deprived of a sufficiently idealized superego, such persons are forever searching for external omnipotent powers from whose support and approval they attempt to derive strength" (84). The obsessive subject of Melville's work is in fact the "reestablishment," as E. H. Miller observes, "of the son's relationship with the father, or friendship. . . . The youths are fatherless and searching for the lost male model. Arrested in adolescence, the young men in story after story struggle toward man's estate, repeating the same struggles, fumbling and failing to complete the same rite of passage. . . . They remain orphans" (1975, 117). Richard Chase has similarly described the novels preceding *Moby-Dick* as "the record of a fatherless boy and young man painfully resurrecting his past and painfully learning about the world and reality. . . . And one often notices that in these pictures the young man assumes a relationship to an older man—an ambiguous figure who is sometimes a patriarchal hero and sometimes a satyr or a killer" (1949, 2). The extreme ambivalence toward the idealized object reflects a background in which intense attachment to the other is fraught with the dread of shame, rage, physical abuse, and the constant threat of betrayal and abandonment. The idealized object cannot, in short, be trusted: one will be shamed, rejected, abandoned—because (and this would seem to be the fear behind all shame) one cannot be loved.

Years later, shame mixed with grief must have affected Melville again in the tragic downfall and death of his brother Gansevoort, whose troubled life, like Herman's, reveals a pattern consistent with a family environment affected by narcissistic disorder and chronic shame. Herman's own feelings toward his brother must have been complicated and ambivalent. The attention and hopes of both parents were from the beginning unhealthily focused on their eldest son. As McCarthy summarizes the situation: "Gansevoort, the oldest of the eight Melvill children, overshadowed everyone else in the family. He was a perennial winner of classroom firsts and scholarship prizes and the idol of his parents. Herman, four years younger, naturally felt inferior and resentful" (1990, 5). Melville's father, in his letters, remarks upon Herman's slowness of speech and unexceptional intelligence, praising instead his innocence and good nature. Indeed, the demeaning word that appears to have haunted Herman from the day of his birth was "docile," a word that recurs in his work. This "ugly duckling" syndrome, as E. H. Miller dubs it, also involved a painful sense of physical unattractiveness, as he measured his own appearance against the "graceful Gansevoort," who seems to have "had the Apollonian and hermaphroditic elegance of his father" (1975, 107). He thus found himself, according to the exacting terms of the family mythology, unavoidably placed in a reduced position, typecast, in relation to his older brother, in the supporting role of the tractable but not very brilliant younger brother.

Gansevoort, however, suffered from the same Procrustean myth, and was only sporadically able to live up to his parents' expectations. After undergoing "the humiliation of bankruptcy, a failure in a business he inherited from an unsuccessful father" (272), he turned ambitiously to a career in politics. It was the golden age of American political stumping and oratory, and his apparent exhibitionism, undoubtedly fostered by the excessive (and perhaps inconsistent) parental attention he had received from birth, was given a somewhat freer rein than was possible in the business world. He turned out to be a highly successful and spellbinding orator, drawing "spectacular crowds and [holding] them for three and four hours" (Rogin 1983, 53). Intensely ambitious, he "embraced the heroic leader [Polk] and his mass following. He employed the emotionally charged, egalitarian language of war and salvation in the West" (58). Horace Greeley, for example, who instinctively distrusted the young demagogue, put his finger on the psychological symptoms of grandiosity and exhibitionism: "He develops too much gas and glory—talks too much of himself, Mr. Van Buren and Gen. Jackson—and says too little of the great questions before the People" (quoted in E. H. Miller 1975, 99). In the light of Gansevoort's dismal fate, we might recall that it is the same General Jackson who figures so prominently in the "gas and glory" of Melville's own idealizing invocation to the great god of Democracy ("Thou who didst pick up Andrew Jackson from the pebbles" [MD, 117]) that brings to an emotional conclusion chapter 26 of Moby-Dick, in which Starbuck's failure of courage is so painfully and tactfully touched upon. Gansevoort's mesmerizing oratory helped to sweep James Polk to power, but his grandiose ambitions met with bitter disappointment when, in an age of shameless political patronage (a state of affairs that Hawthorne satirized so severely in "The Custom House"), he was left unrewarded by the expected appointment after the election. He felt betrayed and harbored a feeling of deep personal injury. He was finally given a minor post in London. Embittered by his fortunes, he was to die shortly after this crushing personal defeat, a deeply depressed man, his reputation ruined by extravagant outbreaks of paranoid and antagonistic behavior. Melville was no stranger, then, to the "undraped spectacle" (MD, 117) afforded by the humiliating public downfall of those closest to him.

The other significant event mentioned by biographers is Melville's brief but intense friendship with Hawthorne, in which he seems to have invested a great deal only to be deeply disappointed, if not to feel betrayed, and this during a period in which the public failed to respond positively to the work—*Mardi, Moby-Dick,* and *Pierre*—that he considered his most serious and truthful.[15] Melville's hunger for understanding and recognition appears to have excited and elated him in his relationship with Hawthorne. At a certain point, however, something like a "sudden loss of distance or the threat of it" (Tomkins 1963, 193), a typical source of shame, may have provoked shame in both parties, followed by an increased distance between the two and a painful sense of rejection on Melville's part. As Robert K. Martin puts it, "The encounter with Hawthorne, and his enthusiastic response to the older writer, indicate the one occasion when he may have felt it possible that his feelings might be satisfied within his world as a writer and an American" (1986, 14). It was this possibility that then seemed so abruptly removed.

In the depiction of the relations between Clarel and Vine in *Clarel,* the autobiographical import of which has long been recognized, Melville pictures the way in which deep longings for intimacy may be frustrated by the other party's timid, even obtuse protectiveness of self:

> Prior advances unreturned
> Not here he recked of, while he yearned—
> O, now but for communion true
> And close; let go each alien theme;
> Give me thyself!
>> But Vine, at will
> Dwelling upon his wayward dream,
> Nor as suspecting Clarel's thrill
> Of personal longing, rambled still.
>> (2.27.66–74)

Feeling vaguely rebuked, Clarel's longing for "confidings that should wed / Our souls in one" (2.27.106–7) is subsequently aroused and then just as quickly dashed when "glancing up, unwarned he saw/ What serious softness in those eyes/ Bent on him. Shyly they withdraw" (2.27.131–33). Rejection of a longing for intimacy and closeness—Vine protectively shrinks from deeper communion, and withdraws his gaze—is an obvious trigger of shame. Incompatible here is Clarel's intense desire for union with the other and Vine's fear of intimacy, which for him signifies too painful exposure. Such a relationship would seem doomed from the start.

Something of an analogous nature seems to have occurred in terms of Melville's creative work. Encouraged by the early reception of his work, Melville felt confident in making more adventurous forays into the world of fiction and thought, only to be severely disappointed. Of the reception of *Mardi*,[16] for example, the book that first shook Melville's trust in the public, he wrote to Evert Duyckinck (14 December 1849):

> And when he attempts anything higher [than *Redburn*]—God help
> & save him! . . . Hereafter I shall no more stab at a book (in print, I
> mean) than I would stab at a man. . . . Had I not written & printed
> 'Mardi', in all likelihood, I would not be as wise as I am now, or
> may be. For that thing was stabbed *at* (I do not say *through*)—&
> therefore, I am the wiser for it. (*Corr.*, 149)

Moby-Dick was another popular failure, receiving in both his own country and England "reviews that, in their particular tone of contemptuous hostility, cannot have failed to give the sharpest kind of pain to a man who was, as he himself confessed in *Mardi*, 'far more keenly alive to censure than to praise'" (Arwin 1957, 200). Melville's sense of narcissistic injury, his painful feelings of humiliation concerning what he must have considered a betrayal by the literary establishment, is reflected in *Pierre*. One of the things that sends Pierre over the brink of sanity at the end of the novel is the rejection from his publishers, who viciously attack him and his work—"the sheets of a blasphemous rhapsody" (*P*, 357)—void their contract, and sue for expenses. The imagery of stabbing that we find in the letter to Duyckinck quoted above—a clear image of the inflicting of a narcissistic wound—recurs here as the protagonist, who even before receiving the final mortifying blow is already anticipating the necessity of a murderous retaliation, ponders the letters from his publishers and his two old friends: "[I]n these hands I feel that I now hold the final poniards that shall stab me; and by stabbing me, make me too a most swift stabber in the recoil. Which point first?" (*P*, 356). Melville himself had his share of quarrels with publishers and, as his correspondence shows, was constantly wrangling with them over their (in his view) unreasonable and unjust conditions and requests. With the faltering of his reputation, he could no longer command terms he felt at all happy with. He was insulted by the extremely ungenerous offer for *Pierre*, at a time when he was still smarting from the bad reviews of *Moby-Dick*, and in a rage interpolated the entire section in the novel concerning Pierre's career as a novelist. The rather condescending review of *Moby-Dick* in the *Literary World* undoubtedly contributed to his growing sense of alienation from his old friends the Duyckincks. Melville's "long-festering but previously controlled resentment at Duyckinck's patronizing treatment" (Branch et al. 1984, 270) found expression in *Pierre* and its biting satirical portrait of the literary world, in particular of a pompous and presumptuous joint editor of the *Captain Kidd Monthly*, a figure likely modeled on Evert Duyckinck. In the later years, the abused and tyrannized Elizabeth alludes more than once in her letters to her husband's morbidly sensitive nature, but even in his early years Melville seems to have suffered from the propensity to take insult, and, like many of his characters, found himself resenting "real and fancied slights by his publishers" (270) and others. After his initial, extremely promising success as a writer of popular stories of adventure and travel, the failure to elicit the public's approval and enthusiasm would have come as a severely wounding defeat. Melville, it seems, did not have the emotional fortitude to sustain the blows of a series of such setbacks, and the extremely disappointing public reception of his most artistically ambitious works paralyzed him creatively and undoubtedly robbed him of much of his enormous potential as an author.

IV

I have not, it should be noted, dealt with the Melville corpus evenly. With the exception of *Redburn*, I have only touched in passing on the novels before *Moby-Dick*, and I have left in the background a large chunk of the later work, such as *Israel Potter*, *Clarel*, and most of the poetry. This decision has been dictated in part by the wish to manage an already expansive analysis, and in part by the extent to which particular texts betray most insistently those elements of disordered narcissism and chronic feelings of shame that are often apparent throughout Melville's work in a much less dramatic and revealing form. In this connection, I am doubtless guilty of having cast a rather intense light on one aspect of Melville's work and left much that is interesting, but not directly relevant to my focus, in the shadows. This narrowing of scope would seem to be inevitable in any study. However, it is perhaps telling that the symptomatology of shame is most dramatically revealed precisely in those works that have been recognized as having a lasting artistic power. Melville's "creative powers," as E. H. Miller justly observes, "were most penetrating in his engagement with the life-negating tactics of 'heroes' like Ahab, Pierre, and Bartleby" (1975, 109).

Part 1 of the book, "Shame and Attachment," deals with the relationship between shame and the affectionate and social ties that link human beings to one another. Chapter 1 ("How to Make a Misanthrope") concerns itself with the theme of betrayal, ostracism, and abandonment as the threat in shame, and some of its effects on the personality: in particular, misanthropy and depression. Chapter 2 ("Mortifying Inter-Indebtedness") focuses on two versions of mortification in *Moby-Dick:* the comic and the tragic. They are two contrasting attitudes to narcissistic injury: the isolation and rage of Ahab in contrast with the humor and sociability of Ishmael, whose relationship with Queequeg exemplifies the alter-ego transference in which acceptance by one's fellow human beings is paramount. Chapter 3 ("The Inexorable Self") examines the possibility of overcoming shame through a strengthening of the self based on a healthy identification with an idealized parental imago. The first part of the chapter examines the example of Jonah in Father Mapple's sermon in *Moby-Dick* and touches on the transcendence of shame through the courageous attachment to ideals; the second part concerns the circumstances that result in a failure to live up to those ideals and overcome shame, a subject most pessimistically treated in Melville's *Pierre.*

Part 2, "Shame, Resentment, and Envy," deals with the "shamers," the series of villains, or antagonists, such as Babo, Radney, Claggart, and Ahab, who parade through Melville's theater of the unconscious and who, as victims of humiliation themselves, have learned to use shame and contempt as a weapon against others. Chapter 4 ("Motiveless Malignity") explores the psychological motivation of resentment as a product of chronic shame and buried narcissistic rage at humiliating defeat and mortification. Chapter 5 ("Turning the Tables") focuses on the susceptibility to slight as a manifestation of shame-proneness and the counter-shaming mechanism of "turning the tables," as this defensive and particularly destructive response to shame has been so aptly described, in which the victim of shame aggressively turns the passive into the active and inflicts on others the humiliation that has been, and that he most fears will continue to be, inflicted on him.

Part 3, "The Evil Eye," explores in depth the imagery of perception and expression in Melville's work, which I relate to the symptoms of both idealization and grandiosity in so many of his characters. These symptoms are characteristic of the expressive and perceptual drives when they have been blocked by traumatic shame and have become "mere vehicles for union, power, and destruction" (Wurmser 1987, 83). In chapter 6 ("Dangerous Mergers") I show how looking and seeing are profoundly linked in Melville to the idealizing tendencies in his work. As a wish, the desire to look appears in the form of merger through idealization and through the gaze; as a fear, it takes the form of an overwhelming fascination that has the power to numb and petrify its victim. Chapter 7 ("The Evil Eye") is devoted to the expressive drive, which is manifested in the distorted form of grandiosity and exhibitionism. These tendencies of Melville's characters appear either as a desire to merge with others by exerting an overwhelming fascination, or as a fear of being exposed to staring, devouring eyes. The examination of this fascinatory drive sets the stage for the analysis of a sort of primal encounter dominated by an envious-fascinating-shaming gaze or "evil eye." The confrontation in *Billy Budd* between Claggart and Billy in Vere's cabin serves as the supreme example of such an instance.

A brief epilogue touches on Melville's yearning for frankness and truth, as he expresses it in his work and correspondence. This yearning is not simply an intellectual abstraction; it is, we can conclude, a unique and very genuine expression of the desire to overcome shame, a desire most triumphantly realized in his most successful writings, where the creative impulse has been strong enough to release the capacity to communicate from the constraints imposed by crippling feelings of humiliation and failure. Melville reached out to others and sought recognition and love through literary expression; the intensity of this quest was perhaps most apparent, in personal terms, in his relationship with Hawthorne. In reaching out, he produced a body of work that courageously explores the need to overcome destructive shame and narcissism. In the later years, *Clarel* and *Billy Budd* stand out as notable victories in face of the guilt and shame he must have felt for perpetuating a family history of abuse and failure: in the tragic deaths of both his sons in their early manhood—Malcolm at eighteen, and Stanwix, after years of drifting, at thirty-five—he doubtless saw "reflected," in Paul McCarthy's words, "his own failures and these in turn [must have been] related in his own mind to failures of his father over fifty years before" (1990, 126). The long-awaited signs of some public recognition of the importance of his work began to emerge only as he approached death. His bitterness must have been great. Crippling depression and rage, the symptoms of an emotional disturbance that manifested itself in the abusive treatment of those closest to him seems to have dogged him throughout his adult years. In his work, however, something else takes place: a creative transmutation that signifies, as Wurmser puts it, the heroic transcendence of shame.

PART ONE

Shame
and
Attachment

CHAPTER ONE

How to Make a Misanthrope

I

According to Richard Chase, "Melville created two kinds of hero, one of whom may be called Ishmael and the other, Prometheus" (1949, 3). It is the former that immediately interests us. Ishmael—the elder son of Abraham, rejected by his father and heartlessly cast out with his mother into the wilderness—is a byword for the socially ostracized. Forced to live in a state of perpetual quarrel and conflict, the biblical Ishmael turns into a "wild man," a misanthrope whose "hand will be against every man, and every man's hand against him" (Gen. 16:12). One of the best descriptions of this man-hating outcast, a figure that so persistently haunts Melville's work, is supplied in chapter 32 of *Moby-Dick* ("Cetology"), where the finback whale is depicted in terms suggesting a cetacean counterpart to the splenetic and misanthropic Ishmael whom we encounter in a state of suicidal desperation at the beginning of Melville's novel:

> The Fin-Back is not gregarious. He seems a whale-hater, as some men are man-haters. Very shy, always going solitary; unexpectedly rising to the surface in the remotest and most sullen waters; his straight and single lofty jet rising like a tall misanthropic spear upon a barren plain; gifted with such wondrous power and velocity in swimming, as to defy all present pursuit from man; this leviathan seems the banished and unconquerable Cain of his race, bearing for his mark that style upon his back. (*MD*, 139)

In its shy withdrawal and systematic avoidance of others, gifted as it is "with such wondrous power and velocity in swimming," the misanthropic finback whale displays the most obvious symptom of shame: flight or withdrawal. Intense shyness, a form of shame anxiety, is, of course, the form taken by the fear of being shamed in interpersonal relations, of being rejected by others. To be shamed by a group or entire society is to be ostracized, and the last image explicitly links misanthropy and social ostracism: the whale's "lofty jet," like a "misanthropic spear," marks it, as the scarlet letter does Hester Prynne, as a *pharmakos* or social outcast.[1]

Combined in Melville's image of the misanthrope, as illustrated in this passage, are thus two important emotional or psychological elements: shame anxiety—the fear of being shamed and rejected—and the feelings of resentment and hurt, the sense of betrayal, that result from being rejected. As Gerhardt Piers points out:

> Behind the feeling of shame stands not the fear of hatred, but the fear of contempt which, on an even deeper level of the unconscious, spells fear of abandonment, the death by emotional starvation. . . . Accordingly, on a higher social and more conscious level of individual development, it is again not fear of active punishment by superiors which is implied in shame anxiety, but social expulsion, like ostracism. (Piers and Singer 1971, 29)

The misanthropic response is thus a combination of a fear of rejection and the hatred of human society that is itself a reaction to having been betrayed and rejected.

Melville depicts the misanthropic leviathan in the passage quoted above as "the banished and unconquerable Cain of his race." The figures of Cain and Ishmael are, of course, part of the romantic inheritance of which Melville, along with so many other American writers of the period, was such a receptive and creative beneficiary. The presence of Byron's Cain, as Wyn Kelly has shown, is present throughout Melville's work and informs his depictions of both Ahab and Claggart. Melville's reading would have included works such as Bulwer-Lytton's "Ishmael" and his *Timon* as well, which, as Murray documents in his preface to *Pierre*, "enjoyed a great vogue in the late forties" (lxvi). Murray notes that "Ishmael was also a much discussed character in Cooper's *Prairie* (1827)" (1962, xli). Both these figures, Ishmael and Timon, and related ones were extremely popular in Melville's time. As Northrop Frye points out: "With the Romantic movement there comes a large-scale renewal of sympathy for these rejected but at least quasi-tragic Biblical figures, who may be sent into exile and yet are in another context the rightful heirs. Cain, Ishmael, Esau, Saul, even Lucifer himself, are all romantic heroes" (1981, 182). The psychological significance of the titanism that is often such an important part of these figures will be treated more extensively in a later chapter. For the moment I would like to concentrate on the theme of rejection and abandonment, and on the misanthropic state of mind that is the result of being rejected or betrayed by one's fellow human beings. It is worth noting in passing, however, that in *Moby-Dick* the Byronic image of a defiant and titanic Cain, associated with Ahab, is clearly contrasted with a less-heroic Ishmael figure, and this contrast may touch on one of the most important themes in the novel: the difference, as we hope to show, between the shame that is tempered by love and that which has been irreversibly corrupted by defiance, contempt, and hate.

The misanthropic theme of "Timonism," as Charles N. Watson Jr. calls it, "took its name from [Melville's] reading of Shakespeare's *Timon of Athens*" (1988, 173), and became increasingly prominent in Melville's work as he struggled with what he felt was a betrayal and desertion by his public, friends, and family. As Tomkins and others remind us, one of the functions of shame in a social context, whether it is external or internalized, is to encourage the individual to repent and seek reconciliation and reaffiliation with the group. But in its most searing and traumatic forms, it is capable of creating deep-rooted resentment and destroying all trust. The misanthropic response—the decision not to reestablish communion with others—is ultimately an expression of deep-seated resentment at some original, unforgivable injury, usually some form of mortifying betrayal or abandonment by others. Timonism in Melville, as Watson sees it, involves two diametrically opposed responses: either the injured party undertakes "a misanthropic withdrawal into spiritual isolation" or he seeks revenge through a "cunning game of literary imposture" (175). The confidence man's use of imposture is a good example of the latter: he vindictively *turns the tables* on his victimizers, other human beings: he has been betrayed, and so he betrays, by deceiving, those who have broken trust and deserted him. As Watson demonstrates, Timonism, in one or both of these two forms, is an extraordinarily consistent feature in Melville's work after *Moby-Dick*. *Pierre*, of course, recounts "a series of Timon-like betrayals" perpetrated on the central character by his family and friends, until "Pierre at last feels deserted by 'even the paternal gods,'" and ends up retreating "into spiritual isolation" (174). In *Israel Potter* as well, as Watson observes, the central character "responds to betrayal by a stoical withdrawal that conceals an underlying bitterness" (177). The stories of Hunilla and Oberlus in "The Encantadas" represent

alternative polar responses to "Timon's misfortune of betrayal and desertion" (175). Hunilla's abandonment is reminiscent of the story of Philoctetes:
she is deserted by companions on an island in the middle of nowhere, and
her ultimate reaction to this betrayal is one of defiance in the face of mortification and deeply wounded pride: "There was something which seemed
strangely haughty in her air, and yet it was the air of woe. A Spanish and an
Indian grief, which would not visibly lament. Pride's height in vain abased
to proneness on the rack; nature's pride subduing nature's torture" (*PT*, 161).
In "Bartleby, the Scrivener" there is defiance as well in the central character's
stubborn refusal to acquiesce, which finally leaves him betrayed and abandoned "to a Timon-like isolation and death" (Watson 1988, 176). The image of Bartleby—"he seemed alone, absolutely alone in the universe. A bit
of wreck in the mid Atlantic" (*PT*, 32)—recalls the epitome of betrayal and
desertion in *Moby-Dick*: the image of helpless Pip abandoned in the midst of
an endless oceanic waste. The final image of Bartleby "Strangely huddled
at the base of the wall, his knees drawn up, and lying on his side, his
head touching the cold stones" (*PT*, 44) is a devastating image of social
abandonment and human betrayal, and is only surpassed in Melville's
work by Redburn's discovery in Launcelott's-Hey of the abandoned "figure
of what had been a woman. Her blue arms folded to her livid bosom two
shrunken things like children, that leaned toward her, one on each side" (*R*,
180).

The nature of betrayal and abandonment in Melville may range from
the intensely personal to the more broadly social and human. When the
experience takes a more personal form it involves deep narcissistic mortification. In "Benito Cereno," for example, we have a most dramatic instance
of deception and betrayal practiced on the innocent and the trusting: Babo,
another one of Melville's confidence men, deceives Delano, that too-trust-
ing man of confidence, with the charming spectacle "of simple-hearted attachment" (*PT*, 64); and he does so in order to hide the treachery he has
practiced on his master, who has unwisely placed trust in his servant. (It is,
however, fairly obvious to the modern reader—if not to the undiscerning
narrator—that Babo is really only turning the tables on a man and a people
who have brutally enslaved and humiliated him in the first place). Cereno's
reaction to betrayal is a misanthropic withdrawal into monastic solitude,
shortly after which he dies. He thus presents the melancholic alternative to
Babo's vindictive response.

Trust is the primary foundation of human attachment: the ability to form a bond with another human being presupposes the ability to trust another, and the severe hurt caused by the betrayal of trust is, to be precise, a form of shame or humiliation: one feels helpless, powerless, abandoned—deeply mortified. After he has been betrayed and abandoned by his friends, Shakespeare's Timon acts like someone who has been horrendously shamed: he withdraws from human society and hides like a hermit in a cave. This is what Ahab does, of course, after his encounter with Moby Dick, and he reacts the same way after he is injured by the violent displacement of his ivory leg which "had stake-wise smitten, and all but pierced his groin" (*MD*, 463). He hides, and cloaks himself in a "Grand Lama-like exclusiveness; and, for that one interval, sought speechless refuge, as it were, among the marble senate of the dead" (464). The captain's cabin is generally associated in Melville with a hermitlike reclusiveness, and this is most particularly the case with the misanthropic Ahab. According to the narrator, the crew of the Pequod loses nothing for being little welcomed in it, for in it

> was no companionship; socially, Ahab was inaccessible. Though nominally included in the census of Christendom, he was still an alien to it. He lived in the world, as the last of the Grizzly Bears lived in settled Missouri. And as when Spring and Summer had departed, that wild Logan of the woods, burying himself in the hollow of a tree, lived out the winter there, sucking his own paws; so, in his inclement, howling old age, Ahab's soul, shut up in the caved trunk of his body, there fed upon the sullen paws of his gloom! (153)

The association of bears and melancholic gloom is a conventional and popular one, and in Melville bear imagery is invariably associated with depression, misanthropy, and solitude. In *The Confidence-Man* the man of many masks refers to "the growling, the hypocritical growling, of the bears" on the floor of the stock market—a metaphor still very much with us, of course—"scoundrelly bears," "professors of the wicked art of manufacturing depressions" (48). He thus associates them with splenetic "low spirits" and depression, economic and otherwise; and later in the same chapter he picks up the same refrain, deploring "some gloomy philosopher here, some theological bear, forever taking occasion to growl down the stock of human nature" (48, 50). Bear imagery recurs with the appearance of the Missouri bachelor who, "somewhat ursine in aspect," is another gloomy misanthrope. He responds to his insinuating interlocutor at one point with "the low, half-suppressed growl, as of Bruin in a hollow trunk" (106, 121), and at one point warns him by "paw-like thrusting out his bearskin arm" (122). A related imagery surrounds the suspicious man (who, like Ahab, is one-legged) admonished for his distrust by the Methodist preacher at the beginning of the novel:

> "Nothing; the foiled wolf's parting howl," said the Methodist, "Spleen, much spleen, which is the rickety child of his evil heart of unbelief; it has made him mad. . . . I have been in mad-houses full of tragic mopers, and seen there the end of suspicion: the cynic, in the moody madness muttering in the corner; for years a barren fixture there; head lopped over, gnawing his own lip, vulture of himself." (16)

"Might deter Timon," is the preacher's conclusion. The Promethean imagery of being a vulture of oneself also surrounds Ahab: "whose intense thinking . . . makes him a Prometheus; a vulture feeds upon that heart for ever; that vulture the very creature he creates" (MD, 202).

The withdrawal associated with misanthropy is also a way of defending against possible mortification in the future; one hides to avoid a repetition of shame and humiliation. The character Nord in *White-Jacket*, for example, has an overwhelming fear of the scourge, a form of physical punishment that involves shameful exposure and public humiliation. "[A]dded to whatever incommunicable grief which might have been his," this fear

> made this Nord such a wandering recluse, even among our man-of-war mob. Nor could he have long swung his hammock on board, ere he must have found that, to insure his exemption from that thing which alone affrighted him, *he must be content for the most part to turn a man-hater, and socially expatriate himself from many things, which might have rendered his situation more tolerable.* Still more, several events that took place must have horrified him, at times, with the thought that, *however he might isolate and entomb himself,* yet for all this, the improbability of his being overtaken by what he

most dreaded never advanced to the infallibility of the impossible.
(51–52; emphasis added)

Nord thus exemplifies the misanthropic response as the result of a wounding mortification: in reaction to a perceived injustice and a feeling akin to that of being betrayed—"whatever incommunicable grief might have been his"—he isolates himself out of resentment, incapacitated by the overwhelming anxiety that the mortification might occur again. His wish to "isolate and entomb himself" concerns that extreme area of shame touching on "wishes and fears about closeness," as Nathanson describes it, and ultimately involves the "sense of being shorn from all humanity," a "feeling that one is unlovable," the "wish to be left alone forever" (1992, 317).

The same fear and the same wish turn up in *Redburn*, written more or less at the same time as *White-Jacket*. Redburn's initial strategy for dealing with shame is a form of *avoidance*, to use Nathanson's term; it involves the denial of shame through an unrealistic overvaluation or presentation of the self. Redburn's narcissistic tendencies, his vanity, his apparent arrogance and self-love, are all masking defenses against painful feelings of shame. The archaic basis of these feelings becomes clear after Jackson's hatred has turned him into an Ishmael by setting the crew aboard the *Highlander* against him. Redburn fears that ostracism will turn him into a monster—someone who cannot be loved—like his fiendishly misanthropic persecutor. In *The Anatomy of Melancholy*—a text that Melville had a particular fondness for, as is clear from the influence of its exuberant anatomical structure on *Moby-Dick*—Robert Burton's warnings against the destructiveness of voluntary isolation describe just such a process of being converted by solitude into a monster: "woe be to him that is so alone. These wretches do frequently degenerate from men, and of sociable creatures become beasts, monsters, inhuman, ugly to behold, *misanthropi*; they do even loathe themselves, and hate the company of men, as so many Timons, Nebuchadnezzars, by too much indulging to these pleasing humours, and through their own default" (1977, pt. 1, 248–49). The explanation doubtless applies a fortiori to a societally enforced solitariness:

And his being my foe, set many of the rest against me; or at least they were afraid to speak out for me before Jackson; so that at last I found myself a sort of Ishmael in the ship, without a single friend or companion; and I began to feel a hatred growing up in me against the whole crew—so much so, that I prayed against it, that it might not master my heart completely, and so make a fiend of me, something like Jackson. (113–14)

This passage reveals how a misanthrope like Jackson is produced in the first place: by being treated as an object of disgust to be shunned and avoided, by being administered, for an extended period of time, toxic doses of shame. Jackson understands all too well the process by which human beings are turned into Ishmaels; his treatment of Redburn is merely the active form of what he has himself passively endured. An outcast from human society, the supreme Ishmael, at one point he is compared to "King Antiochus of Syria, who died a worse death, history says, than if he had been stung out of the world by wasps and hornets" (108). The image of being "stung out of the world," of being cast out from the world itself, is an extravagant hyperbole of social expulsion. Redburn uses a similar image earlier to describe his feeling as the ship leaves the Narrows of New York Harbor: "About sunset we got fairly 'outside,' and well may it so be called; for I felt thrust out of the world" (83).

II

The Confidence-Man, the culminating work in Melville's relentless procession of images of misanthropy, is "a profound examination of confidence or trust on a personal, psychological level" (E. H. Miller 1975, 273). In this terrible satire the relationship between shame and the betrayal of trust or confidence is made dramatically clear. The description, at the beginning of the novel, of the pasteboard sign proclaiming "No Trust," which hangs over the entrance to the barbershop, is the inscription over the gateway to Melville's particular hell, while the name of the riverboat on which the action takes place, the *Fidèle*, is only there to remind us of an ideal that exists, in the novel, only to be flouted and mocked. *The Confidence-Man* offers a bleakly ironic vision of a society in bondage either, as regards humanity, to the most foolish confidence or to the most bitter cynicism. There seems no middle ground, and by the end of the novel the assumption of trust in others, the bond that holds society together, has been completely undermined by a vision of the ubiquity of betrayal and desertion. The suspicious one-legged man sums up the absurdity when he tells a story about the dangers of an unexamined confidence and trust in others: an old Frenchman from New Orleans blindly dotes on a young wife who, his friends advise, is regularly betraying him; he refuses to believe it until, arriving home one night, a stranger bursts from the alcove of their apartment, at which he exclaims: "Begar! . . . now I *begin* to suspec" (*CM*, 30). The sense of absurdity concerning the pervasiveness of betrayal that we get at the end of Melville's novel is very much like what we experience at the end of Shakespeare's *Timon*; it is characteristic of what Frye calls "satire of the low norm," and "arises as a kind of backfire or recall after the work has been seen or read. Once we have finished with it, deserts of futility open up on all sides, and we have, in spite of the humor, a sense of nightmare and a close proximity to something demonic" (1957, 226).

One of the most extraordinary case histories in the novel, and one that powerfully underlines the relationship between shame, betrayal, and loss of trust, is the story of Goneril (*CM*, chap. 12). The tale concerns an extremely sinister woman who through her "manipulation"—the word should be taken quite literally, since it is through the poisonous power of her evil "touch" that she exercises control—manages to isolate her mortified and baffled husband from all human contact. It is, of course, quite appropriate that she should be the namesake of one of Lear's malevolent daughters, since Shakespeare's tragedy focuses on the betrayal and abandonment of a father by his children, an analogous case of the severance of the sacred human bonds of love. In Melville's universe of treacherous human relations, as in the world of *King Lear*, the promise to love according to one's bond, however purely political and legalistic it may sound, is by no means an insignificant gesture. Ultimately, the operations of Goneril have the effect of progressively *ostracizing* her husband, who by the end of the story has been deserted by all his friends. To rescue the child from her mother, the husband is forced to flee with the girl and as a result is shunned by society for abandoning his wife. His wife then sues him for desertion, takes custody of the child, and leaves the husband penniless, in the course of which she destroys his reputation, leaving him alone and disgraced. Threatened with being declared insane and institutionalized, he finds himself—his wife has since died—"an innocent outcast, wandering forlorn in the great valley of the Mississippi with a weed on his hat for the loss of his Goneril" (*CM*, 63).

Object loss, suggested here by the imagery of bereavement, conceals the much deeper scars left by shame and betrayal. We are told that "it largely redounded to his fair-mindedness, as well as piety, that under the alleged dissuasives, apparently so, from philanthropy, he had not, in a moment of excitement, been warped over to the ranks of the misanthropes" (65). The original narrator of the story, however, is the "man with the weed," one of the avatars of the confidence man, and a warping to the misanthropic position seems the most probable result of such a narcissistically mortifying experience, shattering and destroying, as it would, one's feelings of trust in others. Indeed, the figure of the husband in this story is perhaps only matched in Melville's work, in terms of being the passive victim of a compounding of outrageous and often apparently deliberate humiliating blows, by the hapless Pierre Glendinning, the definitive victim of shame, betrayal, and ostracism; in the latter's case, there is, of course, as we shall see, the added complicating factor of a significant element of externalization and self-destructive masochism.

The other most dramatic episode of a personal betrayal inflicting deep disappointment and shame is the story of China Aster. Autobiographically, the story appears to recall a number of important events in Melville's life: his father's bankruptcy and death when Herman was twelve, his brief but intense friendship with Hawthorne, and his discouraging career as an author after a beginning of great promise and public enthusiasm.[2] The fact that Melville condenses and weaves together these several events suggests that he saw them as intimately related in some way, and the thing that relates them—Allan Melvill and his family, disgraced and abandoned by relations, friends, and society; young Herman, deeply disappointed and wounded by his father's downfall and death, and again by the encouraging older friend whom he believed understood him; and Melville the author, stabbed and deserted by the public and the critics—is that all these incidents are associated with a deep sense of betrayal and the humiliating feeling of helplessness and rejection.

The protagonist of the story is China Aster, a candle-maker, who is encouraged by his friend Orchis to expand his little business into something more ambitious. Orchis all but forces him to accept the offer of a generous loan with the promise that he may repay him when he can. This is done on mere trust, on confidence, since no papers are signed. The predictable happens: China Aster runs into unforeseen difficulties, is forced to borrow from another creditor at exorbitant rates, and when he approaches his friend for assistance is met by the unfeeling request that he start repaying interest on the loan immediately. Eventually, he goes bankrupt, collapses, and dies. The circumstances of Aster's end are strikingly similar to those of Alan Melville's last days: financial ruin followed by physical collapse and delirium. In the same way the theme of Aster's reputation of honesty, which encourages a usurious farmer to trust him in the first place and enter into a shady agreement—"had China Aster been something else than what he was, he would not have been trusted" (CM, 215)—seems to be modeled on the illegal transactions undertaken by Allan Melvill, transactions that helped to speed his financial downfall.[3] Melville's father died with both his finances and reputation in ruins, and "the straits in which China Aster had left his family had, besides apparently dimming the world's regard, likewise seemed to dim its sense of the probity of its deceased head" (218). The stigma of dishonesty, one can imagine, can only add to the shame of bankruptcy and destitution and to the deep feeling of betrayal in being deserted by one's friends and society.

The details that recall the circumstances of Melville's friendship with Hawthorne are equally notable. Orchis is associated with the experiment of a quasi-religious sect, as Hawthorne was with Brook Farm, and China Aster is encouraged by his friend to progress from tallow candles to spermacetti, in the way Melville was encouraged by his early success, and perhaps by the example of Hawthorne, boldly to move from trivial things like Redburn to the more serious affairs of Moby-Dick.[4] Orchis, who has a flowery name like Hawthorne's, is a shoemaker, "one whose calling it is to defend the understandings of men from naked contact with the substance of things" (CM, 208). The image suggests other depictions of Hawthorne by Melville (not to mention by other contemporaries), such as the "shyest grape" of "Monody," or the depiction of Vine, "the recluse," in Clarel, both of which emphasize his shadowy, shy, screenlike, or veiling timidity. Hawthorne himself portrayed these aspects of his personality in characters such as Arthur Dimmesdale in The Scarlet Letter and Clifford Pyncheon in The House of the Seven Gables. (The central role of shame in Hawthorne's work requires an elaborate study of its own.) The shyness of such a person—"Vine's manner shy / A clog, a hindrance might imply" (Clarel, 1.29.9–10)—appears to be caused by a deep-rooted fear of exposure, a wish to keep one's secret self concealed:

> Like to the nunnery's denizen
> His virgin soul communed with men
> But thro' the wicket. Was it clear
> This coyness bordered not on fear—
> Fear or an apprehensive sense?
> Not wholly seemed it diffidence
> Recluse. Nor less did strangely wind
> Ambiguous elfishness behind
> All that: an Ariel unknown.
>
> (1.29.43–51)

What lies behind this "coyness" of Vine is, it would seem, a narcissistically protected core, a hidden self very reluctant to reveal itself in genuine communion with other. In Orchis, there appears to be something worse: a fundamental dishonesty and bad faith, which barely disguises a deep selfishness and heartless lack of empathy or genuine human feeling. When Aster is at his most helpless, the narcissistically self-engrossed Orchis, feeling the pull of the other's need, is unable to give anything and becomes evasive, refusing to grasp the reality of his friend's difficulty: "But he could not drive the truth into Orchis—Orchis being very obtuse here, and, at the same time, strange to say, very melancholy. Finally, Orchis glanced off from so unpleasing a subject into the most unexpected reflections, taken from a religious point of view, upon the unstableness and deceitfulness of the human heart" (216). Similarly, the elusive Vine, in his later encounter with Clarel, "Dwelling upon his wayward dream" (2.27.72) and rambling, discourages, with a "rebukeful dusking" (2.27.116), the central character's attempt at intimacy, his poignant desire "for communion true / and close" (68–69).

The story of China Aster is part of the conversation between the cosmopolitan and Mark Winsome as they act out the dialogue between the two hypothetical friends, Frank and Charlie, and is recounted by the latter as an illustration of the foolishness of being either borrower or lender. The satirical point of this hypothetical debate, which casts such an absurd degree of doubt on the advisability of coming to the financial aid of friends, is that sociable relations, like financial relations, depend on trust and confidence, and that without them society collapses. In this regard, Charlie's refusal to lend money to a friend is the same thing as withdrawing the basis of trust not only in their relationship but in the social contract. We will explore this economic metaphor in greater detail in the next chapter when we look at the theme of human inter-indebtedness, a theme that Melville adapted, it seems, from Panurge's great disquisition on the virtue of being in debt in Rabelais's *Tiers Livre*. Panurge's comic thesis, the idea that social and human relations depend on indebtedness, is the very reverse of Charlie's argument that credit destroys friendship. What threatens Frank and Charlie's friendship, in fact, is that one of the parties is forced into a reduced and potentially humiliating position of helplessness and need: like China Aster, Frank is rudely rejected when he approaches his friend for assistance, and thus made to feel shame, shame here carrying the most explicit threat of abandonment, not just personal but social, given the supplicant's financial situation. Indeed, Charlie treats Frank's state of helplessness as itself a source of shame. Comparing a friend in need to a friend in love, Charlie asks: "Would you not instinctively say of your dripping friend in the entry, 'I have been deceived, fraudulently deceived, in this man; he is no true friend that, in platonic love to demand love-rites?'" (*CM*, 206). He concludes that "there is something wrong about the man who wants help. There is somewhere a defect, a want, in brief, a need, a crying need, somewhere about that man" (206). This entire episode is an excellent illustration of the way shame regulates attachment by "governing the interpersonal effect produced when one member of a dyad assumes a *self-image* unjustified by what can be validated consensually or accepted within the bounds of the relationship as previously agreed" (Nathanson 1987b, 32). As Frank desperately sums up his dilemma, "[H]ow foolish a cry, when to implore help, is itself the proof of undesert of it" (*CM*, 206). We are reminded here that unrequited love is a paradigmatic example of just such a needy and humiliating state. When we are in love we are in a state of helplessness, in which our worth depends entirely on the other's recognition; and therefore we find ourselves automatically under threat of abandonment, and in fear of being confirmed in the suspicion, which lies at the very core of shame, that we are defective and unlovable after all.

III

Depression, according to Bibring, as Lewis summarizes his views, is "an affective reaction to what is perceived as helplessness. . . . As to the specifics of what the ego is helpless to do, Bibring emphasizes its powerlessness to maintain, at any psychosexual stage, its narcissistic goals or aspirations, from the oral wish to be loved, to the anal wish for mastery, or the phallic wish to be admired" (Lewis 1978a, 38). These three "narcissistic goals or aspirations" play a particularly important part in Melville's work. Oral imagery—images of ingestion and incorporation—insistently crops up. The anal wish for mastery finds its most dramatic incarnation in Ahab's unlimited will to dominate and be above all others. Finally, the phallic wish to be admired can be observed, for example, in the inappropriate exhibitionism of Redburn, or, as a wish fulfilled, in the successful exhibitionistic display of Billy Budd. In each of these cases (and they are by no means exhaustive), these "narcissistic goals or aspirations" assume a somewhat distorted or prominent form.

In Lewis's view, the powerlessness to maintain narcissistic aspirations is better understood as the helplessness of the ego "to maintain its position of being loved in the other's and its own eyes. It has fallen victim to shame. The secondary aggression that results is humiliated fury, an inevitable accompaniment of shame" (1987, 38). It is this self-directed fury that would appear to be the root cause of Ishmael's depression at the beginning of *Moby-Dick*, which takes the form of a splenetic melancholia, with its attendant conventional imagery (reference to humors, the "damp, drizzly November," the funereal theme, the grimness of mood). This is followed by the revelation of a hostile antisocial impulse to go about knocking people's hats off, and finally by Ishmael's declaration that he is off to sea in order to avoid killing himself:

> Call me Ishmael. Some years ago—never mind how long precisely—having little or no money in my purse, and nothing particular to interest me on shore, I thought I would sail about a little and see the watery part of the world. It is a way I have of driving off the spleen, and regulating the circulation. Whenever I find myself growing grim about the mouth; whenever it is a damp, drizzly November in my soul; whenever I find myself involuntarily passing before coffin warehouses, and bringing up the rear of every funeral I meet; and especially whenever my hypos get such a upper hand of me, that it requires a strong moral principle to prevent me from deliberately stepping into the street, and methodically knocking people's

hats off—then, I account it high time to get to sea as soon as I can. This is my substitute for pistol and ball. (*MD*, 3)

Feeling that one is an object of scorn, contempt, and hatred, one may learn, out of the fear and guilt that accompany the wish to retaliate, to attack and hate oneself instead, which leads to chronic depression. The resentment and self-hatred grow to such proportions that these painful feelings about the self must be discharged by being directed outside onto others: the whole crew of the ship for the ostracized Redburn—"I began to feel a hatred growing up in me against the whole crew" (*R*, 62)—or innocent passers-by in the street for Ishmael. When this fails, and self-loathing, the conviction that one is unlovable, takes over, self-annihilation becomes the only available solution. Melville, in his last meeting with Hawthorne in London, told his estranged friend he had pretty well made up his mind about self-annihilation, and one of his sons, it seems, finally committed himself to it entirely.

In the opening pages of *Moby-Dick*, then, Ishmael displays all the signs of a dangerously precarious narcissistic disequilibrium, a state of shame that expresses itself as the shyness and depression of withdrawal and self-attack, or alternately a sudden impulse to attack others in anger. The novel opens with the curing of Ishmael of this imbalance. It is overcome when he establishes a lasting bond with Queequeg, a loving affiliation that cures him of his misanthropy: "I began to be sensible of strange feelings. I felt a melting in me. No more my splintered heart and maddened hand were turned against the wolfish world. This soothing savage had redeemed it" (51). The allusion to the passage in Genesis—"his hand against every man and every man's hand against him" (Gen. 16:12)—stresses the reversal that takes place: Ishmael may not ever leave the wilderness, but at this point the wilderness leaves him.

Thus, as more than one commentator has noted, it is important to make a distinction between two Ishmaels: Ishmael-sailor and Ishmael-narrator-and-anatomist, the narrated and the narrating Ishmael, the latter being in some sense a "cured" version of the former.[5] As shame among the Melvills and Gansevoorts was bound up with family name and social pretensions, and with secret feelings of personal ambition and grandiosity, one highly creative way in which Herman seems to have disarmed its effects was, as can be seen often in his letters, the adoption of a comic, self-deprecating attitude to such posturing. This is the very special province of the outcast

Ishmael's narrative voice in *Moby-Dick*. The narrator's self-depreciation, his humility, modesty, and humorous self-underestimation, are all variants of shame, but *comic* and, generally speaking, positive ones; they represent a healthy alternative to his initial misanthropy and rage. Ishmael, for example, tells us that he never goes to sea as "a Commodore, or a Captain, or a Cook. I abandon the glory and distinction of such offices to those who like them. . . . What of it, if some old hunks of a sea-captain orders me to get a broom and sweep down the decks? What does that indignity amount to, weighted, I mean, in the scales of the New Testament?" (5–6). In "The Town-Ho's Story," recounted later in the novel, Radney deliberately humiliates his subordinate, Steelkilt, by asking him to "get a broom and sweep down the planks, and also a shovel, and remove some offensive matters consequent upon allowing a pig to run at large" (246). This insulting order provokes a tragic quarrel with fatal consequences. In contrast, Ishmael's self-deprecating equanimity makes him, it appears, largely immune to narcissistic injury and therefore to such conflict. He cannot be 'put down' since he has already put himself down, as when he mocks his own importance in light of the grand design of Providence and Fate: "I cannot tell why it was exactly that those stage managers, the Fates, put me down for this shabby part of a whaling voyage, when others were set down for magnificent parts in high tragedies, and short and easy parts in genteel comedies, and jolly parts in farces" (7). This attitude is clearly not without its resentful and subversive side, but the revenge envisioned is a purely comic one: the reference to Dives and Lazarus at the end of chapter 2 ("The Carpet Bag") evokes a bitter state of social injustice that is, however, ultimately contained by the Gospel vision of an upside-down world in which the low are comically exalted and the superior thrust down. The earlier allusion to the scales of the New Testament evokes the same carnivalesque vision of the social hierarchy overturned.[6]

Ishmael's ironic defense of his conspicuous lack of ambition is thus a comic answer to the resentful sense of defeat and failure that we find in the embittered Redburn, who, at the beginning of his life, declares himself to be "as unambitious as a man of sixty" (*R*, 10). We noted how Redburn tries to escape shame by a strategy of avoidance, specifically a narcissistic overvaluation of the self that is manifested in his transparently pretentious social ambitions and aspirations. In contrast, Ishmael, who at the opening of the novel seems to be swinging back and forth between the modes of "attack self" and "attack others," comes to adopt an alternative strategy; he no longer tries to escape shame, but learns to accept it. His sense of irony thus counters the sort of tragically unrealistic grandiosity that we find, for example, in a character like Ahab, a grandiosity that disguises or masks deep shame and the haunting fear of mortification. Ishmael's credo—"Who aint a slave? Tell me that" (*MD*, 6)—reflects an unambitious acceptance of low status, and is thus the perfect comic reply to the towering ambitions summed up in Ahab's defiant question: "Who's over me? Truth hath no confines" (164). Ishmael has discovered that there are, to use Nathanson's terms, "bargains to be achieved from the open acceptance of shame" (1992, 326–27). In this spirit, he eschews hierarchical social distinctions and celebrates human contact and sociability. When he is cured, it is to sociable life that he is restored, epitomized in the comic image of a human brotherhood that, after a sort of universal comic drubbing, engages in a collective mutual massage:

> Who aint a slave? Tell me that. Well, then, however the old sea-captains may order me about—however they may thump and punch me about, I have the satisfaction of knowing that it is all right; that everybody else is one way or other served in much same way—either in a physical or metaphysical point of view, that is; and so the universal thump is passed around, and all hands should rub each other's shoulder-blades, and be content. (*MD*, 6)

The process of restoration for Ishmael begins when he arrives at the Spouter-Inn, at the beginning of his voyage, and finds himself the victim of some good-natured teasing by the landlord concerning the prospective partner with whom he is to share his bed. Still in a state of melancholic spleen, he responds to this teasing with *exasperation*. The latter word, used twice in this passage, is a particularly resonant one in Melville's work, and invariably signals the presence of humiliated fury or shame-anger. Ishmael breaks into a "towering rage," and flies "into a passion" (18), all of this in a comic key, of course, and in instructive contrast to the narcissistic rage to which Ahab gives such unrelenting expression in the rest of the novel. The next day, having spent the night with Queequeg and survived, Ishmael cherishes "no malice" toward the landlord, and is able now to laugh at himself, to enjoy the teasing and joking that the day before his more vulnerable self had taken as so injurious an assault on his pride.

> However, a good laugh is a mighty good thing, and rather too scarce a good thing; the more's the pity. So, if any one man, in his own proper person, afford stuff for a good joke to anybody, let him not be backward, but let him cheerfully allow himself to spend and be spent in that way. And the man that has anything bountifully laugh-able about him, be sure there is more than you perhaps think for. (29)

The practical joke that the landlord plays on Ishmael is, then, ultimately therapeutic. The melancholic misanthrope learns the trick of turning one's "personal embarrassment" into a source of laughter and thus bringing "plea-sure and comfort to an entire group that now views the "jokester" with increased respect" (Nathanson 1992, 326). This "rueful willingness to ac-cept the laughter" of others and thus fashion "an even stronger connection to them" (326) is worth comparing to the theme of contrition and repen-tance that is the subject of Father Mapple's sermon on Jonah, which Ishmael hears before boarding the *Pequod*.[7]

Coffin's joke seems particularly well aimed at Ishmael's dangerous self-absorption and his inhibiting fear of embarrassment and intense shame anxiety. It is, significantly, explicitly focused on a delicate source of shame for a man in the Victorian culture of nineteenth-century America: the issue of being physically intimate with a male partner, an *intimacy* that the land-lord parodically compares to the sexual intercourse of a married couple. It is the unbecomingness, the untoward nature, of such intimacy, the sharing of a bed with a male *stranger,* that makes Ishmael so uncomfortable, and the fact that Queequeg is a dark-skinned "savage" only adds to the nagging fear of possible mortification:

> I told him that I never liked to sleep two in a bed. . . . I could not help it, but I began to feel suspicious of this "dark complexioned" harpooneer. At any rate, I made up my mind that if it so turned out that we should sleep together, he must undress and get into bed before I did. . . . No man prefers to sleep two in a bed. In fact, you

would a good deal rather not sleep with your own brother. I don't know how it is, but people like to be private when they are sleeping. And when it comes to sleeping with an unknown stranger, in a strange inn, in a strange town, and that stranger a harpooner, then your objections indefinitely multiply. . . . To be sure [sailors] sleep together in one apartment, but you have your own hammock, and cover yourself with your own blanket, and sleep in your own skin. (*MD*, 14, 15, 16)

In reaction to the helpless and embarrassing position that he has been put into by the landlord, Ishmael, "cool as Mt. Hecla in a snow storm," strikes an attitude of icy haughtiness and chastises his tormentor: "And about the harpooner, whom I have not yet seen, you persist in telling me the most mystifying and exasperating stories, tending to beget in me an uncomfortable feeling towards the man whom you design for my bedfellow—a sort of connection, landlord, which is an intimate and confidential one in the highest degree" (18). Ishmael's defensive reaction here, and his suspicion and "uncomfortable feeling" towards this stranger, his anxiety about such "an intimate and confidential" connection with a stranger, his emphasis of the strangeness of the stranger and the situation (unknown stranger, strange inn, strange town, etc.), his fear of exposure (the stranger must undress, expose himself, before he will) and of being uncovered (even sailors have their own blanket with which to cover themselves)—all of this adds up to an intense case of shame anxiety. Ishmael's growing "uncomfortableness" (23)—a type of shame affect, a feeling of inhibition, in Tomkins's terms, activated by an incomplete reduction of positive affect—anticipates his sensation of uncanniness the next morning when he wakes up in Queequeg's arms, his sense of modesty being rudely shocked by his companion's explicitly matrimonial style of grasp. "My sensations were strange" (25), as he puts it. Shame anxiety, the fear that one is in danger of being suddenly exposed in a vulnerable area, is, in fact, often described as an awkward, funny, or strange, feeling, and Ishmael, in the embrace of the sleeping Queequeg, seems to be making an unconscious connection between this uncomfortable feeling and the memory of an apparently traumatic episode in his childhood: the memory of being banished to his room by his stepmother and of the terrible sense of isolation and frightening disorientation experienced upon awakening in the pitch darkness.

The analogy of the child who *makes strange* when faced with someone unfamiliar—*stranger anxiety,* as it is called—may seem rather fanciful, but it most certainly illuminates the dynamics of Ishmael's initial encounter with Queequeg, in which Ishmael's precautions against being put in an embarrassing situation come to naught and he eventually finds himself in bed with, and at the mercy of, his sleeping companion, this frightening "stranger" who unexpectedly enters the room and begins to undress: "But I lay perfectly still, and resolved not to say a word till spoken to. . . . I was all eagerness to see his face, but he kept it averted for some time while employed in unlacing the bag's mouth. This accomplished, however, he turned round—when, good heavens! what a sight! Such a face!" (20–21). Interestingly enough, Ishmael's action here—playing dead, lying still and saying nothing—recalls his childhood memory; it is precisely what he did when, isolated in the darkness of his room, he awakened to find his hand in the frozen clasp of a mysterious phantom. The difference is that the reaction of gaze aversion typical of shame was, in the latter case, so composed of fear and terror as to leave Ishmael in a state of physical paralysis, incapable of interaction. His terror of Queequeg, on the other hand, is countered from the beginning by a strong element of curiosity, precisely as a child will hide and then look, and then hide again, when making strange. Thus Ishmael shyly *hides* at first, peeking through his hands, until this strategy of withdrawal, of lying still and silent and concealing his presence, is overcome by his curiosity, to the point of his becoming *fascinated* with the awesome marvel of his roommate's gradually exposed anatomy. Ishmael's terror and paralysis in the presence of the phantom figure suggests an explicit contrast to this growing interest in Queequeg. As shame necessarily reduces interest and a healthy, curious interaction with one's environment, drawing an inhibiting, self-conscious attention to the self instead, so the active drives of interest and curiosity may, in turn, overcome shame. And so Ishmael conquers his shyness and embarrassment in these opening chapters and ends up in Queequeg's matrimonial arms. This is no small achievement. As Nathanson writes: "Shame haunts our every dream of love. The more we wish for communion, so much more are we vulnerable to the painful augmentation of any impediment, however real or fancied" (1992, 251). Ishmael moves from extremely uncomfortable feelings of embarrassment, strangeness, and even terror to a growing interest in, and eventual intimate familiarity with, the other, and his intense attentiveness to Queequeg's unusual facial and body markings turns out to part of a process whereby shame is eventually overcome and replaced by a healing communion with the other through mutual enjoyment and love.

IV

The preliminary curing of Ishmael through loving friendship is an emotional oasis in the desert of *Moby-Dick*, where the threat of betrayal is never an idle one and the fear of abandonment always looms large. It is no accident that Melville should open *Moby-Dick* with the theme of the outcast ("Call me Ishmael") and end it with the theme of the castaway, the rescue of Ishmael by the "devious-cruising Rachel, that in her retracing search after her missing children, only found another orphan" (573). The theme of abandonment appears to have been insistent in Melville's imagination. Perhaps the most disturbing image of this fear is offered in chapter 93 ("The Castaway") in *Moby-Dick*. On his first lowering, Pip jumps from the boat in fear after a whale has been struck. With great reluctance, Stubb orders Tashtego, the harpooner, to cut the line, save Pip, and lose the whale. Disgusted, the second mate reprimands him sharply and gives him fair warning: "Stick to the boat, Pip, or by the Lord, I wont pick you up if you jump; mind that. We can't afford to lose whales by the likes of you; a whale would sell for thirty times what you would, Pip, in Alabama. Bear that in mind, and don't jump any more" (413). Pip jumps again, of course, and Stubb is, like so many parental figures in Melville, a severe disciplinarian and as good as his word.

> No boat-knife was lifted when he fell so rapidly astern. Stubb's inexorable back was turned upon him; and the whale was winged. In three minutes, a whole mile of shoreless ocean was between Pip and Stubb. Out from the centre of the sea, poor Pip turned his crisp, curling, black head to the sun, another lonely castaway, though the loftiest and the brightest. (413)

Pip's only orientation is the sun, itself described as "another lonely castaway." As Cameron observes, "[W]hat drives Pip to the depths of reason is not the actual danger into which he is fallen, nor the arduousness of keeping afloat, but the pure horror of abandonment" (1991, 25). He finds himself cast out by his "society," a castaway in the measureless expanse of an inhuman wilderness. Interestingly enough, Melville, in describing the loss of Pip's sanity, suggests, with his choice of adverb, the idea of being deliberately taunted and shamed: "The sea had *jeeringly* kept his finite body up, but drowned the infinite of his soul" (*MD*, 414; emphasis added). Later in the novel, Ahab uses the explicit image of abandonment by heartless, omnipotent parental figures, those "omniscient gods oblivious of suffering man" (522), to describe the plight of the pathetic Pip: "There can be no hearts above the snow-line. Oh, ye frozen heavens! look down here. Ye did beget this luckless child, and have abandoned him, ye creative libertines" (522).[8] The tie between Ahab and Pip—"thou art tied to me by cords woven of my heart-strings" (522)—includes the explicit and essential promise of nondesertion. As Pip says to Ahab before the latter does in fact betray and desert him out of fear of being so moved by pity as to abandon his demonic quest : "They tell me, sir, that Stubb did once desert poor little Pip, whose-drowned bones now show white, for all the blackness of his living skin. But I will never desert ye, sir, as Stubb did him. Sir, I must go with ye" (534).

In Melville's work, as the abandonment of Pip illustrates, the boat, from which one is always threatened with separation, often plays a role analogous to that of the mother as a vital object of attachment. The best example is Captain Delano's shifting sense of security aboard the *San Dominick* in "Benito Cereno," in which his anxieties and feelings of mistrust are keenly attuned to the proximity of his faithful *Rover*.

> The less distant sight of that well-known boat—showing it, not as before, half blended with the haze, but with outline defined, so that its individuality, like a man's, was manifest; that boat, Rover by name, which, though now in strange seas, had often pressed the beach of Captain Delano's home, and, brought to its threshold for repairs, had familiarly lain there, as a Newfoundland dog; the sight of that household boat evoked a thousand trustful associations, which, contrasted with previous suspicions, filled him not only with lightsome confidence, but somehow with half humorous self-reproaches at his former lack of it. (*PT*, 77)

The sight of the "well-known" boat awakens feelings of trust ("a thousand trustful associations") and confidence ("lightsome confidence") that eradicate the "previous suspicions"; for the boat is associated with "home," a home away from home in "strange seas," with a familiar ("familiarly lain there") and intimate world. In *Moby-Dick* one of the parts played by Queequeg is that of a life preserver, for Ishmael and for others. Here again we can see the importance of trust and confidence, the presence or absence of the unquestioned assurance that one will not be betrayed or abandoned. It is no accident that Delano's boat *Rover* and Queequeg are both associated with man's best friend, specifically Newfoundland dogs, faithful animals who rescue those in distress and peril from imminent death. Queequeg acts as such a rescuer on a number of occasions: on the way to Nantucket when he saves a man from drowning on the boat; when he leaps into the whale's head and saves Tashtego; and when, *in absentia*, he miraculously saves Ishmael at the end of the novel, his empty coffin serving the castaway as a life buoy. Ironically, the same canine image occurs with reference to Delano's paternalistic and racist interpretation of the relationship that exists between Cereno and the treacherous Babo, a parody of the Queequeg-Ishmael dyad: "In fact, like most men of a good, blithe heart, Captain Delano took to negroes, not philanthropically, but genially, just as other men to Newfoundland dogs" (*PT,* 84).

Typically in Melville, whenever the themes of trust and confidence are too reassuringly sounded, one can be fairly certain that the poignantly discordant notes of betrayal and treachery are about to jar. The irony of the situation in "Benito Cereno" is clearly Gothic in its literary design, as the lurid Spanish motif and the insistently monachal and medieval imagery of the story suggest. But there is deep psychological significance in the story. In the case of Delano, for example, the most striking thing is the benignity of his personality, his hungry sociability, his readiness to assume a humanity brimming with goodness and gratitude. At one point, for example, he comes upon, as he sees it, a natural, "pleasant sort of sunny sight, quite sociable, too," "pure tenderness and love," a slumbering negress, with a child "sprawling at her lapped breasts" (73); we later learn, of course, that this woman is an eager participant in a treacherous and blood-thirsty conspiracy.

The fact that Delano is so obtuse as to ignore the most manifest signs of the real situation and place his confidence and trust in the very person who is secretly intent on assassinating him points, it would seem, to a rather gross act of denial. It is worth quoting here Lynd's eloquent depiction of loss of trust as a consequence of traumatic shame:

> Shattering of trust in the dependability of one's immediate world means loss of trust in other persons, who are the transmitters and interpreters of that world. We have relied on the picture of the world they have given us and it has proved mistaken; we have turned for response in what we thought was a relation of mutuality and have found our expectation misinterpreted or distorted; we have opened ourselves in anticipation of a response that was not forthcoming. With every recurrent violation of trust we become again children unsure of ourselves in an alien world. (1958, 47)

This quotation, which concerns the way shame shatters our trust in the world, is, in many ways, a description of the theme of all of Melville's fiction. As Lynd observes, "[E]xperiences that shake trusted anticipations and give rise to doubt may be of lasting importance. . . . Thus shame, an experience of violation of trust in oneself and in the world, may go deeper than guilt for a specific act" (46–47). As loving responsiveness, according to Erik Erikson, encourages "a sense of basic trust," so shame leads to *basic mistrust,*

> the sum of all those diffuse experiences which are not somehow successfully balanced by the experience of integration. One cannot know what happens in a baby, but direct observation as well as overwhelming clinical evidence indicate that early mistrust is accompanied by an experience of 'total' rage, with fantasies of the total domination or even destruction of the sources of pleasure and provision; and that such fantasies and rages live on in the individual and are revived in extreme states and situations. (1968, 82)

The application of these observations to Ahab's case is clear. They also explain Starbuck's fundamental lack of faith that ultimately makes him unable to withstand Ahab's overwhelming personality. In the person of Delano, on the other hand, we can observe one way of defending against the primal insecurity born of such experiences. His exaggerated and inappropriate sense of confidence, which makes him incapable of recognizing the true situation aboard the slave ship, could be interpreted as a way of avoiding and denying archaic fears of betrayal.

This entire thematic complex of trust, confidence, and faith versus doubt, mistrust, and suspiciousness is treated extensively in Melville's *Clarel*. There it takes the sublimated and often bloodless form of a struggle with questions of metaphysical and religious faith and doubt, questions typical of the nineteenth-century crisis of belief. Ultimately, however, these concerns are rooted in fundamental psychological realities, specifically the primal anxiety that comes with shame, the fear of being betrayed by another or others, of finding oneself helplessly rejected, powerless, and abandoned. Even when he expresses such concerns in religious terms, Melville invariably poses them in terms of the strength of one's faith or trust that, in the end, one will not be dealt falsely with. This is the human ground of all faith, religious or otherwise. "In Elizabethan England," Lynd reminds us, "doubt and fear were synonymous. 'Do not doubt that,' says Desdemona, meaning 'Trust; do not fear.' Doubt replacing basic trust in the way of life of one's social group or in one's place in it can undermine the sense of one's own identity" (1958, 47). It is precisely this deep-seated fear that haunts Melville's writings: the fear that one will be betrayed and rejected even by that other—maternal, paternal, fraternal, amorous or divine—in whom one has placed one's most certain hopes.

V

Behind this primal insecurity, this deep-seated fear of a betrayal of affection or trust, and of being left helpless and abandoned, lies the terrible suspicion that one can never be loved. This theme is certainly notable enough in Melville's work. It can be detected, for example, in Ishmael's nightmarish memory of an episode from his childhood described in "The Counterpane" chapter of *Moby-Dick*. In this dream or memory, his "stepmother"—his "mother," as he calls her in the very next breath ("my stepmother who, somehow or other, was all the time whipping me, or sending me to bed supperless,—my mother . . .")—sends him to his room without his supper for "trying to crawl up the chimney" (*MD*, 25) in imitation of a sweep he had seen do the same thing the day before. The theme of the "stepmother" suggests, of course, a splitting of the mother into a good and a bad maternal figure. To be scolded or perhaps even punished for a somewhat immoderate expression of curiosity may not be an uncommon occurrence in the life of a child. But the episode has a certain archaic quality and gives, indeed, the impression of a kind of screen memory. The idea that the child has been similarly punished many times before, the strikingly cold and unforgiving nature of the punitive maternal figure, the child's desperation to be forgiven and his anguished feelings of isolation and abandonment—all these suggest an unempathic and even abusive family environment. Ishmael's stepmother is an unrelenting disciplinarian, and we can perhaps glimpse behind what may seem like a fairly banal incident the baleful influence of the "poisonous pedagogy" that Alice Miller has exposed with such incisiveness. As noted, the child is punished here for a lively if somewhat rambunctious curiosity. Shame, as both Tomkins and Wurmser see it, can block the child's instinctive interest in his environment and the wish to display himself, the wishes to look and to be looked at, to listen and to be heard; if this function takes over, a sort of "petrification" sets in—a central image, as we shall see, in Melville's work.

The punishment recalled by Ishmael—banishment to his room—takes place during the summer solstice, the longest day of the year. The feeling of isolation becomes so unbearable that Ishmael creeps downstairs and falls in desperation at his mother's feet to beg for forgiveness:

> I felt worse and worse—at last I got up, dressed, and softly going down in my stockinged feet, sought out my stepmother, and suddenly threw myself at her feet, beseeching her as a particular favor to give me a good slippering for my misbehavior; anything indeed but condemning me to lie abed such an unendurable length of time. (26)

However, there is no reconciliation, no tearful reunion; Ishmael's stepmother cannot be budged. In this she recalls the empathizing but emotionally unclouded Starry Vere, whose surname, in the lines quoted from Marvell's "Upon Appleton House," rhymes with "severe":

> This 'tis to have been from the first
> In a domestic heaven nursed,

Under the discipline severe
Of Fairfax, and the starry Vere . . .

(ll. 721–24)

She was, the narrator notes, "the best and most conscientious of stepmothers," the starry Vere of her own domestic heaven. Marvell's image of a domestic sphere ruled by two severe disciplinarians suggests to what extent the story of Vere and Billy Budd is a tragic nursery tale, a haunting fantasy that attempts to reconcile the wish for a tender and healing reunion with the inexorable need to inflict punishment. Refusing to bend, she sends Ishmael back to his room, where he finally falls asleep. The next thing he remembers is awakening in complete darkness, completely disoriented: "Instantly I felt a shock running through all my frame; nothing was to be seen, and nothing was to be heard; but a supernatural hand seemed placed in mine. . . . For what seemed ages piled on ages, I lay there, frozen with the most awful fears, not daring to drag away my hand" (*MD*, 26). This sense of bewilderment and terror that Ishmael remembers experiencing as a child, abandoned and left alone with a silent, phantom form in the darkness of his room, is in direct contrast with the almost matrimonial intimacy that he finds on awakening in the morning with "Queequeg's arm thrown over me in the most loving and affectionate manner" (25).

According to Tomkins, shame and even contempt, when they are balanced by love, provide "a way back to the object," while in contempt, "when it is reinforced by anger or terror," there is "no way back other than defiance, reversal or destruction of the oppressor" (1963, 299–300). This may be the difference between Ishmael and Ahab, the difference between "humiliation and love" and "humiliation and hate or fear" (300). As we shall have occasion to observe more than once, Ahab and Ishmael are almost perfect polar opposites in the novel. For example, Ishmael is isolated in his room during the longest day of the year, while Ahab's psychological disintegration, which follows upon his physical dismemberment, takes place during the converse period of the winter solstice: "Ahab and anguish lay stretched together in one hammock, rounding in mid winter that dreary, howling Patagonian Cape" (*MD*, 185). The "phantom hand" that haunts Ishmael in the darkness recalls the opening image of "one grand hooded phantom, like a snow hill in the air" (7), that haunts Ahab in his quest for revenge. And in a similar way, Ishmael's wish for reconciliation with his stepmother is echoed much later in the novel in association with Ahab, in chapter 132 ("The Symphony").

This chapter is a particularly significant turning point in the novel. It opens with images of erotic merger that suggest a desire for excited and joyful communion with the object: "Aloft, like a royal czar and king, the sun seemed giving this gentle air to this bold and rolling sea; even as bride to groom. And at the girdling line of the horizon, a soft and tremulous motion . . . denoted the fond, throbbing trust, the loving alarms, with which the poor bride gave her bosom away" (542). This embrace prepares the way for the image of reconciliation which then follows, as Ahab is tempted to repent of his desire for revenge on the eve of the chase. "That glad, happy air, that winsome sky, did at last stroke and caress him; the *step-mother* world, so long cruel—forbidding—now threw affectionate arms round his stubborn neck, and did seem to joyously sob over him, as if over one, that however wilful and erring, she could yet find it in her heart to save and to bless" (543; emphasis added). The specific image of "affectionate arms" thrown around the sulking Ahab's "stubborn neck" recalls, in almost verbatim form, the image in the earlier chapter of "Queequeg's arm thrown over [Ishmael] in the most loving and affectionate manner." Tomkins speaks of reconciliation fantasies in which "the wish to openly avow the humiliation and distress without surrendering the love and respect of the parent may become the dominant power strategy" (1963, 294). In such fantasies, the recovery of communion, according to Tomkins, often includes "a tearful reunion of the relenting parent and the tearful, ashamed child," a scenario that may "arise either from the imagination of the child or from his memory of actual reconciliations with his parent who was equally anxious to re-establish communion after having ruptured the relationship with his child through his excessive harshness" (294). In "Bartleby" we can detect in the clerk's despair and rage, as E. H. Miller observes, "the child's fantasy, which sometimes does not die in childhood, that when he dies the world, meaning his parents, will mourn him and at last give him the love and attention denied him in life" (1975, 263). If the ultimate fear in shame is that one cannot be loved and will be rejected and abandoned, then the wish is that one will be lovingly reconciled with one's shamer. As we hope to show in a later chapter, it is precisely such a wish and such a fear, however contradictory, that are expressed simultaneously in *Billy Budd*, a story that "at the deepest level," as Simon O. Lesser observes, "is a legend of reconciliation between an erring son and a stern but loving father-figure" (1957, 92). "The austere devotee of military duty, letting himself melt back into what remains primeval in our formalized humanity, may in end have caught Billy to his heart, even as Abraham may have caught young Isaac on the brink of resolutely offering him up in obedience to the exacting behest" (115). In the misanthrope, however, this wish for reconciliation has lost any effective power. Melville's "Timoleon" is a demonstration of this outcome. When Timoleon's native city finally repents and persuades him to return, the great general, embittered by his protracted sojourn in the social wilderness, decides not to forgive and forget, and declines to return home. The story of a rupture in which a child is ostracized by his mother and his mother country, the poem recalls the situation of Ahab in "The Symphony" in that the reconciliation fails to materialize: when the overture takes place, the embittered, Cain-like outcast is no longer interested in reestablishing communion.

After *Pierre*, "Timoleon" is the best example of the theme of maternal betrayal and abandonment in Melville. In both these works, we are offered a trenchant portrait of the ostracizing mother, driven by shame and wielding it as a weapon. This maternal type is characterized by a deeply narcissistic personality. Her overreaching ambitions for her son are an expression of the need to see her own grandiosity flawlessly mirrored in a malleable selfobject. Pierre's "romantic filial love . . . seemed fully returned by the triumphant maternal pride of the widow, who in the clear-cut lineaments and noble air of the son, saw her own graces strangely translated into the opposite sex" (5). She thus treats her son as a kind of phallus, controlling and manipulating him in order to garner the attention and admiration she desires for herself. She has, as Murray puts it, "absorbed most of her son's personality," to the point that "what soul he can rightfully call his own must be a pathetic little waif" (1962, lii). It is only when her son threatens to depart from his prescribed role and escape her control that she transforms herself into a contemptuous and accusing figure of authority. Mrs. Glendinning's relationship to her son is thus an excellent illustration of the conditions that give rise to what Kohut calls the "vertical split" in the self. As Bacal summarizes Kohut's argument:

> The one side of the split entails maintaining a merger-bond with the caretaker that constitutes an adaptation to *his* archaic requirements: in effect, acting as the instrument of his grandiosity. To the

extent that one attempts to save one's self by disavowing or refusing to accept this condition, one may experience one's self, on the
other side of the split, as isolated, depressed, and empty, there being no selfobject support for the assertion of one's real self. (1990,
240)

In "Timoleon," such a split obtains between the two sibling rivals,
Timophanes and Timoleon, the one "maintaining a merger-bond" with the
mother and "acting as the instrument of [her] grandiosity," and the other,
without any support for "the assertion of [his] real self," "isolated, depressed,
and empty." Similar archaic requirements on the mother's part explain the
narcissistic rage with which Mrs. Glendinning threatens ostracism at any
sign of independent will on the part of a son presumed "docile" (the word
she associates with her son) and malleable to her: "I thought it was all guile-
lessness and gentlest docility to me" (P, 193). Pierre's independence is taken
as a narcissistic injury, an unfeeling attack on her, and this response betrays
the disordered basis of her personality: her haughty narcissism is a defensive structure that masks archaic feelings of shame. In one of those ludicrous but remarkable moments that keep threatening this extravagantly
melodramatic novel, Pierre has just walked out in—as his mother sees it—a
provocative act of defiance; in a fit of frustration and rage at her son's will-
ful show of independence, she flings her fork, which accidentally pierces
her portrait, so that the tines "caught in the painted bosom, vibrantly rankled
in the wound" (130). What *stabs* her emotionally is Pierre's "deed of shame,"
as she calls it: "And some deed of shame, or something most dubious and
most dark, is in thy soul, or else some belying specter, with a cloudy, shame-
faced front, sat at yon seat but now" (131). In reacting she is fearful, as she
admits to herself, that "my pride would work me some woe incurable, by
closing both my lips, and varnishing all my front, where I perhaps ought to
be wholly in the melted and invoking mood" (131). But her pride, of course,
wins out—"I will stand on pride, I will not budge"—and she defends herself
against the threat of what she perceives to be her son's defiance with scorn
and contempt, casting the offending one out. Her reaction, in other words,
is to turn the tables and cast shame on the other.

This dangerously narcissistic pride of his mother is recognized by Pierre
from the beginning: "Then, high-up, and towering, and all-forbidding before Pierre grew the before unthought of wonderful edifice of his mother's

immense pride;—her pride of birth, her pride of affluence, her pride of purity, and all the pride of high-born, refined, and wealthy Life, and all the Semiramian pride of woman" (89). As Pierre envisions the magnitude of this pride,

> he felt that deep in him lurked a divine unidentifiableness, that owned no earthly kith or kin. Yet was this feeling entirely lonesome, and orphan-like. Fain, then, for one moment, would he have recalled the thousand sweet illusions of Life; tho' purchased at the price of Life's Truth; so that once more he might not feel himself driven out an infant Ishmael into the desert, with no maternal Hagar to accompany and comfort him. (89)

Behind the queenly pride of Mary Glendinning, a pride that is itself a deep-rooted defense against shame, lie contempt and the threat of abandonment, of an Ishmaelization comparable to the one Redburn was threatened with by Jackson. Just before their later final rupture, Pierre "painted in advance the haughty temper of his offended mother, as all bitterness and scorn toward a son, once the object of her proudest joy, but now become a deep reproach, as not only rebellious to her, but glaringly dishonorable before the world" (179). At this point in the novel, Pierre is struggling with the intimidating prospect of his mother's possible reactions to what she will interpret as an attack on her, and it is not surprising that the telling word *exasperation*—invariably, as we have noted, a sign in Melville that we are in the zone of narcissistic rage—appears at least twice in this passage with reference to her distraught emotional state. Entrapped and paralyzed on all sides by pressures from shame, Pierre is faced by the dilemma that "not to admit Isabel, was now to exclude Pierre, if indeed on independent grounds of exasperation against himself, his mother would not cast him out" (179). The picture he forms of his mother did not "abstain to trace her whole haughty heart as so unrelentingly set against him" (179–80) that she would not hesitate to ostracize him completely and cut him off from all financial support. Indeed,

> so thoroughly did his infallible presentiments paint his mother's character to him, as operated upon and disclosed in all those fiercer traits,—hitherto held in abeyance by the mere chance and felicity

of circumstance,—that he felt assured that her exasperation against him would even meet the test of a public legal contention concerning the Glendinning property. For indeed there was a reserved strength and masculineness in the character of his mother, from which on all these points Pierre had every thing to dread. (180)

Earlier, in their first confrontation, as she looks "indifferently and icily" upon her son, she warns him: "Beware of me, Pierre. There lives not that being in the world of whom thou hast more reason to beware, so you continue but a little longer to act thus with me" (130). Mrs. Glendinning exemplifies, in the most dramatic way, the cold and haughty behavior of a personality in which archaic grandiosity plays a dominant part, haughtiness being, as Wurmser points out, a particularly potent defense against shame: "[I]n cold arrogance or icy withdrawal one fights off the hurt of shame and engages in all those grandiose claims and fantasies now so often lumped together as narcissism" (1987, 86–87). When Pierre tells her of his marriage, she draws herself up, terrible in her pride, "haughtily and repellingly, and with a quivering lip" (P, 185). Her very physical posture, as she struggles with the news—standing tall and erect—exemplifies the explicit antishame attitude of proudly, and defiantly, holding one's head high, as her quivering lip suggests a fight between tearful distress and the sneer of contempt. Her rigidity relaxing for a moment, "she clutched the balluster, bent over, and trembled, for a moment. Then erected all her haughtiness again, and stood before Pierre in incurious, unappeasable grief and scorn for him" (185), casting him out. Her painful feelings of betrayal and rejection, as her emotional struggle here indicates, are thus warded off with scorn and contempt, which serve to relocate shame in the other. And so it does: "in the balluster he held," Pierre feels "the sudden thrill running down to him from his mother's grasp" as she climbs up the stairs; overwhelmed by confusion and shame, staring about him "with an idiot's eye" (feeling stupid, disoriented, the sudden inability to think clearly, to focus, are symptoms of shame affect) he staggers and trips as he crosses the threshold of the house: "He seemed as jeeringly hurled from beneath his own ancestral roof" (185).

As her pride gains ascendency, Mrs. Glendinning becomes the hectoring, phallic mother, wielding the grandfather's baton of patriarchal authority. For this image of "an outraged and pride-poisoned woman" (194), "dilated with her unconquerable pride" (200), Melville seems, quite appropriately, to have drawn on the image of Milton's Satan, who stands forth all "obdúrate pride" and "unconquerable Will" (1.58, 106) when confronted by Gabriel in *Paradise Lost*: "On th' other side *Satan* alarm'd / Collecting all his might dilated stood,/ Like *Teneriff* or *Atlas* unremov'd" (4.985–87). Scorn and contempt, as we have seen, are antishame postures, and when Mrs. Glendinning says that she must "live my nature out" (131), it points to a personality particularly susceptible to "stung pride" (129) and molded at its very foundation by traumatic mortification. To defend herself against unbearable shame, she is willing to separate herself from her own son as though he were a disgusting object only worthy of contempt. Having finally cast him out, she reflects: "Now, if I were less a strong and haughty woman, the fit would have gone by ere now. But deep volcanoes long burn, ere they burn out" (195). The imagery recalls the image of the volcano associated with the narcissistically enraged Ahab in chapter 132 ("The Symphony") of *Moby-Dick:* "But so have I seen little Miriam and Martha, laughing-eyed elves, heedlessly gambol around their old sire; sporting with the circle of singed locks which grew on the marge of that burnt-out crater of his brain" (543). The connection between these two characters—Ahab and Mrs. Glendinning—is by no means a fortuitous one. In her attitude there is, though without the tragic proportions, something of Ahab's defiant speech to the spirit of fire: "In the midst of the personified impersonal, a personality stands here. Though but a point at best; whencesoe'er I came; wheresoe'er I go; yet while I earthly live, the queenly personality lives in me, and feels her royal rights" (*MD*, 507).

An identical image of the ostracizing mother recurs in "Timoleon," with the added complication of a situation of sibling rivalry, the autobiographical relevance of which is clear. Melville's biographers have long pointed to the important psychological conflict in his life that may have led him to give special attention to this theme of "struggling brothers": his parent's primary attention to his brother, Gansevoort, on whom they seem to have pinned all their hopes.[9] The theme runs through Melville's work. There is a condensed version, for example, in the sibling rivalry between Teei and Marjora in *Mardi* (219–22). According to E. H. Miller, "Melville saw himself as a wounded Narcissus, an Ishmael. He grew up in Gansevoort's shadow, the rejected son who observed with envy and anger the older brother's oratorical brilliance, his charm, and his physical attractiveness" (1975, 105).

Melville was particularly attentive to biblical treatments of sibling rivalry, such as the invidious conflict between Joseph and his brothers, or the envy at being supplanted that turns Saul against the comely David; both these stories are alluded to in *Billy Budd*. As Hershel Parker points out, the story of Saul and David "seems to have infused his treatment of Radney and Steelkilt in chapter 54 of *Moby-Dick*" (1990, 123). While struggling with his ultimate treatment of the theme in *Billy Budd*, he marked the following passage in his copy of Balzac's *Two Brothers*: "Philippe, the elder of the two sons, was strikingly like his mother. . . . Joseph, three years younger, was like his father, but only on the defective side. . . . Unconsciously, the mother acquired a habit of scolding Joseph and holding up his brother as an example to him. Agathe did not treat the two children alike. . . ." (see W. Cowan 1987, 1:58–59). Joseph's "defects" drive his mother's "heart into the gulf of maternal preference," while Philippe "flattered the mother's vanity immensely. . . . he was to her mind a man of genius; whereas Joseph, puny and sickly, with unkempt hair and absent mind, and seeking peace, loving quiet, and dreaming of an artist's glory, would only bring her, she thought, worries and anxieties." Double check marks appear beside the following passage: "She loved Joseph, though not blindly; she simply was unable to understand him. Joseph adored his mother; Philippe let his mother adore him."

When Gansevoort, as the eldest son, took the place of his deceased father beside his mother in the family hierarchy, Melville "experienced once again, as he had so often before, the humiliation and dependency upon and subordination to Gansevoort" (E. H. Miller 1975, 110). The many references to the Ishmael figure throughout Melville's work—for example, in the passage from *Pierre* quoted above in which Pierre fears that, in defying his mother, he will be driven out "an infant Ishmael into the desert, with no maternal Hagar to accompany and comfort him" (89)—indicate to what extent the Ishmael-Isaac myth gripped and dominated his imagination. The same configuration, the myth that shaped his particular family romance, keeps recurring in his fiction: the rival sons, the beloved Isaac (Gansevoort) and the rejected Ishmael (Herman); the mother split into two, the "maternal Hagar" and the haughty, ambitious Sarah—the phallic mother; and the ambivalent father Abraham, an idealized figure capable, however, of great weakness and of great betrayal—the ultimate betrayal of abandoning and sacrificing a son.[10] The same configuration obviously struck Melville in the story of Timoleon. In his version of the story, as rivals for the affection of their mother, "brothers, playfellows in youth" who "Develop into variance wide in span," Timophanes and Timoleon are in a situation very close to that of the competitiveness that appears to have existed between Herman and his older brother.

> Timophanes was his mother's pride—
> Her pride, her pet, even all to her
> Who slackly on Timoleon looked:
> Scarce he (she mused) may proud affection stir.
> *(Poems*, 3.1–4)

In "Timoleon," the mother's slack look, her negligence, and her unappreciativeness of her younger son are flagrant. She even fails to show gratitude to Timoleon for having saved his brother's life. In thus favoring Timophanes, she is treating him as a mirror, as Mrs. Glendinning treats Pierre, unashamedly projecting her narcissism on to him, and like Mrs Glendinning, the mother's intense ambition, her desperation to be "an envied dame of power," are shame-driven, her narcissism being a structure that has been built up to ward off the threat of rejection. She thus manipulates her son, and narcissistically holds him up for others to admire and pay homage to:

> But thou, my first-born, thou art I
> In sex translated; joyed, I scan
> My features, mine, expressed in thee;
> Thou art what I would be were I a man.
>
> My brave Timophanes, tis thou
> Who yet the world's fore-front shall win,
> For thine the urgent resolute way,
> Self pushing panoplied self through thick and thin.
> *(Poems*, 3.17–24)

Thus forced to substitute the wish to be admired for the wish to be loved for who he is, Timophanes is a perfect example of "the so-called phallic man," as Alice Miller describes the type: "He is his mother's special son. . . . The 'phallic man' must be a really splendid fellow if he wants to feel like a man at all" (1981, 41). The self, however, is lost in such a bargain, and the feeling of emptiness and the despair at never being recognized as an independent self are denied and masked by an insatiable quest for attention, mirroring, and control; in other words, Timophanes, however much he may be admired, does not feel that he is loved, precisely because he has never had a chance to be himself. In grossly favoring one son and cruelly slighting the other as lacking "the quality keen / To make the mother through the son / An envied dame of power, a social queen" (*Poems*, 3.14–16), the mother does not, indeed, withhold love from one son and give it to another: she withholds genuine caring and love from both. As Miller puts it: "Narcissistic cathexis of her child by the mother does not exclude emotional devotion. On the contrary, she loves the child, as her self-object, excessively, though not in the manner that he needs, and always on the condition that he presents his 'false self'" (1981, 14).

As a manipulated extension of his controlling mother, as someone whose feeling is that the love bestowed upon him is entirely conditional, Timophanes responds to the threat of shame in a frenetic search for power and admiration. His narcissistic defenses thus blot out the legitimate claims of conscience and human caring, and he is consequently ruthless enough to grasp and maintain power:

> Nor here maternal insight erred:
> Forsworn, with heart that did not wince
> At slaying men who kept their vows,
> Her darling strides to power, and reigns—a Prince.
> (*Poems*, 3.25–28)

At the challenge by his brother to his right to commit injustice and not be subject to the same standards of ideal conduct as others, his "merriment gives place to rage" and he pronounces: "I am the Wrong, and lo, I reign" (4.10–11).[11] He thus strikes a posture of defiance, an antishame posture that is one of the most popular ways of combating shame in Melville's characters. Timophanes' attitude here recalls, for example, that of Ahab, who defiantly announces: "What I've dared, I've willed; and what I've willed, I'll do" (*MD*, 168). Timophanes' overbearing will to dominate, like Ahab's, is an expression of what Bibring calls the "anal wish for mastery" and can be explained in the following way: if one cannot be loved, and if one is refused admiration, then one can still dominate, as a substitute for both love and admiration.

Timoleon, for his part, is depicted as the wronged party, as a victim of neglect and aggression—someone who is pushed to fratricide only by the excesses of a tyrannical and unjust brother. The same theme recurs in "The Town-Ho's Story" in *Moby-Dick*, in which the forbearing Steelkilt is pushed to the limit by the domineering Radney, and in *Billy Budd*, in which Billy is provoked by Claggart to an apparently justifiable act of violence. Guilt, in all these cases, is strongly mitigated, as the innocent are forced by circumstances to commit acts of transgression that make them guilty under the law. The absence of any effective mediator appears to be part of the problem. The authority invested in the captain (Captain Riga, the captain of the *Town-Ho*, Captain Delano, Captain Vere) is often ineffectual and the captain is unable to avert the tragic consequences of deep emotional conflict.

Timoleon's punishment for his crime is ostracism. Shunned by his mother and by the society she rules, he is treated as a stranger in his own land. Shamed, he flees and conceals himself, "self-outcast," to live, like an Ishmael, "in wilding place" (*Poems*, 6.26). His punishment is to live as a head cut off from a body, "Estranged" (6.29) by the shame that covers him "From common membership in mart" (6.30), from the vitalizing social community of which he was a part: "In severance he is like a head / Pale after battle trunkless found apart" (6.31–32). In the penultimate section of the poem, Timoleon is painted, in romantic terms, as a rejected or exiled figure cursing his fate and the heartless gods who have betrayed him and abandoned him in the wilderness, those "creative libertines" whom Ahab accuses of cruelly deserting Pip.

> But deign, some little sign be given—
> Low thunder in your tranquil skies;
> Me reassure, nor let me be
> Like a lone dog that for a master cries.
> (7.25–28)

This plaintive expression of helplessness might recall Frank's protest to Charlie's cruel rebuff in *The Confidence-Man:* "How foolish a cry, when to implore help, is itself the proof of undesert of it" (206); or, in its self-pitying tone, Redburn's bitter description of his fate, as he comments on his brother's parting advice to take care of himself: "I solemnly promised I would; for what cast-away will not promise to take care of himself, when he sees that unless he himself does, no one else will" (*R*, 11). It was Lawrance Thompson who first explored the very fruitful idea of Melville's "quarrel with God," the idea, so prominent in his work, of a titanic grudge against a treacherous universe—a theme we shall return to in our discussion of *ressentiment*. But this intense feeling of resentment is, before all else, the result of a deep sense of injustice and feeling of outrage, of betrayal and helplessness, in the face of an all too *human* rejection and abandonment. This feeling, as we noted, is part of the configuration typical of shame as a causal factor in depression. The overwhelming sense of helplessness and powerlessness in the face of rejection and the hostility that is consequently directed at the self are particularly important in the most searing forms of shame, such as the narcissistic mortification that Ahab experiences in his defeat by Moby Dick, to which he responds with the disproportionate anger of the narcissistically enraged. In Ishmael, on the other hand, we witness a very different response to shame and shame-anger. In shame and contempt, as Tomkins points out, if there is love, there is always a way back to the object, and the prospect—the hope—of reaffiliation is maintained; if there is a predominance of contempt and hate, the bridge back to the object is burned, and all that is left is the desire to annihilate the object or shaming other. It is this difference, the difference in Melville's work between the tragic and the comic vision, that we would now like to explore.

CHAPTER TWO

Mortifying Inter-Indebtedness

I

In his original confrontation with Moby Dick, Ahab undergoes a traumatic experience of terror combined with *mortification,* a form of extreme humiliation. The account of the confrontation is placed in the context of the whale's past victims and the intense feeling of outrage that overcomes them. Their sense of betrayal and helpless anger at their own powerlessness is underscored by the image of the sun, indifferent to human suffering, looking on radiantly at the unfolding scene.

> Judge, then, to what pitches of *inflamed, distracted fury* the minds of his more desperate hunters were impelled, when amid the chips of chewed boats, and the sinking limbs of torn comrades, they swam out of the white curds of the whale's direful wrath into *the serene, exasperating sunlight, that smiled on, as if at a birth or a bridal.* (MD, 184; emphasis added)

The word *exasperating* is again linked with the theme of rage or humiliated fury, those "pitches of inflamed, distracted fury" to which the whale's "more desperate hunters"—the most desperate of all being Ahab—"[are] impelled."[1] Cast among the wreckage like so many of the whale's victims before him, Ahab distinguishes himself in that, rather than swim away, he is pushed by his impotent rage to retaliate for the destruction of his boat and crew. He recklessly strikes at his enemy and finds himself all but annihilated by a superior physical force that (as he sees it) mocks and taunts him. The description of his futile attempt to fight back stresses his infuriating sense of helplessness as he dashes blindly at the whale only to watch as his adversary reaps his leg away, "as a mower a blade of grass in the field" (184). The next time Ahab sees the whale, at the outset of the chase in the closing chapters of the novel, the description of this powerful creature as it sails serenely through the water—this serene, maddening image of Moby Dick as omnipotent Jupiter in the shape of a great white bull, gliding away with Europa on his back—serves again to underline his mortifying sense of defeat and impotency (548).

The experience described here is clearly analogous to "the quintessential reaction to the sense of helplessness in the face of the experience of selfobject failure" (Bacal 1990, 236). Such a feeling is so intolerable that it is "quickly erased from consciousness and, at the same time, trigger[s] the expression of narcissistic rage at the offending object." Béla Grunberger defines the experience of narcissistic mortification in a similar way, as the feeling triggered by "the ego's humiliation, for example for submitting passively to what one cannot actively control" (1979, 21). Lewis emphasizes "the bind which is intrinsic in humiliated fury," where the anger that "pushes toward discharge" is "anger which results from [the] feeling of helplessness, i.e., anger of impotence or shame-anger which is directed against the self" (1971, 209–10). This feeling of humiliated fury or shame-anger (or, as Kohut calls it, narcissistic rage) is akin to the feeling that one has been betrayed; there is the same overwhelming sense of *helplessness*, of impotency and utter lack of control in face of the noncompliance of one's human or physical environment. At the end of *Moby-Dick*, significantly enough, the word "helpless" recurs several times, punctuating each agonizing turning point of Ahab's defeat by his rival: "[T]hen it was that monomaniac Ahab, furious with this tantalizing vicinity of his foe, which placed him all alive and *helpless* in the very jaws he hated; frenzied with all this, he seized the long bone with his naked hands, and wildly strove to wrench it from its gripe" (550; emphasis added); "*helpless* Ahab's head was seen, like a tossed bubble which the least chance shock might burst" (551; emphasis added); "the long tension of Ahab's bodily strength did crack, and *helplessly* he yielded to his body's doom: for a time, lying all crushed in the bottom of Stubb's boat, like one trodden under foot of herds of elephants. Far inland, nameless wails came from him, as desolate sounds from out ravines" (551; emphasis added). As these passages suggest, then, it is the feeling of helplessness in the face of his plight, and of the accompanying undischarged anger directed at himself, that is at the heart of Ahab's deep inner sadness. In an earlier passage of the novel, the same feeling floods his voice as he gazes in despair on a passing ghost ship whose entire crew has been destroyed by plague: "There seemed but little in the words, but the tone conveyed more of deep helpless sadness than the insane old man had ever before evinced" (237). *Deep help-*

less sadness is a perfect description of the depression induced by chronic feelings of shame, in which dejection is a result of self-directed hostility (one is ashamed of oneself, one feels worthless and contemptible, one hates oneself). The "terrific, loud, animal sob, like that of a heart-stricken moose" (163) that Ahab heaves as he tells the crew of his defeat and razing by Moby Dick is an expression of the same feeling of searing shame.[2]

In defining mortification as a variety of shame, Lewis offers the "meaning of the term in current, general use" as, according to *The Oxford English Dictionary*, "'the feeling of humiliation caused by a disappointment, a rebuff or a slight, or an untoward accident; the sense of disappointment or vexation. Also, an instance of this; a cause or source of humiliation.' To be mortified means to be humiliated deeply; to be vexed, chagrined" (1971, 72). In contrast with humiliation, however, which is less specific, the source of mortification is "wounded pride" (72). Mortification, for example, is what Redburn is describing when he speaks, at the beginning of the novel, of the "Sad disappointments" (*R*, 13) that he has suffered in his early life, of those blights to the self that "never again can . . . be made good; they strike in too deep, and leave such a scar that the air of Paradise might not erase it" (11). This is an instance, clearly, of the "primary woundedness" (1981, 296) of which Wurmser speaks. The reference to "Paradise" suggests the loss of an irrecoverable elative state of narcissistic equilibrium or homeostasis, a state of well-being that seems to have been maintained, in Redburn's case, largely through the pride afforded by the merger with an idealized father.

It is simply a much more dramatic image of the same thing that appears in Ahab's humiliating defeat by Moby Dick. There is the same idea of a lost paradisal state of elation and joy, and the narcissistic desire to return to this world of bliss from which he is exiled makes Ahab feel, as he gazes in despair on the loveliness of a sunset that no longer soothes, "damned in the midst of Paradise!" (*MD*, 167), like Milton's Satan at the sight of Adam and Eve in the Garden. The same note, along with the theme of a deep psychic "scar" that nothing can erase, is sounded again when he says to the blacksmith, "In no Paradise myself, I am impatient of all misery in others that is not mad" (488), and then passionately pleads with him to use his forging powers to smooth out the "seam" of his "ribbed brow":

" . . . Cans't thou smoothe this seam?"
"Oh! that is the one, sir! Said I not all seams and dents but one?"

> "Aye, blacksmith, it is the one; aye, man, it is unsmoothable;
> for though thou only see'st it here in my flesh, it has worked down
> into the bone of my skull—that is all wrinkles!" (488)

In Ahab, mortification has a focus in the haunting memory of his lost limb and the nagging physical discomfort that it causes him. It thus acts as an enduring, if not penitentially self-imposed, "mortification"—a shaming to death, as it were—of the flesh. It is the unabating persistence of the effects of the original injury that is most difficult to endure, a fact that is highlighted when he splinters his ivory leg in his rush to leave the *Samuel Enderby* and accidentally pierces himself in the groin: at the time, it did not fail "to enter his monomaniac mind, that all the anguish of that then present suffering was but the direct issue of a former woe" (463–64). Indeed, he cannot seem to eradicate the *memory* of the actual physical pain of his dismemberment: "And if I still feel the smart of my crushed leg, though it be now so long dissolved; then, why mayst not thou, carpenter, feel the fiery pains of hell for ever, and without a body? Hah!" (471). But this haunting nature of the pain, its terrible persistence, is, of course, not primarily the consequence of a physical injury; it resembles, rather, the obsessive quality of remembered incidents associated with searing shame or narcissistic injury. Nathan Schwartz-Salant speaks of events that "wounded the ego's self-esteem" as being "remembered with great tenacity" (1982, 39). Kohut similarly remarks upon the "excessive preoccupation" with such events, which enrage the self "even to the point of wishing to do away with oneself in order to wipe out the tormenting memory" (1978, 642).

The loss of his leg has, moreover, the practical disadvantage of making Ahab completely helpless in certain situations, and thus prone to being suddenly and unexpectedly reduced to an inferior position in the eyes of others. The "loss of position in one's own or in the 'other's' eyes" is an important factor in humiliation, where the spectator may be internal or external to the self. If we wish to define what is specific to mortification, "it is easy to see how humiliation might carry one from a loss of esteem in one's own eyes to wounded pride: feeling as if one had received a slight or rebuff from the 'outside' and the 'other' were present to witness mortification" (Lewis 1971, 71, 73). This idea that others are looking on at one in one's helplessness and vulnerability is an essential element in Ahab's mortifying sense of exposure as he attempts to board the *Samuel Enderby*.

"[D]eprived of one leg" and without "the very handy mechanical contrivance peculiar to the Pequod," he is unable to climb up the ship's side, as the boat rises and falls in the swells: "Ahab now found himself abjectly reduced to a clumsy landsman again; hopelessly eyeing the uncertain changeful height he could hardly hope to attain" (*MD*, 437).[3]

Ahab experiences shame here as a result, in the first place, of being physically incapable of completing an action that, before he was disabled, he would have performed without difficulty or hesitation. Involved here is the feeling of "I want, but—" that is essential to shame, shame being triggered whenever "desire outruns fulfillment sufficiently to attenuate interest without destroying it" (Tomkins 1963, 185). To make matters worse, however, Ahab is standing helplessly in the boarding craft, in full view of both crews. He is suddenly disconcerted by "the sight of the two officers of the strange ship, leaning over the side . . . and swinging towards him a pair of tastefully-ornamented man-ropes; for at first they did not seem to bethink them that a one-legged man must be too much of a cripple to use their sea bannisters" (*MD*, 437). It is as though the original mortification inflicted by Moby Dick were being repeated, but in little. As the narrator informs us, "every little untoward circumstance that befel him, and which indirectly sprang from his luckless mishap, almost invariably irritated or *exasperated* Ahab" (437; emphasis added).

Another aspect of this episode, and, indeed, of the entire theme of Ahab's maiming by Moby Dick, is the important motif of maintaining one's legs, which, running throughout Melville's work of this period, bears on the association of human pride with the ability to stand erect. This theme is connected to the widespread imagery in *Moby-Dick* of various "erections" and their dismasting, of proud masts and hubristic towers.[4] It is interesting to compare Ahab's experience in boarding the *Samuel Enderby* with the description of other captains making the journey to "gam" with a friendly vessel. They too find themselves caught in a potentially humiliating predicament and threatened with a loss of the perpendicular dignity expressive of their captainly office. However, here the theme is treated lightheartedly and in the spirit of that comic humility and acceptance evinced in the opening chapter of the novel by Ishmael, who abandons "the glory and distinction of such offices to those who like them" (5). As the boarding vessel journeys from one ship to another, the captain is expected to maintain without external support his erect posture—to stand on his own two legs—and is thus naturally subject to an anxious self-consciousness about his potentially mortifying visibility and exposure.

> And often you will notice that *being conscious of the eyes of the whole visible world resting on him* from the sides of the two ships, this standing captain is all alive to *the importance of sustaining his dignity by maintaining his legs.* . . . Then, again, it would never do *in plain sight of the world's riveted eyes*, it would never do, I say, for this straddling captain to be seen steadying himself the slightest particle by catching hold of anything with his hands. . . . Nevertheless, there have occurred instances . . . where the captain has been known for an uncommonly critical moment or two, in a sudden squall say—to seize hold of the nearest oarsman's hair, and hold on there like grim death. (241; emphasis added)

An analogous example of mortification treated with rather broad humor is one of the "Authentic Anecdotes of 'Old Zack'," a series of sketches in which Melville, as Chase puts it, "parodies Barnum's advertising style and gulls him generally" (1949, 77). A "mischievous young drummer boy" inserts a "sharp iron tack, point upwards, into the august saddle of the hero of Palo Alto" (*PT*, 217); General Taylor jumps into the saddle but does not react until, on dismounting that evening to enter his tent,

> he was most unexpectedly made aware of what must have seemed to him, at the time, a base and pitiful trick of the enemy. The tack caught in the seat of his inexpressibles, and as he sprang to the ground, would not let go, but left the greater part of the garment upon the saddle. Though valiant as Cid, the old hero is as modest as any miss. Instantly muffling up with his coat tails the exposed part, he hurried into his tent, violently and most perfectly enraged at the occurrence. (217)

As Chase puts it, "[T]he general, though impervious to pain, is overcome with mortification" (1949, 77).

We have already discussed the role of comedy and laughter as it applies to the healing of Ishmael in the opening of the novel. Melville often develops a theme by giving it comic and serious contrasts, and the cure of laughter learned in his assiduous reading of Rabelais, Burton, and Sterne, as well as of the frontier humorists, is reflected in the parodic treatment of potentially tragic themes throughout *Moby-Dick*. The letter to his brother Allan (20 February 1849) on the birth of his son Malcolm is a perfect example of this hyperbolic grotesque style: "We desired much to have him weighed, but it was thought that no hay-scales in town were strong enough. It takes three nurses to dress him. . . . If the worst comes to the worst, I shall let him out by the month to Barnum; and take the tour of Europe with him" (*Corr.*, 116).[5] An extensive comic contrast to Ahab's sense of mortifying injury and the implacable need for redress is drawn out humorously in chapter 100 ("Leg and Arm"), the very chapter that opens with the description of his humiliating discomfiture in the eyes of the onlooking crews and that closes with the hasty exit that, we later learn, results in the shattering of his artificial leg.

Captain Boomer's balanced attitude to a situation comparable to Ahab's offers a parodic overturning of the theme of narcissistic injury. Deliberately drawing attention to his disability, in honest acceptance of his humanity, the English captain comes forward "With his ivory arm frankly thrust forth in welcome," a gesture to which Ahab responds by heartily, if grimly, joining in the spirit and crossing his leg with the arm, as the two "shake bones together" in a grotesque image of shared woundedness. In the ensuing conversation, the ironic account of Boomer's loss of an arm explicitly parodies Ahab's more tragically toned, deeply searing encounter with the white whale. Boomer and Bunger's names are clearly burlesque, and their lively repartee is peppered with jokes about drinking ("Water!" cried the captain; "he never drinks it; it's a sort of fits to him; fresh water throws him into the hydrophobia" [440]), as they cheerfully carry on a conversation about serious matters of life and death. This puts them, in Melville's view, squarely in the Rabelais camp, those who, as the narrator puts it in chapter 97 ("The Try-Works"), "throughout a care-free lifetime [swear] by Rabelais as passing wise, and therefore jolly" (424).

Moby-Dick is full of images of wounding, striking, and sundering, of dismemberment and tearing to pieces. The humorous counterpart of this violent imagery would seem to be the verbal alternatives of knocking, thrashing, punching, or thumping, imagery that suggests the countertragic, carnivalesque spirit of a communal comic beating or drubbing. This is the language Ishmael uses to describe beatings administered by sea captains or whales, an expression, it would seem, of comic humility on his part, especially reserved for unavoidable manifestations of superior force, natural or otherwise. There is, for example, this playful depiction of the suggestively named "Thrasher whale": "This gentleman is famous for his tail, which he uses for a ferule in thrashing his foe" (239); or the following jocular description of fishermen who avoid certain whales known to be particularly irritable: "Like some poor devils ashore that happen to know an irascible great man, they make distant unobtrusive salutations to him in the street, lest if they pursued the acquaintance further, they might receive a summary thump for their presumption" (204).

It is precisely this lighthearted tone and cheerful view of things that Boomer and Bunger adopt. The ship's surgeon, for example, in the midst of describing the "ugly gaping wound" inflicted on the captain's arm by Moby Dick, good-naturedly alludes to being knocked about one day by his former patient with his "club-hammer" and receiving a dent in his skull, which he obligingly exposes to Ahab, offering the explanation:

> "[H]e had that club-hammer there put to the end, to knock some one's brains out with, I suppose, as he tried mine once. He flies into diabolical passions sometimes. Do you see this dent, sir"—removing his hat, and brushing aside his hair, and exposing a bowl-like cavity in his skull, but which bore not the slightest scarry trace, or any token of ever having been a wound—"Well, the captain there will tell you how that came here; he knows."
>
> "No, I don't," said the captain, "but his mother did; he was born with it. Oh, you solemn rogue, you—you Bunger! was there ever such another Bunger in the watery world? Bunger, when you die, you ought to die in pickle, you dog; you should be preserved to future ages, you rascal." (440)

Ahab laments to the blacksmith that the seam or dent in his brow can never be healed, for it has worn itself into his skull. Bunger's scar, however, bears "no token of ever having been a wound." It is a clear parody of Ahab's mysterious mark of Cain, the rodlike scar of this world's woe that appears to thread its way down his entire body. The provenance of Ahab's mark is the object of much speculation aboard the *Pequod:* the crew is uncertain as to "whether that mark was born with him, or whether it was the scar left by some desperate wound" (123). Earlier in the novel, as he watches Queequeg prostrate before his idol, Ishmael comments that "we are all somehow dreadfully cracked about the head, and sadly need mending" (81). This is the observation of a man living in a world where thrashing and beating are the norm, but who, in contrast with the enraged Ahab, assumes a comically balanced attitude towards the inevitable concussions of this world. As Ishmael puts it in the opening chapter of the novel, "[A]nd so the universal thump is passed round, and all hands should rub each others shoulder-blades, and be content" (6).

Throughout the entire *Samuel Enderby* episode, then, what is tragic in Ahab is put in an often ludicrously comic key. Particularly noteworthy is Boomer's decision to forswear any attempt to redress the wrong by taking revenge. In an explicit parody of Ahab's retaliatory and vindictive strategy, Bunger and Boomer joke about the captain's trying to use his left arm for bait to get back the right. "Ahab's tragedy," as Merlin Bowen observes, lies in "a nature which must take from the event a personal and unforgivable affront. Captain Boomer of the 'Enderby' can lose an arm to the same monster, spend his convalescence drinking rum toddies with the ship's surgeons, and cheerfully call the matter quits" (1960, 148). Bunger imagines the whale vomiting up the indigestible arm, a comically grotesque image of that stage in the mythical dragon-killing story when the monster or leviathan gives up his dead after being slain by the hero. "No, thank ye, Bunger," Boomer concludes, "he's welcome to the arm he has, since *I can't help it*, and didn't know him then; but not to another one" (441; emphasis added). In chapter 31 ("Queen Mab") the old merman in Stubb's dreams uses the same words when advising him to stop stubbing his toe against Ahab's "pyramid" and humorously to count it an honor, not a humiliation, to be kicked by the ivory leg of such a mighty man: "Remember what I say; *be* kicked by him; account his kicks honors; and on no account kick back; for *you can't help yourself*, wise Stubb" (132; second emphasis added). This nonretaliatory attitude may seem ignoble from a certain point of view—it is a good example of the use of jocularity to deny the starkness of reality, which is criticized by the narrator elsewhere in the novel—but here it serves as a foil, showing a comic acceptance of the *helplessness* which for Ahab is an insufferable and outrageous condition.

The encounter between Stubb and Ahab (chapter 29) and the dream that Stubb recounts to Flask (chapter 31) are comparable in several details to the comic overturning of Ahab's tragic stance in the meeting with the *Samuel Enderby*. Stubb's dream is, like the conversation between Boomer and Bunger, deliberately constructed as a parody of Ahab's desire to redress and revenge a narcissistic injury, the parody being underlined, among other things, by the pyramid he keeps kicking (Moby Dick's hump is shaped like a pyramid) and the bristle of harpoons in the backside of the merman. Boomer alludes to the same bristling badge of honor in identifying Moby Dick: "And harpoons sticking in near his starboard fin" (438). The episode begins with the ill-advised Stubb, his sleep disturbed by the thumping of Ahab's ivory leg on the deck, tactlessly asking his superior to muffle the noise, thus conspicuously drawing attention to the latter's impairment. This is a perfect example of one of those "little untoward circumstances" that "almost invariably irritated or exasperated Ahab" (437). Humiliated, Ahab adopts a countershaming response; he discharges his anger by shaming his shamer. He threatens him physically and treats him with the most scornful contempt ("Down, dog, and kennel!"), and when there is objection, insults him in the most humiliating terms: "Then be called ten times a donkey, and a mule, and an ass, and begone, or I'll clear the world of thee!" (127). Later, Stubb tells Flask of his dream, in which Ahab "kicked me with [his ivory leg]; and when I tried to kick back, upon my soul, my little man, I kicked my leg right off!" (131). (The parody of Ahab's wounding by Moby Dick is quite explicit here.) The mortified Stubb deals with the experience of wounded pride in a very different way from his captain, of course. His first impulse, immediately checked, is to retaliate: "I was never served so before without giving a hard blow for it" (128). The impulse to "go back and strike him" is tempered, among other things, by Stubb's acute awareness of the distinctive nature of Ahab's narcissistic rage. Thanks to his dream and the propitious intervention of the casuistic Mr. Humpback, he dissuades himself from the feeling that he should seek redress. Recognizing that Ahab is an impersonal force, like Moby Dick himself, he concludes that "the best thing you can do, Flask, is to *let that old man alone*" (132; emphasis added). George Boomer uses the same words to Ahab in referring to the white whale: "There would be great glory in killing him, I know that; and there is a shipload of precious sperm in him, but, hark ye, *he's best let alone*; don't you think so, Captain?" (441; emphasis added).

The *Samuel Enderby* interlude ends with a telling incident. Like Ahab, Boomer is, as the surgeon note, prone to fits of rage and "flies into diabolical passions sometimes" (440). But it is comic rage, a noisy but harmless fury, quick to subside. The narcissistic rage of Ahab, interminable and lethal, is another matter. During their discussion of Moby Dick, Bunger notices Ahab's heated agitation and playfully teases him about it: "this man's blood—bring the thermometer;—it's at the boiling point!—his pulse makes these planks beat!" (441). "A hot old man!" is how Stubb puts it after he has been insulted, muttering that Ahab's pillow is "a sort of frightful hot, as though a baked brick had been on it" (128). The "gam" on the *Enderby* suddenly ends when Bunger, waving his surgeon's lancet, jokingly draws close to Ahab; Ahab shows that, in a state of exasperation, he is no man to tease: he explodes in anger and dashes the good-natured doctor against the bulwarks.

As this and countless other episodes serve to underscore, Ahab's chronic shame and rage is so deep-rooted that he is incapable of accepting himself as a human being beset by universal limitations that—this is the recurrent theme—*cannot be helped*. Instead, he interprets such obstacles to his will as narcissistic injuries. As he mutters in the closing moments of the chase (with that inevitable word appearing once more): "Would now the wind had but had a body; but all the things that most *exasperate* and outrage mortal man, all these things are bodiless, but only bodiless as objects, not as agents" (564; emphasis added). In other words, behind the "pasteboard mask" of the visible world a malignant force is at work that deliberately seeks to frustrate and humiliate "mortal man." What Kohut calls the grandiose self must be understood as inhabiting an archaic realm in which it insists on absolute control over its environment. When the object or environment does not comply, rage ensues (1978, 656). This rage may be so intense that the ego refuses any longer to accept "the inherent limitations of the power of the self" (657). Rather than admit these limitations, it blames any reduction in power on "the malevolence and corruption of the uncooperative archaic object" (657). Thus, "in his frantic morbidness," Ahab identifies with Moby Dick "not only all his bodily woes, but all his intellectual and spiritual exasperations" (283). If there are eventualities that are beyond one's control, they can only be, in Ahab's mind, the handiwork of some supernatural malignant agent, some personified power who is out to humiliate his victim in the most infuriating manner.

In the great speech from "The Quarter-Deck" ("Hark ye yet again,—the little lower layer"), Ahab expresses this irrational susceptibility to narcissistic injury and rage in the language of high metaphysical seriousness:

"Sometimes I think there's naught beyond. But 'tis enough. He tasks me; he heaps me; I see in him outrageous strength, with an inscrutable malice sinewing it. That inscrutable thing is chiefly what I hate; and be the white whale agent, or be the white whale principal, I will wreak that hate upon him. Talk not to me of blasphemy, man; I'd strike the sun if it insulted me" (164). As we have seen, however, Melville's incessant contrasting of the comic and the tragic helps to put the narcissism of Ahab's paranoid view of the universe in focus. Accordingly, in the opening paragraph of chapter 49 ("The Hyena") this grandly tragic theme finds its perfect comic double in Ishmael's self-deprecating metaphysics of the joke:

> There are certain queer times and occasions in this strange mixed affair we call life when a man takes this whole universe for a vast practical joke, though the wit thereof he but dimly discerns, and more than suspects that the joke is at nobody's expense but his own. . . . And as for small difficulties and worrying, prospects of sudden disaster, peril of life and limb; all these, and death itself, seem to him only sly, good-natured hits, and jolly punches in the side bestowed by the unseen and unaccountable old joker. That odd sort of wayward mood I am speaking of comes over a man only in some time of extreme tribulation; it comes in the very midst of his earnestness, so that what just before might have seemed to him a thing most momentous, now seems but a part of the general joke. (226)

Bainard Cowan has justly demonstrated the relevance of Mikhail Bakhtin's theory of laughter to an understanding of *Moby-Dick*: "The motif of hitting and punching captures precisely that jollity and perception of relativity that dominates the carnival, and Bakhtin documents the traditions of good-natured drubbing in medieval festivals as well as in Rabelais" (1982, 118). Thus couched in the imagery of a comic drubbing—"sly, good-natured hits, and jolly punches in the side bestowed by the unseen and unaccountable old joker"—Ishmael's equanimity and acceptance here are the humorous counterpoint to Ahab's paranoid interpretation of the universe. From this competing perspective, inevitable setbacks are perceived not as personal attacks but as good-natured pranks, and instead of unforgiving fury they are met with laughter—a laughter directed at oneself above all ("the joke is at nobody's expense but his own"). As Suzanne M. Retzinger has suggested, the ability to laugh at themselves is a healthy indication that those dominated by narcissistic rage and resentment, incurably mirthless as they are, are on the road to recovery: "In the sharing of laughter we find a common ground, can transform our shame into laughter, and become unified with others" (1987, 167). Reconnecting broken bonds, laughter has the power to release us from the spiral of shame and rage (177).[6]

II

The trauma of searing mortification, and the anxiety it produces—namely, that it will happen again—explains Ahab's extravagant fantasy-vision of an invulnerable, omnipotent titanic body in chapter 108 ("Ahab and the Carpenter"). Ahab hails the carpenter, who is presented as a parody of Ovid's Prometheus, the Titan who molded man out of clay ("Well, manmaker!"), and puts in an order for a custom-made artificial man that would be proof against all injury, physical and emotional. Mary Shelley's *Frankenstein*, with its subtitle *The Modern Prometheus*, naturally comes to mind here.

> Hold; while Prometheus is about it, I'll order a complete man after a desirable pattern. Imprimis, fifty feet high in his socks; then, chest modelled after the Thames Tunnel; then, legs with roots to 'em, to stay in one place; then, arms three feet through the wrist; no heart at all, brass forehead, and about a quarter of an acre of fine brains; and let me see—shall I order eyes to see outwards? No, but put a sky-light on top of his head to illuminate inwards. There, take the order, and away. (*MD*, 470)

In the very next chapter, Starbuck confronts Ahab when the ship is seriously put in danger by leaking barrels, asking him to put off his quest long enough to complete the necessary repairs. Ahab replies: "Let it leak! I'm all aleak myself. Aye! leaks in leaks! not only full of leaky casks, but those leaky casks are in a leaky ship. . . . Yet I don't stop to plug my leak; for who can find it in the deep-loaded hull; or how hope to plug it, even if found, in this life's howling gale?" (474). This anxiety about a disintegrating body-self explains the counterfantasy of a body and ego completely isolated, self-contained, self-sufficient, a fortress-self armored against all injury: not eyes to see outwards, but a sky-light to "illuminate inwards."[7] It is the image of a universe in oneself, impervious to the assaults of the outside world, a human citadel or tower, heartless for fear of mortifying injury. The narcissistic fear of being helpless and in need of others has converted itself into the absolutism of isolation and omnipotence. This is the tragic import of Fedellah's equivocal prophecy; it encourages Ahab, as the witch's prophecy encourages Macbeth, in the grandiose delusion of his invulnerability and unconquerable power: "Nor white whale, nor man, nor fiend, can so much as graze old Ahab in his own proper and inaccessible being" (560). Gored by the splinters of his shattered leg of bone, he cries: "Accursed fate! that *the unconquerable captain in the soul* should have such a craven mate!" (560; emphasis added).

Grunberger speaks of a "negative" object relation in narcissism, that "feeling of 'splendid isolation'" (1979, 15) that paradoxically contrasts with the narcissist's longing for fusion with others. This is one pole of the conflict in Melville between the wish for self-assertion and the wish to belong, between the fear of isolation and the fear that one will be engulfed by the other. As Grunberger explains it, the narcissist wants

> to be loved for himself and not for his abilities, or even his qualities, though he may be very proud of them. . . . The fact is that the longing to be loved in this fashion, that is, the need for narcissistic gratification from outside is in itself a sign of trouble in the narcissistic equilibrium, for the "pure" narcissist is in perfect equilibrium with himself and has no such need. . . . (15–16)

In similar terms, Nathan Schwartz-Salant speaks of the pride narcissistic characters take in having no needs; they reject "feelings of need for another human being, for experiencing such needs can unleash rage and envy that could flood the weak ego structure. . . . If their own needs for sympathy or relatedness are kindled, this often is experienced as a blow to their self-esteem, and can lead to depression and loss of energy" (1982, 39). It is this need of others that Ahab experiences as particularly humiliating, and his rage and resentment naturally focus on the physical incapacity that makes him dependent on help from outside.

We are reminded of the words of the faithless Charlie in *The Confidence-Man:* "There is something wrong about the man who wants help. There is somewhere a defect, a want, in brief, a need, a crying need, somewhere about that man" (206). Ahab's pride makes him find it humiliating to accept that to be human is to be inter-indebted, physically and socially. As he oversees the manufacture of his new leg, he expresses his exasperation in a grotesquely hyperbolic parody of Emerson's gospel of self-reliance:

> Oh, Life! Here I am, proud as a Greek god, and yet standing debtor to this blockhead for a bone to stand on! Cursed be that mortal inter-indebtedness which will not do away with ledgers. I would be free as air; and I'm down in the whole world's books. I am so rich, I could have given bid for bid with the wealthiest Praetorians at the auction of the Roman empire (which was the world's); and yet I owe for the flesh in the tongue I brag with. By heavens! I'll get a crucible, and into it, and dissolve myself down to one small, compendious vertebra. So. (*MD*, 471–72)

The theme of standing erect—the pride at being able to stand on one's own legs, and the fear of being humiliated by a reliance on the support of others—is explicitly connected here to issues of dependency and independence. "Here I am, proud as a Greek god, and yet standing debtor to this blockhead for a bone to stand on!" Ahab's mutilated body reminds him that without others he is as helpless as an infant, unable to walk or talk: he needs the carpenter to make him a limb; he owes the creator for his ability to speak. The organization of the body into different, mutually supporting members is a perfect image of this inter-indebtedness, and thus in a narcissistic defense against this humiliating knowledge Ahab dreams of a blissful condensation into one "small, compendious vertebra."

We might compare this desperate narcissistic isolationism, absolutist in character, with the attitude of the one character in *Moby-Dick* who most unconsciously exemplifies an attitude of genuine independence: Queequeg. In the early passages of the novel Ishmael paints his newfound friend as a somewhat "overawing" figure who comes closest to Ahab's ideal of splendid isolation, exemplifying as he does a "calm self-collectedness of simplicity" and appearing self-sufficient to the point of seeming to have no needs or debts to others: "He looked like a man who had never cringed and never had had a creditor" (50). Melville's noble savage is an individual "entirely at his ease; preserving the utmost serenity; content with his own companionship; always equal to himself" (50). However unrealistic this romantic image of the utterly "natural" man may be—this image of a human being devoid of all anxious self-consciousness and sense of estrangement from himself—it is an ideal that expresses the deep-seated wish to transcend shame at last, to be completely at home with oneself and unashamed of who one is. We feel ashamed of ourselves when there is any significant discrepancy between the self we perceive ourselves to be and the ego ideal against which we measure that self, and it is the relative lack of tension between these two poles that would appear to explain the *nobility* of Queequeg's character. Shame here is what the Greeks call *aidos*, "the guardian that protects the core of integrity" and that expresses itself as "consistent self-restraint under the abiding guidance of an ideal" (Wurmser 1987, 88). It implies a core of the personality that, according to Ruth Benedict, the Japanese know as the "self without shame." We will have occasion to explore this idea of self-loyalty in more detail in the next chapter.

Part of this preventive sense of shame—an attitude, as Wurmser defines it, "of respect toward others and towards oneself" (1987, 68–69)—is reverence and awe for one's place in the larger scheme of the human and natural worlds. It is this positive sense of shame, then, that makes Queequeg—perfectly aware that he is as helpless as the next man, and as helpful as he can be when occasion arises—so superbly *unashamed* of being part of that great network of mortal interdependency that Ahab so furiously resents as a humiliation and an injury. Whereas Ahab is tragically torn apart by the absolute claims of self-assertion, autonomy, and power, Queequeg exemplifies the paradoxical balance between a pride in independence and an acceptance of interdependency. Ishmael describes him in the most admiring terms after his companion has, without so much as a second thought, saved a man from drowning on their passage to Nantucket, a man who a few moments before had been maliciously poking fun at Queequeg's outlandish appearance:

> Was there ever such unconsciousness? He did not seem to think
> that he at all deserved a medal from the Humane and Magnani-

mous Societies. He only asked for water—fresh water—something to wipe the brine off; that done, he put on dry clothes, lighted his pipe, and leaning against the bulwarks, and mildly eyeing those around him, seemed to be saying to himself—"It's a mutual, joint-stock world, in all meridians. We cannibals must help these Christians." (61–62)

This image of "a mutual, joint-stock world" appears to be a knowing dig at Emerson's "Self-Reliance," where the image is pejoratively used to denigrate social conformity: "Society everywhere is in conspiracy against the manhood of every one of its members. Society is a joint-stock company, in which the members agree, for the better securing of his bread to each shareholder, to surrender the liberty and culture of the eater" (Emerson 1957, 149). Emerson's criticisms of social conformity are part of his general assertion of the freedom of the independent self, a myth that, rooted in Western culture, had, of course, one of its most exuberant flowerings in the period of American romanticism. In *The Anatomy of Dependence*, the Japanese psychoanalyst Takeo Doi has demonstrated how relative and culturally specific this idea of the self really may be. Doi argues that the concept does not come naturally in Japanese society, where freedom depends on recognizing one's interpersonal "debts" and of accepting one's social obligations to "creditors." Melville's view of freedom in a social context would appear to be much closer to this conception than to the individualist vision of his New England contemporary. As has been widely argued, Ahab's absolute wish for autonomy stands as a devastating parody of self-reliance, inasmuch as it is precisely this sense of being inevitably constrained and limited by obligation, of finding oneself, at one time or another, in a reduced position of gratitude, of having to say thank you for a kindness, of being indebted to others for anything at all—in other words, of being in a state of socially regulated shame—against which the entirely self-obsessed Ahab despairingly protests when he curses "that moral inter-indebtedness which will not do away with ledgers" (*MD*, 471–72).

In Japanese society, the complex system of social obligation is automatically suspended in what Doi calls the private circle of *amae*, where dependency is accepted as the rule. However, in neither the private circle nor in wider society is there any sense of not being socially interdependent, even if one does not feel indebted but simply indulged (the word *amae* in

Japanese carries the sense of an expectation of "indulgence" as well as "dependence"). The other—Kohut's idea of the selfobject comes to mind here—is experienced more or less as a part of oneself.

> Now the habit of the Japanese of feeling as a burden the kindness of *tanin* towards whom they feel some constraint yet accepting without so much as a "thank you" the kindness of their private circle with whom they feel at one is so completely natural to the Japanese themselves that they may even find it odd that there could be any other way of feeling. In such a world, there is no freedom and independence of the individual in the strict sense of the word. What appears to be freedom and independence of the individual is no more than an illusion. (Doi 1973, 91–92)

Doi's description of the suspension of normal obligations and restraints in *amae* strikingly resembles the tender indulgence that operates in the merger between the bosom friends Ishmael and Queequeg. In their mutual acceptance of the human need for help and love, they offer a dramatic counterexample to Ahab's unbalanced insistence on independence and self-sufficiency. The tragic consequences of the latter's absolute assertion of autonomy give weight to Doi's critique of "the faith in freedom of the modern Western man" in contrast with the Japanese, for whom "freedom in practice existed only in death" (95). Ahab, who puts the freedom of the self before all else, would seem to be a perfect illustration of what Doi means when he claims that

> all the attempts of modern Western man to deny or to sidestep *amae* have not be enough to transcend it, much less to conquer the lure of death. Both in the religious and secular fields, the faiths that have sustained the West may have been deceptions, a kind of opiate, and realization of this may have driven Western men at times to their deaths. If that is so, then they too, I would conclude, have been prey to a hidden *amae*. (95)

The image of a joint-stock company or world comes up on two other occasions in *Moby-Dick*. It is employed in what appears to be a direct allusion to its Emersonian context in chapter 26 ("Knights and Squires") when Starbuck's ruined valor is under discussion: "Men may seem detestable as joint stock-companies and nations . . . but man, in the ideal, is so noble and so sparkling, such a grand and glowing creature" (*MD*, 117). The other occasion of its use is the "Monkey-rope" chapter when Ishmael finds himself in the "humorously perilous business" of holding Queequeg "down there in the sea, by what is technically called in the fishery a monkey-rope, attached to a strong strip of canvas belted round his waist" (320), while the latter, in a "hard-scrabble scramble upon the dead whale's back" (320), goes about the unenviable duty of inserting the blubber-hook into the whale.

> So that for better or for worse, we two, for the time, were wedded; and should poor Queequeg sink to rise no more, then both usage and honor demanded, that instead of cutting the cord, it should drag me down in his wake. So, then, an elongated Siamese ligature united us. Queequeg was my own inseparable twin brother. . . . I seemed distinctly to perceive that *my own individuality was now merged in a joint-stock company of two: that my free will had received a mortal wound*; and that another's mistake or misfortune might plunge innocent me into unmerited disaster and death. (320; emphasis added)

The image of Siamese twins recalls the struggling brothers theme, but only to reverse its implications: instead of rivalry there is interdependency. The passage is one more example of how Melville, throughout *Moby-Dick*, comically subverts the tragic seriousness of Ahab's monomaniacal quest. Helplessly tied to Queequeg, Ishmael finds himself in a situation that meets very precisely the condition of what Grunberger calls "narcissistic mortification," defined as "the ego's humiliation, for example for submitting passively to what one cannot actively control" (1979, 21). Indeed, the closest analogy to the situation of dependency here is that of a helpless infant's dependency on its mother, which the infant may, indeed, find terribly humiliating at times. In contrast with Ahab, however, who responds with shame and rage to any situation in which he finds himself incapacitated and helplessly dependent on others, Ishmael adopts a self-deprecating posture and takes an unperturbed, narcissistically balanced view of this injury to his self-esteem, this "mortal wound" to his "free will." His ironic and equanimous assessment of the situation involves a recognition of his ultimate helplessness and impotency, but it also represents a powerful affirmation of human interconnectedness:

> I saw that this situation of mine was the precise situation of every mortal that breathes; only, in most cases, he, one way or other, has this Siamese connexion with a plurality of other mortals. If your banker breaks, you snap; if your apothecary by mistake sends you poison in your pills, you die. True, you may say that, by exceeding caution, you may possibly escape these and the multitudinous other evil chances of life. But handle Queequeg's monkey-rope heedfully as I would, sometimes he jerked it so, that I came very near sliding overboard. Nor could I possibly forget that, do what I would, I only had the management of one end of it. (*MD*, 320)

Ishmael's acceptance, indeed, comic celebration of human inter-indebtedness may itself be in debt, as it were, for what it owes to Melville's reading of Rabelais, specifically Panurge's preposterous disquisition on debt in the Third Book of *Gargantua and Pantagruel*. It is there that we find the grotesque image of a great inter-indebted ancestral body in which all of humanity takes on the aspect of one's indulgent personal circle:

> But," quoth Pantagruel, "when will you be out of debt?" At the ensuing terms of the Greek calends," answered Panurge, "when all the world shall be content, and that it be your fate to become your own heir. The Lord forbid that I should be out of debt, as if, indeed, I could not be trusted. . . .
>
> Be still indebted to somebody or other, that there may be somebody always to pray for you; that the giver of all good things may grant unto you a blessed, long and prosperous life: fearing if fortune should deal crossly with you, that it might be his chance to come short of being paid by you; he will always speak good of you in every company, ever and anon purchase new creditors unto you; to the end that through their means you may make a shift by borrowing from Peter to pay Paul, and with other folks' earth fill up his ditch. (Rabelais 1970, 288; bk. 3, chap. 3)

The guiding principle of "No Trust" that dominates the cynical world of *The Confidence-Man* is here countered by a celebratory view of the endless goodness produced in a society founded on the purchasing of credit. Credit here is an economic metaphor for the trust on which all human relationship and friendship is founded. In Ishmael's words: "If your banker breaks, you snap; if your apothecary by mistake sends you poison in your pills, you die" (*MD*, 320). Interestingly enough, Panurge's contrasting vision of a world out of debt is a world of Ishmaels, in which every man's hand is raised against his brother, a wolfish world of conflict and confusion: "Lucifer will break loose, and issuing forth of the depth of hell, accompanied with his furies, fiends, and horned devils, will go about to unnestle and drive out of heaven all the gods, as well of the greater as of the lesser nations. Such a world, without lending, will be no better than a dog-kennel, a place of contention and wrangling . . ." (Rabelais 1970, 291). Jupiter, Panurge warns, "reckoning himself to be nothing indebted unto Saturn, will go near to detrude him out of his sphere" (290). The image of Lucifer driving all the gods out of heaven recalls the hubristic Ahab's quarrelsome question: "Who's over me?" (*MD*, 164). This theme of titanic conflict, which is so grandly and tragically toned in Ahab, is comically parodied at the very beginning of *Moby-Dick* in the prefatory "Extracts," where the sociable narrator exhorts the lowly sub-sub-librarians of the world, busy at their thankless task of grubbing about on earth in search of knowledge, once and for all to "Give it up" and lift up their hearts: "Here ye strike but splintered hearts together—there, ye shall strike unsplinterable glasses!" (xvii–xviii). This enthusiastic proclamation recalls the long sought-after wisdom of the quest of the Holy Bottle in Rabelais's Fourth Book: "Trinquez!" It is a thoroughly sociable wisdom, and characteristic of Melville, who consistently associates loving friendship with incorporation and the communion-like sharing of drink and food. As we shall see, there is an obsessive and aggressive side to this orality, this intense desire to "incorporate" idealized objects. But here it is cheerful in tone and evokes a fraternal and democratic vision, as once again we are offered a comic double for a tragic theme: a festive Saturnalia for the humble, instead of a reckless storming of the heavens for the proud.

"Such a world, without lending, will be no better than a dog-kennel" (Rabelais 1970, 236), Panurge concludes. A "rat-pit of quarrels" (*BB*, 46) is how Captain Graveling describes the invidious world of squabbling and dispute into which Billy Budd is dropped aboard the *Rights of Man*. The world as "a place of contention and wrangling" is a comic version of the Hobbesian image of human society given over to perpetual quarrel, conflict, and violence. Out of debt, "Men unto men will be wolves," Panurge warns. Citing, among others, Ishmael and Timon, the two man-haters given particular prominence in Melville's work, he exuberantly continues: "hobthrushers and goblins (as were Lycaon, Bellerophon, Nebuchodnosor), plunderers, highway-robbers, cut-throats, rapperees, murderers, poisoners, assassinators, lewd, wicked, malevolent, pernicious haters, set against everybody, like to Ishmael, Metabus, or Timon the Athenian, who for that cause was named Misanthropos" (Rabelais 1970, 291). Then, to conclude his vision of the wolfish world of conflict and hatred that would result from the disappearance of debt, Panurge employs an elaborate metaphor of the body and its members:

> The head will not lend the sight of his eyes to guide the feet and hands; the legs will refuse to bear up the body; the hands will leave off working any more for the rest of the members; the heart will be weary of its continual motion for the beating of the pulse, and will no longer lend his assistance; the lungs will withdraw the use of their bellows; the liver will desist from conveying any more blood through the veins, for the good of the whole; the bladder will not be indebted to the kidneys so that the urine thereby will be totally stopped. . . . Briefly, in such a world, without order and array, owing nothing, lending nothing, and borrowing nothing, you would see a more dangerous conspiration than that which Aesop exposed in his apologue. Such a world will perish undoubtedly; and not only perish, but perish very quickly. (291–92)

When Panurge praises a world founded on debt in the next chapter he uses the same image of the body and its members. In a cheerful parody of the Eucharist, we see the harmonious members of a giant human body engaged in the cultivation and preparation of food, and, most importantly, in the productive process of digestion, excretion, and circulation through the blood. The description of this harmonious machine ends with the image of marriage: "All this is done by loans and debts of the one unto the other; and hence have we this word, the debt of marriage" (295; bk. 3; chap. 4). As

Richard Slotkin points out, "the archetypal myths of the Eucharist and the sacred marriage" (1973, 543) are the two symbols of the bond between Ishmael and Queequeg. It is immediately after Queequeg's feat of heroic rescue on board the Nantucket schooner, an epiphany of the law of mutuality and inter-indebtedness, that the marriage of the two friends is spiritually consummated, as Ishmael parodically evokes the phraseology of marriage that speaks of the cleaving of man and woman unto one another until death do them part: "From that hour I clove to Queequeg like a barnacle; yea, till poor Queequeg took his last long dive" (*MD*, 157). The weddedness of the two, most graphically portrayed when they are tied together by the monkey-rope, is an image of that great joint-stock company that is one's common humanity, a vision of the world as a giant collective body in which "debt"—but debt without shame, without the humiliation and resentment produced by the unjustly imposed sense of obligation—exists as a guarantee of the sociability of the members.[8]

This Rabelaisian vision stands in deliberate contrast to the Hobbesian vision offered by the "wolfish world" of *Moby-Dick*. For Hobbes, the social covenant is an agreement to tyranny, the wills of the people being formed, under their sovereign, as those of the crew under the dictatorial Ahab, to "peace at home and mutual aid against their enemies abroad" (Hobbes 1937, 143). In "Extracts," Melville quotes the initial clause of the opening of *Leviathan:* "By art is created that great Leviathan called a Common-Wealth, or State—in Latin, Civitas—which is but an artificial man, though of greater stature and strength than the natural, for whose protection and defence it was intended. . . ." (*MD*, 23). At the end of chapter 17, Hobbes has recourse to the same metaphor:

> This done, the multitude so united in one person is called a Commonwealth, in Latin Civitas. This is the generation of the great Leviathan (or rather, to speak more reverently, of that *mortal god*) to which we owe, under the immortal God, our peace and defense. . . . And in him consists the essence of the commonwealth, which, to define it, is one person, of whose acts a great multitude, by mutual covenants one with another, have made themselves every one the author, to the end he may use the strength and means of them

all as he shall think expedient for their peace and common defense. (Hobbes 1937, 143)

This political metaphor of a self-enclosed "artificial man" that defends itself against a hostile outside world finds its psychological counterpart in Ahab's fantasy of a titanic human form, this dream of an omnipotent fortress-self, of a body without members or organs, to match a self without needs or obligations. There is an explicit allusion to Hobbes' treatise in chapter 87 ("The Grand Armada") of *Moby-Dick*. The extensive herds of whales are seen, from afar, to be "sometimes embracing so great a multitude, that it would almost seem as if numerous nations of them had sworn solemn league and covenant for mutual assistance and protection" (382). As applied here, the image is deceiving. More appropriate to their role as the unsuspecting victims of bloodthirsty human predators is the simile that follows, the glimpse of a peaceful and industrious human settlement as it innocently awakens to a new day:

> Seen from the Pequod's deck, then, as she would rise on a high hill of the sea, this host of vapory spouts, individually curling up into the air, and beheld through a blending atmosphere of bluish haze, showed like the thousand cheerful chimneys of some dense metropolis, descried of a balmy autumnal morning, by some horseman on a height. (382–83)

It is, ironically, in the midst of this Hobbesian world, in which "the condition of man . . . is a condition of war of every one against every one" (Hobbes 1937, 110), that Ishmael glimpses beneath the surface the harmonious life of whale mothers with their nurslings. There he watches as the young gaze up, "as human infants while suckling will calmly and fixedly gaze away from the breast, as if leading two different lives at the time; and while yet drawing mortal nourishment, be still spiritually feasting upon some unearthly reminiscence" (*MD*, 388). The prenatal world alluded to here is one in which, in Grunberger's words, the infant "seems to live in a cosmos filled solely with his own being, which is both megalomaniacal and intangible, merging with his own bliss" (1979, 21). Evoked is a condition of perfect narcissistic equilibrium, "an elative state that constitutes a perfect homeostasis, without needs, for, since needs are satisfied automatically, they do not have to be formed as such" (14). This is the world of "wholeness and omnipotence" for which Ahab nostalgically yearns, and which, as "the feeling of uniqueness, self-love, megalomania, omnipotence, invulnerability, autonomy" (21), he projects in his fantasy of an unconquerable and impenetrable body and self.

According to Kohut, narcissism—the original narcissism of the infant—is not overcome. It must be transformed. He speaks, for example, of the process of idealization

> in which the child attempts to save the original narcissism by giving it over to a narcissistically experienced omnipotent and perfect self-object. Under favorable circumstances the child gradually faces the realistic limitations of the idealized self-object, gives up the idealizations, and *pari passu* makes transmuting reinternalizations. (1971, 105)

As a commentary on his vision of peace in the midst of storm and conflict, Ishmael evokes the lost paradise of narcissistic harmony as something that now resides *within*: "But even so, amid the tornadoed Atlantic of my being, do I myself still for ever centrally disport in mute calm; and while ponderous planets of unwaning woe revolve round me, *deep down and deep inland* there I still bathe me in eternal mildness of joy" (*MD*, 389; emphasis added).[9] The wording here calls to mind the very different description, as quoted earlier, of the moans that come from Ahab in his final struggle with Moby Dick: "*Far inland*, nameless wails came from him, as desolate sounds from out ravines" (551; emphasis added). In contrast with Ahab's desolate feelings of abandonment and helplessness, Ishmael's profound sense of inner security is the psychological counterpart of his comic acceptance of human inter-indebtedness, his willingness to rely on others. For he has managed to transmute the lost world of narcissistic bliss and power into an abiding, internalized structure of the self. In the final account, this is undoubtedly much closer to what Emerson meant by that instinctive trust in "an aboriginal Self" (1957, 156), or self-reliance, than some vain and fatal dream of absolute freedom and autonomy.

> In that deep force, the last fact behind which analysis cannot go, all things find their common origin. For the sense of being which

in calm hours rises, we know not how, in the soul, is not diverse from things, from space, from light, from time, from man, but one with them, and proceedeth obviously from the same source whence their life and being also proceedeth. (156)

CHAPTER THREE

The Inexorable Self

I

The function of shame as a regulator of the equilibrium of the self is the central theme of Father Mapple's sermon in *Moby-Dick*. The story of Jonah, as Mapple depicts it, involves a case of disobedience and punishment in which shame and the threat of abandonment play an important part in adjusting personal conduct. In contrast with the traumatic episode recalled by Ishmael in "The Counterpane," this story ends in reconciliation, in a "recovery of communion" and a "reunion of the relenting parent" and the "ashamed child" (Tomkins 1963, 294). Mapple's sermon is, indeed, a psychologically revealing meditation on the meaning of Jonah's repentance, focusing on his vain attempt to flee and hide from God. Repentance has an essential link to shame in that it seeks a restoration of relations on a new and higher ground based on self-respect, in accordance with the exacting standards of the ego ideal, while Jonah's initial response of flight and concealment are a straightforward expression of what Wurmser calls *shame simpliciter*, "shame itself, shame as withdrawal" (Nathanson 1992, 314).

Critical discussions of Mapple's sermon have naturally enough explored its thematic relationship to the novel as a whole. In this spirit, the theme of Jonah's repentance suggests a direct contrast to the refusal to repent that we find in Ahab. The latter's biblical namesake is, of course, an idolatrous and unrepentant king of Israel, one of those "sons of pride" (Job 41:34) ruled over by Leviathan, those "proud gods and commodores of this earth" (*MD*, 48) as Mapple calls them in his final exhortation. The pride referred to here, and which lies behind Ahab's refusal to repent is, of course, not that healthy feeling of excitement and heightened self-esteem that stems from the enjoyment in oneself and one's activities; the latter indicates, in fact, an absence of shame. The pride that drives Ahab is, rather, one of the most obdurate narcissistic defenses against shame affect. Pride so easily becomes a defense because, as Nathanson observes, "anything that can give us a moment of pride is capable of acting as an antidote for what amounts to a chronic sense of shame" (1992, 86).

Kohut has made a very useful distinction between Freud's conceptualization of so-called guilty man, who is the victim of conflict among competing instinctual drives, and his own conceptualization of tragic man, who is "blocked in his attempt to achieve self-realization" (1978, 754). In tragedy, human self-realization is blocked by the limitations of the natural and social orders; tragedy presents us with the image, as Frye puts it, of a "'Dionysiac,' aggressive will, intoxicated by dreams of its own omnipotence, impinging upon an 'Apollonian' sense of external and immovable order" (1957, 214–15). However, this order, as a social and therefore human order, is internalized as conscience and guilt, as the limits represented by the genuine pity and sense of justice from which feelings of guilt stem; thus tragedy would often arise not so much from the failure to achieve self-realization as from the conflict between guilt and shame. This is part of the tragic import of hubris. Tragedy may occur when the self's compulsive need to experience pride and expand its power conflicts with pity in the form of "caring and identification with the other as suffering" (Wurmser 1992, 36), and there results a dangerous disregard for "the needs to belong, to love, to care and to be cared for; and the needs to be treated with justice or fairness and hence to treat others fairly too" (37).

From the onset of his quest to hunt down and annihilate the white whale, Ahab is tempted from time to time to repent, but he blots out feelings of guilt in favor of the more dominant concerns bearing on the self's perceived power or weakness. One of the most dramatic instances of this is in chapter 128 ("The Pequod meets the Rachel") in which Captain Gardiner is unable, in spite of the most desperate and humiliating appeals, to persuade Ahab to put aside his vendetta, if only for a short time, in order to assist him in his search for a son abandoned at sea: "Meantime, now the stranger was still beseeching his poor boon of Ahab; and Ahab still stood like an anvil, received every shock, but without the least quivering of his own" (*MD*, 532). The description of Ahab's resistance here is a graphic depiction of what Nathanson calls the empathic wall, as the overriding nature of his pride makes him shut out the terrible pain that guilt for his unconscionable refusal causes him. The distinction between guilt and shame in terms of the "polarity of power and weakness," as Wurmser describes it, throws light on Ahab's reaction: "*Guilt limits strength; shame covers weakness.*

Guilt follows and blocks the expansion of power; shame is caused by and stops the reduction of power" (1981, 62).

We can see how this functions in the Rachel episode: "shame and the struggle for power" (63) are such a central aspect of Ahab's personality that his natural impulse to empathize with Captain Gardiner, which is real enough, is simply blocked and neutralized by that part of his personality controlled by the fear of shame. Ahab differs from those truly narcissistic personalities who, as Kohut describes them, seem never to suffer from feelings of guilt, as though they were entirely without a conscience (1978, 830). It is clear that Ahab, unlike, for example, a character such as Claggart, recognizes the infringement that has taken place—the act of injustice he has committed, this inconceivable refusal to recognize the most legitimate of all human claims made by the stranger captain—and that his conscience feels guilt for the hurt he is causing, and for the wrong he does. As he pronounces: "God bless ye, man, and *may I forgive myself*, but I must go" (*MD*, 532; emphasis added). Ashamed of himself, he then hurriedly turns away, "with averted face" (533). Indeed, it is the fact that Ahab has such feelings of guilt, and yet they still prove to be powerless to bend his pride, that is perhaps the most frightening measure of the control that shame has over his personality. Ahab's conscience, highly developed as it is, has no capacity to check the self's desire to abolish shame through the expansion of its power, and the relative weakness of his own conscience in this regard is incarnated in Starbuck, who represents a kind of choral norm but whose protestations are ineffective.

Jonah's situation differs, of course, from Ahab's in that it is not that his pride and shame come into conflict with feelings of guilt—in his case shame and guilt are complementary—but rather that two sets of expectations, two sources of shame, this world's and God's, conflict in an absolute way with one another. For Jonah to fulfill his prophetic function he must incur the disapprobation of the world, and when he lacks the courage to do this he feels shame and guilt in the eyes of God. The violation of what Wurmser describes as the *ideal relationship*, which involves conformity to "a system of actions that either ought to be done or ought to be avoided if such a desired relationship should prevail," produces guilt. The *ideal self*, on the other hand, "serves as the measure failing which one would experience shame" (quoted in Nathanson 1987b, 33). Jonah's sense of wrong can be referred to both these realms, but in the description of his feelings and behavior there seems to be a predominance of shame imagery, and in particular of imagery pertaining to a fear of visual exposure:

> Jonah still further flouts at God, by seeking to *flee* from Him. . . . He *skulks* about the wharves of Joppa. . . . Jonah *sought to flee* worldwide from God. . . . Oh! most *contemptible and worthy of all scorn*; with *slouched hat and guilty eye, skulking* from God; prowling among the shipping like a vile burglar hastening to cross the sea. So disordered, *self-condemning* is his look. . . . How plainly he's a *fugitive*! . . . all the sailors for the moment desist from hoisting in the goods, to mark the stranger's *evil eye*. Jonah sees this; but in vain he tries to look all ease and confidence; in vain essays his wretched smile. . . . Frighted Jonah trembles, and *summoning all his boldness to his face*, only looks so much the more a coward. . . . For the instant he almost turns *to flee again*. . . . no sooner does he [the captain] hear that hollow voice, than he darts a scrutinizing glance. . . . at last he slowly answered, *still intently eyeing him*. . . . *The lamp alarms* and frightens Jonah; as lying in his berth his tormented eyes roll round the place, and this thus far successful *fugitive finds no refuge for his restless glance*. . . . a deep stupor steals over him, *as over the man who bleeds to death, for conscience is the wound, and there's naught to staunch it*. . . . In all his cringing attitudes, the *God-fugitive* is now too plainly known. (*MD*, 43–46; emphasis added)

The actions of skulking, slouching, and averting the eyes are physical expressions of shame, and there is an overwhelming sense of painful visual exposure and loss of face: the vicarious experience of being seen by others in a detracting and condemning light, of being exposed to an intrusive gaze, of feeling conspicuous and painfully visible to unsympathetic eyes and scornful glances. Jonah is described as being worthy of scorn and contempt, and unable to keep face by trying to look confident or defiantly putting a bold face forth, he is forced instead to skulk and cringe as he tries in vain to hide and conceal himself, his entire manner betraying that he flees in shame. The image of his hat "slouched" over a "guilty eye" and of his "evil eye" marked by the sailors is typical of the gaze imagery—the idea of being known by the other's look—that is essential to the sense of exposure in shame.

Jonah's relationship to God is very much that of a child to his parent, and thus the sense he has of his "badness" recalls those episodes in Melville where a child is shamed as punishment for disobedience. In "The Counterpane" chapter of *Moby-Dick*, as we have seen, Ishmael's disobedience for cutting "some caper or other" is punished by what is clearly a shaming technique: banishment and a severing of the empathic bond. The "glass ship" episode in *Redburn* suggests a similar situation, though the child is simply restrained and prevented from satisfying his somewhat compulsive curiosity, not punished per se. The most dramatic example is, of course, the execution of the childlike Billy Budd, who, after being falsely accused, is condemned and abandoned to a disgraceful death. The significance of such episodes involving children or the child-like is illuminated by Martin Luther's description of shame as, in Erik Erikson's words, "an emotion first experienced when the infant stands naked in space and feels belittled" (1958, 256). In *Young Man Luther*, Erikson quotes the following passage by Luther concerning the predicament of the sinner:

> He is put to sin and shame before God . . . this shame is now a thousand times greater, that a man must blush in the presence of God. For this means that there is no corner or hole in the whole of creation into which a man might creep, not even in hell, but he must let himself be exposed to the gaze of the whole creation, and stand in the open with all his shame, as a bad conscience feels when it is really struck. . . . (256)

The pain of visual exposure, the feeling in shame of "being stared at, being overcome and devoured by the looks of others" (Wurmser 1981, 162), is portrayed here in all its terror. Erikson goes on to quote a comparable description by Luther of guilt, which involves an allusion to Jonah; we find the same emphasis on the impulse to flee in the face of the unbearable critical scrutiny and judgment:

> And this is the worst of all these ills, that the conscience cannot run away from itself, but it is always present to itself and knows all the terrors of the creature which such things bring even in this present life, because the ungodly man is like a raging sea. The third and greatest of these horrors and the worst of all ills is to have a judge. (Erikson 1958, 258)

There is the following passage as well: "For this is the nature of a guilty conscience, to fly and to be terrified, even when all is safe and prosperous, to convert all into peril and death" (258).[1]

Jonah's guilty reaction demonstrates the role of the superego as, in the form of one's conscience, a critical inner eye severely judging and condemning the self for transgression. However, equally, if not more important here, is the relationship between ego and ego ideal, which involves feelings of self-respect, self-regard, self-esteem, and which, according to Morrison, "is more accurately seen as the experience of shame" (1984, 28). More precisely, the type of shame that Jonah feels is close to the feeling of dishonor, but dishonor in the eyes of God, not of society, the two being in perpetual conflict; as Mapple exhorts, "Woe to him who, in this world, courts not dishonor!" (MD, 48) Lewis discusses among the shame family of feeling, "dishonor, disgrace, ignominy, infamy," which, according to Webster's Dictionary, all "express the loss of good fame" (1971, 69). "The loss of good fame in the eyes or mind of the 'other' is the central feature of experience in this group of shame synonyms" (69). According to the dictionary, "[D]ishonor retains to a greater degree than disgrace a negative force, and expresses deprivation or violation of honor, reputation or dignity. Disgrace expresses positive shame or reproach. Ignominy connotes public infamy, notorious disgrace or dishonor" (69). As Lewis observes, "Implied in these terms, then, is the self's reaction to, i.e., acceptance of, loss of others' respect, with the implication of grave moral transgression as the reason for the self's concurrence" (69–70). It is this aspect of dishonor or disgrace that explains the difficulty of separating shame from guilt in Jonah's reaction: he is in flight from the shame he has incurred for "grave moral transgression" in the eyes of God, and in his own eyes, by his failure to obey God's hard command. The superego, in such an instance, is composed of both a set of rules to be obeyed and an ideal self. The latter aspect is emphasized by the way that Mapple, in his sermon, presents the repentant Jonah—one "who against the proud gods and commodores of this earth, ever stands forth his own inexorable self" (MD, 48)—as a model self to the congregation, as an ideal self or standard that one should try to live up to. "Very close to nobility," Wurmser observes, "is . . . loyalty to oneself, self-loyalty, remaining faithful to the best within oneself" (1987, 88). Jonah, one might say, has simply been disobedient and is therefore punished for transgression. His punishment, however, consists of feeling unbearable shame and guilt and then of being abandoned by God, so that he is forced to experience his complete dependency and utter helplessness in relation to his creator. As we have seen, the threat to attachment is what lies behind shame in an interpersonal context, and this threat is explicit in dishonor and disgrace: the other abandons the one who has disgraced himself.

Wurmser's discussion of the role of dishonor in Plato's *Apology* clarifies this aspect of shame (1981, 61). Explaining his decision to accept his sentence of death, Socrates states: "Where a man has once taken up his stand, either because it seems best to him or in obedience to his orders, there I believe he is bound to remain and face the danger, taking no account of death or anything else before dishonour" (Plato 1969, 60). Thus, in the dramatic exhortation that concludes his sermon, Father Mapple extols that self which, through its conduct, has all but abolished the tension between what this "other" expects of one and what one does. As he speaks of the woe that befalls "him who would not be true, even though to be false were salvation" and "who, as the great pilot Paul has it, while preaching to others is himself a castaway!" (*MD*, 48), Mapple's body is in the classic posture of shame[2]— "bowing his head lowly, with an aspect of the deepest yet manliest humility"— and it is in the same posture of humility and unworthiness that he ends his sermon: "He said no more, but slowly waving a benediction, covered his face with his hands, and so remained kneeling" (48). However, as he turns to the peroration, where he will uplift his parishioners in an emotional expression of admiration and awe for the heroic figure who should be the object of our most sober admiration, his posture and facial expression are dramatically altered: "He drooped and fell away from himself for a moment; then lifting his face to them again, showed a deep joy in his eyes, as he cried out with a heavenly enthusiasm" (48). "Aplomb," Nathanson observes, "means the ability to stand proud and straight, rather than droop in shame" (1992, 210). Mapple's "deep joy" and "heavenly enthusiasm" are, significantly enough, precisely the emotions—"enthusiasm and overwhelming joy"— that, according to Wurmser, accompany the "successful consummation" of the idealizing merger (1981, 165), that point of final equilibrium, as Kohut puts it, "when the central narcissistic structure achieves its total victory and a tranquil joy pervades the total personality" (1990, 154).

But oh! shipmates! on the starboard hand of every woe, there is a sure delight; and higher the top of that delight, than the bottom of the woe is deep. Is not the main-truck higher than the kelson is low? Delight is to him—a far, far upward, and inward delight— who against the proud gods and commodores of this earth, ever stands forth his own inexorable self. Delight is to him whose strong arms yet support him, when the ship of this base treacherous world has gone down beneath him. . . . Delight,—top-gallant delight is to him, who acknowledges no law or lord, but the Lord his God, and is only a patriot to heaven. Delight is to him, whom all the waves of the billows of the seas of the boisterous mob can never shake from this sure Keel of the Ages. (*MD*, 48)

II

It is important, if not always easy, to distinguish the heroic capacity of *self-loyalty* celebrated by Mapple, and exemplified by the repentance of Jonah, from what are clearly tragic and pathological cases of *self-assertion*. The most obvious example, of course, is Ahab, who could certainly be said to stand forth "his own inexorable self," but who draws his power and strength from deeply destructive, narcissistic fantasies of omnipotence. A perhaps less obvious case, to be discussed in more detail below, is the idealistic Pierre, who defends "the cause of Holy Right" (*P*. 170) but who defends it grandiosely and to the point of masochistic self-destruction. A more ambiguous instance is a character conceived of more than three decades after the composition of Mapple's sermon: the deeply principled and value-oriented Captain Vere, who exemplifies great steadfastness of character in his agonizing inner struggle to decide the fate of Billy Budd, but whose psychological stability has been a subject of interpretation.

Much has been made of the motivation behind Vere's decision and of the ambiguity his character adds to a story that is seemingly tormented by the author's own uncertain intentions. A significant amount of this uncertainty is doubtless due, of course, to the fact that story is unfinished.[3] But Melville's inability to complete the story is perhaps significant in itself, and is perhaps a sign of the conflict that motivated the writing in the first place. How Vere is to be judged has largely depended on whether one reads *Billy Budd* ironically or as a so-called testament of acceptance, whether one sees Vere as a rigid servant of "social expediency," as Bowen, for example, argues, or—as he summarizes the opposing argument—as "a brooding and compassionate Lincoln, courageously facing up to the hard necessities of action and responsibility, as a sort of latter-day Abraham 'resolutely offering [young Isaac] up in obedience to the exacting behest'" (216).[4] Supporters of the latter argument, as one critic divides the issue, "would likely see nothing more unexpected or unnatural in Vere's behaviour than a temporary excitement or at most a possible confusion. They would regard his judgments as essentially sound. Supporters of the irony argument might find in his behaviour something not only mysterious but mentally suspect as well" (McCarthy 1990, 130).

Vere is such a controversial character, I would argue, precisely because the particular nature of his relationship with Billy Budd appears to be the manifestation of a deeply painful and unresolved conflict in Melville himself: the struggle between that part of the self which expresses itself in a severely punitive and unrelenting manner (the abusive and authoritarian side of Melville's personality) and that part of the self which is "punished" and which has not given up the desire to find a bridge back to the object; it continues to yearn for reaffiliation and reconciliation. This explains the signs of emotional distress and painful psychological struggle that Vere displays. The "excited manner" (*BB*, 100) of Vere upon the death of Claggart, his "passionate interjections, mere incoherences to the listener as yet unapprised of the antecedents" (101), and the unaccountability and strangeness of his requests so discompose the *Bellipotent*'s surgeon as to fill him with "disquietude and misgiving" (101) and force him to consider if his superior has been "suddenly affected in his mind. . . . He recalled the unwonted agitation of Captain Vere and his excited exclamations, so at variance with his normal manner. Was he unhinged?" (101–2). Later, when the senior lieutenant encounters Vere in the "act of leaving the compartment" after the verdict has been decided, "The face he beheld, for the moment one expressive of the agony of the strong, was to that officer, though a man of fifty, a startling revelation, that the condemned one suffered less than he who mainly had effected the condemnation" (115). Such details, which point to a certain psychological disequilibrium, appear to be signs of a hidden conflict in Vere that exceptional events have somehow brought to the surface. The lack of resolution, in light of the terrible conflict in question, is captured in the *petrified* image of Vere as he stands at the moment of Billy's execution, when the latter's benediction is echoed by the crew: "At the pronounced words and the spontaneous echo that voluminously re-bounded them, Captain Vere, either through stoic self-control or a sort of momentary paralysis induced by emotional shock, stood erectly rigid as a musket in the ship-armorer's rack" (124). The image recalls the rigidity of Ahab, in the passage quoted earlier, as he resists the piteous request of Captain Gardiner for help in finding his son lost at sea: "Ahab still stood like an anvil, receiving every shock, but without the least quivering of his own" (*MD*, 532). The context is the same: a tender and loving father, a lost or abandoned son, and a captain who remains unmoved by the seemingly transcendent claims of an instinctive sense of justice. In *Billy Budd*, Vere is in the position of both Gardiner and Ahab, but in both stories the image of rigidity suggests a deep inner conflict between the internalized punish-ing and humiliating parent and the internalized abused and humiliated child.

We can see here the importance of idealization in Melville as a defense against rage (directed at the self) and the fear of helplessness and abandon-ment. If Claggart's relationship to Billy suggests the most frightening and vindictive aspects of an archaic superego, Vere as a character exemplifies the role played by protector figures in Melville's work. It is a topic we shall treat in more detail later. But it seems fairly clear that, whether one accepts the judgment or not, Vere, from the author's perspective, is an "exceptional character" (*BB*, 62) and displays the attributes of an ideal leader. Melville's point of view here is clarified by what Northrop Frye has to say about Blake's apocalyptic view of the historical figures of the revolutionary period: "[Blake's] Exhibition of 1809 contained pictures of the spiritual form of Pitt, the leader of Albion on land, guiding Behemoth, and the spiritual form of Nelson, the leader on the sea, guiding Leviathan. . . . A figure guiding such monsters would not always be a tyrant: he could be simply a leader doing what he can in a world where such monsters exist" (1993, 77). This is, per-haps, the perfect depiction of Vere—"a leader doing what he can in a world where such monsters exist." Though his spirit, as the narrator speculates at the end of *Billy Budd*, "may yet have indulged in the most secret of all pas-sions, ambition" (129), Vere is clearly to be contrasted with a grandiose and charismatic leader like Ahab. The latter's power resides in the activation of archaic claims of a grandiose self with which his crew merges in a group fantasy of omnipotence. In contrast, Vere's strength—the strength that al-lows him to resist "those invading waters of novel opinion social, political, and otherwise, which carried away as in a torrent no few minds in those days, minds by nature not inferior to his own" (62)—would seem to derive from a merger of the self with internalized idealized objects, in his case, an entire, complex set of civilized ideals. "His settled convictions were as a dike" (62) is how the sentence quoted above begins, a phrase that points to the defensive and protective function of idealization in this case: it is warding off something frightening and archaic that threatens to destroy the self. Vere's love of books, his absorption through reading of the strength and values of other men's accumulation of knowledge and experience, is an important manifestation of this idealizing core of his personality. It is also a detail that connects him quite obviously with Melville.

The narrator of *Billy Budd* lavishly praises Nelson (58) and explicitly links him with Vere in chapter 7: "Upon any chance withdrawal from their company one would be apt to say to another something like this: 'Vere is a noble fellow, Starry Vere. 'Spite the gazettes, Sir Horatio' (meaning him who became Lord Nelson) 'is at bottom scarce a better seaman or fighter'" (63). Nelson sacrifices himself for the sake of a higher cause, an ideal object, as Vere sacrifices his natural and most tender impulses to the "exacting bequest" of a higher order. The explicit allusion to Abraham in chapter 23, the chapter including Vere's "reconciliation" with Billy, is highly significant in this context; like Abraham, Vere obeys the command of the Law, even though it goes against his most natural and humane impulses.[5]

Vere, like Nelson, evinces great courage. He is "intrepid to the verge of temerity, though never injudiciously so" (60). Chapter 7 especially, as Hershel Parker notes in his study of *Billy Budd*, treats Vere with the greatest admiration. His awe before institutions and his uncanny ability to keep in perspective higher ideals and goals are clearly the sign of a personality whose strengths derive from its idealizing capacity. The "honesty [of such personalities] prescribes to them directness, sometimes far-reaching, like that of a migratory fowl that in its flight never heeds when it crosses a frontier" (*BB*, 63). Vere, even when uniformed, has the air of being a civilian, the king's guest aboard the ship, and we learn of his reading and his intense absorption in the history of law and civilization, and his incorporation of principles and precedents. His ideals and values are ultimately concretized in the king, a transformed omnipotent parental imago. This imago, which appears to form the core of Vere's personality, encourages him to remain firm in spite of the opposition of the crew, his own officers, and even his own 'natural' instincts. His identification with the king prevails—"But do these buttons that we wear attest that our allegiance is to Nature? No, to the King" (110)—and this in spite of the sympathy he shares with the jurors. "[P]rompted by duty and the law," he steadfastly exhorts them not to succumb: "But I beseech you, my friends, do not take me amiss. I feel as you do for this unfortunate boy. But did he know our hearts, I take him to be of that generous nature that he would feel even for us on whom in this military necessity so heavy a compulsion is laid" (113).

However much we may balk at the heroic depiction of a character whose ideals are aligned with the most reactionary forces and push him to act in such a severely punitive and authoritarian manner, there is no denying that we, as readers, are meant to recognize that Vere evinces tremendous courage in acting as he does and not wavering. Whatever the contradictions arising from the tension between the deep yearning for communion and the authoritarian's contrasting impulse to punish and punish severely, they do not change the fact that Vere, from the author's point of view at any rate, represents an exemplary instance of leadership, of the kind of ideal self that Mapple holds up in his sermon. He is one of those "whom all the waves of the billows of the seas of the boisterous mob can never shake from this sure Keel of the Ages." And thus it is not Vere's remorse or guilt, but his "martyrdom" that is suggested by his death scene. The narrator has prepared us for it through the earlier digression concerning the martyr-hero Nelson, whom "a sort of priestly motive led . . . to dress his person in the jewelled vouchers of his own shining deeds" and "thus to have adorned himself for the altar and sacrifice" (58). Nelson's death, like Billy's, represents not only the sacrifice of an individual for the sake of an idealized object, but the sacrifice of an idealized object, which is then incorporated by the group in a strengthening merger. Wounded in action, and on the verge of death, Vere "was heard to murmur words inexplicable to his attendant: 'Billy Budd, Billy Budd.'" The narrator makes it clear that "these were not the accents of remorse" (129). The words suggest, indeed, the confession of a vitalizing merger. As Kohut sees it, to the individual who has achieved a state of narcissistic equilibrium in blending "the personality with the central values of the self," such an identification with the idealized object brings a "sense of profound inner peace . . . and even the experience of conscious pleasure that his ideals and his total personality have now become one" (1990, 146).

III

The most obvious point of Mapple's sermon, absorbed by Ishmael on the eve of his voyage, is that it is precisely such an individual, capable of standing forth "his own inexorable self," that might be capable of resisting the charisma and terror, the overwhelming fascination of a grandiose personality like Ahab's. The courage to resist, to refuse the tragic course of Ahab's demonic quest, is, of course, nowhere to be found in *Moby-Dick*. Starbuck plays his functional role of critic of the tragic action, but his resistance is, in the final account, to no avail. There is one character, however, who, dramatically invoked and abruptly withdrawn by the narrator, seems to offer some kind of alternative perspective. His fleeting appearance offers us the briefest glimpse of the courage that will be absent on this doomed voyage: the mysterious Bulkington.

Ishmael first observes him among "a wild set of mariners" as one who "held somewhat aloof." An early version of the "handsome sailor," a sort of melancholic and brooding Billy Budd, he is pursued and admired by his comrades, but remains apart in his own desire for withdrawal and isolation. It is the sign, as we have seen, of *shame simpliciter*, and the choice of the misanthrope: flight from human society. Like Ahab, Bulkington is haunted by the memory of some deeply painful personal injury, some mortifying grief or grievance: "[I]n the deep shadows of his eyes floated some reminiscences that did not seem to give him much joy" (*MD*, 16). More than any other character, however, he seems to meet Kohut's criteria for courage. Indeed, Kohut's observation that in tragedy "it is the hero's innermost self which strives towards its ascendency" (1990, 172) is the very point of the famous salute to Bulkington in the chapter "The Lee Shore": "Know ye, now, Bulkington? Glimpses do you seem to see of that mortally intolerable truth; that all deep, earnest thinking is but the intrepid effort of the soul to keep the open independence of her sea; while the wildest winds of heaven and earth conspire to cast her on the treacherous, slavish shore?" (*MD*, 107). The "treacherous, slavish shore" is the world opposed to the self in its tragic course, the world, as Kohut describes it, of "work and love and everyday morality" (1990, 175). Henry Murray speaks of Melville's establishment of an "uncompromising dichotomy." On the one side, associated with the sea, there is "Open space, freedom, adventure, danger, the heart, spontaneity, selfless benevolence, singlehearted dedication, passionate undirected thought, truth-seeking, zeal for heaven and immortality, God, and insanity." On the other side, associated with the land, there is "closed or structured space, slavishness, family obligations, domestic comforts, safety, the head, cool directed thinking, the calculations of self-interest, propriety, the world, and conventional commonsense" (1962, xxvi–xxvii). It is this latter world, with all its safety and comforts, but all its conventionality and slavishness as well—the world, ultimately, that in his life Melville himself seems to have opted for, and felt entrapped in—that Ahab glimpses in the magic glass of Starbuck's eye. At this point in the novel, Ahab yearns momentarily for "the green land," "the bright hearth-stone," and is tempted to put down the bitter cup, before he turns instead like a setting sun to the inevitable "unrolling of the predestinated life" (Kohut 1990, 175) that is the tragic hero's. As Murray concludes: "Over and over again, in multifarious rhetorical forms, Melville contrasts these two clusters of value and always champions [the tragic one]". This setting and opposing of conflicting absolute values is, as Wurmser has pointed out, one of the most salient characteristics of the tragic character. In what he calls "hybris in the pursuit of a value," "one value becomes so exaggerated and eventually ('tragically') self-defeating because it is a narcissistic value, an idea with which one's self has become totally, absolutely, radically identified—at the exclusion of all the other consciously maintained values" (1978, 327). The values with which Bulkington radically identifies himself would seem to be intellectual freedom and independence, and the tragic consequence of such an exclusive pursuit is hinted at, foreshadowing the central tragedy of Ahab in the novel. It is the same self-defeating pursuit that defines the course of Pierre, and to some extent the tragic conflict of Captain Vere.

But in defeat the tragic hero also finds his triumph. All these figures—Bulkington, Ahab, Pierre, Vere—exemplify Kohut's definition of the tragic hero as "a man who, despite the breakdown of his physical and mental powers (e.g., Oedipus) and even despite his biological death (e.g., Hamlet), is triumphant because his nuclear self achieved an ascendancy which never will, indeed, which never can, be undone" (1990, 166). As Bowen observes of Ahab's tragic heroism: "Oddly, though, we find in his death a sense of fulfilment, not loss. For defeat is his only who accepts defeat, and this Ahab has not done. He 'stands forth his own inexorable self' even in the irreversible moment of final failure. His integrity is his victory" (1960, 157).[6] The whole movement of tragedy, according to Kohut, is towards "the glorified narcissistic triumph which permanently transforms the humiliated, suffering seeker into the god" (Kohut 1990, 175). It is precisely this divine transformation that is so eloquently evoked in the closing paragraph of the Bulkington passage:

> But as in landlessness alone resides the highest truth, shoreless, indefinite as God—so, better is it to perish in that howling infinite, than be ingloriously dashed upon the lee, even if that were safety! For worm-like, then, oh! who would craven crawl to land! Terrors of the terrible! Is all this agony so vain? Take heart, take heart, O Bulkington! Bear thee grimly, demigod! Up from the spray of thy ocean-perishing—straight up, leaps thy apotheosis! (*MD*, 107)

The imagery of defiance invoked here, an explicit antishame posture, is an essential part of the titanic attitude of characters such as Ahab and Pierre. In Bulkington, as in them, the sense of striving emanates not primarily from the idealized parental imago but from the grandiose self, the primary source, in Kohut's view, of the sense of power that drives the most adventurous forms of intellectual activity (that "deep earnest thinking" of which the narrator of *Moby-Dick* speaks). In embodying "the intrepid effort of the soul to keep the open independence of her sea," Bulkington's fate stands as a monument to the destiny of the creative self in its most ambitious and adventurous strivings. As Kohut sees it, the most original thought and creativity are "energized predominantly from the grandiose self" (1978, 801), and thus the ultimate significance of the figure of Bulkington is that he represents, in many ways, the self that took the enormous creative risk of writing a book like *Moby-Dick*.

The ambitious striving and expansive urge of the creative self are the opening theme of book 21 in *Pierre*. Pierre "was resolved to give the world a book, which the world should hail with surprise and delight," and his first step in such an uncertain venture was—like Melville's—"A varied scope of reading, little suspected by his friends, and randomly acquired by a random but lynx-eyed mind, in the course of the multifarious, incidental, bibliographic encounterings of almost any civilized young inquirer after Truth" (*P*, 283). This reading, however, as Pierre as yet is unable to foresee, is only a transition, and that "new and wonderful element of Beauty and Power ... once fairly gained, *then books no more are needed for buoys to our souls; our own strong limbs support us, and we float over all bottomlessnesses with a jeering impunity"* (283; emphasis added). Books, in this passage, serve, in psychological terms, the function of supporting idealized objects that the creative personality, when he feels sufficiently empowered, dares to leave behind: then he walks—nay, he floats—on his own power, unconquerable and proud. This image of fearlessly, defiantly ("with a jeering impunity"), floating over an abyss suggests a flying fantasy that, according to Kohut, "appears to be a frequent feature of unmodified infantile grandiosity" (1971, 144).

The same kind of depiction of the creative process appears in *Mardi* in the midst of a discussion of the author Lombardo. Babbalanja speaks of the two ingredients of creative activity: "Primus and forever, a full heart:—brimful, bubbling, sparkling; and running over like a flagon in your hand, my lord. Secundo, the necessity of bestirring himself to procure his yams" (592). He thus touches on the two poles of the creative self as Kohut sees it. The "soul's overflowings" touch on the idealizing impulse which is so strong in Melville. But this impulse is impotent, "not for lack of power, but for lack of omnipotent volition, to move his strength" (593). To the Lord Abrazza, Babbalanja explains:

> And as with your own golden scepter, at times upon your royal teeth, indolent tattoos you beat; then, potent, sway it o'er your isle; so, Lombardo. And ere Necessity plunged spur and trowel into him, he knew not his own paces. That churned him into consciousness; and brought ambition, ere then dormant, seething to the top, till he trembled at himself. (593)

In *Pierre*, the other important metaphor associated with Pierre's creative ambitions is that of climbing the Alps. Mountainous height connotes the sense of power and domination, but also, ironically, of isolation and abandonment. What it means to compose an original book is ultimately described in the contrasting imagery of the most frightening loneliness and abandonment: "Appalling is the soul of a man! Better might one be pushed off into the material space beyond the uttermost orbit of our sun, than once feel himself fairly afloat in himself!" (*P*, 284). In such a situation, according to Kohut, the self, enfeebled in having cut loose from all recognizable landmarks, as it daringly ventures forth—Kohut's imagery here is almost identical to Melville's—to explore "the moon landscapes of the unknown, will seek the temporary aid that comes to it from the relation with an archaic selfobject" (1978, 824). For Melville, as we shall show in more detail in a later chapter, the role of this imago—this protective, supportive, omnipotent figure, bearing him in his arms through the "daring exploratory venture" (835) that was *Moby-Dick*—seems to have been filled by Hawthorne.

The distinction between the two archaic images of the idealized object and of the grandiose self, these two important narcissistic configurations of the developing self, is, as we hope to have sufficiently demonstrated, enormously useful if we are to make our way through the complicated psychological terrain of Melville's work. The pole of the grandiose self, as we have noted, is the force behind Ahab's sense of unconquerable power, as opposed to any identification with ideals and values. "The firm tower," as he confidently asserts, gazing into the mirror of the doubloon, "that is Ahab; the volcano, that is Ahab; the courageous, the undaunted, and victorious fowl, that, too, is Ahab" (*MD*, 431). Courage, here, is a function, not of an absorption of the self in one's ideals and values, but of one's feelings of power and unconquerability, this being the source as well of Ahab's mystifying, charismatic power over the crew of the *Pequod*.

The image, on the other hand, of being lifted or borne up and carried by a powerful protective force or imago is a sign, in Melville's work, that we are in the zone of the idealized object. We find this image, for example, in the closing passage of the chapter "Knights and Squires," which concerns the apotheosis of the ascendent or triumphant self linked to tragic art: "If, then, to meanest mariners, and renegades and castaways, I shall hereafter ascribe high qualities, though dark; weave round them tragic graces" (117). The paragraph then concludes with the apostrophe to the "Just Spirit of Equality" and, along with those of Bunyan and Cervantes, the image of Andrew Jackson raised from the mud below: "Thou who didst pick up Andrew Jackson from the pebbles; who didst hurl him upon a war-horse; who didst thunder him higher than a throne! Thou who, in all Thy mighty, earthly marchings, ever cullest Thy selectest champions from the kingly commons; bear me out in it, O God!" (117) The idealizing rhetoric of the invocation is characteristic of Melville, as is the enthusiastic appeal to the great God of Democracy, which suggests the need to be borne up by an omnipotent supernatural force, an expression of "the idealized parent imago" in the form of embodied ideals and values.[7]

This invocation comes about at the conclusion of Starbuck's introduction as a character, and the discussion of the latter's personality focuses quite precisely on the question of courage, on the ability of an individual, exemplified by Bulkington, "despite intimidation from within and without"—as Kohut puts it in his essay "On Courage"—"to proceed on his lonely road, even if it means his individual destruction, because he must shape the pattern of his life—his thoughts, deeds, and attitudes—in accordance with the design of his nuclear self" (1990, 134). Right reason, as Melville notes, is not enough, and when it comes to the crisis, Starbuck's courage fails; unable to resist his own inner doubts, he is unable to resist Ahab. This failure is the theme of Starbuck's revealing encounter with the doubloon, where, his basic trust in life having been tainted by doubt, he looks in vain for the concretization of those ideals in some transcendent support, in the form of "God," "the sun of Righteousness."[8] Kohut might say that in Starbuck the transmuting internalization of the idealized object is incomplete. Unlike Mapple's inexorable self, whose ideals are fused with the self so that his own "strong arms support him," unlike Vere who walks proudly in the shadow of a king whose power he identifies with civil law and civilized values, the expectant but uncertain Starbuck, when he looks into the mirror of the doubloon searching for the uplifting support of the parental imago, feels let down and disappointed, abandoned and alone.

> So in this vale of Death, God girds us round; and over all our gloom, the sun of Righteousness still shines a beacon and a hope. If we bend down our eyes, the dark vale shows her mouldy soil; but if we lift them, the bright sun meets our glance half way, to cheer. Yet, oh, the great sun is no fixture; and if, at midnight, we would fain snatch some sweet solace from him, we gaze for him in vain! This coin speaks wisely, mildly, truly, but still sadly to me. I will quit it lest Truth shake me falsely. (MD, 432)

The bowed head and averted eyes, followed by the uplifted head raised towards the sun, repeat Father Mapple's actions near the end of his sermon. However, in Starbuck's case the fear that he will be deserted prevails. When the self realizes its nuclear ambitions and ideals, the fulfillment that it attains "does not bring *pleasure*, as does the satisfaction of a drive, but triumph and the glow of joy. And its blocking does not evoke the sign of *anxiety* . . . but the anticipation of *despair* (e.g., of shame and empty depression—anticipatory despair about the crushing of the self and of the ultimate defeat of its aspirations)" (1978, 757). As we have seen, in the triumphant conclusion to his sermon Mapple is uplifted from his drooping posture and radiates with enthusiasm and joy. In contrast, it is the *despair* of "shame and empty depression," in anticipation of the defeat and crushing of the self, that we can detect in Starbuck's reaction before the coin: "This coin speaks wisely, mildly, truly, but still sadly to me. I will quit it, lest Truth shake me falsely" (*MD*, 432). It is Starbuck's sense of basic trust that fails him here, that "original 'optimism,'" as Erikson puts it, "that assumption that 'somebody is there,' without which we cannot live" (1958, 118).

Starbuck does resist to some extent, it is true, the influence of Ahab's charisma. His identification with transcendent ideals and values allows him largely to withstand the appeal of what Kohut calls "shared archaic grandiosity" (1990, 108). However, like Redburn and his companions who cannot withstand the display of Jackson's seething anger, he is unable finally to resist the spectacle of Ahab's terror and rage:

> But it was not in reasonable nature that a man so organized, and with such terrible experiences and remembrances as he had; it was not in nature that these things should fail in latently engendering *an element in him, which, under suitable circumstances, would break out from its confinement, and burn all his courage up.* And brave as he might be, it was that sort of bravery chiefly, visible in some intrepid men, which, while generally abiding firm in the conflict with seas, or winds, or whales, or any of the ordinary irrational horrors of the world, yet *cannot withstand those more terrific, because more spiritual terrors, which sometimes menace you from the concentrating brow of an enraged and mighty man.* (*MD*, 116–17; emphasis added)

Starbuck's loss of courage exposes a flaw in his personality, that "element in him, which, under suitable circumstances, would break out from its confinement, and burn all his courage up" (116–17). This element is the traumatic scar left by the loss of both his father and brother, a bereavement that

Melville shared at the time of composing the novel: "What doom was his own father's? Where in the bottomless deeps, could he find the torn limbs of his brother?" Shame is an important affect in grief: one bows one's head in shame, and one feels defeated, crushed, and abandoned. We can see, indeed, how Starbuck's grief represents a deeply mortifying injury—though it may have nothing like the same unabating intensity—comparable to the one received by Ahab in his encounter with Moby Dick. The image of an element within him that, in certain circumstances, will *burn all his courage up* suggests the searing quality that accompanies intense shame or mortification. Starbuck is someone whose basic trust in the world has been shaken at the core, and thus his courage is particularly susceptible to being broken by the overwhelming power of a personality such as Ahab's.

It is interesting—especially in the light of Melville's loss of a father and a brother, both of whom died in somewhat disgraceful circumstances—that the paragraph that follows should go on to discuss the potential humiliation involved in exposing someone's dishonorable "fall of valor" to the public gaze: "But were the coming narrative to reveal, in any instance, the complete abasement of poor Starbuck's fortitude, scarce might I have the heart to write it; for it is a thing most sorrowful, nay shocking, to expose the fall of valor in the soul" (117). We touch here on one of the most sacred functions of shame. In its most mature and healthy form, shame serves to protect and guard the innermost self from invasion by others; and, in turn, as an impediment to our own curiosity and fascination, it serves to prevent us from shamelessly intruding on other selves. The obligation to be sensitive to the dignity of other selves, the sense of the inappropriateness of witnessing another in their shame, is central, it seems to me, to the most intimate psychological concerns of Melville's work. One form of shame is "an attitude of respect towards others and towards oneself, a stance of reverence—the highest form of such reverence being . . . reverence for oneself. . . . It is respect and a sense of awe" (Wurmser 1987, 68). Out of what Carl Schneider calls mature shame—the fundamental respect for human dignity, for the inviolability of other selves—we avoid looking at someone in a particularly intimate, vulnerable, or potentially shame-provoking moment. There are certain things, we instinctively recognize, that should be kept from the eyes of others.

A notable instance of this taboo on looking in Melville's work—averting one's gaze from that which should not be seen—is the narrator's decision in *Billy Budd* to draw the curtain before the potentially intrusive and voyeuristic reader, who might be curious enough to want to witness in all its detail the tender "melting" between Vere and Billy: "But there is no telling the sacrament, seldom if in any case revealed to the gadding world wherever under circumstances at all akin to those here attempted to be set forth two of great Nature's nobler order embrace. *There is privacy at the time, inviolable to the survivor; and holy oblivion, the sequel to each diviner magnanimity, providentially covers all at last*" (BB, 115; emphasis added). The narrator's tactfulness here is a good example of shame in its function, as Schneider describes it, of safeguarding "the individual from the potential violation entailed in the public display of these intrinsically private experiences" (1977, 55). Biographically, of course, there were good reasons for Melville's acute sensitivity in this regard. As Cohen and Yannella observe with reference to precisely the same passage concerning Starbuck's failure of courage: "In addition to personal pain and a willingness to gloss over the facts for clannish reasons, his regard for what he has Ishmael call 'man, in the ideal' gave him reason to cast a cloak 'over any ignominious blemish' discovered in men he esteemed and loved" (1992, 72). This aspect of shame is clearly connected to the prominent idealizing dimension of Melville's work, as can be seen, for example, in the grandiloquent rhetoric that takes over the remaining part of the same passage in *Moby-Dick:*

> Men may seem detestable as joint stock-companies and nations; knaves, fools, and murders there may be; men may have mean meagre faces; but man, in the ideal, is so noble and so sparkling, such a grand and glowing creature, that over any ignominious blemish in him all his fellows should run to throw their costliest robes. That immaculate manliness we feel within ourselves, so far within us, that it remains intact though all the outer character seem gone; bleeds with keenest anguish at the undraped spectacle of a valor-ruined man. Nor can piety itself, at such a shameful sight, completely stifle her upbraidings against the permitting stars. (117)

The grandiloquent image of our running to throw our "costliest robes" over any "ignominious blemish" in our fellow creatures gives expression to the sacred quality of the privacy protected by the emotion of shame. Faced with those situations "that remind us of our inability to live up to our ego-ideal. . . . the individual needs protection from those who are uninvolved and from the inquiring gaze that reduces him or her to an object of pity" (Schneider 1977, 80).

Lewis observes that "Shame, by its nature, is contagious. Moreover, just as shame has an intrinsic tendency to encourage hiding, so there is a tendency for the observer of another's shame to turn away from it" (1971, 15–16). In the period preceding the writing of *Moby-Dick*, Melville's reading included the Greek tragedies as well as Shakespeare, and one possible source for the particular language and imagery that Melville uses in the passage quoted above is a speech from the end of *Oedipus the King*. Here Creon, discovering the self-mutilated Oedipus in all his shame and humiliation, gives expression to his horror at the latter's exposure:

> You there,
> have you lost all respect for human feelings?
> At least revere the Sun, the holy fire
> that keeps us all alive. Never expose a thing
> of guilt and holy dread so great it appalls
> the earth, the rain from heaven, the light of day!
> Get him into the halls—quickly as you can.
> Piety demands no less. Kindred alone
> should see a kinsman's shame. This is obscene.
>
> (ll. 1558–66)

Our "immaculate manliness," as Melville puts it, "bleeds with keenest anguish at the undraped spectacle of a valor-ruined man." The image brings to mind the proverb that Wurmser quotes from Baba Metzia in the Talmud: "Shaming another in public is like shedding blood" (quoted in Wurmser 1981, vi).[9] The mortifying violation of the innermost area of the self instigates a furious sense of outrage at what amounts to a scandalous lapse of justice: "Nor can piety itself, at such a shameful sight, completely stifle her upbraidings against the permitting stars." Shame here is the greatest guardian of the self, protecting that innermost core "we feel within ourselves, so far within us, that it remains intact though all the outer character seem gone."[10]

IV

In this protective function, shame is the central affect involved in the taboo on looking and being looked at, which involves first of all, as Tomkins has observed, a taboo on intimacy. As Wurmser observes, "If one . . . crosses another's inner limits, one violates his privacy, and he feels shame" (1981, 62). A good example of such a violation of privacy occurs in *Pierre*, when in the throes of his moral struggle, and in search of some spiritual guidance, Pierre aggressively intrudes on Falsgrave, causing shame to both of them. The fact that this character's name is close to that of Holgrave in *The Blithedale Romance* suggests, perhaps, some connection between this character and Hawthorne. It may have been—one can only speculate—some such sense of guilty violation, combined with the shame felt by Melville when his over-tures were rebuffed by the withdrawing Hawthorne, that led to the disruption of their friendship and the subsequent distancing between the two. Pierre's first reaction is to experience shame-guilt for having invaded the other's privacy: "Yielding to that unwarrantable mood, he had invaded the profound midnight slumbers of the Reverend Mr. Falsgrave, and most dis-courteously made war upon that really amiable and estimable person" (*P*. 166). He repents of "his impulsive intrusion upon the respectable clergy-man" (166). He upbraids himself for "his thoughtlessness" and becomes "distrustful of that radical change in his general sentiments, which had thus hurried him into a glaring impropriety and folly; as distrustful of himself, the most wretched distrust of all" (167). This shattering feeling of self-dis-trust and distrust of the world that begins to overcome Pierre at this point in the novel is part of the shame experience that Lynd focuses on in with particularly keen insight: "What we have thought we could count on in ourselves, and what we have thought to be the boundaries and contours of the world, turn out suddenly not to be the 'real' outlines of ourselves or of the world, or those that others accept" (1958, 46). The growing alienation and estrangement that befalls Pierre in the course of the novel is precisely this experience of becoming a stranger "in a world where we thought we were at home. We experience anxiety in becoming aware that we cannot trust our answers to the questions Who am I? Where do I belong?" (46).

We can see here as well how a reaction to shame causes more shame: Pierre's sense of shame and self-righteous rage at the abandonment of Delly by Falsgrave and his mother leads him to intrude upon Falsgrave in the first place, and he then reacts by feeling ashamed that he has transgressed. This is a perfect illustration of Wurmser's analysis: "The transgressor himself may now feel both guilt—for the transgression of the first boundary, for having inflicted hurt—and shame, owing to identification with the exposed object" (1981, 62). Pierre ends up returning home in a defeated mood and, in the classic posture of shame affect, "with a hanging head." In the middle of the night, he despondently rummages among his books, and after turning from the inscription over the gates of Hell in a copy of Dante's *Inferno*, he finds an opened copy of *Hamlet* "in his hand, and his eyes met the following lines: 'The time is out of joint;—Oh cursed spite, / That ever I was born to set it right!'" (*P*, 168).[11] As he feels the crushing weight of the knowledge of his father's disgraceful past, and of his own self-condemnation at his continuing inaction, a frozenness—freezing or numbing oneself is here a way of disappearing or escaping overwhelming shame—steals upon Pierre's heart as "He dropped the too true volume from his hand; his petrifying heart dropped hollowly within him, as a pebble down Carrisbrook well" (168).

Pierre or, The Ambiguities, in many ways (in spite of its fantastically melodramatic story line) Melville's most autobiographical novel, represents a dramatic portrayal of the destructive impact of shame and the extraordinary efforts made to defend against it. The "ambiguities" of the title refer to the dilemma of someone caught in an irresolvable conflict between shame-inducing positions. When Pierre finds out that the father he has idealized throughout his life has a dishonorable and disgraceful secret—that he is the father of an illegitimate child whose mother died in childbirth and who has grown up as a destitute orphan—he reacts with deep outrage at his father's actions. In the wake of this revelation, he tries to reconcile the impossible demands on himself: to keep his father's secret from becoming public knowledge, in order both to keep his father's public image unsullied and thus to spare his mother from the humiliating consequences of such a revelation; *and*, in order to satisfy the demands of his ego ideal, to make a public acknowledgment of his love for his sister Isabel.

Eight-and-forty hours and more had passed. Was Isabel acknowledged? Had she yet hung on his public arm? Who knew yet of Isabel but Pierre? Like a skulking coward he had gone prowling in the woods by day, and like a skulking coward he had stolen to her haunt by night! Like a thief he had sat and stammered and turned pale before his mother, and in the cause of Holy Right, permitted a woman to grow tall and hector over him. Ah? Easy for man to think like a hero; but hard for man to act like one. All imaginable audacities readily enter into his soul; few come boldly forth from it. (170)

Like Father Mapple in his sermon, Pierre enthusiastically holds up an image of the ideal self to which he aspires: "For Pierre is a warrior too; Life his campaign, and three fierce allies, Woe and Scorn and Want, his foes. The whole world is banded against him; for lo you! he holds up the Standard of Right, and swears by the Eternal and True!" (270). The enthusiasm with which he eventually champions Isabel's cause is the sign of a deep conflict in his personality. It is a case of what Wurmser calls "the heroic but self-defeating fight for a value" or "defence by exaggeration of a value," one of the "indispensable forms of defences" that, combined, make up the tragic character: "a pursuit of a value to its extreme, to its excess, where the value itself and its defender become destructive and destroyed" (1978, 331). Pierre's fate, we discover by the end of the novel, is to be destroyed by the insurmountable conflicts involved in his own struggle to transcend his father's disgrace and be true to himself. At first, he finds himself, like Jonah, in a cowardly flight from the shame he feels in having fallen miserably short of the demands made by his ego ideal; the imagery that Pierre applies to himself—"Like a skulking coward," "Like a thief"—is virtually identical to Mapple's rhetoric concerning Jonah: "Oh! most contemptible and worthy of all scorn; with slouched hat and guilty eye, skulking from his God; prowling among the shipping like a vile burglar hastening to cross the sea. So disordered, self-condemning is his look" (*MD*, 43). Like Jonah, who at first fails to stand forth his inexorable self, Pierre condemns himself for his dishonor in failing to live up to an ideal self, true to the "cause of Holy Right." This shame emanating from the idealizing pole of the self is, however, in conflict with the threat of shame at the grandiose-exhibitionistic pole. The image of being caught "like a thief," stammering and turning pale before the shaming gaze of his mother, recalls Ishmael's memory in "The Counterpane" of being shamed as a boy by his stepmother who, like Mrs. Glendinning, grows tall and "hectors over him."

Pierre thus offers us a singular view of the conflict raging between the two poles of the self: the idealizing pole that, transmuted and internalized, forms the core of one's ideals and values, and the grandiose-exhibitionistic pole that is the source of ambition and expresses itself as a desire for narcissistic mirroring, for admiration and praise. In trying to satisfy the claims of the one pole, Pierre must enter into the most terrible conflict with the other. If he decides to live up to the values and ideals that demand that he publicly acknowledge Isabel, then he faces the terrible scorn of his "proud mother," who "spurning the reflection on his father, would likewise spurn Pierre and Isabel, as unnatural accomplices against the good name of the purest of husbands and parents" (*P*, 170). If he yields to the pressure to avoid being ostracized by his mother, then he must experience the personal shame and loss of self-respect from treating his own sister as an object of disgrace to be concealed and covered in sordid secrecy. Everywhere the self turns in this scenario, it is disabled and paralyzed by shame (and guilt): the fear of hurting his mother and the threat of being treated with scorn and contempt by her for confronting her with the shameful dishonor and disgrace of his father; the fear of covering his father's memory with shame; and the threat of being ashamed of himself for disgracefully treating his own sister as an object of shame out of a contemptible fear of being ostracized for the public acknowledgment.

> Thy two grand resolutions—the public acknowledgement of Isabel, and the charitable withholding of her existence from thy own mother,—these are impossible adjuncts.—Likewise, thy so magnanimous purpose to screen thy father's honorable memory from reproach, and thy other intention, the open vindication of thy fraternalness to Isabel,—these also are impossible adjuncts. And the having individually entertained four such resolves, without perceiving that once brought together, they all mutually expire; this, this ineffable folly, Pierre, brands thee in the forehead for an unaccountable infatuate! (171)

This image of the tragically branded infatuate, marked for sacrifice, recalls the image attached to Radney in "The Town-Ho's Story" in *Moby-Dick*. He is "the foolish and infatuated man" who tempts Steelkilt beyond reason and pays the price: "But, gentleman, the fool had been branded for the slaughter by the gods" (248). Pierre then collapses under the unbearable weight of his conviction that he is completely contemptible and worthy only of disgust and hate: "The cheeks of his soul collapsed in him: he dashed himself in blind fury and swift madness against the wall, and fell dabbing in the vomit of his loathed identity" (*P*, 171).

Paralyzed by utterly incompatible goals, Pierre plunges headlong into a conflict between opposed absolute claims. He wants "to hold his father's fair fame inviolate from any thing he should do in reference to protecting Isabel" and at the same time extend "to her a brother's utmost devotedness and love." He wants "not to shake his mother's lasting peace by any useless exposure of unwelcome facts; and yet vowed in his deepest soul some way to embrace Isabel before the world" (172–73). It is not surprising that the provisory solution he comes up with to harmonize these goals—marriage to Isabel—is completely unsatisfactory. Indeed, this solution only results in an even more intensely shame-provoking situation, with shame covering himself and others: in deciding to make his half-sister his wife, he commits "a most singular act of pious imposture, which he thought all heaven would justify in him, since he himself was to be the grand self-renouncing victim" (173). He thus answers in as satisfying a way as possible the demands of his ego ideal (the "heavenly claim" that Isabel has on him) and escapes to some extent his own self-condemnation and contempt, while at the same time avoiding casting "world-wide and irremediable dishonour—so it seemed to him—upon his departed father" (173). However, "part of the unavoidable vast price of his enthusiastic virtue," of his idealism, is enormous in its consequences: it causes his mother a deep personal injury to which she reacts, in narcissistic rage, by casting him out.

The tone and imagery of these passages recalls Father Mapple's emotional and enthusiastic appeal to self-loyalty, to an authenticity of self, but there is the immeasurable complication in *Pierre* of a much more painful consciousness of the terrible perplexity of "unitedly impossible designs." In the words of Murray, whose extremely perceptive reading of the novel remains of great psychological value: "Wearied and exasperated by the relentless underlying conflict and confounded by the constant inversions of value from positive to negative and negative to positive, the man may finally arrive at a state of virtual paralysis with no capacity for decision" (1962, xv). "Lucy or God?" (*P*, 181) is Pierre's simplistic way of formulating this paralyzing dilemma of incompatible loyalties, and it recalls the kind of choice presented by Mapple—the choice of being a patriot to this world or to heaven—in much less ambiguous terms. Pierre's temporary paralysis is a sign that acceptance and mediation are called for, but this wisdom is completely overruled by Pierre's all-or-nothing approach to the question. He insists on the absolute necessity of choice and on the absolute value of that choice. "I have bought," he tells Isabel after choosing, "inner love and glory by a price, which, large or small, I would not now have paid me back, so I must return the thing I bought" (191). The defense here, as Wurmser describes it, would be "an exaggerated concern for certain external, especially social boundaries, which then is supposed to justify the breaking of other boundaries which—for the rest of society—appear equally important" (1978, 331). The question of Isabel's honor becomes absolute and eventually overrides all other concerns, even at the cost of destroying the most intimate ties with others. The willingness to enter into such an absolute conflict is depicted in terms that, in their trenchancy, recall Mapple's enthusiastic language of martyrdom:

> There is an inevitable keen cruelty in the loftier heroism. It is not heroism only to stand unflinched ourselves in the hours of suffering; but it is heroism to stand unflinched both at our own and at some loved one's united suffering; a united suffering, which we could put an instant period to, if we would but renounce the glorious cause for which ourselves do bleed, and see our most loved one bleed. If he would not reveal his father's shame to the common world, whose favorable opinion for himself, Pierre now despised. How then reveal it to the woman he adored? . . . So Pierre turned round and tied Lucy to the same stake which must hold himself, for he too plainly saw, that it could not be, but that both their hearts must burn. (*P*, 178)

The imagery of martyrdom is, as we have seen, a sign that we are touching on the courage that derives, originally, from merger with the idealized object. Mapple's "patriot to heaven"; Vere, who belongs to the king; and Nelson, who sacrifices himself to victory—all exemplify the same posture of obeisance to the object's "heavenly claim." But Pierre's all too ready willingness to sacrifice himself *and others* makes it impossible to overlook what may be, in the end, the most determining psychological factor in his doomed efforts to manage an impossible dilemma: the hidden pleasure he derives from the amount of pain and suffering that his impossibly idealistic demands cause in both himself and those dearest to him. The imagery of bleeding from a wound—"the glorious cause for which ourselves do bleed, and see our most loved one bleed"—is, as we have already seen more than once now, an image of searing shame or mortification. This type of image occurs with great frequency in *Moby-Dick*: there is the occurrence in Mapple's sermon and in the passage concerning Starbuck and "the fall of valour in the soul"; there is the image of Ahab's physical and psychic goring by Moby Dick—"then it was, that his torn body and gashed soul bled into one another" (*MD*, 185)—and of his later being wounded in the groin by his splintered ivory leg, as well as the image of the scar that appears when he is first introduced, to have divided him in two ; and there is, in a less tragic vein, the "mortal wound" suffered by Ishmael in "The Monkey-Rope." A like image—"such a scar that the air of Paradise might not erase it" (11)—also recurs at the beginning of *Redburn*. Fatally wounded pride by which the soul bleeds to death is the cost that Pierre, "hurt by a wound, never to be completely healed but in heaven" (*P*, 65), must pay in the end to protect himself and others from what he takes to be the greater shame associated with the exposure of his father's disgrace. But this cost has its own narcissistic gains, and is perhaps as much something Pierre has sought out as something to which he has resigned himself.

The sense of injury in Pierre's case is, like Redburn's—and Melville's—triggered first of all by the shame associated with his father, whose image and memory have been irretrievably shattered by the exposure of his shameful secret life. Beginning with his mother's casting him out, a series of blows to the self rain down as a consequence of the complications that follow this discovery. Pierre, snubbed and abandoned by friends, betrayed by those closest to him, feels deeply and unjustly rejected. In New York, he reacts to his feelings of shame and mortification by falling back on archaic grandiosity, on images of his own fascinating power and omnipotence. As absolute as his commitment to Isabel was originally, he now virtually abandons her in his own obsessive ambition to write his book. As Murray observes, "[H]e believes he is motivated by love and the will to uphold truth whereas actually this is but a veil of vapor overlying a volcano of pride and hate and the will to destroy falsehoods" (1962, ci). His ideals of honor and right and then his ambitious will to truth become absolutes in turn, to the point that he sacrifices all other human concerns to them. He is finally pushed over the edge when he receives a double blow in the form of two letters denouncing him, one from his publishers, who dissolve their contract and reject his most personal work with the most insulting contempt, and the other signed by his two closest boyhood friends, Frederic Tartan and Glendinning Stanly, who cruelly denounce him and break off all relations. His anger has been building up through the course of the novel as he finds himself faced with one humiliation or slight after another; these deep feelings of narcissistic rage finally explode when he feels that he has been rejected by those he had placed his last hopes and trust in.

But there is from the beginning—and this may be the most important factor in the end—a deeply *masochistic* element in the logic that guides Pierre's actions and in the humiliation and wounding of his pride that are the consequences. Wurmser indeed views this sort of martyrdom, this "masochistic, totemistic self-sacrifice in a heroic (narcissistic) shine or halo [as] the cardinal, most specific hallmark of the tragic character" (1978, 330). In this connection, Pierre epitomizes what has been called, in another context, "the nobility of failure," the enormous pleasures of self-justification and self-vindication that come from humiliating defeat, when defeat might indeed have been avoided if there were more to life than avoiding shame.[12] Masochism, as Wurmser points out, appears as a solution to so many shame conflicts precisely because of the many gains it offers (1981, 182–85). He lists five in all: turning passive to active, superego gratification, the sexualization of the trauma, the narcissistic gain, and the archaic identification with the victim. All of these are doubtless of importance here, and are combined with externalization, in which the shame that rules the individual's inner life is made to come from the outside, through "the active provocation of punishment and rejection, the invitation of defeat, the turning of traumatically suffered insult, mutilation, humiliation and rejection into an active provoking of attacks" (1978, 333) on oneself. Pierre's impossible situation, which makes necessary a strategy that aims at escaping or fighting off one shame or humiliation by undergoing another, would seem to make the masochistic answer a most compelling one indeed. The active provocation of rejection may have been the motivation all along behind Pierre's puzzling willingness to enter into conflicts that are clearly impossible to resolve in the first place. We opened this chapter with a discussion of Mapple's Jonah as offering us the image of heroically transcended shame and loyalty to self; to be a patriot to heaven, in these terms, is to be a patriot to one's genuine self. It is, however, more faithful perhaps to the pessimistic but psychologically profound insight of Melville's work that we should conclude the chapter with *Pierre*, the gloomy and melancholy tragedy of a human being whose apparently principled and reasoned effort to transcend shame—whose resolution "to live," as Kohut puts it, "in accordance with the central purposes of the self and in harmony with the highest idealized value" (1990, 143)—is ruled at the same time by the aggressive forces of ambition and grandiosity, and by a deep wish for destruction. The tragic character seeks atonement, as Wurmser describes it, "for his oedipal (and preoedipal, especially narcissistic) wishes in such a masochistically exaggerated form because in his own history the oedipal drama had been a bloody chain of traumata" (1978, 330). Melville's own abusive and shame-bound family history undoubtedly looms behind the gloominess of *Pierre*, the story of an individual who is forced to seek out defeat by one mortifying blow after another, until by the end of the novel his homicidal and suicidal outburst arrives as nothing less than a dark but joyous release.

PART TWO

Shame, Resentment, and Envy

CHAPTER FOUR

Motiveless Malignity

I

The theme, so essential to *Pierre*, of heroism in defeat, with its fundamentally masochistic logic, brings us to Richard Chase's second category of hero in Melville: "Prometheus, the Titan who fled from heaven to bring light to man and to suffer on earth in his behalf" (1949, 3). As Murray points out, however, it is not Prometheus but the titanic Satan who is a more fitting model here, since "although both of Melville's heroes [Ahab and Pierre] are against the gods, they are not for humanity" (1962, lxxxvi). The posture of titanic heroes such as Ahab and Pierre exemplifies, in the face of defeat, the attitude of defiance, a particularly potent defense against shame. Defiance in particular is intimately linked to the theme of the Titans, as it is in the famous "Enceladus" chapter in *Pierre*, where such imagery is perhaps most fully developed.[1] At the end of the novel, we find Pierre—the precursor of the resentment-riddled Travis Bickle in Martin Scorsese's *Taxi-Driver*—enraged and wandering the mean streets of New York, the entire universe polarized for him along the shame/pride axis (as Nathanson calls it) of triumph or defeat: "Stemming such tempests through the deserted streets, Pierre felt a dark, triumphant joy, that while others had crawled in fear to their kennels, he alone defied the storm-admiral, whose most vindictive peltings of hail-stones,—striking his iron-framed fiery furnace of a body,—melted into soft dew, and so, harmlessly trickled from off him" (*P*, 340).

The rhetoric and imagery in *Pierre* is often remarkably close to the exhortative style in Father Mapple's sermon in *Moby-Dick*, especially its closing flourishes. The euphoria of both Mapple and Pierre is due to the imagined dissolution of the tension between what Freud would call the ego and the ego ideal, through their projected merger. As Mapple bravely overcomes his momentary despondency and lifts up his face with deep joy and heavenly enthusiasm showing in his eyes, so for a moment, through the adoption of a defiant stance, Pierre manically pulls himself out of his mood of shame and depression and feels, accordingly, a "dark, triumphant joy." This defiant posture, as it appears in both Pierre and Ahab, involves a fighting stance that is part of the magnetic appeal of those who fail but fail nobly, who lose but lose heroically. In cases of charisma, the group, as Irvine Schiffer explains this dynamic,

> demands that the potential leader be prepared to win something or lose something—and with action! It matters not for charisma what may be the ultimate fate awaiting such a figure; the key element is that he symbolize, in his image, someone who is taking an active stand, taking one side against another. His personality, in fact, may have all the markings of a heroic loser; and just because of this, he may fit the ideal image of followers who look to project the heroics of their own polarized stance of losers. (1973, 38)

In exhorting his congregation to stand forth their inexorable selves, Mapple has in mind what Leon Wurmser calls "the striving for self-integrity, self-loyalty, or authenticity" (1981, 299), the heroic transcendence of shame through the healing power of idealization. In contrast, the overwhelming pressures in *Pierre*, as we have seen, are exerted predominantly by the grandiose self, and Pierre is ultimately overcome by rage and the desire for revenge. Pierre does not repent, like Jonah; he chooses, rather, scorn and defiance. He is like the titanic Ahab, who worships—and does so, appropriately, not by bowing down to, but by defying—the "clear spirit of clear fire." Its "right worship," Ahab proclaims, "is defiance" (507). "I leap with thee; I burn with thee; would fain be welded with thee; defyingly I worship thee" (*MD*, 508). Doubtless, Melville based the conflicting forms of heroism of Mapple and Ahab to some extent on *Paradise Lost*, where the idealism exemplified by the heroism of Christ is contrasted with the grandiosity propelling the titanic heroism of Satan. Satan's defiance depends on the hierarchical opposition, associated with the attitude of contempt, of those who defiantly stand up, however overwhelming the odds, and those who withdraw shamefacedly from the fight, who crawl "in fear to their kennels," as Pierre contemptuously views it. This image recalls Ahab's contemptuous dismissal of the abject Stubb in chapter 31 ("Queen Mab") of *Moby-Dick*: "Down, dog, and kennel!" Satan's defiance is outlined in his first speech in Book One; it shows all the marks of a reaction to a deeply mortified narcissism.

> . . . yet not for those,
> Nor what the Potent victor in his rage
> Can else inflict, do I repent or change,
> Though chang'd in outward luster; that fixt mind
> And high disdain, from sense of injur'd merit,
> That with the mightiest rais'd me to contend,
> And to that fierce contention brought along
> Innumerable force of Spirits arm'd
> That durst dislike his reign, and me preferring,
> His utmost power with adverse power oppos'd
> In dubious Battle on the Plains of Heav'n,
> And shook his throne. What though the field be lost?
> All is not lost; the unconquerable Will,
> And study of revenge, immortal hate,
> And courage never to submit or yield:
> And what else is not to be overcome?
> That Glory never shall his wrath or might
> Extort from me. To bow and sue for grace
> With suppliant knee, and deify his power
> Who from the terror of his Arm so late
> Doubted his Empire, that were low indeed,
> That were an ignomiy and shame beneath
> This downfall . . .
> (*Paradise Lost*, 1.94–116)

Echoing Satan's "Better to reign in Hell, than serve in Heav'n" (1.263), and "Which way I fly is Hell; myself am Hell" (4.75), Pierre, imprisoned at the end of the novel, defiantly declares: "Now, 'tis merely hell in both worlds. Well, be it hell. I will mold a trumpet of the flames, and, with my breath of flame, breathe back my defiance!" (*P*, 360). Mapple's enthusiastic exhortation begins and ends in the contrition of shame, which seeks propitiation and reconciliation with the alienated idealized object, but Pierre, like Satan, is beyond repentance. Repentance is possible "but by submission; and that word / Disdain forbids me, and my dread of shame" (*Paradise Lost* 4.81-82). Pierre's euphoria in the passage quoted above, his "dark, triumphant joy"— a perfect way of expressing the masochism that resides at the core of Pierre's antishame posture—is part of a cycle that begins and ends in depression; it is a manic state in which the restrictions of the ego ideal have been artificially blotted out and fused with the ego, "so that the person, in a mood of triumph and self-satisfaction, disturbed by *no self-criticism*, can enjoy the abolition of his inhibitions, his feelings of consideration for others, and his *self-reproaches*" (Freud, quoted in Morrison 1989, 27). It is the joy of perverse pride, the last refuge of a proud but defeated self, whose main affect is, as the "iron-framed fiery furnace" of Pierre's body suggests, humiliated fury, the explosive rage that arises from searing narcissistic injury.

The image of Pierre's "iron-framed fiery furnace of a body" is a powerful image of rage, but it also belongs to the titanic archetype, an archetype made popular in the Byronism that was fashionable during the decades of the 1830s and '40s and that Melville would have fully absorbed in his intense and wide reading.[2] Indeed, Pierre's very being at this point in the novel, as he finds himself in the terrible throes of writing his book, is depicted in terms of a struggle between his body and his titanic soul. During one of his enraged walks in "the utter night-desolation of the obscurest warehousing lanes," he is suddenly overcome by "a combined blindness, and vertigo, and staggering," and comes to later "lying crosswise in the gutter, dabbled with mud and slime" (*P*, 341). After this event, he is physically unable to write: "But now at last since the very blood in his body had in vain rebelled against his titanic soul; now the only visible outward symbols of that soul—his eyes—did also turn downright traitors to him, and with more success than the rebellious blood" (341). His abused eyes "absolutely refused to look on paper. He turned them on paper, and they blinked and shut" (341). The shame, depression, and rage that contend within him have made the normal exercise of perception impossible, and Pierre sinks into a state of paralysis or unconscious trance, as his eyes stop seeing and refuse to take anything more in. The next day, "he returned to the charge. But again the pupils of his eyes rolled away from him in their orbits; and now a general and nameless torpor—some horrible foretaste of death itself—seemed stealing upon him" (342).

This imagery of blindness and torpor—of losing both sight and consciousness—can be explained by a reaction to shame: it is the defensive refusal to see or to be aware anymore of that which overwhelms one with shame or self-contempt. It is connected to the imagery of immobilization and rigidification, of being frozen and petrified, associated with images of stone and stony ruin, that runs throughout *Pierre* and corresponds to the nightmarish fear in shame: that massive disappointment and defeat will leave one exposed to unmitigated feelings of shame and self-contempt, and that one will be frozen in fascination or exposure and turned to stone. Having fallen into a "state of semi-consciousness, or rather trance," Pierre has "a remarkable dream or vision" (342) of the Titans, archetypal figures of crushing and conspicuous defeat, who, in a desperate effort to abolish their shame and abjection, undertake a reckless assault on heaven, only to be cast down again in humiliating defeat. He recalls a mountain from his childhood haunts, whose sublime desolation caused the local inhabitants to change its name from the Bunyan-inspired Delectable (an image inspired by Christian idealism) to the more ominous Titanic (a grandiose image of unconquerable power). The most impressive jutting boulder of this mountain was popularly known as Enceladus:

> You paused; fixed by a form defiant, a form of awfulness. You saw Enceladus the Titan, the most potent of all the giants, writhing from out the imprisoning Earth;—turbaned with upborne moss he writhed; still, though armless, resisting with his whole striving trunk, the Pelion and the Ossa hurled back at him;—turbaned with upborne moss he writhed; still turning his unconquerable front toward that majestic mount eternally in vain assailed by him, and which, when it had stormed him off, had heaved his undoffable incubus upon him, and deridingly left him there to bay out his ineffectual howl. (345)

The sense of unconquerable power derives from the grandiose self, which, as we have seen, comes to play the dominant role in Pierre's personality; his idealism turns out to be a mask for a controlling narcissism and wish for absolute self-vindication. Pierre comes by his pride honestly; the "unconquerable front" of Enceladus recalls the "unconquerable pride" of the dreaded Mrs. Glendinning. The image of the routed Titan is, of course, an image of Pierre's own shameful defeat. The same derision and howl are, not surprisingly, part of the imagery surrounding Ahab in his mortification and despair at being defeated by Moby Dick.

   Kohut describes the narcissistically injured as persons who do not seem subject to feelings of guilt, but who, in their archaic experience of reality, feel that the world has done them some grievous and unforgivable injury in depriving them of a perfectly controlled narcissistic reality, "having first, as if to tease them, given them a taste of its security and delights" (1978, 831). This is why people injured in this way appear to have feelings only for themselves and for their needs; they are compensating for what was originally withdrawn from them, and they continue to be "enraged about a world that has tried to take from them something they consider to be rightfully their own: the response of the selfobject." Thus, what others perceive as actions for which they should feel guilty, are, from their point of view, a justified response to "the prior injustice they suffered" (832). In the same way, the Titans rebelled against a brutal father, and ruled with their mother in a paradisal world, until this special state of well-being, comparable to the narcissistic feeling of wholeness and omnipotence that Grunberger associates with the infant's memory of "a unique and privileged state of elation" (1979, 20), was shattered by the revolt of their own progeny, who, inflicting a crushing defeat upon them, evicted them from heaven and took their place. This myth is, among other things, an expression of the narcissistic injury that befalls the self wrapped up in its "illusion of uniqueness," an essentially "megalomaniacal position" (20). Melville appears to confuse the Titans and the Giants, an understandable and even time-honored error; the two myths are separate but closely related stories, part of the same cycle of rivalry and treacherous reversal. The Titans, subjected to the injustices of a tyrannical father (Uranus), rebelled and deposed him, only to be betrayed by their children in turn. The Giants were half-brothers of the defeated Titans; according to some accounts, their mother "bore [them] . . . out of rage at Zeus's destruction of the Titans" (Tripp 1970, 250). They were possessed of the desire to redress the wrong by taking revenge and thus to recapture the nostalgically yearned-for paradise lost. They vowed vengeance and set out, but all in vain, to overthrow their overthrowers. Milton associates the myth of the Titans with the story of the fallen rebel angels in *Paradise Lost:* Satan, eaten up by envy when God the Father passes him over and places the Christ at his right hand, gathers around him an army of rebel angels who wage war in heaven; defeated in a final battle he is hurled down with his companions into Hell. From there he plots revenge; his plan is to tempt Adam and Eve to eat of the Tree of Knowledge so that they will be expelled from paradise. He who cannot mend his own case, harms another's.

This theme is clearly related, of course, to our earlier discussion of Melville's interest in those rejected figures in the Bible who are forced to live out their exile in the wilderness, victims of an equally unjust dispossession. Claggart, for example, is associated with both Saul and one of the elder brothers of Joseph, the Joseph story offering another instance of this theme of rejection or, as Frye puts it, "passing over of the firstborn son, who normally has the legal right of primogeniture, in favor of a younger one" (1981, 180). In both cases the allusion is made with reference to an intensely scrutinizing look of resentment and envy. Claggart's envy is problematic, the narrator informs us, because it is so deeply rooted in his personality: "Nor, as directed toward Billy Budd, did it partake of that streak of apprehensive jealousy that marred Saul's visage perturbedly brooding on the comely young David" (*BB*, 78–79). And as Vere ruminates on the accusations of the master-at-arms, Claggart steadily regards him with "a look curious of the operation of his tactics, a look such as might have been that of the spokesman of the envious children of Jacob deceptively imposing upon the troubled patriarch the blood-dyed coat of young Joseph" (96).

An important part of the titanic imagery in Melville concerns the assault on heaven, the abortive attempt to overthrow and replace those "above," who have unjustifiably usurped one's position. In this connection, the image of conspicuous defeat also becomes an image of burial, and this in turn is part of the imagery of shame we would like to insist upon: it is the image of a sort of unconquerable self that, like Milton's Satan, has been thrown down in a shameful reversal and buried alive. The opening passage of *Paradise Lost*, would seem to be, for Melville at any rate, the paradigm of this imagery of a titanic fall:

> . . . what time his Pride
> Had cast him out from heav'n, with all his Host
> Of Rebel Angels, by whose aid aspiring
> To set himself in Glory above his Peers,
> He trusted to have equall'd the Most High
> If he oppos'd; and with ambitious aim
> Against the Throne and Monarchy of God
> Rais'd impious War in Heav'n and Battle proud
> With vain attempt. Him the almighty Power
> Hurl'd headlong flaming from th' Ethereal Sky
> With hideous ruin and combustion down
> To bottomless perdition, there to dwell

> In Adamantine Chains and penal Fire,
> Who durst defy th' Omnipotent to Arms.
>
> (1.36–49)

In *Pierre*, the theme of the assault on heaven appears in the description of Pierre's memory of an unsuccessful attempt by a group of schoolboys to unearth or dig up the *fallen and buried* Enceladus. In this particular passage, the element of shame brought on by humiliating conspicuous defeat is prominent:

> At that point the wearied young collegians gave over their enterprise in despair. With all their toil, they had not yet come to the girdle of Enceladus. But they had *bared* good part of his mighty chest, and *exposed* his mutilated shoulders, and the stumps of his once audacious arms. Thus far *uncovering his shame*, in that cruel plight they had abandoned him, leaving stark naked his in vain indignant chest to the defilements of the birds, which for untold ages had cast their foulness on his vanquished crest. (345; emphasis added)

Here we find the explicit imagery of uncovering and exposure, of humiliation, and of abandonment felt by the unprotected victim of ridicule and scorn. The same imagery surrounds the defeated Ahab—a figure who embodies, of course, the very essence of a titanic unconquerable ambition and will—when he is all but destroyed in his initial contest with Moby Dick.

The titanic theme culminates in Pierre's dream vision, in which the overthrown Titans awaken from the stony earth and make one last catastrophic assault on heaven:

> Such was the wild scenery—the Mount of Titans, and the repulsed group of heaven-assaulters, with Enceladus in their midst *shamefully recumbent at its base;*—such was the wild scenery, which now to Pierre, in his strange vision, displaced the four blank walls, the desk, and camp-bed, and domineered upon his trance. But no longer *petrified in all their ignominious attitudes*, the herded Titans now sprung to their feet; flung themselves up the slope; and anew

battered at the precipice's unresounding wall. Foremost among them all, he saw a moss-turbaned, armless giant, who despairing of any other mode of wreaking his immitigable hate, turned his vast trunk into a battering-ram, and hurled his own arched-out ribs again and yet again against the invulnerable steep.

"Enceladus! it is Enceladus!"—Pierre cried out in his sleep. (346; emphasis added)

As we have already observed, the imagery of *petrification* in *Pierre*—the name of the central hero is, of course, part of that imagery[3]—is linked to the experience of shame. We find this image of being *frozen* or entranced, unable to move, in a humiliating or shaming gaze: the indomitable Enceladus is "fast frozen into the earth at the junction of the neck" (345), and the Titans are "petrified in all their ignominious attitudes" (346). When Pierre is in prison, he appears in precisely the same attitude, frozen beneath the stony earth and as if he had himself been turned to stone: "The cumbersome stone ceiling almost rested on his brow; so that the long tiers of massive cell-galleries above seemed partly piled on him. His immortal, immovable, bleached cheek was dry; but the stone cheeks of the walls were trickling" (360). The same image appears in "Bartleby," whose utterly passive but unyielding and unrepentant hero's mechanical response—"I would prefer not to"—is, as Bowen justly points out, "defiance nonetheless" (1960, 134): "The Egyptian character of the masonry weighed upon me in its gloom. . . . Strangely huddled at the base of the wall, his knees drawn up, and lying on his side, his head touching the cold stones" (*PT,* 44). The imagery of being petrified and buried under the earth, eternally benumbed and frozen, appears as well, of course, in the famous "captive king" passage of *Moby-Dick:* "[S]o like a Caryatid, he patient sits, upholding on his frozen brow the piled entablatures of ages." The very same series of images—stone-brow-piled-immovable—appears as in the passage from *Pierre.* There is another instance of this imagery in chapter 132 ("The Symphony") of *Moby-Dick:* "Adam, staggering beneath the piled centuries since Paradise" (544) is how Ahab describes to Starbuck his feeling of being burdened down by his own "undoffable incubus." The same combination of imagery recurs when Claggart shames Billy as they confront one another in Vere's cabin: there is the image of being paralyzed and frozen ("impaled and gagged in the mesmeristic glance") and the image of being buried alive. Billy's face is described as "like that of a condemned vestal priestess in the moment of being buried alive, and in the first struggle against suffocation" (*BB*, 376). This is the fear, again, that haunts those who are helplessly overcome by searing shame: the fear of being turned to stone, of being overwhelmed with shame to the point of petrification.[4]

In *Pierre*, we see how a certain kind of personality comes into being, a personality that, invariably associated with the titanic theme and its attendant imagery, is marked by a number of distinguishing features. First, there is the defiance and the paranoid sense of being pitted against a world of enemies. Second, there is the feeling of entitlement, of having been shamefully supplanted and robbed of one's due by others. This experience of being supplanted is focused on Glen Stanly, who betrays Pierre by abandoning him when he is in the most dire need; he refuses even to recognize him, dispossesses him of his patrimony, and attempts to usurp his place in Lucy's affections. Third, there is the tendency for such a personality to react to everything in terms of the shame/pride axis. Everything is seen in terms of triumph and defeat. There is fear of being defeated and made the conspicuous object of mockery and scorn. In the counterfantasy there is an omnipotent and triumphant turning of the tables, in which one turns from being humiliated to being the humiliator. This type of personality, eaten away by buried narcissistic rage and smoldering resentment, is the fundamental matrix for Melville's protagonists, whether tragic heroes or depraved villains.[5]

More than a hint of Pierre's "reckless sky-assaulting mood" (*P*, 347), or of Ahab's "heaven-insulting purpose" (169), clings, for example, to the shame-ravaged and resentment-ridden Jackson, who "was a brave desperado" and "seemed to run a muck at heaven and earth. He was a Cain afloat; branded on his yellow brow with some inscrutable curse; and going about corrupting and searing every heart that beat near him" (104). Linking Jackson to the titanic theme is the image of running amuck at heaven and the comparison to Cain. Supplanted in his parent's affections by his brother, Cain is a figure who, branded and outcast by God, particularly feels the sting of omnipotent authority. That Jackson is a victim of shame and humiliation is further suggested by the image of being "branded" and by the "searing" mortification that he inflicts on others, an obvious counter-shaming. The idea of having been seared appears in the description of the Promethean Ahab when he is first introduced: "He looked like a man cut away from the stake, when the fire has overrunningly wasted all the limbs without consuming them, or taking away one particle from their compacted aged robustness" (*MD*, 123). This description recalls the Miltonic imagery of Satan hurled down from heaven in flame and combustion, to dwell below in "penal Fire," and suggests the dark psychological web in which the burning of shame and anger is entangled with ambition—the burning ambition, for example, of he who "with ambitious aim" aspired "To set himself to have equall'd the most High."

At the very beginning of *Moby-Dick* the narrator singles out the titanic theme for comic treatment in the concluding exhortation of the "Extracts": "Would that I could clear out Hampton Court and Tuileries for ye! But gulp down your tears and hie aloft to the royal-mast with your hearts; for your friends who have gone before are clearing out the seven-storied heavens, and making refugees of long-pampered Gabriel, Michael, and Raphael, against your coming" (xvii–xviii). The point here is a comic reversal in which Milton's long-pampered angels, instead of the rebel angels, are the ones who are unceremoniously evicted: in *this* heaven, a festive and carnivalized image, the teetotalling Sub-Sub, who occupies the basement of a sort of towering library of Babel, will become a hearty Rabelaisian drinker in a cheerful upside-down world. Here, the narcissistic resentment of an Ahab, a Claggart, or a Pierre is comically answered by laughter and the wisdom that comes with it. With humor, and the ability to laugh at oneself, comes sociability; in its absence, Melville constantly reminds us, we live in a world of murderous rage and deadly quarrel. Implied here as well is the role of creativity and idealization in the healing of what Wurmser calls primary woundedness. It is significant that an earlier version of this comic image—in which those whose creative labors go thankless in this world will be promoted in the next—appears in one of Melville's letters to Evert Duyckinck (24 February 1849), in which "the divine William" is compared to Jesus: "Ah. He's full of sermons-on-the mount, and gentle, aye, almost as Jesus. I take such men to be inspired. I fancy that this moment Shakespeare in heaven ranks with Gabriel Raphael and Michael. And if another Messiah ever comes twill be in Shakespere's person" (*Corr.*, 119).

II

As Nathanson observes of the conditions of competition and rivalry that provoke shame, to "be defeated by an equal is shameful; to be defeated through an 'act of God' is not, for there was no attempt to claim equality with deity. Destruction by a rival produces shame reflecting a heightened sense of a defective self, a decrease in self image and self esteem; 'natural disaster' produces more a sense of loss and mourning" (Nathanson 1987a, 194). As we have seen, Melville's own personal history reflects the conditions of competition and rivalry, as they are outlined by Nathanson, that tend to produce shame in our culture. Social status would seem to be the most relevant area here. Rank is, in Nathanson's terms, "a symbol system balancing power and pride against weakness and shame" (194). To recapitulate, we offer the following list: following a period of prosperity and social success, his father's bankruptcy, ruined reputation, followed by shameful insanity and death; his status-conscious mother's consequent feeling of intense social humiliation; his beloved Uncle Thomas's humiliating failure in business and disgraceful imprisonment for debt, in spite of a past of adventure and romantic promise; his ambitious brother's business failure and later disgraceful fall from political grace after a meteoric rise, followed by a bizarre nervous disorder, loss of reputation, and death; not to mention Herman's own relative failure to attain the attention of the public as a writer after 1850. The precipitous fall in social status of the Melvill family, when both Allan and Maria had such strong narcissistic identifications with the social importance of their families, must have had a significant psychological effect on their children.

The realm of comparison and competition is, of course, of central importance in Melville. The blasphemy of which Starbuck accuses Ahab, who has vowed vengeance on the white whale, is quite precisely, as Nathanson puts it, "to claim equality with deity" and take an act of God as something shameful incurred in competition with a hated opponent: "He tasks me; he heaps he; I see in him outrageous strength, with an inscrutable malice sinewing it. That inscrutable thing is chiefly what I hate; and be the white whale agent, or be the white whale principal, I will wreak that hate upon him" (*MD*, 164). That Ahab's defeat by Moby Dick results in a feeling of humiliation instead of "a sense of loss and mourning" is characteristic of Melville's work in general, in which the imagery of bereavement is always colored by intense shame; a painful feeling of disappointment and of having failed in one's ambitions, associated with the loss of a father, is, for example, a central theme in both *Redburn* and *Pierre*.

The shame felt by Claggart in the presence of Billy Budd is an instance of the same thing: it is the result of his unconsciously measuring himself against the narcissistic ideal represented by his rival, who outshines him and thus causes him "a heightened sense of defective self," to use Nathanson's terms. In the story both Red Whiskers and Claggart are, in the homoerotic context of shipboard life, the incumbent objects of admiration who find themselves suddenly supplanted by a usurping interloper, and Red Whiskers, like Claggart, clearly dislikes the "newcomer" "out of envy" (*BB*, 47). "Where there is envy," as Wurmser observes, "you find shame underneath" (1986, 87). The important link between shame and envy can, indeed, often be detected in the way that Melville's narrators tend to emphasize comparative elements when contrasting rivals, envy being a feeling in which a person is made to acknowledge "inferiority with respect to another; He measures himself against something else, and finds himself wanting" (George Foster, quoted in Berke 1987, 325). In "The Town-Ho's Story," for example, Steelkilt appears as a rudimentary prototype for the narcissistic ideal of the beautiful golden sailor Billy Budd, a figure associated with solar imagery. The description of Steelkilt as "a tall and noble animal with a head like a Roman, and a flowing golden beard like the tasseled housings of your last viceroys snorting charger" (*MD*, 246) is also reminiscent of the imagery surrounding the Phoebus-like Pierre, in his prelapsarian state, who is also associated with his fiery horses. Radney, on the other hand, is as "ugly as a mule" (246). This comparative element is even more pronounced in *Billy Budd*. The narrator makes a point of depicting Billy and Claggart as invidiously compared solar and lunar twins. The image of Siamese twins is, in fact, used to describe the relationship between envy and antipathy: "Now envy and antipathy, passions irreconcilable in reason, nevertheless in fact may spring conjoined like Chang and Eng in one birth" (*BB*, 77). They are "irreconcilable in reason" because envy is presumably based on the recognition of the good that the other possesses. The struggling brothers theme, the image of a Jacob and Esau struggling in the womb—"The children struggled together within her" (Gen. 25:22)—is explicit in the image of Chang and Eng. The "marked contrast between the persons of the twain" (*BB*, 77), as the narrator puts it, between Billy and Claggart, is remarked upon in the phallic terms of physical beauty: "That Claggart's figure was not amiss, and his face, save the chin, well moulded, has already been said. Of these favorable points he seemed not insensible, for he was not only neat but careful in his dress. But the form of Billy was heroic" (77). We will have more to say of Shakespeare's *Othello*, but it is worth noting here Iago's observation, duly mentioned by Hayford and Sealts (1962, 164), that Cassio "has a daily beauty in his life / That makes me ugly" (*Othello* 5.1.19–20).

In an early version of *Billy Budd* Melville made allusion to Spenser's allegorical depiction of Envy in *The Faerie Queene*:

> And next to him malicious Envy rode
> Upon a ravenous wolfe, and still did chaw
> Between his cankred teeth a venemous tode,
> Then all the poison ran about his jaw;
> But inwardly he chawéd his owne maw
> At neighbours wealth, that made him ever sad;
> For death it was, when any good he saw,
> And wept, that cause of weeping none he had,
> But when he heard of harme, he wexéd wondrous glad.
>   (1.4.30)[6]

The last line of the canto, along with the image of chawing "a venemous tode" and inwardly "his own maw," brings to mind the sinister and envy-ridden shamer Goneril in *The Confidence Man*: "[I]dly she chewed her blue clay, and you could mark that she chuckled" (61). In the next canto of Spenser's poem, Envy is "ypainted full of eyes" (1.4.31). The origin of the word *envy* is the Latin *invidia*, a derivation of *invidere* (to look askance), envy being associated in folklore with a certain *look*, specifically that malignant looking known as the evil eye, that restless looking that "invidiously" compares to the self everything that it happens to lights on. But the pronounced visual aspect that inheres in envy involves first of all the *sight* of that which provokes the look itself. Recalling Spenser's lines is Max Scheler's illustration of what constitutes a sufficient motive for revenge in someone riddled with envy and resentment: "A typical cause would be the continual deflation of one's ego by the constant sight of [a] neighbor's rich and beautiful farm" (1961, 65). It is his neighbor's wealth that makes Claggart sad, that strangely suffuses "his eyes with incipient feverish tears" and makes him "look like the man of sorrows" (*BB,* 88). It is, to be precise, the continual deflation of his ego by the constant sight of Billy's rich and beautiful *form*—to adapt Scheler's example—the alluring distillation of the freshness of innocence and a narcissistically balanced enjoyment of life, that awakens his deadly madness to action. We noted earlier the same sense in Ahab of being supplanted and excluded from a paradisal bliss and power, although the element of envy in Ahab's rivalry with Moby Dick remains in the background only: "No more. This lovely light, it lights not me; all loveliness is anguish to me, since I can ne'ere enjoy. Gifted with the high perception, I lack the low, enjoying power; damned, most subtly and most malignantly! damned in the midst of Paradise!" (*MD,* 167). It is this sight of "paradise" that awakens Claggart's look of envy: "If *askance he eyed* the good looks, cheery health, and frank enjoyment of young life in Billy Budd, it was because these went along with a nature that, as Claggart magnetically felt, had in its simplicity never willed malice or experienced the reactionary bite of that serpent" (*BB,* 78; emphasis added). Claggart, "in an aesthetic way," "saw the charm of it, the courageous free-and-easy temper of it, and fain would have shared it, but he despaired of it" (78). It is the despair of "shame and empty depression," "despair about the crushing of the self and of the ultimate defeat of its aspirations" (Kohut 1978, 757); it is the despair of Satan as he plots the downfall of the inhabitants of Eden: "Thus while he spake, each passion dimm'd his face, / Thrice chang'd with pale, ire, envy, and despair" (*Paradise Lost* 4.115). In the manuscript Melville cited these five words—"Pale ire, envy, and despair"—as a title to chapter 12 of *Billy Budd,* the 'envy' chapter. The look with which Claggart observes Billy is—the identification is explicit—the look of Satan gazing on Adam and Eve in the Garden, as his excruciating grief tears him apart:

> O Hell! what do mine eyes with grief behold,
> Into our room of bliss thus high advanc't
> Creatures of other mould, earth-born perhaps,
> Not Spirits, yet to heav'nly Spirits bright
> Little inferior; whom my thoughts pursue
> With wonder, and could love. . . .
>   (*Paradise Lost* 4.358–63)

As what Claggart most despairs of, is most ashamed of, is his own deprav-ity—a form of monstrous defectiveness—which he thus keeps concealed, hidden, shut up, what he is most disdainful of, even beyond Billy's con-spicuous beauty, is the innocence and frank enjoyment that the spontane-ous young sailor exudes just by being alive. The paradigm is, again, Milton's Satan:

> Sight hateful, sight tormenting! thus these two
> Imparadis't in one another's arms
> The happier Eden, shall enjoy thir fill
> Of bliss on bliss, while I to Hell am thrust,
> Where neither joy nor love, but fierce desire,
> Among our other torments not the least,
> Still unfulfill'd with pain of longing pines. . . .
>   (4.505–11)

The deadly nature of the envious feelings that Claggart harbors, charac-terized as they are by "the fanaticism of the need for revenge and the un-ending compulsion of having to square the account after an offense," is understandable only in terms of "an archaic perception of reality" (Kohut 1978, 643). In such a framework, according to Kohut, the offending person is seen not as an autonomous center of initiative "but as a *flaw in a narcis-sistically perceived reality*" (644). The person's mere independence or differ-ence is experienced almost as an attack on the self. The narcissistically in-jured "cannot rest until he has blotted out a vaguely experienced offender who dared to oppose him, to disagree with him, or to outshine him." The grandiose self—Kohut compares it to the evil stepmother in "Snow White"— can never escape its torment "because it can never wipe out the evidence that has contradicted its conviction that it is unique and perfect" (644). "Claggart's [envy]," the narrator insists, "was no vulgar form of the passion. . . . Claggart's envy struck deeper" (*BB*, 77). The deep-rooted and pathologi-cal nature of Claggart's resentful feelings are underscored by the contrast with Red Whiskers who, in his quarrel with Billy on the *Rights of Man*, is cured of his resentment and ends up becoming one of the young sailor's most ardent admirers. In its peculiar virulence, Claggart's brand of envy corresponds very clearly to Joseph Berke's description of the envious: "The envious person feels inferior, rather than empty. He can't stand to see others full of life and goodness, because he is preoccupied with his own limitations and defects. So he aims to debunk, debase, and defile what others have" (1987, 325). Envy is "aroused by the awareness of vitality and prosperity, indeed, by life itself. The envier aims to eliminate the torment in himself or herself by forceful, attacking, annihilatory behaviour" (323). In such personalities, in other words, we are dealing most assuredly with what Max Scheler is referring to when he observes that

> the most powerless envy is also the most terrible. Therefore existential envy, which is directed against the other person's very nature, is the strongest source of ressentiment. It is as if it whispers continually: "I can forgive everything, but not that you are—that you are what you are—that I am not what you are—indeed, that I am not you." This form of envy strips the opponent of his very existence, for this existence as such is felt to be a "pressure," a "reproach," and an unbearable humiliation. (1961, 53)

III

In *Moby-Dick*, "Benito Cereno," and *Billy Budd*, Melville evokes the question of the motiveless villain, an issue raised by Coleridge in his discussion of Shakespeare's Iago. *Othello* is a play that Melville returned to throughout his life. Though over thirty years separate their conception, both Babo in "Benito Cereno" and Claggart in *Billy Budd* must acknowledge Iago as their model. Melville's voracious assimilation of other authors is well known (a fact that, as we shall argue in another chapter, is perhaps connected to the incorporative nature of the idealizing pole in his personality). His absorption of *Othello* can be *heard*, for example, in a passage such as the following from chapter 87 ("The Grand Armada") in *Moby-Dick*. Ahab ponders the significance of the spectacle unfolding before his eyes, as, "glass under arm," he "to-and-fro" paces the deck; "in his forward turn" he beholds "the monsters he chased, and in the after one the bloodthirsty pirates chasing *him*" (383). This then gives birth to the bleakly ironic fancy that through the gate beyond which lay the route to his vengeance . . . he was now both chasing and being chased to his deadly end; and not only that, but a herd of remorseless wild pirates and inhuman atheistical devils were infernally cheering him on with their curses;— when all these *conceits* had passed through his *brain*, Ahab's *brow* was left gaunt and ribbed, like the black sand beach after some stormy tide has been gnawing it, without being able to drag the firm thing from its place. (383–84; emphasis added)

When Iago baits the trap of jealousy by hinting at Desdemona's infidelity, Othello tries to "drag" from him his hidden meaning:

> By heaven, he echoes me,
> As if there were some monster in his thought
> Too hideous to be shown.—Thou didst mean something.
> I heard thee say but now, thou lik'st not that,
> When Cassio left my wife. What didst not like?
> And when I told thee he was of my counsel
> In my whole course of wooing, thou criest 'Indeed?'
> *And didst contract and purse thy brow together,*
> *As if thou then hadst shut up in thy brain*
> *Some horrible conceit.* If thou dost love me,
> Show me thy thought.
> (Othello 3.3.105; emphasis added)

The image of the pursed and contracted brow and the idea of some "horrible conceit" being "shut up in [the] brain" that cannot be dragged, even with great effort, from its place, and the actual occurrence in both texts, in close proximity, of the words *conceit, brain,* and *brow* taken together points to the unmistakable presence of the *Othello* intertext in the passage from *Moby-Dick*.

Another instructive instance is an echoing of Othello's words in two passages in Melville. The words are the Moor's very last:

> And say besides, that in Aleppo once,
> Where a malignant and a turban'd Turk
> Beat a Venetian and traduc'd the state,

I took by the throat the circumcised dog,
And smote him thus.

                    (5.2.352–56)

"No turbaned Turk, no hired Venetian or Malay," the narrator of *Moby-Dick* comments, remarking on the reaping away of Ahab's leg, "could have smote him with more seeming malice" (184). The same passage appears to be echoed in "Benito Cereno": "He smote Babo's hand down, but his own heart smote him harder" (99). In both cases, the somewhat archaic *smote* indicates the presence of the intertext. In "Benito Cereno," indeed, the blow is directed against the betrayal or treachery of an Iago-like villain, and Ahab's blow is, similarly, in retaliation for the perceived treachery of a "beast" endowed, in the mind of its victim at any rate, with an "inscrutable malice." Delano's blow is also, metaphorically, self-directed ("his own heart smote him harder"), as it is, literally, in *Othello*.

Melville had, of course, a fondness for seventeenth-century diction, but the selection of this particular word, it seems to me, is determined by the theme of betrayal combined with that of mortification. We have shown to what extent Ahab, in his traumatic encounter with Moby Dick, is subjected to a *mortifying* experience of humiliating helplessness and powerlessness. The same may be said of Delano in his encounter with Babo; his heart is smitten or mortified by an insidious act of betrayal. Cereno, however, is smitten even harder by the same treachery. Shame and shame-anger, or humiliated fury, triggered by betrayal, can flood the self with overwhelming, often suicidal feelings of helplessness and depression, and in the end Cereno, the powerless witness of the terror and violence of the insurrection aboard the ship, can be said to die from a kind of literal mortification; he dies from the knowledge of the horrors he has seen. He is overcome— "shamed-to-death," feeling abandoned and alone in a world that can no longer be trusted—by an unhealable mortal wound to his free will.[7]

Melville's dialogue with Shakespeare included his commentators as well. He admired, for example, the writings of Charles Lamb, and the question of motive that is raised by Melville in essaying his portraits of Ahab, Babo, and Claggart involves, of course, not so much a reference to Shakespeare's play as to the critical discussion surrounding it. Coleridge explicitly addresses the question of the so-called motiveless villain in commenting on the way that Iago rationalizes to himself his own irrational hatred of the Moor: "The last speech, Iago's soliloquy, shows the motive-hunting of motiveless malignity—how awful!" (1969, 190); and this, he exclaims, "Shakespeare has attempted—executed—without disgust, without scandal!" Hazlitt's discussion of Iago as "one of the supererogations of Shakespeare's genius" makes the same point as Coleridge. He refers to critics who, "more nice than wise, have thought this whole character unnatural, because his villainy is without a sufficient motive" (1948, 211), and counters by arguing that Shakespeare "knew that the love of power, which is another name for the love of mischief, is natural to man. He would know this as well or better than if it had been demonstrated to him by a logical diagram, merely from seeing children paddle in the dirt or kill flies for sport" (211). Coleridge's point is the point made by the narrator in *Billy Budd* when he says to "invent something touching the more private career of Claggart, something involving Billy Budd . . . might avail in a way more or less interesting to account for whatever of enigma may appear to lurk in the case. But in fact there was nothing of the sort" (*BB*, 73–74). What cannot be doubted, however, is the psychological accuracy of such mysterious malignity.

With both Claggart and Iago, we are quite clearly dealing with a type of personality best described by Max Scheler in his remarkable little study of the psychology of *ressentiment*: "Ressentiment is a basic impulse only in crimes of spite. These are crimes which require only a minimum of action and risk and from which the criminal draws no advantage, since they are inspired by nothing but the desire to do harm" (1961, 65). This description reads almost like a gloss of Melville's own terms in *Billy Budd* in probing the mystery of evil in Claggart: "For what can more partake of the mysterious than an antipathy spontaneous and profound such as is evoked in certain exceptional mortals by the mere aspect of some other mortal, however harmless he may be, if not called forth by this very harmlessness itself?" (*BB*, 74). Indeed, it is Billy's essential harmlessness that brings out Claggart's spite, but the "basic impulse" here is, as Scheler suggests, *ressentiment* or chronic resentment. The same is true of Iago. More than the love of power or mischief for mischief's sake, it is his resentment at the grievous injustice of his position, at his displacement, his being overlooked and slighted—put in a reduced position—by Othello and supplanted, robbed of his place, by Cassio, that motivates his revenge: he feels cheated out of that which, in his mind, properly belongs to him, the recognition that is his due. Iago and Claggart both exemplify personalities who are "enraged about a world that has tried to take from them something they consider to be rightfully their own" (Kohut 1978, 831). Their pathological sense of *entitlement* explains Melville's association of such characters with the titanic theme explored above: paradise lost is the paradise that one's evictor or supplanter now blissfully occupies; it is he, as it were, who now basks and glows with pleasure in the light of the mother's radiant smile and gleaming eye. Iago, for example, is so obsessed by the idea that another has leaped into his seat and robbed him of his due, that, besides resenting Cassio for pushing him out of his office, he fantasizes—however little he actually believes it in the end—that Othello has pushed him out of that other "office" done "twixt the sheets" (*Othello* 1.3.386–87) and robbed him of the affection of his wife. Later, he even goes so far as to suggest that he has been cuckolded by Cassio as well: "For I fear Cassio with my night-cap too" (2.1.310). As Iago's scornful language emphasizes, to be a cuckold is to live in a compound state of shame: cheated out of that which one is entitled to, betrayed and abandoned by a loved one, and forced to live in the glare of ridicule and contempt.

A similar emotional compound—the conviction that one has been robbed, cheated, and betrayed, and now lives in ridicule and scorn—is an implicit aspect of Claggart's feelings as he gazes on Billy Budd, that "signal object" of "significant personal beauty." This compound is also, though the analogy may seem at first a bit forced, a fundamental aspect of Ahab's feelings towards Moby Dick. Indeed, at the end of the novel, when Ahab first sights his omnipotent rival as he swims into view before the final chase, an intriguing epic simile is used that reflects, it seems to me, the same emotional dynamic that we find in Iago and Claggart: the feeling of being cheated and left empty-handed, of being helplessly robbed, and of being an object of derision and contempt:

> A gentle joyousness—a mighty mildness of repose in swiftness, invested the gliding whale. Not the white bull Jupiter swimming away with ravished Europa clinging to his graceful horns; his lovely, leering eyes sideways intent upon the maid; with smooth bewitching fleetness, rippling straight for the nuptial bower in Crete; not Jove, not that great majesty Supreme! did surpass the glorified White Whale as he so divinely swam. (*MD*, 548)

This epiphanic moment, of "whale-as-supreme-and-lovely being" (1986, 62) as Lawrence Buell so aptly puts it, involves just such an envied sight as that which Scheler claims provokes the ressentiment-driven to coldly calculated and explosive action. The enthusiasm of the description and the joyousness of its subject are an indication that we are in the presence of an intensely idealized, omnipotent object. In Melville, the presence of such an object means that two responses are possible: admiration and the enthusiastic wish for merger, or the annihilative contempt and hatred born of envy and shame. There are, indeed, two points of view implied in the description: the narrator, who idealizes the object, and Ahab, whose delusional psychological state is, we would argue, subtly implied in the simile. This classical image— Melville would have read the story in Ovid and may have been familiar with Rubens's *Rape of Europa*—portrays an act of "dispossession," one that is quite comparable, if we adopt Brabantio's point of view, to the elopement of Othello and Desdemona at the beginning of Shakespeare's play: the abduction of King Agenor's daughter by Jupiter, who has assumed the shape of a bull. This image of the abducted woman in the arms of her ravisher, who flees while the dispossessed, robbed of the affection he feels is rightfully his own, looks on helplessly, would seem, most obviously perhaps, to point to a Freudian dynamic of rivalry for sexual possession of the mother. We would suggest, however, that what may seem to be an oedipal contest masks something more deep-seated, and that the compelling nature of the image bears ultimately on Kohut's portrayal of the archaic world inhabited by the narcissistically injured.

If we may be permitted for the purposes of illustration a brief digression, it is worth considering the following scene of "abduction" in Kafka, in which sexual rivalry and competition reveal themselves to be a manifestation of archaic feelings of shame. In *The Trial* Joseph K. and the law student, one of a series of rivals in the novel, have been struggling for possession of the usher's wife:

> "Ah, that's it," said the student, "no, no, you don't get her," and with a strength which one would not have believed him capable of he lifted her in one arm and, gazing up at her tenderly, ran, stooping a little beneath his burden, to the door. A certain fear of K. was unmistakable in this action, and yet he risked infuriating K. further by caressing and clasping the woman's arm with his free hand. K.

ran a few steps after him, ready to seize and if necessary to throttle him, when the woman said: "It's no use, the Examining Magistrate has sent for me; I daren't go with you; this little monster," she patted the student's face, "this little monster won't let me go." "And you don't want to be set free," cried K., laying his hand on the shoulder of the student, who snapped at him with his teeth. "No," cried the woman, pushing K. away with both hands, "No, no, you musn't do that, what are you thinking of? It would be the ruin of me. Let him alone, oh, please let him alone! He's only obeying the orders of the Examining Magistrate and carrying me to him." "Then let him go, and as for you, I never want to see you again," said K., furious with disappointment, and he gave the student a punch in the back that made him stumble for a moment, only to spring off more nimbly than ever out of relief that he had not fallen. K. slowly walked after them, he recognized that this was the first unequivocal defeat that he had received from these people. There was no reason, of course, for him to worry about that, he had received the defeat only because he had insisted on giving battle. While he stayed quietly at home and went about his ordinary vocations he remained superior to all these people and could kick any of them out of his path. (1984, 58–59)

In this passage a number of the themes we have isolated in Melville's work can be detected in their most archaic form: the rival is omnipotent (like the idealized, all-powerful Moby Dick that Ahab pits himself against, the student, an agent of the powerful Examining Magistrate, manifests "a strength one would not have believed him capable of"); K. perceives that, by being excluded and sexually taunted, he is being mocked and scorned (Moby Dick's "leering eyes [are] sideways intent upon the maid"; the student "risked infuriating K. further by" deliberately caressing the disputed objet of affection); K. evinces the contradictory feeling in sexual rivalry that one has been both betrayed by the disputed object ("you don't want to be set free") and robbed by another of a rightful possession; perceived rejection is accompanied by intense shame and shame-anger (K. is "furious with disappointment") and the immediate impulse to retaliate (K. is ready to seize and "throttle" his rival); K. then wards off these painful feelings of shame by relocating it through contempt: "he remained superior to all these people and could kick any of them out of his path." As in Melville, then, sexual rivalry is a manifestation of shame inasmuch as what is at stake here is not primarily an object of sexual love so much as one's self-image, one's self-estimation; rivalry over the object is not aimed at possession of the object but at reducing the negative feelings about oneself (maximizing positive and minimizing negative affect, to use Tomkins's terminology). If one succeeds in winning the object, one temporarily banishes painful feelings of shame through triumphing over another; if one is defeated in the competition, one is subject to "furious disappointment" and increased shame: "[H]e recognized that this was the first unequivocal defeat that he had received from these people. There was no reason, of course, for him to worry about that, he had received the defeat only because he had insisted on giving battle." As Wurmser comments about the use of women in *The Trial:* "More and more the women turn from being instruments of deliverance and lust into those of submission, degrading selfloss, and humiliation" (1995, 5).[8] It is, in a similar way, Ahab's rage at his own perceived submission and humiliation that are implied in the depiction of the white whale as the omnipotent Jupiter swimming off with the disputed Europa on his back.

IV

In "Benito Cereno" the detail of Babo's silence recalls Iago's last words in *Othello:* "Demand me nothing. What you know, you know: / From this time forth I never will speak a word" (5.2.303–4). Babo, like Iago, when his part has been played and his plot exposed, shuts up like a tomb, his secret buried: "Seeing all was over, he uttered no sound, and could not be forced to. His aspect seemed to say, since I cannot do deeds, I will not speak words" (*PT,* 116). The silence of such characters has deep roots, and is connected to an almost instinctive propensity to concealment. Claggart, we are told, was powerless "to annul the elemental evil in him, though readily enough he could hide it" (78). Explaining Claggart's readiness to believe that Billy is scornful of him, the narrator observes: "An uncommon prudence is habitual with the subtler depravity, for it has everything to hide," and this "secretiveness voluntarily cuts it off from enlightenment or disillusion" (80). Claggart is—the theme is insistent—"protectively secret"; he remains "a nut not to be cracked" (76), not even by the worldly narrator's sophisticated probing. When the officer of marines poses the question to Billy of why Claggart "should have so lied, so maliciously lied, since you declare there was no malice between you?" (107), Vere intervenes: "'But how can he rightly answer it?—or anybody else, unless indeed it be he who lies within there,' designating the compartment where lay the corpse. 'But the prone one there will not rise to our summons'" (107). This cryptic and almost tomblike secretiveness is a symptom of what Kierkegaard, in *The Concept of Dread*, calls the shut-up-ness of all true evil. It is incapable of revealing itself, of confessing—not out of guilt (guilt, to a very large extent, motivates and encourages confession), but out of the fear of unbearable shame. "The demoniacal does not shut itself up *with* something, but shuts *itself up*; and in this lies the mystery of existence, the fact that unfreedom makes a prisoner precisely of itself" (1973, 110).

Exposure, in the form of confession, may purge the guilty, but for those who hide because there is something about themselves that they feel they must rigorously keep concealed, it threatens to bring only heavier shame, behind which lurks the ultimate fear of being found out as a "monster." In probing the sources of Claggart's mysterious depravity, the narrator alludes perhaps to *Othello* and "the green-ey'd monster" (3.4.159–60) of jealousy "which doth mock / The meat it feeds on" (3.3.166–67)—"'Tis a monster / Begot upon itself, born on itself" (3.4.159–60)—when he points out that there is nothing as *shameful* as envy: "Is Envy then such a monster? Well, though many an arraigned mortal has in hopes of mitigated penalty pleaded guilty to horrible actions, did ever anybody seriously confess to envy? Something there is in it universally felt to be more shameful than even felonious crime" (*BB*, 77).[9] The narrator's insight here is quite consistent with the psychological view that of the "destructive forces" with which shame puts us in touch "envy is the most shameful experience and the one most defended against" (Berke 1987, 325). We shall have occasion to explore in more detail the special relationship that exists between envy and the experience of humiliation, but what immediately interests us here is the fact that Claggart's envy is an object of shame that must be hidden, buried deep. Shame, in its benign forms, is essentially a reconciliatory emotion that can foster communication and reinforce a sense of belonging. Embarrassment and blushing, for example, tend to evoke sympathy in others, while the one who feels momentarily estranged by shame is, by the same token, encouraged to reaffiliate with others. But traumatic shame, when it is not tempered by positive affects, is another matter: acute feelings of self-contempt and self-disgust, which are focused on a defective self, are naturally denied and avoided through an often complex and rigid defensive structure of hiding, burial, and masking. Thus the mysterious inaccessibility of such personalities. It is not surprising that the narrator admits defeat in trying to explain Claggart's madness, for the master-at-arms has most jealously hidden away as in a tomb his secret self and the malignant nature of his motivations, the shameful feelings of shame itself and self-contempt, along with their equally humiliating companions—envy, rage, and *ressentiment*.

This means that what needs to be hidden must be hidden from oneself perhaps first of all. If "secretiveness voluntarily cuts [the subtler depravity] off from enlightenment or disillusion" (*BB*, 80) that might come from the outside world, the most important factor is that such a personality necessarily spends a good deal of energy rationalizing and justifying—denying, that is—the irrational feelings and actions emanating from the deeply injured part of his personality. This is the point of what Coleridge calls the "motive-hunting of motiveless malignity," and it is what Melville means when he says that "Claggart's conscience being but lawyer to his will, made ogres of trifles," justifying his "animosity into a sort of retributive righteousness" (*BB*, 80). As Kohut describes this process, the ego and the rational and conscious parts of the narcissistically enraged become increasingly called on to justify "the persisting insistence on the limitlessness of the power of the grandiose self" (1978, 657). This means that the self is forced to attribute limitations to the uncooperativeness and malignancy of the selfobject, or to the corruption of the archaic world in which it lives. It is by such a process that "all evil" to Ahab becomes "visibly personified, and made practically assailable in Moby Dick" (*MD*, 184). What Kohut calls "chronic narcissistic rage" thus takes root, either "as grudge and spite, or, externalized and acted out in disconnected vengeful acts or in a cunningly plotted vendetta" (1978, 657).

We can see quite clearly how such rage is "acted out" in both Babo and Claggart, and again, of course, the prototype is Iago. Hazlitt speaks of Shakespeare's villain as a type who is willing to "[run] all risks for a trifling and doubtful advantage; and is himself the dupe and victim of his ruling passion—an insatiable craving after action of the most difficult and dangerous kind" (1948, 211). After he has been overpowered by his captor, Babo's "aspect seemed to say, since I cannot do deeds, I will not speak words" (*PT*,

116). The depiction of Claggart recalls Hazlitt's description on two counts: the great energy and activity of the character's ruling passion ("a nature like Claggart's surcharged with energy as such natures almost invariably are") and the compulsive and self-destructive nature of that passion, there being no recourse "left to it but to recoil upon itself and, like the scorpion for which the Creator alone is responsible, act out to the end the part allotted it" (78); like Iago, Claggart is "himself the dupe and victim of his ruling passion." The theatrical metaphor of acting out a part is of particular importance here. Hazlitt acutely recognizes that Iago "is an amateur of tragedy in real life" who "takes the bolder and more desperate course of getting up his plot at home, [casting] the principal parts among his nearest friends and connections, and [rehearsing] it in downright earnest, with steady nerves and unabated resolution" (1948, 212). In the same way, it is Babo's active and energetic "brain" that "had schemed and led the revolt, with the plot" (*PT,* 116). Both Babo and Claggart are, in one way or another, craftsmen of the stage. "This is thy work," Ludovic says to Iago at the end of the play, referring to the pile of bodies on Desdemona's bed, but the whole play is Iago's "work" in another sense—his dramatic work.[10]

This theatrical aspect of the machination deployed to ensnare the victim is very clear in "Benito Cereno," where an entire drama is staged aboard the ship for the audience and the gaze of one Delano. The "plot" of the drama is in ironic and gruesome contrast to what Delano takes it to be: evil is made to look like the good, treachery like trustworthiness. As Iago makes the innocent and true seem like the shameless and the unfaithful, so Babo makes the faithful and the trustworthy mask their opposites. They are both true confidence men, in Melville's sense. "To such degree may malign machinations and deceptions impose" (115), mournfully concludes the mortified Don Benito Cereno. "You half thought me plotting your murder," he observes to his newfound friend. Plot and plotting are the same thing in such a context, and Cereno's role is aptly described as the difficult playing of a "part."

Claggart, too, is a true Melvillian confidence man who tries to make innocence look like its opposite. In his attempt to play on Vere's confidence and trust, to fascinate him by the picture he paints of conspiracy, he describes Billy as a "man-trap beneath the daisies"—a perfect projection of Claggart himself. The image is used earlier in describing the Dansker's "expression of speculative query as to what might eventually befall a nature like [Billy Budd's], dropped into a world not without some man-traps" (70).

Like the "honest Iago," or the treacherous Titus Oakes, or Henri de Guise, to whom he is at one point compared, Claggart's irrational and deadly goals hide behind the mask of respectability, virtue, and trustworthiness. His so-called depravity "folds itself in the mantle of respectability. It has certain negative virtues serving as silent auxiliaries. It never allows wine to get within its guard. It is not going too far to say that it is without vices or small sins. There is a phenomenal pride in it that excludes them" (75–76).[11] The imagery of a protective cloaking accompanied by "phenomenal pride" and vanity points to deeply buried shame.

The image of the man-trap appears in *The Confidence-Man* when the cosmopolitan asks his boon companion for a loan and his friend responds by "pushing back his chair as from a suddenly-disclosed man-trap or crater" (179). The man-trap is a particularly apt image for this idea of the "confidence game," an idea that runs throughout Melville's work. The deceptive surface that masks beneath a sinister intent is one of the masks of shame that Wurmser speaks about. The most memorable mask in Melville's work is, of course, the one in Ahab's "Quarter-Deck" speech.

> All visible objects, man, are but as pasteboard masks. But in each event—in the living act, the undoubted deed—there, some unknown but still reasoning thing puts forth the moulding of its features from behind the unreasoning mask. If man will strike, strike through the mask! (*MD*, 164)

The image of the mask in this passage is intimately related to shame and the themes of hiding and exposure. From behind the mask of the visible world, some "inscrutable thing" haunts Ahab. This mask, which in Ahab's paranoid imagination has the amplitude of the entire cosmos, is a most powerful image of the kind of loss of trust and estrangement from the universe that a recurrent subjection to shame can cause. "With every recurrent violation of trust," as Lynd puts it, "we become again children unsure of ourselves in an alien world" (1958, 47). And as this passage suggests as well, the mask in Melville is intimately connected to the idea of a resentful and treacherous turning of the tables, to shamelessness and, as in *The Confidence-Man*, to an aggressive and resentful ridiculing and exposing of others.[12]

A mask must be worn first of all to protect oneself from possible shameful exposure, the kind of cruel or violent exposure, for example, that the misanthrope threatens the impostor with in *The Confidence-Man*: "The butterfly is the caterpillar in a gaudy cloak; stripped of which, there lies the impostor's long spindle of a body, pretty much worm-shaped as before" (124). On two occasions in Melville's satire someone suggests that the impostor should be unmasked and exposed. However, a powerful indication of the taboos associated with shame is the sensitivity to the potential *shamelessness*, whatever the overwhelming justification, of subjecting another human being to painful exposure. On the first occasion, a passenger asks: "But do you think it the fair thing to unmask an operator that way? . . . Supposing that at high 'change on the Paris Bourse, Asmodeus should lounge in, distributing hand-bills, revealing the true thoughts and designs of all the operators present—would that be the fair thing in Asmodeus?" (89). He then quotes—slightly misquotes—Horatio's "'Twere to consider too curiously, to consider so" (*Hamlet* 5.1.211–12), a response to Hamlet's rather grotesque musings in the graveyard. Such *curiosity* is presumably shameless: there are, it seems, limits to what one should want to know, and one of the functions of a proper or mature sense of shame is to inhibit such untoward interest or fascination. On the other occasion, a similar recommendation to expose the impostor is cooly challenged by the masquerader himself, newly disguised and incognito, of course. He brazenly casts shame on his interlocutor: "Shame upon you, Dare to expose that poor unfortunate. . . ." (137). It is, of course, the confidence man's own use of deception and disguise that is lacking in shame. The irony is superb. In order to avoid being exposed and shamed oneself, one shamelessly casts shame on others for their shamelessness.[13] For masking in Melville is not only a way of hiding, though it is most certainly that; it is also a way of retaliating.

In both Babo and Claggart, the mask and the almost reflexive instinct of concealment are the signs of deep-rooted feelings of humiliation and resentment, while the mask of confidence and trustworthiness is a part of the strategy of *turning the tables*, of turning the passive into active, of turning the passive fear of betrayal and abandonment into the active betrayal of others. "The stops and breaks," Hazlitt writes of Iago, "the deep workings of treachery under the mask of love and honesty, the anxious watchfulness, the cool earnestness, and if we may so say, the passion of hypocrisy, marked in every line, receive their last finishing in that inconceivable burst of pretended indignation at Othello's doubts of his sincerity" (1948, 133). Scheler's description of the type of personality most representative of those dominated by *ressentiment* is astonishingly close to both Hazlitt's depiction of the honest Iago and Melville's depiction of the proudly abstemious Claggart, whose depravity is masked by the appearance of virtue and respectability:

> The arsonist is the purest type in point, provided that he is not motivated by the pathological urge of watching fire (a rare case) or by the wish to collect insurance. Criminals of this type strangely resemble each other. Usually they are quiet, taciturn, shy, quite settled and hostile to all alcoholic or other excesses. Their criminal act is nearly always a sudden outburst of impulses or revenge or envy which have been repressed for years. A typical cause would be the continual deflation of one's ego by the constant sight of the neighbour's rich and beautiful farm. (1961, 65)

Or as Melville puts it: "These men are madmen, and of the most dangerous sort, for their lunacy is not continuous, but occasional, evoked by some special object; it is protectively secretive, which is as much as to say it is self-contained, so that when, moreover, most active it is to the average mind not distinguishable from sanity" (*BB*, 76). Melville settles on the same type as Scheler's arsonist when he uses the image of the incendiary Guy Fawkes as an analogy to the enraged and smoldering self shut up and buried in the hypocritical Claggart: "The Pharisee is the Guy Fawkes prowling in the hid chambers underlying some natures like Claggart's" (80).

Melville was particularly fond of the figure of Guy Fawkes, perhaps because it fuses the idea of calculated treachery with that of a hidden and deep rage-like explosiveness. A related image is used to describe the humiliated fury of Pierre, who feels betrayed by "the uttermost ideal of moral perfection" and overwhelmed by the mortification he has been made to suffer: "For the rest, let the gods look after their own combustibles. If they have put powder-casks in me—let them look to it! let them look to it!" (*P*, 273). The titanism of the imagery in this passage points, as it does elsewhere in Melville, to the presence of deep-seated feelings of shame and *ressentiment*. In "Benito Cereno," for example, the same image occurs, as the trusting Delano watches his approaching boat. As with the figure of the man-trap beneath the daisies, the Guy Fawkes image is perfectly apt for the treacherous Babo but is ironically misapplied to Cereno. Delano muses, nagged by the seemingly inexplicable ambiguities of Cereno's apparent capriciousness:

"But as a nation . . . these Spaniards are all an odd set; the very word Spaniard has a curious, conspirator, Guy-Fawkish twang to it" (79). Babo's head, "fixed on a pole in the Plaza," is described as "that hive of subtlety" (116)—an apt description, since that hive, buzzing and humming like the wound-up Ahab with the inexorable machinery of revenge, has managed to turn the ship into a "honeycomb" under the feet of the trusting and unsuspecting Delano. As Cereno says to his all too trusting friend:

> Do but think how you walked this deck, how you sat in this cabin, every inch of ground *mined into honey-combs* under you. Had I dropped the least hint, made the least advance towards an understanding between us, death, *explosive death*—yours as mine—would have ended the scene. (115; emphasis added)

The image of an explosive mine that has been excavated under one's feet recurs in association with Ahab and is a suitable one for a hidden self that, like Ahab's, plots a revenge that will be equal to its interminable rage.

Only a theory of archaic rage can account for the motive in such villains, like Claggart and Babo, who gain no apparent advantage by their actions but seem to act only out of pure malignity. As the victim of a humiliating enslavement and oppression, of course, Babo's actions are quite explicable. Indeed, his particular situation speaks quite explicitly to the conditions necessary for the genesis of *ressentiment*, a psychological turn of mind that, in Nietzsche's view, expresses a "slave mentality." As Scheler points out,

> [R]evenge tends to be transformed into *ressentiment* the more it is directed against lasting situations which are felt to be "injurious" but beyond one's control—in other words, the more the injury is experienced as a destiny. This will be most pronounced when a person or group feels that the very fact and quality of its *existence* is a matter which calls for revenge. (1961, 50)

As a slave, Babo is the recipient, in all its force, of the stinging humiliation inflicted by authority and, because he is enslaved, is unable to express his humiliated fury or shame-anger except through a complete overthrow—indeed, *annihilation*—of the situation in which he finds himself.

In his discussion of *Othello,* Hazlitt speaks of Shakespeare's "probing to the quick," and Melville uses the same words—one more sign of his uncanny ability to nourish his own work on other men's books—in the review of Hawthorne's *Mosses.* He speaks of Shakespeare's "short, quick probings at the very axis of reality." Hazlitt depicts Iago as

> a class of character, common to Shakespeare and at the same peculiar to him; whose heads are as acute and active as their hearts are hard and callous. Iago is to be sure an extreme instance of the kind; that is to say, of diseased intellectual activity, with the most perfect indifference to moral good or evil, or rather with a decided preference for the latter, because it falls more readily in with his favourite propensity, gives greater zest to his thoughts and scope to his actions. (1948, 211)

The most distinctive feature of Babo is, of course, his notable brain power: "As for the black—whose brain, not body, had schemed and led the revolt, with the plot—his slight frame, inadequate to that which it held, had at once yielded to the superior muscular strength of his captor, in the boat" (*PT,* 116). The prototype is, again, as Coleridge puts it, "Iago's passionless character, all *will* in intellect" (1969, 189). Claggart's pallid face has an "intellectual look" (*BB,* 77), his brow being "of the sort phrenologically associated with more than average intellect" (64). When he is struck by Billy it is the well-shaped, globular seat of that intellect that receives the full force of the blow: "Whether intentionally or but owing to the young athlete's superior height, the blow had taken effect full upon the forehead, so shapely and intellectual-looking a feature in the master-at-arms" (99). In a letter to Hawthorne (1? June 1851), commenting on "Ethan Brand," Melville protests that "It is a frightful poetical creed that the cultivation of the brain eats out the heart" (*Corr.,* 192). The problem, as Melville suggests, lies not in the head but the capacity to feel, which is precisely what is atrophied in the narcissistically enraged, who evince "an absolute certainty concerning the power of their selves and an absolute conviction concerning the validity of their ideals with an equally absolute lack of empathic understanding for large segments of feelings, needs, and rights of other human beings and for the values cherished by them" (Kohut 1978, 835). Melville, in the same letter, concludes: "To the dogs with the head! I had rather be a fool with a heart, than Jupiter Olympus with his head. The reason the mass of men fear god, and at bottom dislike Him, is because they rather distrust His heart, and fancy Him all brain like a watch" (*Corr.*, 192). This metaphor of the watch may be behind the image of Ahab's "lowly humming to himself," which produces "a sound so strangely muffled and inarticulate that it seemed the mechanical humming of the wheels of his vitality in him" (*MD*, 162).

Of Claggart we are told:

> Though the man's even temper and discreet bearing would seem to intimate a mind peculiarly subject to the law of reason, not the less in heart he would seem to riot in complete exemption from that law, having apparently little to do with reason further than to employ it as an ambidexter implement for effecting the irrational. That is to say: Toward the accomplishment of an aim which in wantonness of atrocity would seem to partake of the insane, he will direct a cool judgment sagacious and sound. (*BB*, 76)

Whatever the aims of Claggart's madness are, "the method and the outward proceeding are always perfectly rational" (76). Kohut observes that the reasoning power is often enhanced when it is subservient to the individual's narcissistic rage, and he connects this phenomenon to "the subordination of the rational class of technicians to a paranoid leader and the efficiency—and even brilliance—of their amoral cooperation in carrying out his purposes" (1978, 640). These observations provide us with a connection between Claggart's use of his reason as, in the narrator's words, "an ambidexter implement for effecting the irrational" and Ahab's dictatorial and charismatic power over the crew of the *Pequod*. As Ahab grimly commands his crew in the closing moments of the chase: "Ye are not other men, but my arms and my legs; and so obey me" (*MD*, 568); or as he describes them in his soliloquy in chapter 37 ("Sunset"), combining the idea of narcissistic control of the group with that of explosive rage and revenge: "Or, if you will, like so many ant-hills of powder, they all stand before me; and I their match. Oh, hard! that to fire others, the match itself must needs be wasting!" (168). Starbuck uses the same explosive imagery: "But he drilled deep down, and blasted all my reason out of me" (169). Both Ahab and Claggart carry out their paranoid purposes with "utter disregard for reasonable limitations and a boundless wish to redress an injury and to obtain revenge" (Kohut 1978,

639–40). They exemplify Coleridge's judicious observation concerning Iago of "how a wicked man employs his real feelings as well as assumes those most alien from his own, as instruments of his purpose" (1969, 187). This is exactly how Kohut describes those who suffer from deep narcissistic injury and who "understand others only insofar—but here with the keenest empathy!—as they can serve as tools towards their own narcissistic ends or insofar as they interfere with their own purposes" (1978, 834). Jackson's mysterious power over the crew, for example, is explained in just this way: "[I]t was quite plain, that he was by nature a marvelously clever, cunning man, though without education; and understood human nature to a kink, and well knew who he had to deal with" (R, 57).

However much they may differ in the degree of tragic self-knowledge, Ahab's type of madness clearly resembles Claggart's; with both, "the method and the outward proceeding are always perfectly rational" (BB, 76). The intellectual part becomes the instrument of an enraged grandiose self: "That certain sultanism of his brain, which had otherwise in a good degree remained unmanifested" becomes, in the context of the authoritarian structure of shipboard command, "incarnate in an irresistible dictatorship" (MD, 147). "All my means are sane, my motive and my object mad" (186), Ahab declares. His sultanic intelligence, like Claggart's, has remained intact—"not one jot of his great natural intellect had perished." However, "That before living agent, now became the living instrument. If such a furious trope may stand, his special lunacy stormed his general sanity, and carried it, and turned all its concentrated cannon upon its own mad mark" (185). The image of a rebellious and enraged storming of "his general sanity" is titanic in inspiration. The idea of a deeply wounded titanic self, defeated, humiliated, and buried, which we looked at in the Enceladus passage of Pierre, is central to the passages concerning Ahab's ultimate motives for revenge on Moby Dick. Ahab's ego, like Claggart's, is not his own. In Ahab, as in Claggart, the narcissistically injured part of the personality has come to exercise full control over his conscious mind: it manipulates the latter from "below," as it were, making it its pliable agent. The rational part of the self, thus controlled, now serves to justify the archaic self's delusional hatred, making the most innocent actions seem like unforgivable slights. As the narrator so aptly observes of Claggart, in the most legalistic manner, it makes "ogres of trifles."

In "The Chart," Ahab is depicted as bursting from his state-room whenever the "hell in himself yawned beneath him" (*MD*, 202), "as though escaping from a bed that was on fire" (202). The narrator concludes that

> the Ahab that had gone to his hammock, was not the agent that so caused him to burst from it in horror again. The latter was the eternal, living principle or soul in him and in sleep, being for the time dissociated from the characterizing mind, which at other times employed it for its outer vehicle or agent, it spontaneously sought escape from the scorching contiguity of the frantic thing, of which, for the time, it was no longer integral. But as the mind does not exist unless leagued with the soul, therefore it must have been that, in Ahab's case, yielding up all his thoughts and fancies to his one supreme purpose; that purpose, by its own sheer inveteracy of will, forced itself against gods and devils into a kind of self-assumed, independent being of its own. Nay, could grimly live and burn, while the common vitality to which it was conjoined, fled horror-stricken from the unbidden and unfathered birth. (202)

In the passage we looked at earlier, when Pierre's "titanic soul" takes ascendancy over his being, his reluctant body—his blood and his eyes—rebel, just as a crew might mutiny against its captain rushing headlong to destruction. Similarly, in Ahab a titanic struggle for control takes place between the "eternal, living principle or soul" and what Melville calls "the characterizing mind"—this "mind" corresponds, it seems, to the "titanic soul" in *Pierre*—an imposing, assertive independent power that makes of the ego an instrument of its will, employing it "for its outer vehicle or agent." This subterranean will is depicted as a mocked and defeated, but ever defiant and raging, titanic power. As the passage concludes: "God help thee, old man, thy thoughts have created a creature in thee; and he whose intense thinking thus makes him a Prometheus; a vulture feeds upon that heart for ever; that vulture the very creature he creates" (202).

The imagery of fire and combustion that runs throughout this part of the text is, as we have seen, based largely on Milton's treatment of Satan, which itself represents an important extension and deepening of the titanic tradition. This kind of imagery haunts Melville's work. In *Redburn*, for example, there is the grotesque and somewhat ludicrous example of the spontaneous combustion of a sailor, which appears in conjunction with the image of Prometheus and the theme of defiance: "The eyes were open and fixed; the mouth was curled like a scroll, and every lean feature firm as in life; while the whole face, now wound in curls of soft blue flame, wore an aspect of grim defiance, and eternal death. Prometheus, blasted by fire on the rock" (244). This kind of "furnace" imagery—which links the titanic thief of fire with he who dwells in "Adamantine Chains and penal Fire"— also suggests, as we have noted earlier, the *burning* that is a common denominator in the psychological trio of shame, ambition, and rage. The burning ambition of Ahab—his refusal to accept any power superior to himself—is a reaction to the searing shame of his defeat by Moby Dick, as is the deep inner rage that takes the form of his "one supreme purpose"; that "frantic thing," which feels "scorching" to his soul, having successfully taken over the ego and assumed an independent being, now "could grimly live and burn" (*MD*, 202). The enraged Pierre, burning with mortification from all the slights and outrages he has imagined or undergone, and obsessed with a dark and destructive ambition in writing his novel, strides defiantly into the storm, its pellets striking and melting against "his iron-framed fiery furnace of a body." We find the same fiery imagery in *Billy Budd*: Claggart's monomania—the offspring of shame, envy, and narcissistic rage—is described as a titanic "subterranean fire" that "was eating its way deeper and deeper in him" towards some "decisive" explosion (90).

In his search for the motive of Claggart's motiveless malignity, the narrator evokes a trackless labyrinth. In the words of his "honest scholar": "I think that to try and get into X——, enter his labyrinth and get out again, without a clue derived from some source other than what is known as 'knowledge of the world'—that was hardly possible, at least for me" (74). The idea of descending into a labyrinth of the self to find the controlling power or agency behind the individual's inexplicable behavior is also found, in much more expansive form, in the famous "captive king" passage in chapter 41 of *Moby-Dick*. The narrator is similarly unable to make sense of the character's madness, and in trying to explain the mystery of his motivation to the readers the same sort of imagery appears: "This is much; yet Ahab's larger, darker, deeper part remains unhinted" (*MD*, 185). The narrator then evokes the image of a Titan-like archaic self, entombed in a deep underground vault, lying frozen beneath the ruins of the ages.[14]

But vain to popularize profundities, and all truth is profound. Winding far down from within the very heart of this spiked Hotel de Cluny where we here stand—however grand and wonderful, now quit it;—and take your way, ye nobler, sadder souls, to those vast roman halls of Thermes; where far beneath the fantastic towers of man's upper earth, his root of grandeur, his whole awful essence sits in bearded state; an antique buried beneath antiquities, and throned on torsoes! So with a broken throne, the great gods mock that captive king; so like a Caryatid, he patient sits, upholding on his frozen brow the piled entablatures of ages. Wind ye down there, ye prouder, sadder souls! question that proud, sad king! A family likeness! aye, he did beget ye, ye young exiled royalties; and from your grim sire only will the old State-secret come. (185–86)

The passage closes with the image of a figure as shut-up and secretive as Claggart—as Vere lugubriously reminds his officers, "[T]he prone one there will not rise to our summons'" (*BB,* 107)—a figure from whose cryptic, tomblike silence no further word will come. The titanic theme is quite explicit here. This archetypal progenitor, man's "root of grandeur," this "antique buried beneath antiquities, and throned on torsoes," is portrayed as some great titanic king, who at the dawn of the ages was hurled down in ignominy and buried deep beneath the earth; frozen in shame, turned to stone, he has been left to nurse his grievance—that "old State-secret"—in an eternity of exile. It is, indeed, the same archetype of wounded pride in defeat—"ye prouder, sadder souls! question that proud, sad king!"—as the image in *Pierre* of the howling Enceladus covered with derision and buried ignominiously under "his undoffable incubus." Ahab is the legitimate scion of this humiliated race: as the "serene, exasperating sunlight" smiles on him in the shame and fury of his defeat, surrounded by the sinking limbs of his torn and scattered comrades, he too is mocked by the "great gods" who mock this "captive king."

When Ahab at last comes forth onto the deck, months after his encounter with Moby Dick, "even then, when he bore that firm, collected front, however pale, and issued his calm order once again; and his mates thanked God the direful madness was now gone; even then, Ahab, in his hidden self, raved on" (185). When he sets out on his final voyage, it is with the "mad secret of his unabated rage bolted and keyed in him" (186). Much later in the novel, in chapter 132 ("The Symphony"), Ahab, echoing Lear, doubts the very possession of himself, as though he were no longer his own agent:

> What is it, what nameless, inscrutable, unearthly thing is it; what cozening, hidden lord and master, and cruel, remorseless emperor commands me; that against all natural lovings and longings, I so keep pushing, and crowding, and jamming myself on all the time; recklessly making me ready to do what in my own proper, natural heart, I durst not so much as dare? Is Ahab Ahab? Is it I, God, or who, that lifts this arm? (545)

At the end of chapter 41 ("Moby-Dick"), the theme of a buried archaic self appears in the image of the molelike "subterranean miner" who dwells in the human psyche, and the narrator raises the question of how it was that the crew "so aboundingly responded to the old man's ire—by what evil magic their souls were possessed, that at times his hate seemed almost theirs" (187). "All this to explain," the narrator evasively concludes,

> would be to dive deeper than Ishmael can go. The subterranean miner that works in us all, how can one tell whither leads his shaft by the every shifting, muffled sound of his pick? Who does not feel the irresistible arm drag? What skiff in tow of a seventy-four can stand still? For one, I gave myself up to the abandonment of the time and the place; but while yet all a-rush to encounter the whale, could see naught in that brute but the deadliest ill. (187)

In certain forms of mass behavior, as Kohut understands it, the group is "predominantly amalgamated by the identity with the archaic grandiose self" (1990, 108). Indeed, in his view "the bulk of mass movements form themselves around shared archaic grandiosity." Mobilized in such group fantasies are, of course, the deep feelings of shame and resentment that motivate aggressivity, that "subterranean miner that works in us all" (*MD*, 187), as Ishmael puts it, whose "irresistible arm" drags. The almost irresistible prospect of abolishing shame, the mysterious motive of our collective motiveless malignity, is capable of moving us all from below. Because of the ubiquitousness of "shame propensity and readiness for rage," according to Kohut, "Individuals seek to melt into the body of a powerful nation (as symbolized by a grandiose leader) to cure their shame and provide them with a feeling of enormous strength, to which they react with relief and triumph. Old fantasies of omnipotence seem suddenly to have become reality" (1990, 110). Those who, like Starbuck, rather than proclaim this "invincible strength," dare to "question the omnipotence of the group and omniscience of its leader" risk being treated like traitors or enemies.

Ahab's ability to magnetize the crew would seem to be a textbook illustration of this phenomenon. With "greedy ears," Ishmael and the rest of the crew listen to the spellbinding oratory of their blasted captain, as he preaches revenge on an enemy irrationally demonized as evil incarnate:

> I, Ishmael, was one of that crew; my shouts had gone up with the rest; my oath had been welded with theirs; and stronger I shouted, and more did I hammer and clinch my oath, because of the dread in my soul. A wild, mystical, sympathetical feeling was in me; Ahab's quenchless feud seemed mine. With greedy ears I learned the history of that murderous monster against whom I and all the others had taken our oaths of violence and revenge. (*MD*, 179)

Ultimately, the motivating wish here is to *turn the tables*, to turn a passive experience of humiliation into an active experience of humiliating others, to turn, in other words, feelings of helplessness and powerlessness into action and power. The mechanism is one of the simplest and most effective means of defending against shame. It is also—in the way that it reproduces the conditions of humiliation that spawned such a reaction in the first place—one of the most destructive. It is to Melville's understanding of this phenomenon that we would now like to turn.

CHAPTER FIVE

Turning the Tables

I

On the first night of his arrival in New York, Pierre has an encounter with a cabdriver by whom he feels insulted and slighted. "To certain temperaments," the narrator explains, "especially when previously agitated by any deep feeling, there is perhaps nothing more exasperating, and which sooner explodes all self-command, than the coarse, jeering insolence of a porter, cabman, or hackdriver" (*P*, 232). Pierre's reaction to what he regards as the insolence of the driver—his rage, and the barely throttled desire to retaliate—is yet another sign of the importance of deep-seated shame as the affective bedrock of personality in Melville's novels. Pierre's reaction is reminiscent of Redburn's paranoia in response to the perceived insult of the gazers who surround him aboard the boat on the Hudson. Like Redburn, Pierre is acutely aware of his impoverished appearance, and his own sense of being in a reduced position makes him, as he projects these feelings of shame and self-contempt outwards, susceptible to find disdain or contempt in the attitudes of others. The idea that the cabman has shown contempt for him "now prompted the highly irritated Pierre to an act, which, in a more benignant hour, his better reason would have restrained him from" (232). Isabel is unable to stop him as, in "his sudden wrath," he rushes from the coach and becomes embroiled in a physical struggle with the driver. A police officer intervenes, and Pierre, for the moment, checks his impulse: "Now, I must not quarrel with this man, thought Pierre to himself, stung at the officer's tone" (235).

In this *checking of the impulse to retaliate* Pierre conforms to a pattern that, if it becomes habitual, may lead to the harboring of chronic resentment or *ressentiment*. The two essential ingredients of this psychological complex are intense rage at a perceived state of injustice and the inability to express one's feelings in actions or words. "Thirst for revenge," as Max Scheler points out, is "the most important source of *ressentiment*" (1961, 46).

Revenge is distinguished by two essential characteristics. First of all, the immediate reactive impulse, with the accompanying emotions of anger and rage, is temporarily or at least momentarily checked and restrained, and the response is consequently postponed to a later time and to a more suitable occasion ("just wait till next time"). This blockage is caused by the reflection that an immediate reaction would lead to defeat, and by a concomitant pronounced feeling of "inability" and "impotence." Thus even revenge as such, based as it is upon an experience of impotence, is always primarily a matter of those who are "weak" in some respect. (46–48)

Ressentiment, however, arises only when the thirst for revenge, or the feelings of rage and envy, "are particularly powerful and yet must be suppressed because they are coupled with the feeling that one is unable to act them out—either because of weakness, physical or mental, or because of fear" (48). In discussing the *attack other* strategy as a response to shame, Nathanson observes that "the decision to enter the realm of *attack other* scripts . . . depends at least partially on our assessment of the interpersonal relationship involved," and that there are situations in which "My ability to sense and test the reality of my existence declares the uselessness of protest and the essential need for submission" (1992, 365). We have already seen a perfect example of the latter situation in Stubb's decision to adopt a posture of submission after being humiliated by Ahab and muttering to himself, "I was never served so before without giving a hard blow for it" (*MD*, 128). The decision not to retaliate is thus explicitly underscored in Stubb's reaction, though his one-sided, jocular view of the world—Stubb's jolliness epitomizes the use of joking to deny reality—is an important tempering factor that allays the buildup of any poisonous feelings of resentment.

"Through its very origin," as Scheler observes, "ressentiment is chiefly confined to those who *serve* and are *dominated* at the moment, who fruitlessly resent the sting of authority" (1961, 48). He offers the example of "an ill-treated servant" who, if he "can vent his spleen in the antechamber," avoids "the inner venom of ressentiment." But, says Scheler, "it will engulf him if he must hide his feelings and keep his negative and hostile emotions to himself" (48). It is no accident that the official positions of all three—Radney, Jackson, and Claggart—make them the underlings and servants of a higher authority, the captain aboard the ship: Radney is a mate, Jackson is a common sailor, however dominant a member of the group, and Claggart is the "master-at-arms," a title that, the narrator makes a point of explaining, is "somewhat equivocal." Its original function having ceased, the master-at-arms has become "a sort of chief of police charged among other matters with the duty of preserving order on the populous lower gun decks" (*BB*, 64). Claggart's position in the hierarchy is not essentially different from Jackson's: he is a bully by any other name, just as Jackson is effectively a keeper of order on the lower decks. It is in this role that the latter is first introduced: "While we sat eating our beef and biscuit, two of the men got into a dispute, about who had been sea-faring the longest; when Jackson, who had mixed the *burgoo*, called upon them in a loud voice to cease their clamour, for he would decide the matter for them" (*R*, 56).

In a more recent study of shame and resentment, Suzanne R. Retzinger speaks of "a circular feeling trap between the desire for revenge (rage) and the inability (shame) to express the rage toward the actual source" (1987, 157). Her observations are especially relevant to an understanding of the inner rage of Melville's characters: "When rage occurs and is not resolved, a residue is left of rage. . . . When many incidents of rage occur without being resolved, layer upon layer may build until the person is in a continuous state of rage, or as we say, an angry mood" (158). This process is explicitly depicted in *Redburn* when the central character encounters the awful Jackson, a supreme example of someone trapped "in a continuous state of rage." Unable to "avoid Jackson's evil eye, nor escape his bitter enmity," Redburn adopts forbearance as his "best plan" (*R*, 62). Dominated at the moment, he decides to try his best "to get along peaceably with every body, and indeed endure a good deal before showing fight." Powerless, he must check the impulse to express his anger, and he prays, aware of the destructive psychological consequences, that hatred "might not master my heart completely, and so make a fiend of me, something like Jackson" (62). With the prospect of being interminably subjected to the hostility and contempt of others without any hope of escape, it is the ultimate effect of his growing resentment and rage—that he will begin to hate himself and turn his self-hatred outwards, like Jackson—that Redburn fears and tries to ward off.

After his altercation with the cabman, Pierre decides to visit Glen Stanly, who has inexplicably reneged on his promise to secure an apartment for his friend, making Pierre feel betrayed in a time of particularly desperate need and helplessness. The significance of this betrayal is underlined by the earlier mention of their childhood friendship as one already susceptible to slights and jealousy:

> Nor is this boy-love without the occasional fillips and spiciness, which at times, by an apparent abatement, enhance the permanent delights of those more advanced lovers who love beneath the cestus of Venus. Jealousies are felt. The sight of another lad too much consorting with the boy's beloved object, shall fill him with emotions akin to those of Othello's; a fancied slight, or lessening of the every-day indications of warm feelings, shall prompt him to bitter upbraidings and reproaches; or shall plunge him into evil moods, for which grim solitude only is congenial. (*P*, 216–17)

When Pierre confronts his old friend, he refuses to recognize Pierre and has him unceremoniously thrown out of his house. A repetition of his mother's ostracism, this contemptuous and scornful disowning—indeed, a refusal literally to recognize him—drives Pierre into a state of humiliated fury. He feels powerless to vent the rage, checks himself, and is forced to withdraw from the scene: "Bolting his rage in him, as impossible to be sated by any conduct, in such a place, Pierre now turned, sprang down the stairs, and fled the house" (239). When he returns to find Isabel and Delly he discovers that they have been discourteously "abandoned to their own protection." He again throttles his anger: "It was no time for Pierre to manifest his indignation at the officer—even if he could now find him—who had thus falsified his individual pledge concerning the precious charge committed to him" (241). Finally, in the cab again, Pierre is, or imagines he is, insulted for a second time by the driver who, "maliciously diverted by what had happened thus far—made some ambiguous and rudely merry rejoinder" (242). Again, checking his rage, "warned by his previous rash quarrel with the stage-driver," the forbearing Pierre "passed this unnoticed, and in a controlled, calm, decided manner repeated his directions" (242).

We have here the perfect recipe for *ressentiment*, a chronic state of negative affect—of shame, rage, or envy—induced by a series of mortifications and humiliations in the face of which one feels helpless and powerless to act. As one critic quite accurately and concisely depicts this process in Melville's heroes: "Repeated disappointments and humiliations breed a smoldering anger of a more personal sort until at last pity gives way to a monomaniac fury which sees nothing but the hated object" (Bowen 1960, 138). Ahab's desire for revenge has the same origin in *ressentiment*, for even if he seems to be taking vengeance on a specific object in retaliation for a particular attack, it is evident that the object, as is so clearly the case with Jackson and the paranoid Claggart, has become the vehicle of an unspecific emotional discharge: "He piled upon the whale's white hump the sum of all the general rage and hate felt by his whole race from Adam down; and then, as if his chest had been a mortar, he burst his hot heart's shell upon it" (*MD*, 184).[1] It is the same "general rage and hate" that Pierre piles on his old friend Glen Stanly. In one situation after another, Pierre feels insulted, slighted, ridiculed, scorned, and treated with contempt. More follows in the form of betrayals by friends and society, and when the letters of professional and personal rejection and denunciation arrive at the end of the novel, we get an explosion of violence that brings to mind modern-day treatments of the same theme of suppressed narcissistic rage and its orgiastic annihilatory release, such as Martin Scorsese's *Taxi-Driver*, a classic study of shame, rage, and *ressentiment*. Pierre, overwhelmed, retaliates and attacks his "shamer," shooting him down in the street in broad daylight.[2]

The relentless humiliation of Pierre, not just in this chapter but throughout the novel, threatens at times to adhere a little too faithfully to the comic principle of unincremental repetition. The bathos that keeps leaking into the novel—an often cited shortcoming of *Pierre*—may reflect a certain indulgence of the protagonist on the author's part. At the same time, as we have seen, it is impossible for the reader not to recognize that there is a significant component of externalization and masochism in Pierre's behavior. The nature of Pierre's deeply injured emotional state brings to mind Scheler's observations concerning the vindictive personality:

> The vindictive person is instinctively and without a conscious act of volition drawn towards events which may give rise to vengefulness, or he tends to see injurious intentions in all kinds of perfectly innocent actions and remarks of others. Great touchiness is indeed frequently a symptom of a vengeful character. The vindictive person is always in search of objects, and in fact he attacks—in the belief that he is simply wreaking vengeance. This vengeance restores his damaged feeling of personal value, his injured "honor,"

or it brings "satisfaction" for the wrongs he has endured. When it is repressed, vindictiveness leads to *ressentiment*, a process which is intensified when the *imagination* of vengeance, too, is repressed—and finally the very emotion of revenge itself. (Scheler 1961, 49)

Like the heroes in Stendhal's novels, such as Julien Sorel and Fabrice del Dongo,[3] many of Melville's characters show a pronounced susceptibility to narcissistic injury and therefore to perceived "slights," imagined or otherwise (though all slights or narcissistic injuries to the self are, if not imagined, at least imaginary, in Lacan's sense, in that they bring into play the vicarious experience of the other's awareness of oneself). In such a paranoid, "generalized state of shame," as Wurmser describes it, the world may seem rejecting and slighting (1981, 207–8). This paranoid state is a defense against internalized feelings of shame and takes the form of denial: one feels ashamed of oneself and, in order to avoid self-criticism, projects the feeling that one is being made to feel shame onto the other. In his rather cryptic manner, Lacan describes this projection, in its pathological form, in terms of

> the two moments when the subject denies himself and when he charges the other, become confused, and one discovers in him that paranoiac structure of the ego that finds its analogue in the fundamental negations described by Freud as the three delusions of jealousy, erotomania, and interpretation. It is the especial delusion of the misanthropic "belle ame," throwing back on to the world the disorder of which his being is composed. (1977, 20)

This mechanism of relocation, a way of protecting oneself against painful feelings of shame, is a structure fundamental to chronic resentment. In Claggart, for example, at least two of these delusional elements are present—namely, jealousy (or envy) and paranoid interpretation—and all, if we include a sort of inverted erotomania.

The "tendency to perceive impersonal and accidental occurrences as personal slights" (1990, 106) is, according to Kohut, characteristic of "certain narcissistic types." In *Billy Budd*, for example, there is no intended slight to Claggart, and the injury in question is clearly imagined. Claggart's susceptibility is clearly evident in the fact that he chooses to take Billy's inadvertent spilling of soup across his path as an affront. He also shows himself too ready to believe that Billy is mocking him behind his back, a scurrilous fiction that the accommodating Squeak obligingly foments by "perverting to his chief certain innocent frolics of the good-natured foretopman, besides inventing for his mouth sundry contumelious epithets he claimed to have over heard him let fall" (*BB*, 79). Contumelious—contemptuous, that is—epithets: Claggart's disavowal of his own shame and self-contempt through his contempt for Billy now returns to its source in the specular form of a paranoid belief that Billy is contemptuous of him. In "The Town-Ho's Story" Radney's similar feeling of being slighted by Steelkilt reveals the same delusionary elements, more or less, except that it involves actual insult and not a complete fiction. The period of almost forty years that separate the composition of these two stories is testimony to the extraordinary insistence of Melville's concern with this theme.

In all the important scenes of aggressive confrontation in Melville's work, the role of the imagined slight is pivotal. It is, as noted earlier, Ahab's proneness to detect slights—which is, of course, of paranoid proportions—that Starbuck brings into focus when he protests to the captain that "Vengeance on a dumb brute . . . that simply smote thee from blindest instinct [is] Madness! To be enraged with a dumb thing, Captain Ahab, seems blasphemous" (*MD*, 163–64). It is characteristic of the resentful personality that this sense of the injury done them is, ultimately, unspecific; it is not simply the loss of his leg that Ahab resents, for the latter simply serves to focus a more global feeling. It is "as if all the world was one person, and had done him some dreadful harm, that was rankling and festering in his heart" (*R*, 61). This is Redburn's description of Jackson. But it is almost a paraphrase of Lewis's description of the paranoid image projected by personalities suffering from shame-induced depression: "This image of the 'whole world against me' is a paranoid image. It is, however, a vague or global, unspecific paranoid image, in which the proportions of the 'other' are swollen by the self-directed hostility" (1971, 209).

What constitutes a perceived slight in such a context is, of course, anything that makes the subject feel ashamed or humiliated. For Claggart, the mere existence of a figure such as Billy Budd represents, in itself, a shame-provoking situation, inasmuch as it tends to produce, by comparison, shame and envy. Such comparison is, in Wurmser's words, a "demonic force," leaving "the person perpetually defeated, constantly a humiliated loser and feeling the sting of envy and jealousy" (1981, 174). We find the same "existential envy," as Scheler calls it, in the emotional disturbance that Redburn and Steelkilt produce in Jackson and Radney, respectively. Jackson's animosity towards Redburn is, in fact, a response to what is commonly known as "smugness." The personality of Redburn is that of someone whose main defense against shame is avoidance through a narcissistic overvaluation of himself, reflected, for example, in his exhibitionistic need to be mirrored by his environment. As he naively—and quite smugly—explains Jackson's dislike of him: "For I was young and handsome, at least my mother so thought me" (*R*, 58). What Jackson resents, of course, is not so much Redburn's physical beauty as, it would seem, this very self-satisfied attitude and pose, which he interprets, erroneously, as a personal attack. Nathanson speaks of

> the humiliated fury of the onlooker at *what is perceived* to be an unjustified assertion of superiority, fury that is always inherent in smugness. . . . the smug person evokes humiliated fury by ignoring all attempts by the other to form a[n interpersonal] bridge and allow even marginal feelings of attachment. Shame at this initial helplessness to have an effect on another person is amplified by the dawning awareness of one's failure to be recognized as a fellow human. (1987a, 202)

Individuals who are themselves severely shame-prone or narcissistically injured are thus particularly susceptible to feelings of anger when they are in the presence of such persons.

There is, of course, no evidence whatsoever that Billy Budd is smug—indeed, the opposite is true: he is the epitome of modesty, frankness, and good nature. However, his air of moral and physical perfection has the same effect on Claggart. If we keep in mind that what is at stake here is Claggart's *perception*, Lewis's description still applies: suffering from a form of delusional paranoia, he acts very much like someone faced with another's "unjustified assertion of superiority." The master-at-arms at first shows signs of intense interest in the new recruit; we are told, indeed, that Claggart would have loved Billy "but for fate and ban" (*BB*, 88). But Claggart is someone who in reaction to the anticipated pain of rebuff has long ago strangled potential feelings of love and longings for intimacy; envy and hate have taken their place. For such a personality, as we have noted, something as innocuous as the other person's independence or difference is enough to constitute an offense (Kohut 1978, 644). The following description by J. A. Arlow, cited by Nathanson, of the reaction of certain patients to the smug person is particularly instructive; its relevance to Claggart's response to Billy should be obvious.

> The smug person is independent. He seems in need of no one. This element arouses envious fascination. But beyond that, the smug person acts as if he were oblivious of his surroundings, even unaware of the people in the immediate vicinity, or aware of them only in a general, undistinguishing way. It is this aspect of the smug person which is most intolerable and infuriating to such patients. Their sense of self-esteem is offended; the blow to their narcissism is compounded with a sense of futile and injured rage. The mere presence of a smug person, they complain, is something they cannot endure. (1987a, 202)

As Nathanson points out, "Arlow derives these attitudes from an ideal prototype of 'the well fed nursling falling asleep at its mother's breast'" and sees smugness as representing "oral satiety with incorporation of the good object" (201–2). Images of oral satiety and of the sleeping child are, interestingly enough, an important part of the complex imagery that surrounds Billy Budd as the very incarnation of narcissistic independence and self-containment.

In "The Town-Ho's Story" something of the same kind of paranoid reaction can be seen in Radney's attitude to Steelkilt, except that the resentment at being outshone by his more handsome and prepossessing rival is brought into focus by an explicit injury or slight. In the most pointed manner, Steelkilt, knowing Radney is in earshot, draws attention to both the internal and the external "defectiveness" of his superior. Here the susceptibility to narcissistic injury can be linked explicitly to the shame felt by Radney for painful personal defects. Steelkilt's insults are, indeed, intensely embarrassing observations about what Radney would most like to *hide from view*, the most vulnerable aspects of his personality: his feelings of shame about perceived physical imperfections (his ugliness) and the contemptible (i.e., anal, dirty) greediness reflected in his inappropriate obsession with his property—his worry that the boat is being injured (greed itself being a defense against deep-seated feelings of shame and envy).

In Claggart the link between greed and chronic envy is suggested metaphorically and through certain images. His antipathy towards Billy, for example, feeds with "the greediness of hate for pabulum" (79-80) on the news from Squeak of Billy's contemptuous insults. Joan Riviere describes the feeling of envy in the following way:

> When a person, whose sense of security is largely based on his greed—on the feeling that he has, or can get, as much as he needs of good things—sees that someone else has more than he, it upsets this self-protective edifice of security; he feels reduced to poverty, as if he had little—"too little good"—in him. Not only has his unconscious protective defence vanished, but he feels in phantasy as if the others who have more must have actually *robbed* him of what had made him feel secure, which now is gone. That is why the feeling of envy is so exceedingly poignant and bitter to those who experience it. They feel they are being forced to submit to robbery and persecution. (1964, 27–28)

We have already touched on this sense of being robbed and persecuted in relation to shame and envy in Ahab and Claggart, who both exemplify delusional hate, the prototype for which, as we have seen, is Shakespeare's Iago. This is the logic, ultimately, of Iago's scandalous motive hunting. As Riviere observes: "It is easy to see that this unconscious belief or suspicion— that others who possess more than oneself have acquired it through robbing oneself—though so illogical, is amazingly soothing" (28). Greed too is related to shame—shame at one's ugliness, or badness, or defectiveness. It is rooted in the desire for the proof of one's goodness as a way of reducing shame:

> The longing or greed for good things can relate to any and every imaginable kind of good—material possessions, bodily or mental gifts, advantages and privileges; but, beside the actual gratification they may bring, in the depths of our minds they all ultimately signify one thing. They stand as proofs to us, if we get them, that we

are ourselves good, and full of good, and so are worthy of love, or respect and honour, in return. Thus they serve as proofs and insurances against our fears of the emptiness inside ourselves, or of our evil impulses which make us feel bad and full of badness to ourselves and others. (27)

Greed is, in other words, a way of compensating for shame and feelings of defectiveness and unlovability. To overcome shame we need the proof that we are worthy of recognition and love.

It is precisely this vulnerable aspect of Radney's personality that Steelkilt deliberately strikes at to antagonize his rival. Affecting "not to notice" Radney but going on with "his gay bantering," he cuttingly observes:

> I tell ye what, men, old Rad's investment must go for it! he had best cut away his part of the hull and tow it home. The fact is, boys, that sword-fish only began the job; he's come back again with a gang of ship-carpenters, saw-fish, and file-fish, and what not; and the whole posse of 'em are now hard at work cutting and slashing at the bottom; making improvements, I suppose. If old Rad were here now, I'd tell him to jump overboard and scatter 'em. They're playing the devil with his estate, I can tell him. But he's a simple old soul,— Rad, and a beauty too. (*MD,* 246)

Radney feels that his subordinate has as good as robbed him of what rightfully belongs to him, of what he is entitled to—the love and admiration of others—and is now deliberating "rubbing it in," cruelly drawing attention to the fact that Radney is devoid precisely of what Steelkilt, *by comparison,* has in plenty. "Shame," as Morrison writes, "is a reflection of feelings about the whole self in failure, as inferior in competition or in comparison with others, as inadequate and defective" (1989, 12). Steelkilt's insults are deliberately shaming ones, focusing on those "comparative elements . . . which, when acknowledged, threaten the envier with a massive loss of self-esteem" (Berke 1987, 325). The source of envy is the "hatred aroused by people's perceived or imagined sense of inferiority in relation to each other" (325), and Steelkilt's insult about Radney's ugly looks explicitly focuses on his comparison with others, at the same time as it emphasizes the injured narcissism and deep feelings of envy awakened in Radney by such a comparison.

"Boys, they say the rest of his property is invested in looking-glasses. I wonder if he'd give a poor devil like me the model of his nose" (*MD*, 246).

The reference to Radney's nose and the emphasis placed on his ugliness ("ugly as a mule," as the narrator describes him) touches, of course, on one of the potentially most highly charged sources of shame. Kohut points out that organ defectiveness or inferiority can be the cause of particularly painful feelings of shame and rage, to the point that the person feeling shame is convinced that the defective part is being stared at and scrutinized by "gloating onlookers" (1978, 632); essentially the same mechanism explains "the paranoid's delusion of being watched" (632). The self-conscious feeling that one is being stared at turns up quite extensively in the early part of *Redburn* and elsewhere, and an acute sensitivity to onlookers is apparent in Ahab's reactions on a number of occasions. The description of Ahab's attempt to board the *Samuel Enderby* is, as we have seen, an excellent example of a manifestation of the shame incurred from the feeling that one is being subjected to glaring visual exposure. In Radney's reaction to Steelkilt there is, however, the very specific perception that the other is *gloating*, and this perception—that the other is staring (*glotzen*, "to stare") and scornfully rubbing it in (*glotta*, "to smile scornfully")[4]—is an important element in Ahab's feeling of having been defeated in competition by Moby Dick. The idea that the other is gloating seems to be implied in the *Rape of Europa* passage that we examined in the last chapter. This projection of a supposedly gloating onlooker is, of course, an essential component of Claggart's delusional hatred of Billy Budd, whom he imagines regards him with a sort of self-satisfied derision and contempt.

The individual who feels that shame is always threatening him from outside, when in fact it is actually being projected from within, may resort in defense to "the active (often anticipatory) inflicting on others of those narcissistic injuries which he is most afraid of suffering himself" (Kohut 1978, 638). The victim of shame visits on others the humiliation that he fears will be visited on him. Claggart, Jackson, and Radney—even though in the latter case the injurious insults in question are actual—all show the same propensity to anticipate and reverse the injury they fear in a potentially shame-provoking situation, a situation that may exist, as we have seen, merely by virtue of the presence of a rival who outshines them. In order to ward off painful feelings of shame, the victim of shame learns to become the shamer. Jackson is the most dramatic example in Melville's work of someone who, to spare himself unbearable shame, turns the tables on his shamer; he avoids his feelings of self-contempt and self-disgust, his feeling of being exposed as hideous, and his anguish at being a monstrous object of contempt and disgust for others by preemptively going on the attack and shaming them, "going about corrupting and searing every heart that beat near him" (*R*, 104). He treats them, that is, with the shame and contempt he has been made to feel for himself, making them suffer the searing mortification that has struck so deep into his own soul.

This mechanism of turning the tables has been well described by Lewis. According to her, humiliated fury "often has just this quality of being throttled in shame, and then appearing at other, unpredictable times, pushing to turn the tables on the humiliating person. . . . Rageful longings create strong tendencies toward retaliation against the person who has evoked them. These retaliatory impulses are expressed in fantasies of humiliating the other, in revenge" (1987c, 34–35). The work of Kafka, once again, illustrates in the most paradigmatic fashion the primal impulse that is awakened here. Let us return for a moment to the episode examined earlier, the struggle between K. and the law student over the usher's wife. Just before the encounter, K. imagines taking revenge on the Examining Magistrate who is preparing the case against him:

> And probably there could be no more fitting revenge on the Examining Magistrate and his henchmen than to wrest this woman from them and take her himself. Then some night the Examining Magistrate, after long and arduous labor on his lying reports about K., might come to the woman's bed and find it empty. Empty because she had gone off with K., because the woman now standing in the window, that supple, voluptuous warm body under the coarse heavy dark dress, belonged to K. and to K. alone. (1984, 56)

We can see again here how the disputed sexual object is ultimately only a vehicle for avoiding shame by turning the tables and triumphing over the other. "The joy in vengeance," as Nathanson accounts for it, "is this sudden reduction in chronic shame by acute reduction in the self-esteem of the person viewed as superior, following an intentionally contemptuous attack on that other" (1987a, 192). Thus here in his fantasy K. already imagines using the woman, in the form of a prized possession or trophy, to humiliate a rival; and the law student who then appears will use her in the same way to humiliate K. After the student has disappeared with his "prize," K., "furious with disappointment" (that is, in the throes of humiliated fury) first avoids the shame by asserting his "superiority" and then invents the following retaliatory fantasy involving his girlfriend Elsa:

> While he stayed quietly at home and went about his ordinary vocations he remained superior to all these people and could kick any of them out of his path. And he pictured to himself the highly comic situation which would arise if, for instance, this wretched student, this puffed-up whippersnapper, this bandy-legged beaver, had to kneel by Elsa's bed some day wringing his hands and begging for favors. This picture pleased K. so much that he decided, if ever the opportunity came, to take the student along to visit Elsa. (Kafka 1984, 58–59)

The throttled fury behind this psychological mechanism is depicted for us in its most virulent and primitive form when K. subsequently meets the usher himself, who is the cuckolded husband of the disputed woman. In their conversation the usher casually offers his own retaliatory fantasy, which is, for all its offhandedness, completely murderous in its desire for revenge: "If my job were not at stake, I would have squashed that student flat against the wall here long ago. Just beside this card. It's a daily dream of mine. I see him squashed flat here, just a little above the floor, his arms wide, his fingers spread, his bandy legs writing in a circle, and splashes of blood all round. But so far it's only been a dream" (76). *If my job were not at stake*, as the usher says: if I were able, in other words, to express and act out my rage; if I were not helpless and powerless. One of the essential ingredients of *ressentiment*—the feeling of powerlessness that prevents one from venting one's shame and rage, either in action or in words—is contained in these apparently banal and innocuous words.

Narcissistic rage, as we see here, must be distinguished from justifiable anger, in that it shows an "utter disregard for reasonable limitations and a boundless wish to redress an injury and to obtain revenge" (Kohut 1978, 639–40). As the narrator in *Billy Budd* observes, "[T]he retaliation is apt to be in monstrous disproportion to the supposed offense; for when in anybody was revenge in its actions aught else but an inordinate usurer?" (80) In every case depicted by Melville—Ahab's revenge on Moby Dick, Radney's humiliation of Steelkilt, Jackson's mortification of the crew, and Claggart's treachery to Billy—the disproportionate reaction to the *perceived* slight or injury reveals that when the only pleasure experienced by the individual is a result of "reducing his humiliation, expressing it or humiliating others, the individual is then caught up in the most deadly of human aims" (Tomkins 1963, 296).

II

The shame-proneness and irascibility so characteristic of such personalities is not, it should be noted, completely absent from the character of Billy Budd, where it takes on a subtle modulation. The narrator hints at the latter's sleeping explosiveness when he compares Claggart and Billy as contrasting twins: "[I]f his face was without the intellectual look of the pallid Claggart's, not the less was it lit, like his, from within, though from a different source. The bonfire in his heart made luminous the rose-tan in his cheek" (*BB*, 77). This fire refers to the energetic and passionate nature of Billy, which expresses itself frankly and spontaneously in all his actions. In the same vein, the narrator refers to Billy's "being of warm blood" (81). Billy is known, when provoked, to be prone to sudden and unrestrained outbursts of physical violence: the swift and fatal blow to Claggart's head— "The next instant, quick as the flame from a discharged cannon at night, his right arm shot out" (99)—is foreshadowed, of course, by the beating summarily administered to the bullying Red Whiskers for an *insulting* dig in the ribs:

> So, in the second dogwatch one day, the Red Whiskers in presence of the others, under pretense of showing Billy just whence a sirloin steak was cut—for the fellow was a butcher—insultingly gave him a dig under the ribs. Quick as lightning Billy let fly his arm. I dare say he never meant to do quite as much as he did, but anyhow he gave the burly fool a terrible drubbing. It took about half a minute, I should think. (47)

In both these episodes, Billy's reflexlike reactions are consistent with the idea of someone who expresses himself in the most natural and unselfconscious fashion. His aggressiveness calls to mind "the fight component of the fight-flight reaction with which biological organisms respond to attack" (Kohut 1978, 636). Pierre's interpretation of *Hamlet* and its application to his own case comes to mind: the idea "that all meditation is worthless, unless it prompt to action," "that in the earliest instant of conviction, the roused man must strike, and, if possible, with the precision and the force of the lightning-bolt" (*P*, 169). In other words, Billy's violence is, in contrast with the hidden and festering, throttled retaliatory impulses of those burdened with resentment and envy, an explicit instance of directly and punctually expressed anger, of an immediate impulse to react that is *not checked* but followed through. "I'd strike the sun if it insulted me" (*MD*, 164), as Ahab boasts.[5]

It is worth contrasting Billy's response to insult to Claggart's automatic decision *to check himself* when Billy spills the soup across his path, as though in the master-at-arms the learned postponing of revenge had become instinctive: "*Pausing, he was about to ejaculate something hasty at the sailor, but checked himself,* and pointing down to the streaming soup, playfully tapped him from behind with his rattan, saying in a low musical voice peculiar to him at times 'Handsomely done, my lad! And handsome is as handsome did it too!'" (*BB*, 72; emphasis added). Claggart stifles the direct expression of his anger; it then surfaces in the equivocal form of a disdainful sarcastic comment, in which "he there let escape an ironic inkling . . . as to what it was that had first moved him against Billy, namely, his significant personal beauty" (77). As we noted in our introduction, the sexual connotations of this suppressed "ejaculation" are undeniable, but it is equally important to underline that it is the sudden discharge of anger, not sperm, that is throttled here; and that this anger or rage, associated with the conflicting feelings of shame, envy, and sexual jealousy, then expresses itself in Claggart's wish to turn the tables and humiliate Billy.

As a prototype of Billy Budd, Steelkilt evinces a similar reflexlike or "fight" reaction to provocation when the sting of the overbearing Radney's arbitrary authority pushes him to express his anger in direct action. Steelkilt has been toiling at the pump and is thus in a "corporeally exasperated state," "his face fiery red, his eyes bloodshot." The description emphasizes a disposition to rage, as does, of course, that resonant word "exasperated":

Now what cozening fiend it was, gentlemen, that possessed Radney to meddle with such a man in that corporeally exasperated state, I know not; but so it happened. Intolerably striding along the deck, the mate commanded him to get a broom and sweep down the planks, and also a shovel, and remove some offensive matters consequent upon allowing a pig to run at large. (*MD,* 246)

In a deliberate attempt to turn the tables and humiliate him, Radney orders his subordinate to sweep the deck, "the prescriptive province of the boys." Steelkilt rightly regards this order "almost as plainly meant to sting and insult [him], as though Radney had spat in his face" (247). As part of his humiliating initiation, Redburn, as a greenhorn, is given a similar order to "clean out that pig-pen in the long-boat" (73), the first order he receives on board the ship and, as he sees it, one insulting to his dignity. He decides it is "best to say nothing; I had bound myself to obey orders, and it was too late to retreat" (73). Steelkilt, in contrast, refuses. In the ensuing confrontation, he warns Radney, who threatens him with a hammer, that "if the hammer but grazed his cheek he (Steelkilt) would murder him" (248). Radney pays no heed and "the next instant the lower jaw of the mate was stove in his head; he fell on the hatch spouting blood like a whale" (248). Though there are a series of provocations leading up to this point, Steelkilt vents his anger from the beginning, and the expression of rage through physical action is a punctual, reflexlike response to the specific and explicit threat of a blow ("Immediately the hammer touched the cheek"). In this it clearly resembles Billy's lightning response both to the insulting dig in the ribs from the Red Whiskers and to the feeling of suffocation exerted by Claggart's accusing eyes, which overwhelm him with shame and anger.

Another example of the same following through of an immediate impulse to react to insult can be seen, but this time in a comic key, in an episode involving Queequeg. On the journey taken by Ishmael and his newfound friend aboard the packet schooner at the beginning of *Moby-Dick*, Queequeg is jeered at by one of the passengers:

So full of this reeling scene were we, as we stood by the plunging bowsprit, that for some time we did not notice the jeering glances of the passengers, a lubber-like assembly, who marvelled that two fellow beings should be so companionable; as though a white man were anything more dignified than a whitewashed negro. But there were some boobies and bumpkins there, who, by their intense greenness, must have come from the heart and centre of all verdure. Queequeg caught one of these young saplings mimicking him behind his back. I thought the bumpkin's hour of doom was come. Dropping his harpoon, the brawny savage caught him in his arms, and by an almost miraculous dexterity and strength, sent him high up bodily into the air; then slightly tapping his stern in midsomerset, the fellow landed with bursting lungs upon his feet, while Queequeg, turning his back upon him, lighted his tomahawk pipe and passed it to me for a puff. (60)

Queequeg, as we have seen, is one of the few characters in Melville who can boast of having an integrated and genuinely balanced sense of himself. This is, of course, the same thing as saying that he is a man without *ressentiment*, and accordingly his reaction is an explicit *turning of the tables* that, with as little ceremony as possible, good-humoredly, and without humiliation, shames his shamer. As the immediate following through of an impulse, his reflexlike action resembles the comic drubbing that Billy Budd gives Red Whiskers. And similar to the effect of Billy's drubbing, Queequeg's response to insult has a comic resolution. A potentially quarrelsome situation is defused and the social group harmonized: moments later, after Queequeg saves the same man's life, "All hands voted Queequeg a noble trump; the captain begged his pardon" (61).[6]

Queequeg's reaction can be instructively contrasted with that of Redburn when the latter finds himself in a more or less identical situation at the beginning of his own journey. Aboard the steamboat on his way to New York, he feels isolated and threatened by the other passengers eyeing him, in his view, with contempt and suspicion. In contrast with Queequeg's ability to dispel any sense of injury through an immediate and appropriate expression of his irritation and anger, Redburn's response clearly depicts the process by which feelings of shame and anger are suppressed until they push for expression in the form of a paranoid and aggressive turning of the tables.

Redburn's sense of himself as a conspicuous object of contempt and disgust takes the form of a sort of primal oral envy, as he watches the others eat while he is excluded and remains hungry. After dinner, "the few passengers, waked up with their roast-beef and mutton, became a little more sociable. Not with me, for the scent and savor of poverty was upon me, and they all cast toward me their evil eyes and cold suspicious glances, as I sat apart, though among them" (*R*, 12). Poverty's "scent and savour" suggests a feeling of being separated out as something shamefully dirty, or excremental, by ostracizing "evil eyes." That the sense of one's defectiveness should be expressed in terms of one's dirtiness and smell is characteristic of the shame felt by someone who is the object of contempt. This feeling of being in a socially reduced position, of being an object of disgust at the bottom of the social pyramid, an untouchable or social "excrement," reveals an anal dimension that plays an important part in Melville's work. The anal relation, as Grunberger notes, "is based on systems of opposites, such as the pairs 'strong and weak,' 'Small and large,' 'rich and poor,' 'stupid and intelligent.'"(1979, 151), two of which are explicitly at play here—rich and poor, and strong and weak (the latter when Redburn asserts himself physically and stares down his shamers). The other one at play here—dirty and clean—is particularly relevant to the anal relation. Tomkins relates contempt specifically to the anal character, "whose primary affect is disgust" (1963, 132). Contempt involves dissmell and disgust with the unappetizing object, in which there is "a literal pulling away from the object" so that "the distance between the face and the object that disgusts the self" (128) is maximized. Involving, then, less self-consciousness than shame, and directing attention to the object, contempt-disgust is particularly good for two things: drawing shame away from the self and relocating it in the other.

The feeling of being dirty and smelly is, of course, most explicitly related to infantile feelings of shame. The oppositions "strong and weak," and "small and large" are of general relevance to the desire for dominance in Melville, and they are equally characteristic of shame imagery; when one feels ashamed one feels "small," "weak," and "stupid," and in a society where wealth is a token of rank and worth, painful feelings of shame are bound to arise from being poor and belonging to a lower status of human beings.

Redburn's feeling of being outcast and exposed to hostile, insolent, shaming gazes comes to focus on the "mighty patch on one leg of [his] trowsers," which he has tried in vain to "hide with the ample skirts of [his] shooting jacket," so that it is "still very obvious and incontrovertible to the eye" (*R*, 12). In an antishame posture of defiance, he thrusts it into view. This aggressive gesture anticipates, in little, the way Jackson turns the tables on those around him, flaunting his own ugliness and defectiveness to advantage in order to mortify and dominate the crew: "This patch I had hitherto studiously endeavoured to hide with ample skirts of my shooting jacket; but now I stretched out my leg boldly, and thrust the patch under their noses, and looked at them so, that they soon looked away, boy though I was. Perhaps the gun that I clenched frightened them into respect; or there might have been something ugly in my eye" (12). This "something ugly" in the eye subtly connects Redburn with Jackson, whose malevolent power is located in his evil eye. As Redburn watches another party over their wine and cigars after dinner, he *enviously* compares their situation to his own: "Their faces were flushed with the good dinner they had eaten; and mine felt pale and wan with a long fast" (12). He then *imagines*, in a paranoid projection of his own feelings of shame, that if he had "solicited something to refresh me," they would have laughed him to scorn and "had the waiters put me out of the cabin, for a beggar, who had no business to be warming himself at their stove" (12). This image of being excluded is like the one, which, on the threshold of a similar voyage, Ishmael evokes to describe his own situation: the image of the outcast beggar Lazarus, from Jesus's parable, who must lie "stranded there on the curbstone before the door of Dives" (*MD*, 11). As Ishmael notes, "[I]t maketh a marvellous difference, whether thou lookest out at it from a glass window where the frost is all on the outside, or whether thou observest it from that sashless window, where the frost is on both sides, and of which the wight Death is the only glazier" (10). Redburn feels injured by this situation, though he notes that the insult is "only a conceit" on his part. (In its paranoia, this is analogous to the sort of conceit that makes Claggart believe that Billy is mocking him behind his back.) On the basis of this imaginary sense of slight, however, he "sat and gazed at them, putting up no petitions for their prosperity," his soul "soured within" him (*R*, 12).

Because he is without a ticket, the captain's clerk, "in a loud angry voice that attracted all eyes," orders him "out of the cabin into the storm. The devil in me than mounted up from my soul, and spread over my frame, till it tingled at my finger ends" (13). Redburn refuses to leave, and decides to stand up and fight, rather than make a shamefaced withdrawal. The idea of a *fighting stance* is alluded to in the immediately preceding passage concerning Redburn's traumatic mortification at being abandoned by his deceased father: "And it is a hard and cruel thing thus in early youth to taste before-hand the pangs which should be reserved for the stout time of manhood, when the gristle has become bone, and *we stand up and fight out our lives. . . .*" (11; emphasis added). The theme of being erect or not, which we examined earlier, is central here. From the beginning of the novel, Redburn presents himself as someone who is trying to find his legs and right himself, like the toppled mariner on the glass ship he is so fascinated by, and this theme brings into play a series of associations associated with growing up: being big and strong, and being able to stand up and walk without external sup-port. As we can see in Redburn's confrontation with his fellow passengers, the theme of standing erect, and all the infantile pride associated with it, is inevitably associated with the theme of "standing up" to the other, of as-suming a fighting stance and being able to "stand up and fight out our lives" (11). Feeling that he is surrounded by an indifferent and even hostile crowd, Redburn flirts with the kind of paranoia that we later discover in Jackson, in which the subject acts "as if all the world was one person, and had done him some dreadful harm" (61). After he faces down the ticket collector, Redburn, having made a spectacle of himself, feels all the more the object of hostile, insolent, shaming gazes, with "every eye fastened upon me" (13). The shame-rage that he has checked until now finally pushes him to adopt a countershaming posture and turn the tables on his shamers. Rather than submit to these shaming gazes, he decides to fight back, match-ing gaze for gaze. "I stood their gazing some time, but at last could stand it no more. I pushed my seat right up before the most insolent gazer . . . and fixing my gaze on his, gave him more gazes than he sent" (13). He notes that "This somewhat embarrassed him" and the man withdraws. He then turns to "the next gazer, and clicking my gun-lock, deliberately presented the piece at him" (13), until this man too takes flight and deserts the field. Afterwards, he feels "heartily ashamed" at having lost control and acted in such a way.

In this countershaming tactic of turning the tables on one's shamers, the gaze, specifically the look of contempt, becomes an aggressive shaming weapon, turned on others like Redburn's fowling gun, to ward off and pro-tect a self that feels vulnerable and perilously exposed to the looks of others. This strategy anticipates, of course, Redburn's later encounter with the sham-ing, contemptuous Jackson, when he finds himself on the other side of such a look.

The great scenes of aggressivity in Melville always seem to take the form of such a confrontation—of "mutually confronting visages" (*BB*, 98) as the narrator describes the face-to-face showdown between Claggart and Billy—in which an injured or slighted party, in a "fighting mood," attempts to make the other back down, forcing his opponent to make a "shamefaced" withdrawal—take flight—or stand up and fight. We have already explored some of the connections between such a fighting stance, the posture of defiance, and the sources of the appeal of certain charismatic leaders. Schiffer locates the source of "the vitality of this imagery of polarized action" in an aggression "derived from . . . pre-oedipal roots springing from old rivalries in the nursery, in which the child would fight his fellow for the favour of the primal mother. Any leader reduces his chances for a charisma if he backs off from the fight that rekindles this childhood ambition in his vicariously organized following" (1973, 39). The sibling rivalry or struggling brothers theme in Melville's work and life comes to mind here, and its obvious link to "envy," an important factor in these scenes of aggressivity. Indeed, Lacan links envy to the aggressivity that is rooted in the imaginary and the mirror-stage, "which in the present stage of our culture is given to us under the dominant species of *resentment*" (1977, 20).

This "posture of polarized aggression" (1973, 37), as Schiffer calls it, this fighting stance, is second nature to a character such as Jackson, so much so that it becomes a weapon in itself. The "three or four who used to stand up sometimes against him" would tell the others ""what a shame and ignominy it was, that such a poor miserable wretch should be such a tyrant over much better men than himself" (*R*, 61).[7] In the end, however,

> finding themselves unbefriended by the rest, they would gradually become silent, and leave the field to the tyrant, who would then fly out worse than ever, and dare them to do their worst, and jeer at them for white-livered poltroons, who did not have a mouthful of heart in them. At such times, there were no bounds to his contempt; and indeed, all the time he seemed to have even more contempt than hatred, for every body and every thing. (61–62)

We can see here quite clearly how Jackson's chronic contempt and hatred for others acts as a defense against his "own readiness to feel ashamed" (Tomkins 1963, 146). Like the mechanism of turning the tables and shaming the other, contempt, then, serves the function of directing shame away from the self and locating it elsewhere. As Andrew Morrison observes, it is "a mechanism for ridding the self of unbearable shame, in this case by projecting the shame out of the self into another person" (1989, 105); it is a more structured form than rage, and takes the form of a "subjective disavowal of one's personal shame experience and its reappearance in feelings toward another person" (105).

Claggart's scornful attitude to Billy illustrates this mechanism, as reflected in the sarcasm of his remark "handsome is as handsome did it, too," or in the "passion," as the narrator calls it, of his intense envy, which assumed "that of cynic disdain, disdain of innocence—to be nothing more than innocent!" (*BB*, 78). Claggart's contempt for Billy's "frank enjoyment," for the simplicity of a nature that "had never willed malice," recalls Iago's contempt for Othello's "free and open nature / That thinks men honest that but seem to be so" (*Othello* 1.3.398–99); this aspect of the Moor's character is, as Sussman points out, his "Achilles's heel . . . which we may think of as an inability to curb his appetite for direct and frank collaboration" (1993, 25). Needless to say, this openness of his nature is Billy's fatal weakness as well. In contrast, the closed and secretive nature of both Iago and Claggart is directly related to what Coleridge calls, with great psychological acuteness, "the dread of contempt habitual to those who encourage in themselves and have their keenest pleasure in the feeling and expression of contempt for others" (1969, 186–87).[8] Contempt as an antishame posture is perfectly depicted here; contempt becomes habitual because it is a way of reducing the shame from self-contempt, which often takes the form of anticipated contempt from outside. Like Iago, who views Othello's simple nature with scorn and seizes on it as a means of leading his victim "by the nose / As asses are" (*Othello* 1.3.400–401), Claggart regards Billy's innocence with disdain and hopes to manipulate the same frankness, honesty, and openness in Billy's character to entrap him unwittingly in conspiracy. At the same time, however, the fact that he "fain would have shared [Billy's beauty and innocence], but he despaired of it" (*BB*, 78) reveals that underneath his envy lie shame and self-contempt, which he rids himself of precisely through an attitude of disgust with and contempt for others. "Even so was it that in to the gall of Claggart's envy he infused the vitriol of his contempt" (79). Claggart's attitude to Billy is, then, a perfect illustration of how contempt is "an attempt to 'relocate' the shame experience from within the self into another person, and, thus, like rage . . . may be an attempt to rid the self of shame. . . . In essence, subjective shame, over failure, inferiority, or defect, is disavowed or repressed and is 'placed' into another, who must then 'accept' and 'contain' the projection" (Morrison 1989, 14).

The case of Jackson is a particularly interesting example of how contempt and hatred for others are used to relocate one's own self-contempt and self-hatred. For here they are turned into overwhelming weapons that humiliate and mortify others, thus weakening their will to resist and making it almost impossible to fight back. This is the source of Jackson's ability to intimidate and manipulate the group; his shameless willingness to control and manipulate others is itself a sign of his contempt.

> They made a point of shouting out, whenever Jackson said any thing with a grin; that being the sign to them that he himself thought it funny; though I heard many good jokes from others pass without a smile; and once Jackson himself . . . told a truly funny story, but with a grave face; when, not knowing how he meant it, whether for a laugh or otherwise, they all sat still, waiting what to do, and looking perplexed enough; till at last Jackson roared out upon them for a parcel of fools and idiots; and told them to their beards, how it was; that he had purposely put on his grave face, to see whether they would not look grave, too; even when he was telling something that ought to split their sides. And with that, he flouted, and jeered at them, and laughed them all to scorn; and broke out in such a rage, that his lips began to glue together at the corners with a fine white foam. (R, 61)[9]

In Jackson the mechanism of ridding oneself of feelings of shame by relocating them in others involves, in particular, the *shameless* display of his own contempt and rage. This shamelessness is perhaps the ultimate source of Jackson's power over the group, and is an excellent example of what Tomkins calls *flaunting;* it is a product of humiliating oppression in which the individual "does the shameful or disgusting act and wallows in his degradation, flaunting both the act and his self-contempt in the face of the oppressor" (1963, 297). Berke speaks of those individuals who "try to turn the tables on shame by flaunting their condition" (1987, 331). Such "aggressive flaunting measures," the ostentatious display of one's own shame and self-hatred, function "to discharge intolerable inner tensions and stick them somewhere else" (332). Berke speaks of a patient whose "outrageous behaviour enabled her to shame her parents and doctors and become more of a persecutor to them than they were to her" (332), and of another who "when he wasn't hiding [in shame] . . . used to pick his nose in public. He loved to watch others' discomfort. . . . The whole point is to avoid shame by becoming the shamer and making others look bad. In this way, shame and envy act in tandem. *Shame rubs one's nose in the dirt, while envy rubs the dirt in one's nose*" (332). Jackson is a perfect example of someone who avoids or reduces shame in this way: turning the tables, he uses self-exposure as a weapon that assumes a fascinating and paralyzing power allowing him to dominate and humiliate his opponents, who are afraid to face up to him. Persecuted by Jackson, Redburn is forced to take flight and make a "shame-faced" retreat into the social wilderness. Like the "remarkably robust and good-humored young man from Belfast in Ireland" (*R*, 59) who is mentioned earlier in the same chapter, he becomes a convenient scapegoat for the shaming and ostracism that Jackson is able to impose through his control of the group. The Belfast man "was hooted at, and trampled upon, and made a butt and a laughing-stock; and more than all, was continually being abused and snubbed by Jackson, who seemed to hate him cordially, because of his great strength and fine person, and particularly because of his red cheeks" (59). The extent of the mortification involved in such abusive and contemptuous treatment becomes particularly clear in the reaction of the sailors when Jackson is lost at sea.

> One and all they seemed tacitly to unite in hushing up his memory among them. Whether it was, that the severity of the bondage under which this man held every one of them, did really corrode in their secret hearts, that they thought to repress the recollection of a thing so degrading, I can not determine; but certain it was, that *his* death was *their* deliverance. (296–97)

Both the "The Town-Ho's Story" and *Billy Budd* stage the same kind of confrontation, though in both cases the "shamer" is overturned. Steelkilt, whose robust physical beauty, golden hair, and frank and open disposition place him squarely in the camp of the narcissistic ideal exemplified by Billy Budd, refuses to back down in face of "the brutal overbearing" (*MD*, 243) of his rival Radney, and the latter's attempt to tyrannize and humiliate cata-strophically (tragically) backfires. A similar tragic reversal takes place when Claggart attempts to intimidate Billy and force him into submission, to face him down and paralyze him with his accusing, slanderous (i.e., shaming) eye.

At the risk of some repetition, it is worth turning again to the very instructive encounter between Ahab and Stubb, where the latter is so uncer-emoniously "put in his place." Both Stubb and Steelkilt are the victims of a shame-provoking indignity inflicted on them by their superiors. Steelkilt, "a mariner, who though a sort of devil indeed, might yet by inflexible firmness, only tempered by that common decency of human recognition which is the meanest slave's right [had] . . . long been retained harmless and docile" (244–45). ("Docile," it may be recalled, is the word that haunted Herman in the Melvill family mythology.) This recognition of course is pre-cisely what Radney deliberately and provocatively withdraws from Steelkilt, when in retaliation for the insults he has received—the recognition, in other words, that he feels has been contemptuously denied *him*—he attempts to humiliate his rival. Ahab, in retaliation for a perceived slight, refuses to afford the same recognition to Stubb; he humiliates him, verbally degrad-ing him and treating him with contempt. Whereas Stubb decides to submit to the humiliation and retreat, Steelkilt stands his ground: unduly provoked, his pride pricked once too often, he knocks down his shamer.

In backing down, Stubb resorts to what Nathanson calls self-attack, counting it an honor to be insulted by such a great man as Ahab. We might compare this logic of self-abasement with the way in which Ahab placates Starbuck when he insults his first mate to his face in the chapter 36 ("The Quarter-Deck") and then counts it "small indignity." In the middle of his "little lower layer" speech, Ahab feels that he is being impertinently stared at and barks out at the bewildered Starbuck, in angry reaction to a sudden feeling of self-consciousness: "Take off thine eye! More intolerable than fiends' glaring is a doltish stare! So, so; thou reddenest and palest; my heat has melted thee to anger-glow. But look ye, Starbuck, what is said in heat, that thing unsays itself. There are men from whom warm words are small indignity. I meant not to incense thee" (164). A similar encounter is de-scribed in chapter 109 ("Ahab and Starbuck in the Cabin"), when the ship is leaking oil; Ahab's reluctance to take action is challenged by Starbuck, who receives a contemptuous rebuke and is peremptorily ordered back on deck.

When the "reddening Starbuck" persists, Ahab points a loaded musket at his head:

> For an instant in the flashing eyes of the mate, and his fiery cheeks, you would have almost thought that he had really received the blaze of the levelled tube. But mastering his emotion, he half calmly rose, and as he quitted the cabin, paused for an instant and said: "Thou hast outraged, not insulted me, sir; but for that I ask thee not to beware of Starbuck; thou wouldst but laugh; but let Ahab beware of Ahab; beware of thyself, old man." (474–75)

In both cases, Starbuck's reasoned forbearance contrasts with Ahab's overbearingness and limitless will to domination and mastery, illustrating Grunberger's description of the anal subject as one who places himself "above the object, to whom the quality of subject is denied." "The anal subject-object couple is, then," according to Grunberger, "in its ideal form that of master and slave ('You are my object, I will do with you what I want, and you will have no way of opposing me')" (149). This is, as we have seen, the defiant and contemptuous attitude of Timophanes in "Timoleon": "I am the Wrong, and lo, I reign / And testily intolerant too in might" (5.11). In relation to the object, a personality of the anal type obsessively seeks a position of superiority as the one way of escaping painful shame and humiliation. "The main point," in Grunberger's words, "is that the subject occupy in relation to the object a position of superiority, which he protects at all cost, especially since it carries, in addition to its energizing value proper, a positive narcissistic confirmation" (1979, 151). It might be more accurate to view this "positive narcissistic confirmation" as a sign that, as Tomkins puts it, the "positive affects experienced [by the individual] are consequences of reducing his humiliation, expressing it or humiliating others" (1963, 296). Ahab's inability to accept that there might be someone over him, outshining or surpassing him, as it were, is experienced as an unbearable shame and is by itself taken as a slight and injury. As he says to Starbuck at the beginning of the same speech: "Talk not to me of blasphemy, man; I'd strike the sun if it insulted me. For could the sun do that, then could I do the other; since there is ever a sort of fair play herein, jealousy presiding over all creations. *But not my master, man, is even that fair play. Who's over me?* Truth hath no confines" (*MD*, 164; emphasis added). In both these encounters with Starbuck, however, Ahab does attempt to mitigate the insult, whether "It may have been," as the narrator speculates, "a flash of honesty in him; or mere prudential policy which, under the circumstance, imperiously forbade the slightest symptom of open disaffection, however transient in the important chief officer of his ship" (475). In the first case, he takes back his words—"What is said in heat, that thing unsays itself. . . . I meant not to incense thee"—and in the second he yields to his first mate's better judgment and gives orders to seek harbor and repair the ship.

III

The anal relation, which in Melville's work plays such an important part in the encounter between contending individuals, has a highly important social dimension as well. The social order aboard ship is, we are constantly reminded, in the shape of a pyramid. On the top is the captain, whose walled-in inaccessibility Melville makes much of throughout his work; from him descends a carefully graded ladder of rank. The introduction of the crew in *Moby-Dick* emphasizes this pyramidical structure of authority, and in the dream that he has after he has been abjectly humiliated by Ahab, whose superiority and towering dominance over him is stressed, Stubb dreams that he is kicking his foot against a pyramid. Melville, like Ishmael, seems to have made a point of scorning all forms of social grandiosity—showed his contempt, that is, for the established forms of social contempt—and his democratic instincts, at least from the point of view of their emotional content, are rooted in his wish to transcend shame through the frankest forms of communion. An attitude of contempt, however, is an impediment to such communion. Tomkins notes that "Contempt will be used sparingly in a democratic society lest it undermine solidarity," whereas in "a hierarchically organized society" it is an indispensable instrument serving "to maintain distance between individuals, classes, and nations" (1963, 140–41). Contempt is thus a psychological barrier that Melville found himself fighting, because he had to fight it first of all within himself.

He begins one letter by openly encouraging the shy, withdrawn Hawthorne to be frank and truthful with him—"With no son of man do I stand upon any etiquette or ceremony, except the Christian ones of charity and honesty"—observing that

there have been those who, while earnest in behalf of political equality, still accept the intellectual estates. And I can well perceive, I
think, how a man of superior mind can, by its intense cultivation,
bring himself, as it were, into a certain spontaneous aristocracy of
feeling,—exceedingly nice and fastidious,—similar to that which,
in an English Howard, conveys a torpedo-fish thrill at the slightest
contact with a social plebian. So, when you see or hear of my ruthless democracy on all sides, you may possibly feel a touch of a shrink,
or something of that sort. (*Corr.,* 190)

This electric shudder or shrink is a reference to the affect of disgust, the
affective basis of contempt. It is, in fact, extraordinary to what extent Melville
conceives of social relationships on the basis of just such archaic emotional
responses. When Billy has his brush with the afterguardsman planted by
Claggart, his discomfiture is described in the following way: "In his disgust-
ful recoil from an overture which, though he but ill comprehended, he instinctively knew must involve evil of some sort, Billy Budd was like a young
horse fresh from the pasture suddenly inhaling a vile whiff from some chemical factory, and by repeated snortings trying to get it out of his nostrils and
lungs" (*BB,* 84). The pastoral imagery here—a horse in the pasture contrasted
with the poisonous stench of a chemical factory—is, of course, quite consistent with the theme of Billy's unfallen innocence. But Billy's recoil is also a
perfect description of the dissmell and disgust responses, as Tomkins calls
them, which are "innate defensive responses, which are auxiliary to the
hunger, thirst and oxygen drives," in which "the upper lip and nose are
raised and the head is drawn away from the apparent source of the offending odor. If the food has been taken into the mouth, it may, if disgusting, be
spit out" (1987, 142). This describes the way in which Billy reacts to the
afterguardsman's overture, in his instinctive rejection of the something dirty
and disgusting detected in his first contact with "evil." It is perhaps worth
noting that, in a similar way, Vere's response to the presence of Claggart is
distaste, a dissmell response, and that the narrator's description of his reaction is particular in the way that it emphasizes facial expression, the face
being, in Tomkins' view, the site of affect: "No sooner did the commander
observe who it was that now deferentially stood awaiting his notice than a
*peculiar expression came over him. It was not unlike that which uncontrollably
will flit across the countenance* of one at unawares encountering a person . . .

something in whose aspect nevertheless now for the first provokes a *vaguely repellent distaste*" (*BB*, 91). In both these cases the distaste or dissmell is directed at Claggart or at his "evil" sphere of influence.

Melville seems to have had an extremely acute sensitivity to the way in which "ideo-affective posture is the result of systematic differences in the socialization of affects," and Tomkins's polarity scale assessing "the individual's normative or humanistic position on a broad spectrum of ideological issues" (1987, 147, 146) would be worth applying to the ideo-affective tensions that we can detect in his work. In his struggle over the fate of Billy Budd, for example, we can recognize the irresolvable tension in Vere's personality between "the humanistic position . . . that attempts to maximize positive affect for individuals and for all their interpersonal relationships" and "the normative position" in which "norm compliance is the primary value" (148). The importance of the socialization of affects in Melville's work applies as well to the positive ones, such as interest-excitement and enjoyment-joy. Billy Budd, as we have seen, is consistently associated with enjoyment and joyousness, as Ishmael's responses to Queequeg at the beginning of *Moby-Dick* largely revolve around the conflict between interest-excitement, to use Tomkins's terms, and the shame and fear that threaten to inhibit curiosity and mutual intimacy.

Characters such as Jackson and Claggart, on the other hand, are all too ready, as a recourse against shame, to fall back on the contempt-disgust response. "Contempt," as Tomkins simply puts it, "is the mark of the oppressor" (1963, 140), and it is, as Melville clearly understood, contempt that is reflected in shipboard hierarchy, where interaction between individuals is rigorously organized by clearly demarcated distinctions in rank and authority. In *White-Jacket* the narrator rails against "the social state in a man-of-war," illustrating social relations aboard ship by taking the flagrant, but nonetheless emblematic, instance of the "mutual contempt and even hatred" in which "the marine and sailor stand toward each other," a relation proudly "held by most Navy officers as the height of the perfection of Navy discipline. . . . Checks and balances, blood against blood, that is the cry and the argument" (374). This oppositional structural principle gives birth to a monstrous

> system of cruel cogs and wheel, systematically grinding up in one common hopper all that might minister to the moral well-being of the crew.

It is the same with both officers and men. If a Captain have a grudge against a Lieutenant, or a Lieutenant against a midshipman, how easy to torture him by official treatment, which shall not lay open the superior officer to legal rebuke. And if a midshipman bears a grudge against a sailor, how easy for him, by cunning practices, born of a boyish spite, to have him degraded at the gangway. Through all the endless ramifications of rank and station, in most men-of-war there runs a sinister vein of bitterness, not exceeded by the fire-side hatreds in a family of step-sons ashore. It were sickening to detail all the paltry irritabilities, jealousies, and cabals, the spiteful detractions and animosities, that lurk far down, and cling to the very kelson of the ship. It is unmanning to think of. The immutable ceremonies and iron etiquette of a man-of-war; the spiked barriers separating the various grades of rank; the delegated absolutism of authority on all hands; the impossibility, on the part of the common seaman, of appeal from incidental abuses, and many more things that might be enumerated, all tend to beget in most armed ships a general social condition which is the precise reverse of what any Christian could desire. (375)

A society born of contempt gives birth, in other words, to the monstrous progeny of humiliation and resentment that its barriers must then desperately strive to protect against.

The anal nature of this oppositionalilty as it is reflected in the trenchancy of shipboard hierarchies and distinctions of rank helps to explain the extensive "rat" imagery in Melville, especially in *Billy Budd*. With all its connotations of anality and greed, "rat" would seem to be the source of *Rad*ney's name in "The Town-Ho's Story." We find "rat" also in *Rat*cliffe, the lieutenant from the *Bellipotent* who impresses Billy into service; he is a character whose brief moment on the story's stage is marked by a certain greediness and the avidity of his eye: "Plump upon Billy at first sight in the gangway the boarding officer, Lieutenant Ratcliffe, pounced" (*BB*, 45). In the captain's cabin he helps himself to a conspicuous "flask from the spirit locker, a receptacle which his experienced eye instantly discovered" (46). His "natural instinct for sensuous enjoyment," we are informed, has not been impaired by "all the hardship and peril of naval life," and demonstrations of that instinct punctuate the scene with the shipmaster. In the same vein, the cat's paw of Claggart is a fellow called "'Squeak,' one of his more cunning corporals, a grizzled little man, so nicknamed by the sailors on account of his squeaky voice and sharp visage ferreting about the dark corners of the lower decks after interlopers, satirically suggesting to them the idea of a rat in a cellar" (79). Billy Budd is dropped into "a rat-pit of quarrels" (46) aboard the *Rights of Man*, and into an even worse one when he lands in the *Bellipotent*, where Claggart, whose name contains a transposed "rat," and his rat-pack are denizens of the lower depths, the bowels of the ship, the anal foundation or fundament of the pyramid of authority and rank.

We thus return to our earlier discussion of one of the most vexatious puzzles posed by Melville's work: the dramatic and unresolved struggle between two separate and contradictory social visions. Melville's deep-rooted liberal, democratic, and communal impulses run counter to the conception of a society based on contempt, separation, and hatred—this wolfish world of resentment and quarrel that is the basis of the Hobbesian political mythology reflected in *Moby-Dick*. Over forty years ago, Richard Chase devoted the introductory chapter of his critical study of Melville to the question of the author's ambiguous political position, which Chase declared liberal but antiprogressive. What is meant by antiprogressive is perhaps better understood in terms of Melville's profound intuition of the potentially destructive influence of narcissistic rage and *ressentiment* in human societies. The vitality of Melville's liberalism on the other hand—the humanistic position, in Tomkins's terms—is reflected, for Chase, in "[his] strong young heroes—the Jack Chases, Bulkingtons, and Ethan Allens" as

> Melville's "common man." They are men of epic size, great in heart, in sensibility, and in the quality of endurance; they are companions, storytellers, defenders of freedom, revolutionaries; their brotherhood with other men is open, frank, and based on the deepest ties of common humanity; they are, in their way, pure; but their purity is in their sensitiveness and in their longing for brotherhood and fatherhood; their purity is not the righteous monomania of Ahab. (1949, x)

These young heroes are representatives of a profoundly egalitarian and democratic vision. The comic world of Ishmael is a world of frank social human communion, and it subsists in spite of the *Pequod*'s trenchant social hierarchy. To put it in terms of its emotional basis: in a world of sperm-squeezing, shame-humiliation, in contrast with contempt, "is the negative affect linked with love and identification" (Tomkins 1963, 140). Shame leaves the door open for reaffiliation with the group, whereas in Ahab's Leviathan world of trenchant oppositions and tyrannical domination, contempt-disgust is "the negative affect linked with individuation and hate" (140), where the separation from the object is complete. Both shame and contempt impede "intimacy and communion," but "shame-humiliation does not renounce the object permanently, whereas contempt-disgust does" (140). Ishmael, at the beginning of *Moby-Dick*, seeks love and intimacy with Queequeg, and in his memory of being punished by his stepmother in chapter 4 ("The Counterpane") we see him seek reconciliation with the alienated object, a reconciliation that his stepmother, in whom contempt appears to dominates, cruelly disallows. The counterexample to Ishmael's conciliatory impulse, as discussed earlier, is Ahab's refusal of the temptation of reaffiliation in chapter 132 ("The Symphony"); he chooses instead a fiery hunt that is pursued with an all-consuming hatred that wishes only to annihilate the object. Ahab is thus, for Chase, the nightmarish image of "a progressive American," the

> terrifying picture of a man rejecting all connection with his family, his culture, his own sexuality even, expunging the colors from the rainbow, rejecting the stained imperfections of life for a vision of spotless purity and rectitude attainable only in death, drifting into the terrible future, jamming himself on like a father turned into a raging child, toward a catastrophe which annihilates a whole world[.] (1949, ix)

This passage from Chase recalls Doi's observations concerning the denial by Western man of the fundamental dependency and human caring that is at the core of human life; Doi claims that "all the attempts of modern Western man to deny or to sidestep *amae* have not be enough to transcend it, much less to conquer the lure of death" (1973, 95). The same drama of the conflict between these two affective bases—contempt-disgust and shame-humiliation—and their opposing social visions is played out again tragically in *Billy Budd*, where Billy is the focus of the most intense democratic communion on the part of the crew at the very moment that he is sacrificed to maintain a hierarchical order threatened by the unbridled, resentment-driven forces of the French Revolution.

Béla Grunberger's observations concerning the social implications of what he calls *anal narcissism* may help to illuminate this sociopolitical dimension of Melville's work:

> An anal society can be compared to a busy well-organized hive that functions according to strict and implacable rules. The crises of anality can also profit from this comparison, but in this case it is a matter of an insane hive. Anality, bound by the whole structuralization of the hive down to its very substance, by its organization, by the ordered activity of its inhabitants, and by the discipline that they undergo and impose at the same time, is unleashed and turns upon them, since they have never learned to integrate it in an authentic and personal mode or to sublimate it. *Therefore, there is panic, rout, and a blind fight of all against all.* The anal character then loses his feeling of security and no longer collaborates. On the contrary, *he sees enemies in everyone and everywhere:* "Are you with me, or must I destroy you, cover you with dirt, and trample on you?" (1979, 164; emphasis added)

In its most dire form, this vision of social frenzy recalls Raskolnikov's last dream in *Crime and Punishment*, in which all the people on the face of earth become victims, like Ahab, of what Chase calls "a vision of spotless purity and rectitude attainable only in death," as they drift "into the terrible future . . . toward a catastrophe which annihilates a whole world." Raskolnikov dreams of a virus that has infected every member of the population with—as Kohut describes the narcissistically enraged—an absolute belief in "the validity of their ideals with an equally absolute lack of empathic understanding" for the feelings, concerns, and values of other human beings (Kohut 1978, 835).

> All were full of anxiety, and none could understand any other; each thought he was the sole repository of truth and was tormented when he looked at the others, beat his breast, wrung his hands, and wept. They did not know how or whom to judge and could not agree what was evil and what good. They did not know whom

to condemn or whom to acquit. Men killed one another in senseless rage. (Dostoevsky 1989, 524)

It is precisely the potential for such a world given over entirely to "senseless
rage" that defines the fragility of social order aboard the *Bellipotent:* when
the sense of security is lost, no one collaborates any longer, and enemies are
seen in "everyone and everywhere." In such a world released from any social or political authority, the treachery and hatred of Claggart becomes the
rule.

It is this ever present, very real possibility of mutiny and collapse of all
civilized sociality, the outbreak of "panic, rout, and a blind fight of all against
all," brought on by a society torn apart by chronic feelings of humiliation
and resentment, that explains Vere's overriding sense of the urgency of order, of maintaining what Grunberger calls "a busy well-organized hive that
functions according to strict and implacable rules." This would seem to be
the significance of the series of Burke-inspired images that run through *Billy
Budd*—that of a besieged England "confronted by those wars which like a
flight of harpies rose shrieking from the din and dust of the fallen Bastille";
of "Camoens' Spirit of the Cape, an eclipsing menace mysterious and prodi-
gious"; and of "this French portentous upstart from the revolutionary chaos
who seemed in act of fulfilling judgment prefigured in the Apocalypse" (*BB*,
66). Such imagery suggests an entirely pragmatic argument for an authoritarian political order: that without such an order the forces of *ressentiment*
will tear society apart. It is an argument that is so unsettling, so redolent of
the worst justifications of dictatorship, and so contradictory to the deep
communal impulses that also run through Melville's work, that it is little
wonder that readers and critics should be defeated again and again by the
insuperable conundrum that is *Billy Budd*. We touch here the uninterpretable
navel, as it were, of Melville's dream, the terrible essence of his tragic vision:
this should not and yet must be. It is the vision of a man who was himself a
battleground for shame and contempt, a man whose best and most loving
impulses were constantly torn apart by severity and rage.

Thus Melville must have it both ways in *Billy Budd*. Though the law
cannot forgive Billy, he is tenderly reconciled with his executioner. Though
Claggart is struck down, his hatred and contempt is allowed to annihilate
its object. For in the political vision of *Billy Budd*, it is but a step from a
world in which contempt for the object is the basis of order to one in which

it and the murderous resentment it spawns are the basis of disorder, and everyone turned into an Ishmael, all against all—a world torn apart by unending hatred and interminable homicidal quarrel. We might recall that Babo's brain, that extraordinary rational machinery devoted to utterly irrational ends, is called "that hive of subtlety" (*PT*, 116), and if the *Bellipotent* is, in Grunberger's terms, "a busy well-organized hive" (1979, 164), it is treacherously close to being an insane one. The particular madness of a Claggart is merely the corollary of the contempt and hatred that is already implied in the sociopolitical order and its child-devouring, sacrificial Law. The reference, after Billy's hanging, to Vere's love of measure and of strict implacable rule—as befits his nickname "Starry," with its suggestion of cosmic order—is made in connection with "the story of Orpheus with his lyre spellbinding the wild denizens of the wood" (*BB*, 128). We cannot help but be reminded, of course, of the fate of Orpheus: violent death and dismemberment. The same image of Orphic song occurs in *Redburn*. On the voyage home, Redburn's ill-fated alter ego, Harry Bolton, a tormented object of the crew, masochistically "yield[s] himself up to the almost passive reception of contumely and contempt" (*R*, 258), yet his beautiful singing voice stills for a moment the savage crew. For a time, they "relinquished their prey": "Hushed, and more hushed they grew, till at last Harry sat among them like Orpheus among the charmed leopards and tigers. Harmless now the fangs with which they were wont to tear my zebra, and backward curled in velvet paws; and fixed their once glaring eyes in fascinated and fascinating brilliancy" (278). We might note the important magical, fascinatory element suggested here in both these allusions to Orpheus. "'With mankind,' [Vere] would say, 'forms, measured forms, are everything. . . .' And this he once applied to the disruption of forms going on across the Channel and the consequences thereof" (*BB*, 128). We touch here on the subject of our next chapter: the potentially harmonizing role of idealization and its dangerous counterpart—the intense fascination with omnipotent objects.

PART THREE

The
Evil
Eye

CHAPTER SIX

Dangerous Mergers

I

Shame is able to wreak so much emotional and psychic damage because, in large doses, it makes impossible the healthy interest and enjoyment in life that is the foundation of a fully developed sense of self. Wurmser in particular has focused on the impact that shame can have on expression and perception, and how the distortion of natural wishes to communicate with others and to explore the world can damage the very core of an individual's self-concept. Wurmser speaks of two "drives" that motivate the self's interactions and development: *delophilia*, which is commonly known as exhibitionism, and *theatophilia*, which is related to *scopophilia* and voyeurism. The active form of *delophilia* or magic exhibitionism is defined as the wish "to express oneself and to fascinate others by one's self-exposure, to show and to impress, to merge with the other through communication" (1981, 158). In Wurmser's view, Kohut's grandiose-exhibitionistic self—a phase of developing self-esteem that in "normal" development is channeled in a realistic direction—corresponds fairly exactly to this active form. The desire to show oneself, to be admired, and to fascinate is "that normal phase of the development of the grandiose self in which the gleam in the mother's eye, which mirrors the child's exhibitionistic display, and other forms of maternal participation in and response to the child's narcissistic-exhibitionistic enjoyment confirm the child's self-esteem" (Kohut 1971, 116; quoted in Wurmser 1981, 153). In both drives, the passive mode is usually expressed as a fear more than as a wish. In the case of exhibitionism the fear is of exposure, of being "stared at, being overcome and devoured by the looks of others," against which the subject "tries to fight back" (Wurmser 1981, 162). In the next chapter we shall examine in detail the way this drive operates in active and passive modes.

The active form of *theatophilia* or scopophilia, the desire to see, is an intense curiosity and attentiveness in which the subject, through looking, wants to conquer and merge "with the partner into an all-powerful, autarkic union, to incorporate the strength and value of the other person and attain control over him" (162). In Wurmser's view, this scopophilic drive correlates to Kohut's image of the idealized selfobject, in which voyeuristic wishes and mergers are "attempts to supply substitutes for the idealized parent imago and its functions . . . attempts to reestablish the union with the narcissistically invested lost object through visual fusion and other archaic forms of identification" (Kohut 1971, 98–99; quoted in Wurmser 1981, 153)). Wurmser points out that this wish often has "a very strong oral tinge" (162). In its passive mode, this mode of attentiveness and curiosity is often expressed as the fear of being unduly fascinated and psychologically overpowered by others, as Starbuck, for example, is overpowered by Ahab, or Redburn by Jackson, or Billy by Claggart. The presence and looks of these overbearing figures exert "a hypnotizing, paralysing spell" that must be fought off in some way.

It is in Redburn perhaps that we find the most explicit example of the bipolar self in Melville, the oscillation in one personality between "solipsistic claims for attention" and the "compelling need for merger" (Kohut 19771, 9) with a powerful object. Redburn's pronounced fear of being overwhelmed by the gazes of others—the phobic counterpart to "the undisguised pleasure in being admired" (25)—is only matched by the voyeuristic and idealizing aspects of his personality. In its most primal form, this manifests itself, in the opening passages of the novel, in the description of his childhood propensity to stare at others. Redburn recounts a memory of *gazing in fascination* at a man whom his aunt points out to him as a famous traveler:

> For I very well remembered *staring at a man* myself, who was pointed out to me by my aunt . . . as the person who had been in Stony Arabia, and passed through strange adventures there, all of which *with my own eyes* I had read in the book which he wrote, an arid-looking book in a pale yellow cover.
> "*See what big eyes he has,*" whispered my aunt, "they got so big, because when he was almost dead with famishing in the desert, *he all at once caught sight of a date tree, with the ripe fruit hanging on it.*"
> Upon this, *I stared at him till I thought his eyes were really of an uncommon size, and stuck out from his head like those of a lobster. I am sure my own eyes must have magnified as I stared. . . .* I never saw this

wonderful Arabian traveller again. But he long haunted me; and several times I dreamt of him, and thought *his great eyes were grown still larger and rounder, and once I had a vision of the date tree.* (*R*, 5–6; emphasis added)

This extraordinary passage is a perfect illustration of the archaic scopophilic drive as the wish "to watch and observe, to admire and to be fascinated, to merge and master through attentive looking" (Wurmser 1981, 158). The repetition of the words "wonder" and "wonderful" emphasize the voyeuristic intensity of Redburn's gaze as he visually merges with the wonderful traveler he so admires. The eyes do not look but "stare," and there is a significant insistence on an almost devouring quality, suggesting a certain aggressiveness of the eye. Tomkins, as we noted, remarks upon the extraordinary taboo in all cultures against looking at others, a taboo that is linked to the idea of the *evil eye*. Staring makes the other uncomfortable, uneasy, nervous, self-conscious, ashamed—reactions that, as we have seen, Redburn exemplifies when later in the novel he himself feels that he has become the object of others' stares. Staring, of course, is a proverbially rude gesture, precisely because it causes shame; and it is something for which children are habitually scolded (that is, shamed) by their parents. By rather rudely pointing out the man to him in the first place, Redburn's aunt seems, however, more intent on encouraging, than correcting, this bad habit in her nephew. She does, of course, dissuade him from following the man home, albeit in a way that, by invoking the repressive law, only serves to locate the place of desire ("she said the constables would take us up, if we did"). This "wonderful Arabian traveller" has himself enormous staring eyes, which the young man imagines "really of an uncommon size, and stuck out from his head like those of a lobster. I am sure my own eyes must have magnified as I stared" (*R*, 5). These goggle eyes seem to be the prototype of Claggart's hypnotic fascinating gaze, which seems to have the power to stun its victim and is compared, as he fixes Billy with his look, to the gelid eyes of some uncataloged creature of the deep. That night, Redburn dreams of his eyes growing "still larger and rounder" as he stares in longing fascination at the ripe fruit of the date tree.

Thus commences a series of images surrounding the eye that run through the chapter, images that suggest a *hunger for merger* that is potentially destructive in its avidity. Redburn visually merges with the omnipotent traveler, whose own fixation with the hungered-after object, the ripe fruit, Redburn repeats in his fantasy. The imagery of an instinctual oral need surrounding the (often visual) merger with an idealized object, evident elsewhere in Melville, is especially marked in this opening chapter of *Redburn*, which bears the title "How Wellingborough Redburn's *Taste* for the Sea was Born and Bred in Him" (emphasis added). In describing how he would gaze at travelogues with what can only be described as avidity, the narrator uses the image of an essentially oral pleasure: "In course of time, my thoughts became more and more prone to dwell upon foreign things; and in a thousand ways I sought to *gratify my tastes*" (6; emphasis added); "The waves were *toasted brown*, and the whole picture looked mellow and old. I used to think a piece of it might *taste good*" (6; emphasis added). Two pages, indeed, are then devoted to Redburn's all-consuming passion for dreamily gazing upon books of travel replete with "colored prints" that he pores over "with never-failing delight":

[A]nd many a time I gazed at the word "*London*" on the title-page. And there was a copy of D'Alembert in French, and I wondered what a great man I would be, if by foreign travel I should ever be able to read straight along without stopping, out of that book, which now was a riddle to every one in the house but my father, whom I so much liked to hear talk French, as he sometimes did to a servant we had. (7)

And he adds: "The servant, too, I used to gaze at with wonder" (7). Redburn's staring and wonder here clearly bears on his desire to be enriched by what he sees: to absorb, in order to share in them, these images of power and knowledge that surround him.

Tomkins discusses the traumatic effects on development when excitement and interest are reduced to the point that the individual feels shame whenever they threaten to be activated. "This source of shame becomes critical when . . . socialization radically restricts the free movement of the child" (1963, 194). "The Counterpane" episode in *Moby-Dick* is a good example of how the natural curiosity and activity of the child might be blocked by a shaming punishment that restricts its freedom of movement. The fascination with the glass ship in *Redburn* involves a similar configuration of elements: an actively—perhaps overly—curious child and the inhibiting presence of the mother. The memory is recalled at the end of the opening chapter, which, as we have shown, is marked by imagery that stresses incorporation through the gaze. The glass ship, the narrator tells us, was for him a particular source of compulsive interest, indulged in until it became destructive.

A similar theme is touched on in *Pierre*, where Isabel describes how, as a child, she felt compelled, by curiosity and the sense of something momentous but undefinable being concealed from her, to dismantle her guitar and examine the inside: "Thou know'st that it is not at all uncommon for children to break their dearest playthings in order to gratify a half-crazy curiosity to find out what is in the hidden heart of them. . . . Seized with this sudden whim, I unscrewed the part I showed thee, and peeped in, and saw 'Isabel'" (148). Here, unconscious curiosity and shame—the shame that motivates the family policy of hiding and covering up that is depicted in the novel—are intimately related: it is through the discovery of her real name that Isabel begins to pierce the secret of her paternity, which had been concealed from her by her father's fear of exposure and disgrace. The same theme of curiosity about something secret and hidden occurs, though in a comic vein, in "I and My Chimney": "Though standing in the heart of this house, though hitherto we have all nestled about it, unsuspicious of aught hidden within, this chimney may or may not have a secret closet. But if it have, it is my kinsman's. To break into that wall, would be to break into his breast" (*PT*, 376). Redburn describes the glass ship as a similarly mysterious and cryptic object, and one that is the focus of the greatest general admiration and even awe:

> This ship, after being the admiration of my father's visitors in the capital, became the wonder and delight of all the people of the village where we now resided, many of whom used to call upon my mother, for no other purpose than to see the ship. And well did it repay the long and curious examination which they were accustomed to give it. (*R*, 7–8)

The repetition of the words "wonder" and "wonderful" in this part of the text, as in the earlier passage, emphasizes, in an almost obsessive manner, a fascination that is clearly analogous to the hungry fixation expressed in the outsized eyes of the "wonderful" traveler. One of the most fascinating things about the ship is that "every bit of it was glass," "a great wonder of itself" (8), and the narrator describes the object in a way that suggests, indeed, a certain compulsiveness and a dangerous mesmerizing fascination, as he lovingly goes over "the tall masts, and yards, and rigging of this famous ship, among whose mazes of spun-glass I used to rove in imagination, till I grew dizzy at the main-truck" (8). The glassiness of the object has a magical quality to it that particularly suggests a visual absorption or devouring, and Redburn displays an intrusive wanting to know that is characteristic of the wish to conquer and incorporate idealized objects. The passage reveals that Redburn wishes to break into the object and become enriched by the contents: "I made no doubt, that if I could but once pry open the hull, and break the glass all to pieces, I would infallibly light upon something wonderful, perhaps some gold guineas, of which I have always been in want, ever since I could remember" (8). Ultimately, his curiosity and fascination threaten to overwhelm him: "And I often used to feel a sort of insane desire to be the death of the glass ship, case, and all, in order to come at the plunder; and one day, throwing out some hint of the kind to my sisters, they ran to my mother in a great clamor; and after that, the ship was placed on the mantle-piece for a time, beyond my reach, and until I should recover my reason" (8).

As Wurmser understands it, then, in those who are subject to severe feelings of shame, wishes for expression and perception—to look and be looked at, to listen and to be listened to—come to focus on the failure to secure a loving response from the object, and thus increasingly take on aggressive urges for union, power, and destruction. The association of looking with wishes for merger and for power and destruction is an important aspect of the visual imagery in *Billy Budd*. The story opens with the theme of the handsome sailor, a charismatic figure who is presented as a cynosure for all admiring eyes. Visual merger and idealization are explicitly linked in this opening passage, as they are elsewhere in the story, whenever it is the crew's love of Billy that is in question. Kohut points out that idealization has a harmonizing role in social groups, as it has the power to curb "certain exquisitely painful experiences of narcissistic imbalance," such as jealousy and envy (1978, 798). This role is exemplified in the conflict between Billy Budd and Red Whiskers on the *Rights of Man,* as recounted by Captain Graveling:

> Before I shipped that young fellow, my forecastle was a rat-pit of quarrels. It was black times, I tell you, aboard the Rights here. . . . But Billy came; and it was like a Catholic priest striking peace in an Irish shindy. Not that he preached to them or said or did anything in particular; but a virtue went out of him, sugaring the sour ones. They took to him like hornets to treacle; all but the buffer of the gang, the big shaggy chap with the fire-red whiskers. He indeed, out of envy, perhaps, of the newcomer . . . must needs bestir himself in trying to get up an ugly row with him. (*BB*, 47)

After Billy gives him a curative drubbing, Red Whiskers is converted as well: "And will you believe it, Lieutenant, the Red Whiskers now really loves Billy—loves him. . . . But they all love him. . . . Anybody will do anything for Billy Budd; and it's the happy family here. . . . Ay, Lieutenant, you are going to take away the jewel of 'em; you are going to take away my peacemaker" (47). The oral imagery in the passage quoted above—"a virtue went out of him, sugaring the sour ones. They took to him like hornets to treacle" (47)—is quite consistent with the idea of an idealizing merger with the charismatic object. Billy, in his role as peacemaker, serves as a sort of commonly held ego ideal "to which all individuals look up, and to whose greatness they all submit in shared admiration and submission" (Kohut 1978, 798). Painful feelings of jealousy and envy are thus averted. This theme culminates in the merger with Billy at the moment of his execution, when the crew responds in unison to his

> conventional felon's benediction directed aft towards the quarters of honor. . . . Without volition, as it were, as if indeed the ship's populace were but the vehicles of some vocal current electric, with one voice from alow and aloft came a resonant sympathetic echo: "God bless Captain Vere!" And yet at that instant Billy alone must have been in their hearts, even as in their eyes. (*BB*, 123)

The counterexample to this harmonizing role is, of course, the tragic theme of the story. The staring of admiration and union, the subject of the opening section of the story, contrasts with the aggressively charged staring manifested in Claggart's look of envy. As noted, the etymology of envy *(invidia, invidere)* suggests the link between this painful feeling and its scopophilic basis. In Claggart, to recapitulate our argument, potential feelings of love towards the idealized object have been converted, through contempt and disgust, into envy and hatred. This transformation is depicted in Claggart's glance as he watches Billy ambling along the deck:

> When Claggart's unobserved glance happened to light on belted Billy rolling along the upper gun deck in the leisure of the second dogwatch, exchanging passing broadsides of fun with other young promenaders in the crowd, that glance would follow the cheerful sea Hyperion with a settled meditative and melancholy expression, his eyes strangely suffused with incipient feverish tears. Then would Claggart look like the man of sorrows. Yes, and sometimes the melancholy expression would have in it a touch of soft yearning, as if Claggart could even have loved Billy but for fate and ban. But this was an evanescence, and quickly repented of, as it were, by an immitigable look, pinching and shrivelling the visage into the momentary semblance of a wrinkled walnut. (87–88)

This "immitigable look" brings to mind the look of envy or resentment as depicted by Lacan, who invokes the famous passage from Augustine's *Confessions* (bk. 1, chap. 7): "I have seen with my own eyes and known very well an infant in the grip of jealousy: he could not yet speak, and already he observed his foster-brother, pale and with an envenomed stare" (quoted in Lacan 1977, 20). As another translation puts it, "he would grow pale with envy" (Augustine 1961, 28). In the envenomed stare of *invidia* we witness a distortion of the scopophilic wish to be enthusiastically enriched, through visual merger, by the strength and value of the idealized object. As Lacan comments on the passage from Augustine: "Thus, with the *infans* (pre-verbal) stage of early childhood, the situation of spectacular absorption is permanently tied: the child observed, the emotional reaction (pale), and this reactivation of images of primordial frustration (with an envenomed stare) that are psychical and somatic co-ordinates of original aggressivity" (1977, 20). "With an envenomed stare" is a translation of *amare conspectu*, literally, 'with a bitter look.' Such a look, as Lacan describes it elsewhere, with reference to the same passage from *The Confessions*, "seems to tear [the subject] to pieces and has on himself the effect of a poison. Such is true envy—the envy that makes the subject pale before the image of a completeness closed upon itself" (1978, 116). And so it is with Claggart's monomania, which, "like a subterranean fire, was eating its way deeper and deeper in him. Something decisive must come of it" (*BB*, 90).

Both Kohut and Wurmser link visual fusion to "the wish to reestablish the omnipotent 'self-object'" (Wurmser 1981, 154), a wish that is clear in Redburn's aggressive looking and his self-assertion through intense identification with idealized figures. The spell the glass ship casts over him, as someone who shores up his vulnerable sense of self through a narcissistic overvaluation of his family's grandeur, is ultimately due to its status as a family heirloom. The aura of the object is derived from its having been passed down from an important idealized figure, the famous Senator Wellingborough. The name of the ship, *La Reine,* is part of a series of references to France in this section of the novel that evoke for the young Redburn an alluring world of curiosity and wonder associated with the travels of idealized, omnipotent figures. As suggested earlier, the mother's role in the episode—she puts the glass ship out of reach—puts her in the contrasting camp of forbidding parental figures, like Ishmael's stepmother in *Moby-Dick.* Her role is that of restricting the child's freedom of movement, and in relation to her little Redburn feels small, weak, and impotent.

This feeling of powerlessness brings his thoughts about the glass ship to their conclusion. Ultimately, the importance of the ship, a symbol associated with the paternal imago and with his own grandiose aspirations associated with travel, is related, as he himself recognizes, to his deep feelings of disappointment at being abandoned by his parents at such a young age: by his father through death, and by a mother who has cast him out into the world. When he solemnly promises his brother he will take care of himself, he observes, "[W]hat cast-away will not promise to take care of himself, when he sees that unless he himself does, no one else will" (*R*, 11). Redburn identifies with the ship's "figure-head, a gallant warrior in a cocked-hat," who "lies pitching head-foremost down into the trough of a calamitous sea under the bows" (9). The figurehead, according to his sisters, "fell from his perch the very day" Redburn left home to go to sea on his first voyage (9). Redburn interprets the "secret sympathy" between the two in terms of his own struggle to escape dependency and the shame that goes with it: "[B]ut I will not have him put on his legs again, till I get on my own" (9). Shame about "a weak self unable to stand on its own two feet," as Wurmser points out, is one the basic forms pertaining to shame's contents: the fear and pain of "a symbiotically bound self that tries to struggle free," along with the shame associated with toilet training and castration anxiety, coincides "developmentally with the first visible emergence of shame" (1987, 85). We have already looked at this imagery of standing on one's own legs in relation to the attempt to overcome shame by aggressively striking a fighting stance; the most dramatic example of this particular manifestation of the shame/pride axis—the attempt, as Nathanson sees it, to master shame through the illusion of pride—is the intensely oppositional and confrontational attitude of the maimed Ahab in *Moby-Dick*. Another defensive structure is apparent in the early parts of Redburn: defense through idealization. Let us explore some of its further implications.

In such a case, as Kohut explains it, the perfection associated with the equilibrium of primary narcissism is transferred "to an admired omnipotent (transitional) self-object: *the idealized parent imago*" (1971, 25). This pattern of idealization—the seeking of personal aggrandizement through merger with an idealized parental surrogate—runs throughout Melville's work, and is a particular source of irony in *Redburn*. The wonderful traveler Redburn rudely stares at is the first in a series of such admired figures in the novel. As we have seen, traveling is generally associated with idealized paternal figures in the novel. Indeed, just before he recalls his fascination with the wonderful traveler, he recounts a scene in which he was standing with his father—basking proudly, as it were, in the shadow of the omnipotent selfobject. "[O]n the wharf when a large ship was getting under way, and rounding the head of the pier. . . . I remembered how I thought of their crossing the great ocean; and that very ship, and those very sailors, so near to me then, would after a time be actually in Europe" (4–5). He reminisces how his father, "now dead, had several times crossed the Atlantic on business affairs" and how "he used to tell my brother and me of the monstrous waves at sea, mountain high; of the masts bending like twigs; and all about Havre, and Liverpool, and about going up into the hall of St Paul's in London" (5). The association of his idealized father with traveling is explicit, of course, when he arrives in Liverpool and uses his father's map and guidebook to tour the city: "Among the old volumes in my father's library, was a collection of old European and English guide-books, which he had bought on his travels, a great many years ago. In my childhood, I went through my courses of studying them, and never tired of gazing at the numerous quaint embellishments and plates, and staring at the strange title-pages" (141). When he folds his father's old map, he does it "reverentially." Earlier in the novel, as he goes through the Narrows of New York Harbor into the Atlantic Ocean, he paints his father in the most idealized terms, as an all-powerful, beneficent, all-knowing figure: "But then I remembered, how many times my own father had said he had crossed the ocean; and I had never dreamed of such a thing as doubting him; for I always thought him *a marvellous being, infinitely purer and greater than I was, who could not by any possibility do wrong, or say an untruth*" (34; emphasis added). In this same passage of the novel, he recalls the uncle who was a "sea-captain, with white hair, who used to sail to a place called Archangel in Russia. . . . he was the very first sea-captain I had ever seen, and his white hair and fine handsome florid face made so strong an impression upon me, that I have never forgotten him, though I only saw him during this one visit of his to New York" (35). He associates this uncle with a visit he made with him and his father to a fort overlooking the Narrows, a place that has become intensely idealized in his memory: "It was a beautiful place, as I remembered it, and very wonderful and romantic, too, as it appeared to me, when I went there with my uncle" (35). At the end of this remembrance, he speaks in the most idealized terms of the "sky overhead" as "blue as my mother's eyes" and muses over the lost paradise of his childhood: "I was so glad and happy then. But I must not think of those delightful days, before my father became a bankrupt, and died, and we removed from the city; for when I think of those days, something rises up in my throat and almost strangles me" (36).

Aboard ship, this hunger for idealized objects is transferred to Captain Riga, who is—at least until he rudely discredits himself in the eyes of his beseeching admirer—an obvious choice as a parental surrogate for Redburn. In his longing to make contact with this inaccessible figure, Redburn displays—it is a small enough detail, but one which shows again the link between idealization and visual merger with the object—a wistful form of voyeuristic peeking: "And here I may as well state, that I never saw the inside of the cabin during the whole interval that elapsed from our sailing till our return to New York; though I often used to get a peep at it through a little pane of glass" (69–70). Redburn is not the only one to take a peek into the captain's cabin, but it is telling that his particular manner of looking evinces a yearning distinctly absent from the amusement and scorn with which the rest of the crew regard the spectacle inside: "And it used to be the great amusement of the sailors to look in through the pane of glass, when they stood at the wheel, and watch the proceedings in the cabin" (70).

Billy's attitude toward Vere, during and after his encounter with Claggart, is clearly an expression of the same archaic idealization that we find in Redburn. However, the tone surrounding Billy's relation to Vere is almost reverential; the depiction is itself highly idealized, and the relation is even more primitive: Billy looks up to Vere with the unselfconsciousness of a child gazing up at his powerful parent, or like a faithful dog eagerly attending its master. During the drumhead court martial, which eventually decides his death sentence, Billy turns, at one point, "an appealing glance towards Captain Vere as deeming him his best helper and friend," and at another, casts a "wistful interrogative look toward" him, a look that is depicted "in its dumb expressiveness" as "not unlike that which a dog of generous breed might turn upon his master" (BB, 107).[1] In reciprocal fashion, during the earlier interrogation in the presence of Claggart, Captain Vere takes a "fatherly tone" with Billy that touches the latter's "heart to the quick" (99). Behind this yearned-for attachment to a parental figure lurks, however, the terrifying threat of an annihilation of the self, as the passive wish for power and union through merger veers abruptly into its phobic form. For Melville's work, along with its ample evidence of an archaic wish for merger, shows all the signs of the converse: the deep-rooted fear of fascination, the fear of being overwhelmed and annihilated by the object.[2]

In its extreme form, this fear may be expressed as a fear of being transfixed, paralyzed, and frozen—turned to stone. It helps to explain, perhaps, much of the enigma of "The Counterpane" chapter in Moby-Dick. Banished to his room, and eventually dozing off in the daylight of the waning afternoon, Ishmael awakens to find himself in complete obscurity and suddenly "felt a shock running through all my frame; nothing was to be seen, and nothing was to be heard; but a supernatural hand seemed placed in mine. My arm hung over the counterpane, and the nameless, unimaginable, silent form or phantom, to which the hand belonged, seemed closely seated by my bedside" (MD, 26). The experience that triggers the nightmarish memory for Ishmael is the vaguely uncomfortable and embarrassing, though otherwise pleasurable, predicament of waking up and finding himself in Queequeg's powerful arms. In the immediately preceding chapter, Queequeg had undressed before him and exhibited his hypnotizing body to the fascinated Ishmael:

> I was all eagerness to see his face, but he kept it averted for some time while employed in unlacing the bag's mouth. This accomplished, however, he turned round—when, good heavens! what a sight! Such a face! It was of a dark, purplish, yellow color, here and there stuck over with large, blackish looking squares. Yes, it's just as I thought, he's a terrible bedfellow. . . . Meanwhile, he continued the business of undressing and at last showed his chest and arms. As I live, these covered parts of him were checkered with the same squares as his face; his back, too, was all over the same dark squares. . . . But there was no time for shuddering, for now the savage went about something that completely fascinated my attention, and convinced me that he must indeed be a heathen. Going to his heavy grego . . . he fumbled in the pockets, and produced at length a curious little deformed image with a hunch on its back. . . . I now screwed my eyes hard towards the half hidden image, feeling but ill at ease meantime—to see what was next to follow. . . . All these queer proceedings increased my uncomfortableness, and seeing him now exhibiting strong symptoms of concluding his business operations, and jumping into bed with me, I thought *it was high time*, now or never, before the light was put out, *to break the spell in which I had so long been bound*. (21–23; emphasis added)

The "spell" in which Ishmael feels he has been "so long been bound" in spying on his roommate contrasts with his frozen state of fascination, bound by another, more terrifying "spell," in the uncanny nightmarish memory that he has the next morning when he awakens in Queequeg's arms: "*For what seemed ages piled on ages*, I lay there, *frozen with the most awful fears*, not daring to drag away my hand; yet ever thinking that *If I could but stir it one single inch, the horrid spell would be broken*" (26; emphasis added).

This is the latent *fear*, then, according to Wurmser, in the realm of the scopophilic drive: the fear of being overwhelmed and petrified by a frightening archaic superego, a theme, as we have seen, most fully developed in *Pierre* with its extensive imagery of lapidary paralysis and stony ruins. As this nightmarish fear is manifested in Ishmael's memory, so, in his blossoming friendship with Queequeg, is it overcome by the *wish* in active curiosity: "Now, *take away the awful fear,* and my sensations at feeling the supernatural hand in mine were very similar, in their strangeness, to those which I experienced on waking up and seeing Queequeg's pagan arm thrown round me" (26; emphasis added). The comic triumph of the wish, of awakening in the "comical predicament" of a state of intimacy with the object of one's fascination, thus recalls for Ishmael the neurotic impediment or obstacle that has been abolished, the fear represented in the traumatic memory of the nightmare: of awakening and being frozen by a horror. Ishmael's active curiosity, to play on Wurmser's terms, triumphs over the passive fear. After recounting his nightmare Ishmael goes about describing, in a way that recalls Redburn's *shameless* staring at the goggle-eyed foreign traveler, the great enjoyment he takes in watching as his new friend gets dressed. He confesses: "I was *guilty of great rudeness; staring at him* from the bed, and watching all his toilette motions; for the time *my curiosity getting the better of my breeding.* Nevertheless, a man like Queequeg you don't see every day, he and his ways were well worth unusual regarding" (27). The point here is that shame is overcome: whereas Redburn's staring is somewhat shameless, Ishmael's unabashed looking would seem to be a healthy sign of his ability to commune again with others.

II

Fascination, then, involves both a wish or a fear, and the one, in Melville, often turns into the other. The state of being fascinated is rarely the excited and joyous communion that Ishmael finds with Queequeg, but turns out, again and again, to be a treacherous situation indeed. The theme of fascination meets us in the opening passages of *Moby-Dick.* The imagery in Ishmael's memory of being paralyzed in horror by the presence of a ghostly figure, mesmerized by a spell, frozen by a "phantom," recalls the imagery surrounding the beguiling and haunting evocation of Moby Dick in the first chapter of the novel.

On the threshold of Ishmael's journey on the *Pequod,* first evoked is the classical image of Narcissus. It is worth noting that Tomkins relates this myth to the evil eye and the taboo on looking; he sees it as an expression of the belief in "[t]he danger of the reflected look for the one who looked at his image in the water or in a mirror" (1963, 163). The image is called forth as a sort of clincher to the opening two-page ode to the fascination of water. Its hyperbolic catalog of interrogatives commencing with "Go visit" is summed up in the following passage:

> And still deeper the meaning of that story of Narcissus, who be-cause he could not grasp the tormenting, mild image he saw in the fountain, plunged into it and was drowned. But the same image, we ourselves see in all rivers and oceans. It is the image of the ungraspable phantom of life, and this is the key to it all. (*MD*, 5)

The idea of being fascinated to the point of plunging into an enchanting illusory reflection[3] recurs in chapter 35 ("The Mast-Head") where the oceanic feeling produced by the view of a glittering expanse of water has a hypnotizing, fascinating, lulling, and ultimately treacherous effect on the gazer. The image of the "ungraspable phantom of life" evokes the implication of futility in Ovid's description of an image "Vain and illusive" (*Metamorphoses* 3.450) that "is only shadow, / Only reflection, lacking any substance" (3.434–35). This ghost image is explicitly linked to the whale at the end of the chapter by the figure of "one grand hooded phantom, like a snow hill in the air" (*MD*, 7); and the same sort of image reappears at the end of chapter 41 ("Moby-Dick"), where the question of the crew's fascination with the same "gliding great demon of the seas of life" is raised and then skirted by the narrator. The whale is depicted throughout as an entrancing and omnipotent object, and the image of Narcissus at the beginning of the novel speaks, it would seem, to the tragic implications of precisely such a fascinatory situation.

Ahab himself is quite often captured in the Narcissus-like pose of fixedly gazing over the edge of the ship into the water. In chapter 132 ("Symphony"), for example, Ahab leans over the side to gaze on his reflection: "Slowly crossing the deck from the scuttle, Ahab leaned over the side, and watched how his shadow in the water sank and sank to his gaze, the more and the more that he strove to pierce the profundity" (543). The image of his reflection elusively sinking to his gaze as he makes a vain effort to grasp it is an explicit repetition of the opening image of a tantalizing phantom image that recedes beyond one's grasp. Like Narcissus, Ahab drops "a tear into the sea, nor did all the Pacific contain such wealth as that one wee drop" (543).

In the same chapter, Ahab also searches for a human image of himself in Starbuck's eye, and unable to find it, "crossed the deck to gaze over on the other side; but stared at two reflected, fixed eyes in the water there. Fedellah was motionless leaning over the same rail" (545). Ahab is both a fascinator himself and subject to fascination; he seems "an independent lord; the Parsee but his slave" (538), and yet, "as Ahab's eyes so awed the crew's, the inscrutable Parsee's glance awed his" (537); together, in a demonic parody of the Ishmael-Queequeg twinship, "both seemed yoked together, and an unseen tyrant driving them; the lean shade siding the solid rib" (538).

Melville's haunting image of Narcissus may also have been inspired by Milton's reworking of the Ovid passage in Eve's narration of her dream in *Paradise Lost*. It includes the idea of being fascinated and drawn magically and irresistibly to water:

> That day I oft remember, when from sleep
> I first awak't, and found myself repos'd
> Under a shade on flow'rs, much wond'ring where
> And what I was, whence thither brought, and how.
> Not distant far from thence a murmuring sound
> Of waters issu'd from a Cave and spread
> Into a liquid Plain, then stood unmov'd
> Pure as th' expanse of Heav'n; I thither went
> With unexperienc't thought, and laid me down
> On the green bank, to look into the clear
> Smooth Lake, that to me seem'd another Sky.
>   (4.449–59)

She says that if left uninterrupted, her attention unbroken, there she would have "fixt" her "eyes till now." This sense of being irresistibly drawn and fixed is, of course, precisely what we get in the disquisition on the magnetic attraction of water that opens *Moby-Dick*:

Once more. Say, you are in the country; in some high land of lakes. Take almost any path you please, and ten to one it carries you down in a dale, and leaves you there by a pool in the stream. There is magic in it. Let the most absent-minded of men be plunged in his deepest reveries—stand that man on his legs, set his feet a-going, and he will infallibly lead you to water, if water there be in all that region. (*MD*, 4)

A single word here—"plunged"—links reverie, through the passage in Ovid, to narcissistic fascination: the image of "the most absent-minded of men . . . plunged in his deepest reveries" and the image, evoked later, of Narcissus who "plunged into [the pool] and was drowned." The allusion to Narcissus, as noted, is posed as an apparently conclusive one at the close of a rhetorical catalog describing a mass exodus of the populace from domestic securities to the treacherous *charms* of the sea.

> Circumambulate the city of a dreamy Sabbath afternoon. . . . What do you see?—Posted like silent sentinels all around the town, stand *thousand upon thousands of mortal men fixed in ocean reveries.* Some leaning against spiles; some seated upon the pier-heads; some looking over the bulwarks of ships from China; some high aloft in the rigging, as if striving to get a still better seaward peep. But these are all landsmen; of week days pent up in lath and plaster—tied to counters, nailed to benches, clinched to desks. How then is this? Are the green fields gone? what do they here?
>
> But look! here come more crowds, pacing straight for the water, and seemingly bound for a dive. Strange! Nothing will content them but the extremest limit of the land; loitering under the shady lee of yonder warehouses will not suffice. No. They must get just as nigh the water as they possibly can without falling in. And there they stand—miles of them—leagues. Inlanders all, they come from lanes and alleys, streets and avenues—north, east, south, and west. Yet here they all unite. Tell me, *does the magnetic virtue in the needles of the compasses of all those ships attract them thither?* (4; emphasis added)

The dreaminess of the "Sabbath afternoon," the fixity of the gaze in reverie, the magnetic attraction of the water, and the possibility of falling in are all characteristic features in Melville of this mesmeric, entrancing mood threatening to hold the attention in a state of dangerous, potentially fatal, fascination. The book moves, as Harold Beaver puts it, "from trance to trance," from its opening in which "the valley of the Saco lies 'thus tranced' to "its demoniac close, when Ahab Narcissus-like is plunged into the sea" (1986, 701).

Over thirty years after *Moby-Dick*, the idea of "men fixed in ocean reveries" reappears in connection with a certain suspicious dreaminess in Captain Vere's character in *Billy Budd:*

> Captain Vere though practical enough upon occasion would at times betray *a certain dreaminess of mood.* Standing alone on the weather side of the quarterdeck, one hand holding by the rigging *he would absently gaze off at the blank sea.* At the presentation to him then of some minor matter interrupting the current of thoughts *he would show more or less irascibility; but instantly he would control it.* (61; emphasis added)

Later, while the troubled drumhead court is making its painful deliberations, Vere "for the time stood—unconsciously with his back toward them, apparently in one of his absent fits—gazing out from a sashed porthole to windward upon the monotonous blank of the twilight sea" (109). Vere's mysterious moments of absence provide us with one more proof that "Meditation and water are wedded for ever," as the narrator proclaims at the beginning of *Moby-Dick.* The show of quickly controlled anger in the captain's reaction to being interrupted in his meditation is also part of the larger paradigm we been trying to outline: it suggests a propensity to rage characteristic of so many of Melville's characters, a propensity, as we have shown, best explained in terms of shame-anger.

We touch here, indirectly, on the biological function of shame. That it is an interruption of his meditation—indeed, of a visual state of fascination—that triggers Vere's anger and brings him back to himself and his surround is thoroughly consistent with Tomkins's understanding of the innate affect *shame-humiliation* as "a mechanism that throws the organism into a painful experience of inner tension by attempting to reduce the possibilities for positive affect in situations when compelling reasons for that positive affect remain" (1963, 139–41). In this way, the organism is able to control "its affective output so that it will not remain interested or content when it may not be safe to do so." However, if the expressive-perceptual drives have been traumatically blocked in some way, their operation may be largely devoted to avoiding or defending against overwhelming and unbearable feelings of shame that have become internalized. Shame as a mechanism, in such a case, may be, in certain contexts, overruled or denied—by the all-compelling need to be at one with another, or to have power over another, or to annihilate another—and the subject may well remain in a state of fascination "by whatever had triggered its interest" even "when it may not be safe to do so." One of the advantages of Wurmser's scheme, with its emphasis on archaic wishes and fears, and on the way that these drives are affected by shame, is that it enables us to relate the yearning for merger with idealized objects, as Kohut conceives it, to the insistent theme, in Melville's work, of that dangerous moment when fascination as a wish turns into its nightmarish opposite—when, in other words, the active wish becomes the passive fear.

A perfect image of such a deadly turning point in fascination is offered in the description of Moby Dick when, near the end of the novel, he makes at last his long anticipated appearance. The whale is portrayed as a fascinating but treacherous object, another one of Melville's confidence men, whose mask of benevolence conceals a most sinister design:

> On each soft side . . . on each bright side, the whale shed off enticings. No wonder there had been some among the hunters who namelessly transported and allured by all this serenity, had ventured to assail it; but had fatally found that quietude but the vesture of tornadoes. Yet calm, enticing calm, oh, whale! thou glidest on, to all who for the first time eye thee, no matter how many in that same way thou may'st have bejuggled and destroyed before. (*MD*, 548)

Such a serene feeling of calm, or "haunted mood" (*PT*, 75) as it is called in "Benito Cereno," is almost always accompanied in Melville by a sense of threat, as though the state of fascination were an inherently dangerous one.

The connection between the overvaluation of idealized objects and such a dangerous state of captivation is perhaps most dramatically dramatized in "Benito Cereno." One critic says that when Babo is present, Cereno is "transfixed by what he sees there, helpless as a bird before the snake," and it is only by "a last spasmodic effort of the will" that at the last moment he "breaks the spell and throws himself overboard" (Bowen 1960, 203). Delano is even more clearly a victim of fascination. Idealistic to a point of *scotoma*, he is held in thrall by an ambiguous spectacle behind which is set a deathly trap. If Babo exploits to his destructive and vindictive ends a fascinatory, exhibitionistic power that aims at magically overwhelming his victim, Captain Delano unwittingly does his very best to help him along. The two illustrate, in a truly cautionary way, what it means when, for the shame-damaged self, the perceptual and expressive drives have become "mere vehicles for union, power, and destruction" (Wurmser 1981, 164). In this connection, there is an emblematic moment in the story when Delano, lulled in the midst of the calm sea into a state of dreamy enchantment, finds himself dreamily gazing out over the water, like Captain Vere meditatively staring out to sea. As one enchanting image after another "flitted through his mind, as the cat's-paw through the calm, gradually he felt rising a dreamy inquietude, like that of one who alone on the prairie feels unrest from the repose of noon" (*PT,* 74). Leaning "against the carved balustrade," he again looks off for his boat, but finds "his eye falling upon the ribbon grass. . . . Trying to break one charm, he was but becharmed anew." Delano's enchantment here is an extension of the general state of captivation that seems to leave him so haplessly perplexed by the enigmatic signs of treachery that crowd in on him from all sides. Thinking that "something moved nigh the chains," "He rubbed his eyes and looked hard," but is unable to make sense of the "imperfect gesture towards the balcony" made by one of the sailors, who then "vanished into the recesses of the hempen forest, like a poacher" (74). Then, as he eagerly bends forward once again to catch sight of his boat, "the balustrade gave way before him like charcoal." Only "an outreaching rope" (75) that he clutches on to prevents him from falling into the sea.

Such visual and meditative engrossment in connection with a catastrophic and fatal drop into the sea is a recurrent theme in Melville, and comes up more than once in *Moby-Dick*. The inducing of such states is usually associated with a certain scopophilic element. "Benito Cereno," like *Billy Budd*, is full of visual imagery. In particular, the deception practiced on Delano by Babo and his agents depends largely on optical effects. We spoke at some length in chapter 4 of the possible intertextual relations of this extraordinary story with Shakespeare's *Othello*. One of the critical turning points in the play is when Othello demands from Iago some "ocular proof"; this allows Iago to set the snare that seals the downfall of his paranoid superior. For the paranoid and the suspicious, seeing is indeed believing. The same goes for the overtrusting. Delano, who is the very reverse of paranoid, resembles the man described in *The Confidence-Man*, who, upon finding his wife in bed with her lover, only *begins* to suspect. In contrast to Othello, Delano's delusions take the form of a sort of anxious denial of all treachery by an at times ludicrous insistence on the ubiquity of trust and gratitude. In his case, the scopophilic drive shows all the signs of having become a mere vehicle for union or merger with others. He idealizes the other; he is—to a pathological extent—all too ready to trust the other; he is overconfident, overgenerous, overgrateful, and his readiness to take as credible proof of reality the trompe-l'oeil that is presented to him makes him the perfect victim of Babo's mesmerizing sleight of hand. Like Othello, he is all too susceptible to visual evidence, no matter how flimsy and circumstantial; the difference is that while Othello believes "the handkerchief" because he is paranoid, Delano overlooks the most manifest signs of treachery because he is not nearly suspicious enough; he prefers instead the heartwarming scene of loving fidelity that is staged for his benefit. The danger of a one-sided view of reality, so clearly demonstrated here, is, of course, one of Melville's most important themes; it is central in *Moby-Dick*, as well as in *The Confidence-Man*, and it is invariably linked to this idea of *denial*, very much in a psychoanalytic sense—the denial of unpleasant and extremely painful truth or reality. This explains the almost remedial insistence, powerfully illustrated in "The Try-Works" and "Doubloon" chapters, on an equilibrium struck among competing one-sided perspectives on reality.

In contrast to Delano is Vere in his dealings with Claggart. In his plot to frame Billy, Claggart paints a fascinating picture of treachery and mutiny; he is clearly relying on the sort of paranoia in the victim of his confidence that, in *Othello*, fits Iago's purposes like a glove. Vere, however, is not an Othello, nor for that matter a Delano. He is Melville's attempt—if not always an entirely convincing one—to show us a deeply judicious and integrated personality, a man not too ready to believe another nor too ready to mistrust his own eyes; for him an incomplete picture is presumptive evidence only and must be put to the test of reality. He is a man whose eyes and ear are for seeing and knowing the world, and not "mere vehicles for union, power, and destruction" (Wurmser 1981, 164).

Doubtless, the most memorable example of the risks that attend those who are too easily fascinated and entranced is chapter 35 ("The Mast-Head") in *Moby-Dick*. This cautionary parable spells out what can happen when the organ of perception is used not to know and explore the world but to bring on a feeling-state of harmonious at-oneness with objects. One of the things that defines shame is the experience of acute and painful self-consciousness or objective self-awareness, just as one of the things that defines contempt is a trenchant pulling away from the object. Thus, in both shame and contempt the separation of subject and object is particularly pronounced. It is therefore easy to see how, in a situation where the most important goal is to minimize negative affect, the inducing of a state of fusion or merger that abolishes this separation might be used as a particularly effective defense against shame.

> Beware of enlisting in your vigilant fisheries any lad with lean brow and hollow eye; given to unseasonable meditativeness. . . . Beware of such an one, I say: your whales must be seen before they can be killed; and this sunken-eyed Platonist will tow you ten wakes round the world, and never make you one pint of sperm the richer. . . . those young Platonists have a notion that their vision is imperfect; they are short-sighted; what use, then, to strain the visual nerve? They have left their opera-glasses at home. . . . lulled into such an opium-like listlessness of vacant, unconscious reverie is this absent-minded youth by the blending cadence of waves with thoughts, that at last he loses his identity; takes the mystic ocean at his feet for the visible image of that deep, blue, bottomless soul, pervading mankind and nature; and every strange, half-seen gliding beautiful thing that eludes him; every dimly-discovered, uprising fin of some undiscernible form, seems to him the embodiment of those elusive thoughts that only people the soul by continually flitting through it. In this enchanted mood, the spirit ebbs away to whence it came. . . . Over Descartian vortices you hover. And perhaps, at mid-day, in the fairest weather, with one half-throttled shriek you drop through that transparent air into the summer sea, no more to rise for ever. Heed it well, ye Pantheists. (*MD*, 158–59)

Melville himself, it should be noted, suffered from great eye strain throughout his life; reading small print made his eyes, as he observes in a letter to Evert Duyckinck, as "tender as young sparrows" (*Corr.*, 119; 24 February

1849). But the problem with Melville's young pantheists is shortsighted-ness, and it is not primarily a sign of physical disability. It is an indication that the "sunken-eyed Platonist" uses his sight not for *seeing* and knowing the world out there but—in taking "the mystic ocean at his feet for the visible image of that deep, blue, bottomless soul, pervading mankind and nature"—for inducing a meditative feeling-state of union with that world. *Platonism* and *pantheism* are merely metaphysical labels for the deep yearn-ing for merger with idealized objects. At the height of enchantment the lulling rhythm of "the blending cadence of waves with thoughts" combined with the eye's captivation by the ocean's blue expanse subtly induces a hyp-notic mood until, consciousness being overwhelmed, "there is no life in thee, now, except that rocking life imparted by a gently rolling ship" (*MD*, 159). The danger of such a fascinatory predicament is then dramatically brought into focus: what breaks the trance is shock and terror, the sudden realization of the danger of imminent death, which suddenly startles the dreamer out of his dream. "But while this sleep, this dream is on ye, move your foot or hand an inch; slip your hold at all; and your identity comes back in horror" (159).

A similar episode occurs in *White-Jacket*, when the narrator, who lies "one hundred feet above," slips into a trance, "now dozing, now dreaming" (77):

> Perhaps I was half conscious at last of a tremulous voice hailing the main-royal-yard from the *top*. But if so, the consciousness glided away from me, and left me in Lethe. But when, like lightning, the yard dropped under me, and instinctively I clung with both hands to the *"tie,"* then I came to myself with a rush, and felt something like a choking hand at my throat. For an instant I thought the Gulf Stream in my head was whirling me away to eternity; but the next moment I found myself standing; the yard had descended to the *cap* and shaking myself in my jacket, I felt unharmed and alive. (77)

In a letter to Hawthorne, Melville cites Goethe's "Live in the all" and employs the same imagery of pantheistic merger that we find in "The Mast-Head" passage: "That is to say, your separate identity is but a wretched one,—good; but get out of yourself, spread and expand yourself, and bring to yourself the tinglings of life that are felt in the flowers and the woods, that are felt in the planets Saturn and Venus, and the Fixed Stars" (*Corr.*, 193; [1? June] 1851). The context—he is addressing Hawthorne—is not incidental here. As we shall explore more fully below, the occasion is quite precisely one in which Melville is drawing strength from a merger with his friend. Melville immediately pokes fun at himself, as though to guard against having perhaps risked a certain embarrassing self-exposure in such an emotional display: "As with all great genius, there is an immense deal of flummery in Goethe, and in proportion to my own contact with him, a monstrous deal of it in me" (193–94). In the postscript, he warns against the dangers of any "universal application of [such a] temporary feeling and opinion" (194). We find the same kind of thing, for example, in his finding himself, after hearing him lecture, "very agreeably disappointed in Mr. Emerson" (121). His grudging admiration of "this Plato who talks thro' his nose" (122) reveals both a sympathy for such an unabashed idealism and an instinctive suspiciousness of such deceiving and potentially dangerous feeling-states.

The theme of dangerous fascination as it is developed in "The Mast-Head" chapter recalls a passage in *Redburn*. There is the same spell cast on the eye by the hypnotic calm of the ocean, powerful enough ultimately to overwhelm the consciousness and completely entrance the subject. "Nor could I imagine," Redburn wonders as he contemplates the gentle rolling of the water, "how any thing that seemed so playful and placid, could be lashed into rage, and troubled into rolling avalanches of foam, and great cascades of waves, such as I saw in the end" (64). Lurking beneath the surface of such reassuring tranquility is, significantly, a treacherous rage. Redburn then describes how he is lulled into a dreamlike state. He depicts it as a state of fascination, a spell in which he is controlled from outside, almost as though he had become a manipulated object under hypnotic command: "I felt as if in a dream all the time; and when I could shut the ship out, almost thought I was in some new, fairy world, and expected to hear myself called to, out of the clear blue air, or from the depths of the deep blue sea" (64). At one point, the spell of fascination is broken and Redburn is brought back to himself and his surroundings. In this case, it is the mate who tears the greenhorn from his dreamy state and triggers what is clearly a feeling of shame—a state of confusion and perplexity that leaves him speechless and makes him feel foolish and stupid. The mate "ordered me to do a great many simple things, none of which could I comprehend, owing to the queer words he used; and then, seeing me stand quite perplexed and confounded, he would roar out to me, and call me all manner of names, and the sailors would laugh and wink to each other" (65).

This pattern of falling into a state of fascination—of enchantment, of charm, of hypnotic trance—that is then suddenly disrupted and revealed to be fraught with peril is particularly notable in *Moby-Dick*. In "The Grand Armada" chapter, for example, Ishmael's boat is drawn by a whale struck in the hunt into the midst of "a still, becharmed calm which it was impossible not to marvel at. Like household dogs [the whales] came snuffling round us, right up to our gunwales, and touching them; till it almost seemed that some spell had suddenly domesticated them" (*MD*, 387). Caught up in their absorption with the wondrous world that "met our eyes as we gazed over the side," the whalers find themselves in close observation of the nursing whales and their cubs engaged in the most intimate domestic pleasures. The vision induces a feeling-state of serene and peaceful harmony in the crew, and in Ishmael, as we noted in our earlier discussion of this passage, it takes the form of a profound state of narcissistic equilibrium and joy. But the spell ("as we thus lay entranced" [389])—consistent with the pattern we are suggesting—is then abruptly and violently broken by the signs of danger, "the occasional sudden frantic spectacles in the distance," and the ensuing eruption of a wounded whale into the heart of the head, "in the extraordinary agony of his wound . . . now dashing among the revolving circle like the lone mounted desperado Arnold, at the battle of Saratoga, carrying dismay wherever he went" (389).

In "The Try-Works" chapter, the fascinating object is not something apparently benign or beautiful, but evil itself. As Melville confesses in his review of Hawthorne's *Mosses:* "Now it is that blackness in Hawthorne, of which I have spoken, that so *fixes and fascinates* me" (*PT*, 244; emphasis added). So Ishmael finds himself fatally transfixed by the hypnotic vision of evil incarnate blazing in the darkness as he stands at the tiller:

> Wrapped, for that interval, in darkness myself, I but the better saw the redness, the madness, the ghastliness of others. The continual sight of the fiend shapes before me, capering half in smoke and half in fire, these at last begat kindred visions in my soul, so soon as I began to yield to that unaccountable drowsiness which ever would come over me at a midnight helm. (*MD*, 423)

Ishmael starts from sleep, "horribly conscious of something fatally wrong" and "A stark, bewildered feeling, as of death, came over me. Convulsively my hands grasped the tiller, but with the crazy conceit that the tiller was, somehow, in some enchanted way, inverted" (424). Righting the ship, he feels glad and grateful at being relieved "from this unnatural hallucination of the night, and the fatal contingency of being brought by the lee!" The proverbial wisdom offered by the narrator at the end of the chapter concerns the dangers of being fascinated by looking "too long in the face of the fire," of becoming engrossed with a demonic image of the human compulsion to self-destruction. The episode is a commentary, of course, on the hypnotic charismatic hold that Ahab, bent on power and self-annihilation, has over the crew. But the optical emphasis in this episode, which is all about looking and not looking, underscores the importance of the scopophilic drive, expressed here as a fear of being overwhelmed by the fascinating object: "Give not thyself up, then, to fire, lest it invert thee, deaden thee; as for the time it did me" (425).

In the idealizing transference, according to Kohut, "the psyche saves a part of the lost experience of global narcissistic perfection by assigning it to an archaic, rudimentary (transitional) self-object, the idealized parent imago. Since all bliss and power now reside in the idealized object, the child feels empty and powerless when he is separated from it and he attempts, therefore, to maintain a continuous union with it" (1971, 37). In Melville, the yearning for such a union often takes on a definite erotic coloring. The poem "After the Pleasure Party," for example, is a poignant if somewhat tortured expression of this deep longing, couched in romantic and explicitly sexual terms. The use of the classical topos based on Aristophanes' account of the origin of love in the *Symposium* evokes a particularly forceful image of the wish for union:

> Could I remake me! or set free
> This sexless bound in sex, then plunge
> Deeper than Sappho, in a lunge
> Piercing Pan's paramount mystery!
> For, Nature, in no shallow surge
> Against thee either sex may urge,
> Why hast thou made us but in halves—
> Co-relatives? This makes us slaves.

If these co-relatives never meet
Selfhood itself seems incomplete.
And such the dicing of blind fate
Few matching halves here meet and mate.
What Cosmic jest or Anarch blunder
The human integral clove asunder
And shied the fractions through life's gate?
                    (*Poems*, 257)

The word "plunge" ("then plunge / deeper than Sappho") recalls Ovid's description of Narcissus, who almost *plunges* into his reflection in the water. The same kind of explicitly sexual imagery appears in "the wonderfully tender erotic fantasy" (1949, 75), as Chase calls it, of the opening passages of chapter 132 ("The Symphony") in *Moby-Dick*. The chapter concerns Ahab's temptation to give up his murderous quest and reconcile himself with a more human world of domestic concerns, and it opens with a memorable description of the union of the "feminine air" and the "murderous sea": "those two seemed one; it was only the sex, as it were, that distinguished them" (*MD*, 542). As in "After the Pleasure Party," erotic union here is primarily the expression of an *affective* longing.

> Aloft, like a royal czar and king, the sun seemed giving his gentle air to this bold and rolling sea; even as bride to groom. And at the girdling line of the horizon, a soft and tremulous motion—most seen here at the equator—denoted the fond, throbbing trust, the loving alarms, with which the poor bride gave her bosom away. (542)

The idealized object may or may not be another person per se. But whatever the catalyzing object, the feeling-state induced—of serenity, bliss, and power—helps to explain the association made by Redburn, in the passage examined earlier, as he gazes entranced at the peacefulness of the boundless sunny expanse of water that spreads out before him: "As I looked at it so mild and sunny, I could not help calling to mind my little brother's face, when he was sleeping an infant in the cradle. It had just such a happy, careless, innocent look" (*R*, 64). Grunberger speaks of the child as, after birth, continuing to live in "a protonarcissistic realm, identical to that of prenatal life," the maintenance of this state being "fostered by almost continual sleep" (1979, 22). This image of the sleeping infant is an idealized image of the "homeostatic narcissistic state" (22), this being the goal of merger with an idealized object. Redburn's fascination, his feeling of being in a dreamy, hypnotic, trancelike state, is linked to "a certain wonderful rising and falling of the sea," to "a sort of wide heaving and swelling and sinking all over the ocean" (*R*, 64). Recalling the fascinating glass ship, "among whose mazes of spun-glass I used to rove in imagination, till I grew dizzy at the main-truck" (8), the movement of the sea makes Redburn "almost dizzy to look at it; and yet I could not keep my eyes off it, it seemed so passing strange and wonderful" (64). The imagery throughout this passage suggests the merger of the infant with the idealized omnipotent parent, the feeling-state of harmony and fusion, for example, when one is being carried or rocked to sleep: "Let me roll around the globe, let me rock upon the sea" (66). The wonderfulness, the uncanny, *unheimlich* quality of it all, suggests, indeed, the return to the *strange, yet very familiar,* unconscious memory of an infantile, even prenatal, state of narcissistic equilibrium.

One of the best examples of such imagery is that which surrounds Billy Budd as he sleeps "like a baby" on the eve of his execution:

> Without movement, he lay as in a trance, that adolescent expression previously noted as his taking on something akin to the look of a slumbering child in the cradle when the warm hearth-glow of the still chamber at night plays on the dimples that at whiles mysteriously form in the cheek, silently coming and going there. For now and then in the gyved one's trance a serene happy light born of some wandering reminiscence or dream would diffuse itself over his face, and then wane away only anew to return. (*BB*, 119–20)

This evocation of the ideal harmony and peace experienced by the sleeping or dreaming child recalls "The Grand Armada" chapter of *Moby-Dick*. There the baby whales are compared to "human infants" who, "while suckling will calmly and fixedly gaze away from the breast, as if leading two different lives at the time; and while yet drawing mortal nourishment, be still spiritually feasting upon some unearthly reminiscence" (388). As this latter image appears to the sailors amid "circle upon circle of consternations and affrights," so the image of Billy Budd as "slumbering child in the cradle" immediately follows the discussion of the agony he has just undergone, as he lies "between the two guns, as nipped in the vice of fate" (*BB*, 119). The word *nipped* here, interestingly enough, is the word Redburn uses to describe the mortifying disappointment he has suffered at his father's sudden death— "the fruit, which with others is only blasted after ripeness, with him is nipped in the first blossom and bud" (*R*, 11)—and in the same passage from *Redburn* the image of "a scar not even the air of Paradise might erase" (11) evokes the loss of precisely the sort of blissful state of narcissistic equilibrium that the self aims at recovering through merger, a state which Redburn associates with the lost and lamented paradise of childhood, "those delightful days, before my father became a bankrupt, and died" (36). In the description of the sleeping Billy, "Billy's agony" is said to proceed "from a generous young heart's virgin experience of the diabolical incarnate and effective in some men—the tension of the agony was over now. It survived not the something healing in the closeted interview with Captain Vere" (*BB*, 119). Successful merger with the object restores narcissistic equilibrium. The merger with Captain Vere heals the scar left by Billy's traumatic encounter with Claggart, a mortifying event analogous, at least in its effect, to the one suffered by Redburn. The other example of such a healing merger we have already examined: the righting of Ishmael's emotional disorder at the beginning of *Moby-Dick* when, depressed and isolated by his feelings of shame, he finds himself suddenly "sensible of strange feelings" as he melts in love for the powerful and protective Queequeg.

III

The fascination depicted in the mass flight to water at the beginning of *Moby-Dick* involves a sort of collective self, and, as suggested earlier, it thus anticipates the group psychology that can be observed in the crew of the *Pequod*. *Moby-Dick* is, in fact, one of the best illustrations in literature of the importance of the leader for the group. Freud, in *Group Psychology and the Analysis of the Ego*, focuses on the role played by the ego ideal in the collective identification with the leader, and he remarks upon the hypnotic fascination and loss of will that accompany the idealization that characterizes "the relation of the individual member of the primal horde to the primal father" (127). Starbuck's inability, for example, to resist the pull of Ahab's

personality would appear to illustrate Freud's point that "what is thus awakened is the idea of a paramount and dangerous personality, toward whom
only a passive-masochistic attitude is possible, to whom one's will has to be
surrendered—while to be alone with him, 'to look him in the face,' appears
a hazardous enterprise" (127). This description recalls the image used in
chapter 26 when Starbuck is described as being unable to "withstand those
more terrific, because more spiritual terrors, which sometimes menace you
from the concentrating brow of an enraged and mighty man" (117). For
Ahab's power goes well beyond his authority as captain. It derives from his
charisma, a word whose dictionary meanings as "a personal magic of leadership arousing special popular loyalty or enthusiasm for a public figure or
political leader" and "a special magnetic appeal or charm"[4] accurately describe the nature of his mesmerizing hold over the crew. In chapter 46 ("Surmises") Ahab's hold on the crew is qualified to some extent; the power of
his personality does not eliminate the requirements of deception ("the full
terror of the voyage must be kept withdrawn into the obscure background")
and of the promise of "food for their more common, daily appetites" (i.e.,
"hopes of cash") (212). Ahab recognizes, with respect to the most resistant
member of that group, that

> however magnetic his ascendency in some respects was over
> Starbuck, yet that ascendency did not cover the complete spiritual
> man any more than mere corporeal superiority involves intellec-
> tual mastery. . . . Starbuck's body and Starbuck's coerced will were
> Ahab's, so long as Ahab kept his magnet at Starbuck's brain; still he
> knew that for all this the chief mate, in his soul, abhorred his
> captain's quest, and could he, would joyfully disintegrate himself
> from it, or even frustrate. (211–12)

In the words of the narrator, it is Ahab's intellect that dominates Starbuck.
It might be more precise to speak of the prevailing force of his magnetic
personality of which, as we have seen, his intellect is an instrument. It en-
feebles and neutralizes the core of the first mate's idealism, and bullies and
coerces his vulnerable "will." Incapable of resisting his own doubts and of
acknowledging, in the end, a higher power, the first mate is swept away in
the end by "the waves of the billows of the seas of the boisterous mob" (48).
    The fascinated state of the crew under Ahab resembles, in accordance

with Freud's description of group psychology, a sort of hypnotic trance, "a psychological state characterized by a relative loss of one's function of will, a phenomenon that especially operates in group structures" (Schiffer 1973, 78). As we can see here, what we call *charisma* depends on the convergence of at least these two things: a group desire for merger or union with an omnipotent selfobject, in order to be "gripped by the power of the awe-inspiring object and [become] enthusiastically enriched" (Wurmser 1981, 165); and a leader whose archaic exhibitionism cooperates with such a wish with the aim of fascinating and spellbinding the object. As a defense, the aim, in both cases, is to abolish shame, as it is in the merger with the idealized selfobject that aims at restoring narcissistic equilibrium. The wish for union may be, but is not necessarily, accompanied by aggressivity, the desire for power and destruction. As we have seen, Ahab's charisma specifically involves the so-called fighting stance or "a posture of polarized aggression," as Schiffer calls it, a posture that can be related to "a certain stage in the evolution of a child's idealizations . . . when in disillusionment, he turns from his parents in search of an extra-familial hero or heroine to adopt" (1973, 37). The polarization of aggressions, the wish

> to take sides, to declare oneself victor or victim, winner or loser, must ultimately express itself at the level of a people's projections onto their leader; the latter must in turn then become invested with a polarized stance; and the stance that heroically disposed people want from a leader is of necessity *a stand for action*. In effect, people looking for a charismatic object for this projection are searching for someone ready to fight with another person or persons and ready to become victor or victim, winner or loser. (38)

In the end, as Starbuck puts it, it is because "all of us are Ahabs" (*MD*, 623) that resistance is broken down: in other words, the group merges with Ahab in a sharing of archaic grandiosity, as his ambitions and designs happen to dovetail with the collective yearning for an archaic omnipotent figure (Kohut 1978, 834). It is precisely in these terms that Starbuck, in his soliloquy in chapter 38 ("Dusk"), admits to himself his inability to resist or oppose Ahab: "My soul is more than matched; she's overmanned; and by a madman! Insufferable sting, that sanity should ground arms on such a field! But he drilled deep down, and blasted all my reason out of me! I think I see his impious end; but feel that I must help him to it. Will I, nill I, the ineffable thing has tied me to him; tows me with a cable I have no knife to cut" (*MD*, 169).

On an individual scale, the element of "charisma," in the form of a transference of creativity, seems to have been an important dimension in Melville's relationship with Hawthorne, who had something like a magnetic hold on the younger man. Freud compares the individual's submission to the leader to the submission of a subject in the hypnotic state and to the "unlimited devotion to someone in love," relations that constitute "a group formation with two members" (115). Common to the relation to the leader and being in love is an idealizing tendency in which "the object serves as a substitute for some unattained ego ideal of our own" (112). *Moby-Dick* is, of course, dedicated to Hawthorne, "in Token of my admiration for his genius"—in token, as Harold Beaver notes, of "the same mystical bond as tied Ishmael to Ahab" (1986, 691). "The divine magnet is on you, and my magnet responds" (*Corr.*, 213), Melville writes to Hawthorne in response to his letter praising *Moby-Dick* ([17?] November 1851). An explicit expression of fascination, it is followed by a dramatic image of merger or fusion, which illustrates the (if only temporary) harmonizing role of idealization: "[W]hich [magnet] is the biggest? A foolish question—they are *One*" (213). Melville's image of magnetic attraction ("my magnet responds") to a divinely inspired figure ("The divine magnet is on you") suggests the pull, on an object-hungry self, of an idealized omnipotent object. Equally symptomatic is the fact that the letter to Hawthorne ends and then obsessively begins again ("I can't stop yet") with the confession that the writer would continue writing the letter indefinitely ("upon that endless riband I should write. . . ."). The same thing occurs in "Hawthorne and His Mosses." "But I cannot leave my subject yet," Melville writes, and prolongs the review even after it has seemed to end: "Twenty-four hours have elapsed since writing the foregoing. I have just returned from the hay mow, charged more and more with love and admiration of Hawthorne" (*PT*, 250). It is as though the subject cannot tear himself away from the object of his interest, like Ovid's Narcissus: "No thought of food, no thought of rest, can make him / Forsake the place" (*Metamorphoses* 3.438–39). As Freud puts it, "From being in love to hypnosis is evidently only a short step" (114). In both, the object is put in place of the ego ideal.

It is, of course, during this period of intense friendship that Melville's most creative and original work—*Moby-Dick* and *Pierre*—was realized. The need for the support of an idealized protector figure may have been particularly urgent at this time, illustrating Kohut's thesis that during the throes of creative struggle certain people "require a specific relationship with another person—a transference of creativity" (1978, 814), as he calls it. Kohut compares this *transference* based on "the temporary needs of the enfeebled self of the creative person" (828) to cases of charisma, citing the example of the British people's merger with Churchill as a temporarily needed charismatic figure; his leadership, in a time of crisis, was also based on shared feelings of omnipotence (828). In particularly creative periods, according to Kohut, the self is often "at the mercy of powerful forces that it cannot control" and may feel itself "helplessly exposed to extreme mood swings" (818). As E. H. Miller describes the correspondence with Hawthorne: "The letters were tender, depressed, exhilarated, the moods in constant flux, not unlike the surface and subterranean rhythms of his masterpiece" (1975, 181). In the letter of [17?] November 1851 there are expressions of the most joyous enthusiasm and exultation, manic in their intensity—"But, believe me, I am not mad, most noble Festus! But truth is ever incoherent"—mixed with references to feelings of solitude and depression. "My dear Hawthorne, the atmospheric skepticisms steal into me now, and make me doubtful of my sanity in writing you thus. . . . Ah! it's a long stage, and no inn in sight, and night coming, and the body cold. But with you for a passenger, I am content and can be happy" (*Corr.*, 213). Melville clearly knew all the fragmentation, isolation, and loneliness of creativity—the "deep sense of isolation" of which Kohut speaks, "frightening experiences, which repeat those overwhelmingly anxious moments of early life when the child felt alone, abandoned, unsupported" (1978, 818). And he had, it seems—The "Counterpane" chapter in *Moby-Dick* comes to mind—a deep intuitive understanding of the connection between the intensity of childhood experience and psychic disintegration; as he comments in a letter to Evert Duyckinck (5 April 1849): "What sort of sensation permanent madness is may be very well imagined—just as we imagine how we felt when were infants, tho' we can not recall it. In both conditions we are irresponsible & riot like gods without fear of fate" (*Corr.*, 128).[5]

The hypothesis of a transference of creativity may help to explain Melville's preoccupation with the story of "Agatha," an anecdotal history recounted by an acquaintance, which he offered to Hawthorne as the latter's "property": "[T]he thing seems naturally to gravitate towards you . . . should of right belong to you" (234; Letter of 13 August 1852). There is in Melville's efforts to arrange the matter, a certain blurring of the borders of self and other: "I do not therefore, My Dear Hawthorne, at all imagine that you will think that I am so silly as to flatter myself *I am giving you anything of my own. I am but restoring to you your own property*—which you would quickly enough have *identified for yourself*—had *you but been on the spot as I happened to be*" (237; emphasis added). Not surprisingly, Melville connects the story with Hawthorne's *Wakefield*, a similar tale of desertion by a husband. In what is his last recorded letter to his friend (December 1852), he asks that the "whole affair" (242) of the story now be returned to him, on the basis of Hawthorne's expressed "uncertainty" concerning the undertaking and his feeling that Melville should write it himself. The story was originally a gift to Hawthorne, and its final return to the donor may represent some sort of symbolic liquidation of the "transference." Thus, the mysterious cooling off in the friendship between the two authors, a source of much speculation for biographers, may be, at least in part, an effect of what Kohut describes as the often temporary nature of this need for a response from the narcissistic object (1978, 810). With the completion of *Moby-Dick* and *Pierre*, this turbulently creative phase in Melville's life, which ended in a disastrous setback for his aspirations as a writer, came to a close. The urgent need of a friend such as Hawthorne, especially in light of his overwhelming sense of defeat, may have ceased, which is certainly not to say that the friendship between them may be reduced entirely to a matter of creative convenience. Its particular intensity and brevity, however, may have been partly due to the specific nature of a transference that, as Kohut concludes regarding the temporary nature of Freud's intense tie to Fliess, ended when the creative work was finished.

However we may view it, Melville's correspondence with Hawthorne and his adulating review of *Mosses from an Old Manse* leave little doubt as to the strength of his feelings. Indeed, if the aim of what Wurmser calls the *theatophilic* drive is to merge with and gain power from the object and if the accompanying affect is admiration or awe (Wurmser 1981, 165), the workings of such a drive could hardly be better illustrated than by Melville's idealization of the older writer. In the same famous letter of [17?] November 1851, Melville strikes an exaggeratedly humble posture in response to the generosity of his friend, with repeated expressions of the most intense desire for merger or union. We noted above the image of magnetic attraction and union. In the same vein, he writes of the emotional effect on him of Hawthorne's appreciation of *Moby-Dick*: "I felt pantheistic then—your heart beat in my ribs and mine in yours, and both in God's. A sense of unspeakable security is in me this moment, on account of your having understood the book" (*Corr.*, 212). This feeling of communion is expressed, in another passage, through the Eucharistic imagery of oral incorporation: "Whence come you, Hawthorne? By what right do you drink from my flagon of life? And when I put it to my lips—lo, they are yours and not mine. I feel that the Godhead is broken up like the bread at the Supper, and that we are the pieces. Hence this infinite fraternity of feeling" (212). That this feeling of awe accompanied by the desire for merger is an expression of the wish to overcome hidden feelings of shame (about personal defectiveness and imperfection) is apparent in another passage. Here, in Melville's implied identification of himself with Socrates, there is the expression of grandiosity as well: "You were archangel enough to despise the imperfect body, and embrace the soul. Once you hugged the ugly Socrates because you saw the flame in the mouth, and heard the rushing of the demon,—and recognized the sound; for you have heard it in your own solitudes" (213). Melville is referring to the book, *Moby-Dick*, but the unconscious thought of a personal union clearly emerges. The shame imagery is instructive: the shame of being physically unlovable ("I am ugly or deformed") is purged by merger, through the recognition and approval bestowed by the idealized object with whom one shares a spiritual understanding.

It is perhaps in the hyperbolic praise bestowed by the "ardent Virginian" of Melville's review of Hawthorne's *Mosses* that we find the most dramatic expression of awe before the idealized object. There is, for example, the following passage: "Now, I do not say that Nathaniel of Salem is a greater than William of Avon, or as great. But the difference between the two men is by no means immeasurable. Not a very great deal more, and Nathaniel were verily William" (*PT,* 246). The state of awe here, a variant of shame, comes very close to the feeling-state of being in love.[6] Melville concludes the review with the extravagant claim: "But even granting all this; and adding to it, the assumption that the books of Hawthorne have sold by the five-thousand,—what does that signify?—They should be sold by the hundred-thousand; and read by the million; and admired by every one who is capable of admiration" (253). The functional importance of this merger with an idealized figure in the sustaining of Melville during a particularly creative spell in his life may be surmised when, in the overtly erotic imagery of a notably intense passage in the review, the incorporation of Hawthorne's work becomes an act of insemination by the author of that work:

> But already I feel that this Hawthorne has dropped germinous seeds into my soul. He expands and deepens down, the more I contemplate him; and further, and further, shoots his strong New-England roots into the hot soil of my Southern soil. (250)

In the process of its own creative growth and expansion, the self is impregnated by the idealized object. It is interesting, given this imagery of organic growth, that in her description of their conversations Sophia Hawthorne refers to Melville as "this growing man." In the letter of [1?] June 1851, Melville confesses to Hawthorne: "My development has been all within a few years past. I am like one of those seeds taken out of the Egyptian Pyramids, which, after being three thousand years a seed and nothing but a seed, being planted in English soil, it developed itself, grew to greenness, and then fell to mould" (*Corr.*, 193). Melville dates his life from his twenty-fifth year, the year he began his first novel. The same organic imagery of growth appears in the letter of [17?] November: "Lord, when shall we be done growing? As long as we have anything more to do, we have done nothing" (213). The imagery of insemination and replanting suggests the intellectual growth and expansion that might in part be enhanced and accelerated through the unconscious merger with a temporary selfobject: Melville's creativity, if we take the metaphor seriously, having been awakened by an intense cross-fertilization with Hawthorne, flourishes dramatically. The letter of June 1851 continues: "Three weeks have scarcely passed, at any time between then and now, that I have not unfolded within myself. But I feel that I am now come to the inmost leaf of the bulb, and that shortly the flower must fall to the mould" (193).

   It is worth noting that a related aspect of this idealizing-incorporating tendency in Melville is his incalculable indebtedness to other texts for the generation of his own. What Carolyn Porter observes of Ishmael applies just as surely to Melville himself: "Ishmael's voice absorbs the authority it is all the while draining from these discourses. . . . Ishmael's voice is . . . a virtual sponge, capable of soaking up an infinite number of voices and squeezing out their discourse into a pool as large as the oceans he sails" (1986, 100). "Melville's books," as Charles Olson puts it, "batten on other men's books" (1947, 36). This seemingly preternatural ability to incorporate the discourses, styles, and words—the entire verbal substance—of others in his being, is part of Melville's unique ability to identify with another as an "embodiment of idealized power" (Kohut 1978, 822) whose strength he borrows for a period of intense creative expansion. Elizabeth Foster describes Melville's creative process, which seems to have begun with the composition of *Mardi* and eventually culminated in the writing of *Moby-Dick*, as "rushing him into such an intellectual expansion and exhilaration that his very being was ringing with the voices of the great dead. At the same time, like his Lombardo in *Mardi*, as he wrote he 'got deeper and deeper into himself.' And there the release of dormant powers and thoughts also released what he later called 'a certain something unmanageable'" (1970, 661–62). As the narrator puts it in *Mardi*: "And like a frigate, I am full with a thousand souls. . . . Ay: many, many souls are in me. In my tropical calms, when my ship lies tranced on Eternity's main, speaking one at a time, then all with one voice. . . . In me, many worthies recline, and converse. . . . My memory is a life beyond birth; my memory, my library of the Vatican, its alcoves all endless perspectives" (367–68). Babbalanja, in the same novel, comes up with the same kind of argument when he is accused of never speaking in his own voice:

> The catalogue of true thoughts is but small; they are ubiquitous; no man's property; and unspoken, or bruited, are the same. When we hear them, why seem they so natural, receiving our spontaneous approval? why do we think we have heard them before? Because they but reiterate ourselves; they were in us, before we were born. The truest poets are but mouth-pieces; and some men are duplicates of each other. (397)

Babbalanja—whose name suggests babble or Babel-tongue—returns to the idea in a later chapter: "We are full of ghosts and spirits; we are as graveyards full of buried dead, that start to life before us. . . . From sire to son, we go on multiplying corpses in ourselves; for all of which, are resurrections. Every thought's a soul of some past poet, hero, sage. We are fuller than a city" (594).

Other passages in Melville's review illustrate this goal of gaining power through incorporation, a process expressed by metaphors of oral gratification and ingestion. It is as if the strength and value of Hawthorne and his work are taken in through the mouth by the act of praise:

> But I am content to leave Hawthorne to himself, and to the infallible finding of posterity; however great may be the praise I have bestowed upon him, I feel, that in so doing, *I have more served and honored myself,* than him. For, at bottom, great excellence is praise enough to itself; but *the feeling of a sincere and appreciative love and admiration* towards it, this is relieved by utterance; and *warm, honest praise ever leaves a pleasant flavor in the mouth;* and it is an honorable thing to confess to what is honorable in others. (*PT,* 249; emphasis added)

The next paragraph continues in the same "oral" and idealizing vein: "No man can read a fine author, and *relish him to his very bones,* while he reads, without subsequently fancying to himself some *ideal image of the man and his mind*" (249; emphasis added). The imagery is quite explicit in another passage—the one that immediately precedes the famous "insemination" image—as Melville rehearses the fantasy of literally *stuffing himself,* as it were, on Hawthorne's work: "To what infinite height of loving wonder and admiration I may yet be borne, when by *repeatedly banquetting on these Mosses, I shall have thoroughly incorporated their whole stuff into my being*" (250; emphasis added). As E. H. Miller points out, "The extravagant praise and, more specifically, the desire to 'incorporate' Hawthorne constituted a kind of attack" (1975, 181). The image, indeed, is of an outright intellectual cannibalism, the joyous and enriching absorption of another's spiritual essence into oneself.[7] Here and elsewhere, Melville's fascination with his idealized friend clearly manifests the desire, in Wurmser's terms, "to conquer and to merge with the partner into an all powerful, autarchic union, and thus to incorporate the other person's strength and value" (1981, 162).

There seem to be two aspects to this intense idealization in Melville. On the one hand, the desire to merge with the object appears to be the expression of a frustrated archaic wish; on the other hand, it acts as a powerful defensive structure against intensely painful feelings of shame. Rather than stressing the images of self and object, as Kohut does, Wurmser understands these images as "expression of deep desires" and as "defensive structures against overwhelming anxiety (helplessness)" (164). Idealized figures often play the role of "archaic protectors," idealization serving "to defend against devastating rage and annihilating contempt" (164).

It is an overwhelming anxiety about his helplessness and powerlessness that defines Ahab's feeling of mortification at being mauled and defeated by Moby Dick. But the defensive structure here, of course, stems almost entirely from images of the grandiose self. In the same novel, however, in the role played by Queequeg, we discover a particularly instructive example of the idealized object as an archaic protector. From the beginning, as we have seen, Queequeg is depicted as a particularly powerful figure. A man without needs, indebted to no one, who looked like he had never cringed or had a creditor, his pride stems from being eminently *independent*; physically strong and courageous of heart, he is associated throughout with a sustaining function and with heroic acts of deliverance in assisting those in situations of distress and helplessness. Ishmael's awestruck attitude before Queequeg appears in their first encounter at The Spouter-Inn, and as their friendship blossoms into love the imagery of melting and of magnetic attraction expresses the theme of merger and fascination: "I began to be sensible of strange feelings. I felt *a melting in me*. . . . I began to feel myself *mysteriously drawn towards him*. And those same things that would have repelled most others they were *the very magnets that thus drew me*" (*MD*, 51; emphasis added). The chapter "A Bosom Friend" finishes with these "solitary twain" in bed engaged in "*confidential disclosures* between friends. Man and wife, they say, there open the very bottom of their souls to each other and some old couples often lie and chat over old times till nearly morning. Thus, then, in our hearts' honeymoon, lay I and Queequeg—a cozy, loving pair" (52; emphasis added).

Israel Potter is an exemplary illustration of this pattern that runs through Melville's work of a passive young innocent, "the passive victim of his own failures" (1975, 265), as E. H. Miller puts it, who seeks the protection of a series of father figures, all of whom turn out to be, in one way or another, as disappointing as Captain Riga is to Redburn. The relationship between Israel and John Millet, his elderly, patriarchal protector in his first flight from home, would seem to be a depiction of the wished-for ideal of such a relationship, and it is, like Ishmael and Queequeg's budding friendship, characterized by an amorous melting and the intimacy of "confidential disclosures." The merger between the young man and his mentor, achieved through recognition and approval by the older man, characteristically involves the imagery, in displaced form, of oral incorporation, in this case—in anticipation of the sacrificial Billy Budd—in the passive mode. A sacrificial note is even suggested by the image of Israel's having, "in the course of two or three weeks so *fattened his flanks*, that he was able completely to fill Sir John's old buckskin breeches" (*IP*, 27; emphasis added). Sir John is at first a somewhat frightening figure of authority with a "penetrating glance" (26), but he soon shows an affectionate protectiveness toward the young fugitive.

> And often, of mild, sunny afternoons, the knight, *genial and gentle with dinner*, would stroll bareheaded to the pleasant strawberry bed, and have *nice little confidential chats* with Israel; while Israel, charmed by *the patriarchal demeanor of this true Abrahamic gentleman*, with a smile on his lip, and *tears of gratitude in his eyes, offered him*, from time to time, *the plumpest berries of the bed*. (27)

A kindly old Abraham and a helpless Isaac who, grateful to be spared, offers his protector "the plumpest berries of the bed" as they pass the hours in "confidential chats"—this is the imagery of a wish fulfilled and suggests an ambivalent splitting of the father figure that, indeed, is apparent from the beginning of the novel: Israel's natural father is a tyrannical and severe individual whose oppression of his son drives him away from home; in his fugitive state of exile Israel runs into his first protector, the kindly John Millet, who temporarily adopts the boy.[8]

A similar episode is recounted in *Billy Budd*, when Captain Vere has his own "confidential chat" with Billy after the sentence of death has been decided. (The theme of a confidential merger with one's protector also occurs in *Redburn*, but only in the form of an unrealistic fantasy.) The same cluster of associations appears. There is the joy of appreciation and gratitude at being approved and recognized—"Not without a sort of joy, indeed, he might have appreciated the brave opinion of him implied in his captain's making such a confidant of him" (*BB*, 115)—and there is the *melting* of love on the part of a captain who is both father and sacrificial priest, attentive and tender parent and austere military devotee: "He was old enough to have been Billy's father. The *austere devotee of military duty,* letting himself *melt back into* what remains primaeval in our formalized humanity, may in end have caught Billy to his heart, *even as Abraham may have caught young Isaac* on the brink of resolutely offering him up in obedience to the exacting behest." It is here that the narrator speaks of the "*sacrament,* seldom if in any case revealed to the gadding world, wherever under circumstances at all akin to those here attempted to be set forth two of great Nature's nobler order embrace. There is privacy at the time, inviolable to the survivor; and holy oblivion, the sequel to each *diviner magnanimity,* providentially covers all at last" (115; emphasis added). The idea of "divine magnanimity," with its strong idealizing note, occurs—the expression is almost the same, the order and form of the words simply being reversed—in connection with the merger in the chapter "A Bosom Friend" ("the magnanimous God of heaven and earth" [*MD,* 52]), as well as in Melville's letter of [17?] November 1851. In the letter the same words are used, but in the plural—where the sacrificial *sacrament* of the Eucharist is evoked to express the gratitude or "infinite fraternity of feeling," the "divine magnanimities," that Hawthorne's appreciation has produced in him: "I feel that the Godhead is broken up like the bread at the Supper, and that we are the pieces" (*Corr.,* 212).

The archaic function of the idealized selfobject as a defensive structure is apparent in an episode in *Typee.* Tommo's physical incapacity symbolizes the regression to a state of protected and dependent helplessness in which the passive oral wish to be loved appears to play a central part.[9] Tommo becomes the ward of Kory-Kory, who feeds him and carries him about like an infant. This protected state of dependency involves at the same time the primary anxiety of being devoured by one's protectors. Rogin describes this as "the danger of a devouring, maternal power. Cannibalism perfectly embodies Tommo's primitive fears, for the island has awakened the boundaryless, devouring infant within him. The infant eats, and is afraid it will be eaten" (48). The fear of being devoured is particularly acute when Tommo feels as though Marnoo has outshone him—the way Red Whiskers and Claggart feel supplanted by Billy Budd— and that he will no longer be loved and admired: "When I observed the striking devotion of the natives to him, and their temporary withdrawal of all attention from myself, I felt not a little piqued. The glory of Tommo is departed, thought I, and the sooner he removes from the valley the better" (137). As is usual in Melville, the situation of rivalry involves an incumbent and an intruder, awakening in the former an underlying fear of rejection—particularly terrifying in this case since, as Tommo surmises, the loss of one's preeminence may lead to one's being cannibalized. "Influenced by these feelings," Tommo recounts, "I now felt a strong desire to avail myself of the stranger's protection. . . ." (140). Feeling, then, that his ability to elicit admiration has been seriously threatened, Tommo now looks for an intercessor or protector; idealization, to follow Wurmser, often is a defensive structure against the overwhelming anxiety of being helpless and abandoned.

The protector, however, is always potentially the devourer as well, as we can see in the treacherous uncertainty of characters such as Captain Riga—his threat is a mock or comic one, but it is certainly part of the same paradigm—and Captain Vere. On the one hand they are surrogate fathers and fill the reassuring role of "archaic protectors," while, on the other, their additional role as Abrahamic, sacrificing, or devouring fathers reflects the very defensive structure of which Wurmser speaks. These figures combine, as it were, a wish (that one will be protected by the loving and all-powerful other) and a fear (that one will be abandoned and perish, sacrificed even, because one is unlovable). They represent at once a defense and the threat defended against: as idealized protector, the figure wards off that which, as terrible father, he threatens. This splitting is explicit in the change of attitude that instantaneously overcomes Vere after Billy lands his fatal blow. When Claggart is tragically struck dead, Vere's fatherly role is suddenly eclipsed by the terrible figure of authority.: "Slowly he uncovered his face; and the effect was as if the moon emerging from eclipse should reappear with quite another aspect than that which had gone into hiding. The father in him, manifested towards Billy thus far in the scene, was replaced by the military disciplinarian" (*BB*, 99–100). The same splitting of the father figure is explicit in *Redburn*, in which the "fatherly" Riga is associated with the identical theme of a dutiful figure of authority condemning a son to death. Redburn looks to Captain Riga for protection on his journey and is ultimately deceived when he hails him with easy familiarity on deck and the captain turns on him in fury, shattering his naive fantasy of intimacy: "I never saw a man fly into such a rage; I thought he was going to knock me down; but after standing speechless awhile, he all at once plucked his cap from his head and threw it at me" (*R*, 70). At the beginning of the chapter, there is, significantly enough, the casually offered motif of the devouring father:

I had no doubt that he would in some special manner take me under his protection, and prove a kind friend and benefactor to me; as I had heard that some sea-captains are fathers to their crew; and so they are; but such fathers as Solomon's precepts tend to make—severe and chastising fathers, fathers whose sense of duty overcomes the sense of love, and who every day, in some sort, play the part of Brutus, who ordered his son away to execution as I have read in our old family Plutarch. (67)

At the very heart of this theme, as this passage suggests, lies the most terrible human fear of being rejected and abandoned, destroyed even by one's protector.

The severity of such figures is linked to shame in a number of ways. For one thing, the form of punishment with which they are associated is not just physical (often including execution) but relies on public humiliation. The "value of privacy" (Nathanson 1992, 319)—precisely what the narrator of *Moby-Dick* upholds when, in introducing Starbuck as a character, he tactfully passes over the spectacle of "a valour-ruined man"—is outlined by Nathanson in a discussion of shame-laden forms of punishment. He mentions crucifixion as "one epitome of public humiliation," along with the witch trials of Salem, "the public stocks of colonial Williamsburg, arrest, trial, and imprisonment of any sort, public spanking or reprimand, any form of punishment by exposure to public censure," in which "the culprit is denied the recourse of privacy" (319). Billy is shaken by the spectacle of just such a public humiliation when he and the rest of the crew are forced as a matter of naval policy to witness a formal gangway-punishment: "When Billy saw the culprit's naked back under the scourge, gridironed with red welts and worse, when he marked the dire expression in the liberated man's face as with his woolen shirt flung over him by the executioner he rushed forward from the spot to bury himself in the crowd, Billy was horrified" (*BB*, 68). The shame of the spectacle is emphasized by the fact that the man rushes to "bury himself in the crowd" and hide his face. The spectacle, of course, foreshadows Billy's humiliating public execution, which clearly suggests the ostracism and sacrifice of a *pharmakos* figure, the adjudication, in Vere's words, "to summary and shameful death of a creature innocent before God" (110).

There is a comic modulation of this archaic fear of rejection and abandonment in *Redburn*. At one point in the course of his initiation aboard ship, the young recruit inadvertently finds himself a cause for quarrel between the chief mate and second mate. The experience is a particularly humiliating one—one that anyone who has been passed over in the choosing of sides in an athletic contest will be all too painfully familiar with—inasmuch as the two are fighting to decide not who will take him under his wing but who will be relieved of the burden: "While this scene was going one, I felt shabby enough; there I stood, just like a silly sheep, over whom two butchers are bargaining" (86). This shabby feeling of foolishness and "sheepishness," of contemptible docility, is combined here with the implication of sacrifice—of being a pathetic sheep branded for the slaughter. The situation, comical as it is, captures perhaps what is manifest in all these scenes where the yearning for closeness, love, and belonging struggles with a most terrible suspicion: the underlying fear that one cannot be loved. This sense, in Nathanson's words, "of being shorn from all humanity" is a feeling that, when it becomes unbearable, results in that most nightmarish of human wishes, "the wish to be left alone forever" (1992, 317).

CHAPTER SEVEN

The Evil Eye

I

Redburn is a work that Melville, perhaps for defensive reasons, singled out for particular depreciation: "a plain, straightforward, amusing narrative of personal experience—the son of a gentleman on his first voyage to sea as a sailor—no metaphysics, no conic-sections, nothing but cakes & ale" (*Corr.*, 132) is how he described it in a letter to his English publisher, Richard Bentley (5 June 1849). At the same time, as he wrote to his father-in-law, Lemuel Shaw, with reference to both *Redburn* and *White-Jacket*: "I have not repressed myself much . . . but have spoken pretty much as I feel" (139). The frankly autobiographical import of the novel is clearly suggested by the name of its protagonist, Wellingborough Redburn: Wellingborough is a thinly disguised play on Melville, while we find the same use of a patronymic as a first name in the name of Herman's older brother Gansevoort. The details of the story, of course, are clearly consistent with what we know of the early events and experiences in Melville's life.

The opening parts of the novel revolve around the theme of the *disappointed* or defeated self. The narrator begins his story by speaking of the "Sad disappointments in several plans which I had sketched for my future life," which have led him to go "to sea as a sailor" (*R*, 3), and as he sets out on his voyage Redburn is a figure very much like Ishmael at the beginning of *Moby-Dick*: winter has descended in his soul and he is deeply embittered and misanthropically disposed to turn away from all human society. The theme of grievous disappointment is picked up again at the beginning of the second chapter:

> I had learned to think much and bitterly before my time; all my young mounting dreams of glory had left me; and at that early age, I was as unambitious as a man of sixty. . . . Cold, bitter cold as December, and bleak as its blasts, seemed the world then to me;

there is no misanthrope like a boy disappointed; and such was I,
with the warm soul of me flogged out by adversity. (10)

The "sad disappointments" touch most directly on the death of Redburn's
father, which has left the family in a financially desperate state. This traumatic event represents a compound blow to his personal pride: he finds
himself abandoned at an early age through the loss of an idealized father,
while suffering at the same time from the disgrace associated with his family's
dramatic social demotion and financial destitution. The effect has been to
turn him into a singularly unambitious young man: "I was as unambitious
as a man of sixty" (10). His "young mounting dreams of glory" may have
departed, but their existence in the first place may be a sign of a frustrated
wish for admiration and attention, and thus his father's financial ruin and
untimely death, together with his family's social degradation, are the source
of particularly painful feelings of mournful defeat and shame. We have already touched on certain images in the following passage, but it is worth
quoting at length and discussing again here:

> Talk not of the bitterness of middle-age and after life; a boy can feel
> all that, and much more, when upon his young soul the mildew
> has fallen; and the fruit, which with others is only blasted after
> ripeness, with him is nipped in the first blossom and bud. And
> never again can such blights be made good; they strike in too deep,
> and leave such a scar that the air of Paradise might not erase it. And
> it is a hard and cruel thing thus in early youth to taste beforehand
> the pangs which should be reserved for the stout time of man-
> hood, when the gristle has become bone, and we stand up and
> fight out our lives, as a thing tried before and foreseen; for then we
> are veterans used to sieges and battles, and not green recruits, re-
> coiling at the first shock of the encounter. (11)

"If distress," as Tomkins observes, "is the affect of suffering, shame is
the affect of indignity, of defeat, of transgression, and of alienation. Though
terror speaks to life and death and distress makes of the world a vale of tears,
yet shame strikes deepest into the heart of man" (1963, 118). This is because
"shame is felt as an inner torment, a sickness of the soul" in which the
subject "feels himself naked, defeated, alienated, lacking in dignity or worth"

(118). The "conspicuous defeat" suffered by Redburn is received with all the searing shame of mortification. The imagery of premature battle and defeat (the nipped, blighted, blasted "first blossom and bud") anticipates the dark theme of *Pierre*. The "shock" of a deep narcissistic blow to the self is a calamity for which the youth is unprepared and which has struck deep enough to leave an unhealable scar. What strikes at Redburn is the loss and failure of an idealized object, but this grievous event is experienced not just as a bereavement but also, in perhaps a more damaging way, as an unjust and resented crushing defeat of the self.

The sense of isolation and the tone of self-pitying bitterness suggest that the loss of a father here is not mitigated by the effective presence of any reassuring maternal presence. The allusions to the mother in *Redburn* are primarily associated with the grandiose-exhibitionistic part of his personality, his naive desire to "shine" and be the glint in the (m)other's eye. They recall a blissful state of narcissistic wholeness, a world of security and delight in which the self was admired as unique and special. The mother that Redburn paints, in other words, is an idealized object of nostalgic yearning, an imagined, not a real, mother—a sign, indeed, that the maternal imago, like the paternal one, is deeply split. As we have seen, the intensely proud and ambitious mothers in *Pierre* and "Timoleon," as well as the stepmother of "The Counterpane" chapter in *Moby-Dick*, are depicted as punitive and unempathic narcissistic figures; the mother may also be depicted as a "dead mother," like Ahab's "crazy, widowed mother, who," as we learn from Peleg, "died when he was only a twelvemonth old" (*MD*, 79).

Damaged in his object relations, and therefore in his self-image, Redburn, as we have seen, is compelled to look outside himself for protection. We return, yet again, to those issues of dependence and independence associated with the theme of standing erect—here, the idea of being able to "stand up and fight out our lives"—that are such important specific sources of shame in Melville. The following passage from *Pierre* concerning the development of the soul is an excellent expression of the psychological situation that we also find at the beginning of *Redburn*:

Watch yon little toddler, how long it is learning to stand by itself! First it shrieks and implores, and will not try to stand at all, unless both father and mother uphold it; then a little more bold, it must, at least, feel one parental hand, else again the cry and the tremble;

long time is it ere by degrees this child comes to stand without any support. But, by-and-by, grown up to man's estate, it shall leave the very mother that bore it, and the father that begot it, and cross the seas, or settle in far Oregon lands. There now, do you see the soul. . . . it is born from the world-husk, but still now outwardly clings to it;—still clamors for the support of its mother the world, and its father the Deity. But it shall yet learn to stand independent, though not without many a bitter wail, and many a miserable fall. (296)

What follows seems to undermine the confidence expressed, as it focuses on the image of being abandoned before finding one's feet: "That hour of the life of a man when first the help of humanity fails him, and he learns that in his obscurity and indigence humanity holds him a dog and no man; that hour is a hard one. . . ." The image recalls the figure of Timoleon who, abandoned by mother, friends, and human society, is shorn from humanity and pleads that the gods not "let me be / Like a lone dog that for a master cries." But that hour is "not the hardest." The narrator continues: "There is still another hour which follows, when he learns that in his infinite comparative minuteness and abjectness, the gods do likewise despise him, and own him not of their clan" (296). Like the image of Pip deserted by his companions and by God, and left with his soul drowning like a speck, lost and engulfed in the midst of the jeering infinite, the image here is of both cosmic and human abandonment: "Divinity and humanity then are equally willing that he should starve in the street for all that either will do for him. Now cruel father and mother have both let go of his hand, and the little soul-toddler, now you shall hear his shriek and his wail, and often his fall" (296).

The pathetic tone and the imagery here are characteristic as well of the initial psychological state and affective mood of the young Redburn. It is no accident that Melville referred to the novel, in a letter to Richard Dana, as "A little nursery tale of mine" (*Corr.*, 93). This somewhat demeaning attitude to his own literary offspring is, indeed, reflected in the depiction of its protagonist who, from the beginning, comes across as what is commonly and contemptuously referred to as a "mama's boy." Redburn's smugness and his expectations of coddling and special treatment aboard ship—a treatment appropriate only to a private familial circle where a certain indulgence can be assumed—are interpreted as an arrogant provocation by the crew. He becomes, indeed, the butt of a good deal of scornful and humiliating humor precisely because of this prominent aspect of his character. The humor is focused on his ineptness and helplessness, on matters of dependency and competence that are associated with infantile sources of shame. Redburn is given humiliating names—"Buttons" (a reference to the grandiosity he reveals in wearing his ridiculous jacket) and "Pillgarlic"—and he is ordered to perform degrading tasks, such as cleaning out the pigpens. He is particularly susceptible to this kind of treatment because his grandiosity makes him both highly self-conscious and extremely oblivious to the reality of his environment: he seems unaware of how inappropriate and ridiculous are certain of his assumptions, how unsuitable it is, for example, to dress up and go make a social call on the captain.

His perceived smugness and arrogance represent, in fact, a general strategy of shame avoidance or denial. We can see, for example, how Redburn bolsters his shaken sense of self through an identification with his family, from whose social pretensions he derives a superficial sense of his value as a person.[1] According to Nathanson, narcissism, "a protection against shame," is "the name we give to the broad array of scripts through which people prevent themselves from "knowing" about anything that might increase an already unbearable amount of shame" (1992, 349). The manifestations of grandiosity—self-inflation, exaggeration and false embellishment of one's self-image—serve

> the function of drawing attention away from a centrally damaged self-concept. Narcissism is a term that must be reserved for that part of our self-image that would be relinquished were we to accept shame. It is an ill-fitting mask or a badly made toupee (indeed, a mask or toupee of any sort), a girdle or corset designed to show us as we wish to be rather than as we are, a swagger meant to disguise the slump of disgrace, a house full of imitation fine art and fake jewelry, a phony accent. (349)

Or it is the red shooting-jacket worn by a member of the gentleman class, which looks so ridiculous on a declassé young man who has just joined the merchant marine as a common sailor. White-Jacket's garment seems to function in the same way; it draws attention to the self but away from a "centrally damaged self-concept." The famous green jacket that Melville wore on his trip to London in 1849 may have served a similar purpose[2]—"anything," Nathanson concludes, "we do to call attention to the self we wish to assume rather than the person we are" (349).

Redburn's desire to be admired, to be seen as someone special and unique, as someone particularly worthy of attention and praise, is, of course, not just a defensive structure. It also represents—as does the impulse to idealize the other as omnipotent and perfect—a genuine wish that needs to be filled. Wurmser calls it active, magic exhibitionism, the desire to impress and fascinate others. In Redburn's case, as we noted, it is associated with the approving maternal gaze, the sparkle or gleam in the mother's eye. Grunberger observes that the child "clings to the narcissistic components of his economy" and reads "his narcissistic confirmation in his mother's eyes, confirmation of the fact that he is still the one and only, that he is valued because of his intrinsic worth" (1979, 22–23). As he sets out on the Hudson, Redburn grows nostalgic for his childhood and thinks of a particularly beautiful June day when "everything looked as if it was waiting for something, and the sky overhead was blue as my mother's eye, and I was so glad and happy then" (R, 35–36). We meet the passive and inverted form of this desire to be mirrored when Jackson's particular dislike of him is expressed in the latter's horrible squinting eye. As we have seen, Redburn ascribes this hostility, which makes him feel painfully exposed, to envy of his physical attractiveness, which he associates with his mother's admiration: "For I was young and handsome, at least my mother so thought me" (58). He then goes on to contrast his own beauty with Jackson's physical defectiveness: "I began to have my old color in my cheeks, and, spite of misfortune, to appear well and hearty; whereas *he* was being consumed by an incurable malady, that was eating up his vitals, and was more fit for a hospital than a ship" (58). This narcissism in the area of personal attractiveness is, of course, another manifestation of disavowed shame.

In the last chapter we tried to establish the importance of the idealized selfobject in the psychological makeup of Redburn. We are now concerned to show the equally pronounced role of the grandiose self. These two images are often hard to separate. Redburn's desire to go traveling, for example, is, as we have seen, the expression of an impulse to imitate his idealized father and other older male figures, such as the explorer his aunt points out to him at church. But this desire also reveals the fantasy of being mirrored and of producing a state of fascination in others. When Redburn dreams of traveling, for example, what he primarily focuses on is returning home and finding himself an object of wonder and awe for having undergone such a wonderful experience:

> As I grew older my thoughts took a larger flight, and I frequently fell into long reveries about distant voyages and travels, and thought how fine it would be, to be able to talk about remote and barbarous countries; with what reverence and wonder people would regard me, if I had just returned from the coast of Africa or New Zealand; how dark and romantic my sunburnt cheeks would look; how I would bring home with me foreign clothes of a rich fabric and princely make, and wear them up and down the streets, and how grocers' boys would turn back their heads to look at me, as I went by. (5)

We can see quite clearly here that the source of Redburn's fascination with the wonderful traveler is, in fact, his own fantasy of being equally fascinating in the future. The barely repressed exhibitionism of the grandiose self is humorously apparent in the idea that, on his return, he will become the admiration of all the grocery boys as he struts down the streets in gorgeous exotic costume. His desire to learn French, which might be ascribed to a healthy curiosity, also reveals the influence of the grandiose self: "I wondered what a great man I would be, if by foreign travel I should ever be able to read straight along without stopping, out of that book, which now was a riddle to every one in the house but my father, whom I so much liked to hear talk French, as he sometimes did to a servant we had" (7). Thus his father's role as an idealized selfobject is inseparably bound up with Redburn's fantasy of becoming "a great man." Similarly, he looks forward to recounting his exotic travels and imagines that "just as my father used to entertain strange gentlemen over their wine after dinner, I would hereafter be telling my own adventures to an eager auditory. And I have no doubt that this presentiment had something do with bringing about my subsequent rovings" (7). The theme of flight and travel is thus connected to a regression into the imaginary and to a fascination that may stem, not just from the idealizing pole, but from the chronic need of the grandiose self to display itself and produce in others a state of fascination.

It is clear, indeed, from the beginning of Redburn's departure from home to what extent his self-esteem depends on feedback from those surrounding him. We have already shown how Captain Riga plays the part of an idealized protector figure. But in terms of Redburn's need for narcissistic confirmation, Captain Riga plays the role of an archaic mirroring selfobject. In seeking out the captain, Redburn's assumption is that this powerful and fatherly figure, fascinated by him, will indulgently provide him with the admiring response demanded by the grandiose self. He fantasizes, for example, that the captain expects a social call from him and the imagined communion between the two strikingly foreshadows—four decades separate the composition of the two works—the merger between Billy and Vere:

> Yes, I thought that Captain Riga, for Riga was his name, would be attentive and considerate to me, and strive to cheer me up, and comfort me in my lonesomeness. I did not even deem it at all impossible that he would invite me down into the cabin of a pleasant night, to ask me questions concerning my parents, and prospects in life; besides obtaining from me some anecdotes touching my great-uncle, the illustrious senator; or give me a slate and pencil, and teach me problems in navigation; or perhaps engage me at a game of chess. I even thought he might invite me to dinner on a sunny Sunday. . . . (67–68)

Like the patriarchal and protective John Millet in *Israel Potter*, Captain Riga is (in Redburn's fantasy) an attentive fatherly figure, offering cheer and comfort, while Redburn is the center of attention in a fantasized conversation focused on his parents, his ambitions, and the adventures of his "illustrious" great-uncle. The captain wants to know who he is, who his family is, what he will become. He takes an interest in his education and recreation. Riga, indeed, plays the part in Redburn's imagination of a highly cooperative selfobject and is explicitly associated with the indulgent environment of the familial private circle: "And I could not help regarding him with peculiar emotions, almost of tenderness and love, as the last visible link in the chain of associations which bound me to my home. For, while yet in port, I had seen him and Mr Jones, my brother's friend, standing together and conversing; so that from the captain to my brother there was but one intermediate step; and my brother and mother and sisters were one" (68).

Redburn's subsequent disappointment in Riga, who for the merest breach of decorum—his unwitting attempt to pay the captain a social call—turns on him in a violent rage and humiliates him, represents a reactivation, in a sense, of the deep disappointments spoken of in the opening chapters. Redburn is disillusioned as the captain loses in his eyes the "gloss" of idealization. This is not, however, a particularly notable step in the young man's maturation. Redburn continues, especially in the early parts of the novel, to remain blind to his own blocking narcissistic grandiosity and the obtrusive need for attention and approval that led to his disappointment in the captain in the first place. Indeed, his own grandiosity is reflected in his scornful dismissal of Captain Riga. He resolves "to let the captain alone for the future, particularly as he had shown himself so deficient in the ordinary breeding of a gentleman." Seeing him later in the middle of an emergency during a storm in his "nightcap, and nothing else but his shirt on," cursing and swearing at the men, he concludes that Riga is "just like a common loafer in the street" (71). He concludes, more defensively of course than snobbishly: "Yes, Captain Riga, thought I, you are no gentleman, and you know it!" (71). What is revealed here, of course, is Redburn's own "narcissistic vulnerability . . . the 'underside' of exhibitionism, grandiosity, and haughtiness— the low self-esteem, self-doubt, and fragility of self-cohesion that defines the narcissistic condition" (Morrison 1989, 14–15), as Redburn avoids and disavows his feelings of shame through contempt and scorn.

> Indeed, I began to think that he was but a shabby fellow after all; particularly as his whiskers lost their gloss, and he went days together without shaving; and his hair, by a sort of miracle, began to grow of a pepper and salt color, which might have been owing, though, to his discontinuing the use of some kind of dye while at sea. I put him down as a sort of impostor; and while ashore, a gentleman on false pretenses; for no gentleman would have treated another gentleman as he did me. (*R*, 71)

The relocation in the captain of the inferiority he himself feels reflects the strategy of Hegel's *belle âme*. As Lacan defines it: "[I]n the depressive disruptions of the experienced reverses of inferiority, [the ego] engenders essentially the mortal negations that fix it in its formalism: 'I am nothing of what happens to me. You are nothing of value'" (1977, 20).

II

We have emphasized the element of idealization in Melville's friendship with Hawthorne. Just as significant, however, seems to have been his desire for an open and frank self-display, for an uninhibited revelation of himself. "A sense of unspeakable security is in me this moment, on account of your having understood the book" (*Corr.*, 212), he tells his friend, and the way he then goes on to assign himself the role of the fascinating Socrates while Hawthorne plays the captivated Alcibiades suggests quite precisely a wish to be seen, to use Lacan's formulation, in the form he likes to be seen. Hawthorne, he believes, has glimpsed the beauty of his soul. Sophia Hawthorne's letters suggest that Melville may, indeed, have sought merger with her husband, and not simply through idealization but through the wish to fascinate the older writer—with his speech, his thought, his physical presence.

> Nothing pleases me better than to sit & hear this growing man dash his tumultuous waves of thought up against Mr Hawthorne's great, genial, comprehending silences—out of the profound of which a wonderful smile, or one powerful word sends back the foam & fury into a peaceful booming, calm—or perchance not into a calm—but a murmuring expostulation—for there is never a "mush of concession" in him. yet such love & reverence & admiration for Mr Hawthorne as is really beautiful to witness—& without doing anything on his own part, except merely *being*, it is astonishing how people make him their innermost Father Confessor. (Quoted in E. H. Miller 1975, 42–43)

It is, of course, not only Melville who seems to have treated Hawthorne as an idealized object, but Sophia herself, who is clearly doing much of the admiring and adulating here. It is, nevertheless, true that this "brilliant picture of an excitable son in the presence of a judicious father" (43), as E. H. Miller puts it, is quite consistent with the intense enthusiasm and imagery of incorporation that overflow in the letters and in the review of *Mosses*. However, as we found with Redburn, there are perhaps more powerful grandiose and exhibitionistic wishes that, from time to time, protrude from beneath what appears to be at first an idealizing core of the self. It is as though

Melville wished to unite with Hawthorne both by gaining power from him through the absorption of his strength and value, and by gripping and fascinating him with his own spellbinding power of expression. Indeed, Melville seems to have shared with his brother Gansevoort an aggressive self-assertiveness that could become threatening and intrusive. E. H. Miller speculates that "Melville's love . . . was intertwined with rivalry" (1975, 181) and that his "exuberance was almost an assault"; Hawthorne's "role of 'Father Confessor'"—as the object of a transference in which he would have been expected to fit a certain preestablished part—"was a kind of anomalous personality and at the same time opened his own reserved nature to invasion" (43).

Melville's aggressiveness seems to have manifested itself, for Sophia Hawthorne, most dramatically in Melville's unsettling "look." In a letter to her mother, she describes him as having

> very keen perceptive power, but what astonishes me is, that his eyes are not large & deep—He seems to see every thing very accurately & how he can do so with his small eyes, I cannot tell. They are not keen eyes, either, but quite undistinguished in any way. . . . When conversing, he is full of gesture & force, & loses himself in his subject—There is no grace nor polish—once in a while, his animation gives place to a singularly quiet expression out of those eyes, to which I have objected. (Quoted in Wilson 1991, 3)

The physical animation, "full of gesture and force," suggests an intense desire to express himself and the consequent excitement of a successful exhibitionism in the presence of a cooperative audience. The eyes, for their part, do not pierce or penetrate—as, indeed, Hawthorne's very different but equally off-putting gaze appears to have done—but they betray, it seems, a disquieting, almost threatening intrusiveness and power nonetheless. They appear to possess a perceptual intensity ("keen perceptive power") as well as a certain hypnotic, fascinatory quality. In the same letter, Sophia goes on to speak of them as having "an indrawn, dim look, but which at the same time makes you feel—that he is at that instant taking deepest note of what is before him—It is a strange, lazy glance, but with a power in it quite unique" (quoted in Wilson 1991, 3). This look "does not seem to penetrate through you, but to take you into himself." We are relying on little more than conjecture here, of course, but, if we take Sophia as a fairly accurate if particularly sensitive observer, we may conclude that Melville's peculiar way of looking, introjective, even "devouring" in character, reflects perhaps an aggressive aspect of his personality that may have emerged in his more intimate relations with others.

With all the veiling protectiveness with which he covered his "inmost Me" (4), as he calls it at the beginning of *The Scarlet Letter,* Sophia's husband may have felt overpowered and intruded upon, and thus rejected Melville's enthusiastic and perhaps ardent attempts at greater intimacy and closeness. Critics have suggested that the reclusive Coverdale's rejection of Hollingsworth's demand for a mergerlike bond in *The Blithedale Romance* may be some kind of fictionalized depiction of Hawthorne's rejection of Melville's "advances"; as Hawthorne leaves the Berkshires suddenly and without explanation, so Coverdale takes flight from Blithedale. As Wurmser describes the psychodynamics of such a transgression of personal boundaries, "an aggressive move to intrude upon and overpower the other can and should evoke guilt in us. Yet if this move is turned down, shrugged off, given the cold shoulder, we feel profound shame" (1981, 62). In the relationship between Hawthorne and Melville, these two different kinds of shame may have been at work: in Hawthorne, where "shame guards the separate, private self with its boundaries and prevents intrusions and merger" (65), "the self's integrity" would have been threatened by the other's unwanted intrusion; in Melville, it would have been the rejection in one's "inmost area" that caused shame, the feeling of a loss of love and rejection: "To be rejected in one's inmost area means that the other turns away in contempt and disappears. Ultimately radical abandonment by the other also means disappearance of the self . . ." (63).[3]

Melville's dream of gripping others—of eliciting, in his relationships and through his writings, their attention and intense admiration—did not perhaps meet with the success he had hoped for. Such success was for the world of his fiction. The prototype of this delophilic or exhibitionistic wish would seem to be the figure of Jack Chase, the handsome sailor of *White Jacket:* "No man ever had a better heart or a bolder. He was loved by the seamen and admired by the officers; and even when the Captain spoke to him, it was with a slight air of respect. Jack was a frank and charming man" (13). Frankness—the sign of a personality whose expression and perception has not been inhibited or paralyzed by shame—is perhaps the most positive quality in Melville's assessment of the psychological health of personality. It is, of course, an important feature in the character of Billy Budd, who is resented by Claggart quite precisely for his "frank enjoyment" of life. Other features tie these two characters together. Billy is impressed while on the *Rights of Man* and removed to the *Bellipotent,* and Jack leaves the Peruvian *Fight for Independence* to rejoin the American *Man of War.* Both are suspected of being by-blows of a nobleman. Both are the idealized object of an enthusiastic and joyful merger with an admiring crew:

> But at the first appearance of that universal favorite, Jack Chase, in the chivalric character of *"Percy Royal-Mast,"* the whole audience simultaneously rose to their feet, and greeted him with three hearty cheers, that almost took the main-top-sail aback.
>
> Matchless Jack, *in full fig,* bowed again and again. . . . Matchless Jack stepped forward, and, with his lips moving in pantomime, plunged into the thick of the part. Silence soon followed, but was fifty times broken by uncontrollable bursts of applause. . . . At length . . . the audience leaped to their feet, overturned the capstan bars, and to a man hurled their hats on the stage in a delirium of delight. (94)

In *Typee,* we find the same type of character in Marnoo, who, when he makes his striking appearance among the Typee, threatens to supplant Tommo as the center of attention: "So vain had I become by the lavish attention to which I had been accustomed, that I felt half inclined, as a punishment for such neglect, to give this Marnoo a cold reception, when the excited throng came within view, convoying one of the most striking specimens of humanity that I ever beheld" (135). Marnoo's power to fascinate others is not limited to his looks. Like Ahab, he is a riveting orator: "Never, certainly, had I beheld so powerful an exhibition of natural eloquence as Marnoo displayed during the course of this oration. . . . The effect he produced upon his audience was electric; one and all they stood regarding him with sparkling eyes and trembling limbs, as though they were listening to the inspired voice of a prophet" (137–38). In Tommo's initial reaction to the appearance of this rival we can see the connection between envy and the feeling of shame and narcissistic injury that results from the unsuccessful exhibition of oneself: I envy the other on whom the admiration I covet is bestowed. Envy, as clearly shown here, is rooted in the exhibitionistic drive, the area of the grandiose self. The invidiousness that defines Claggart's attitude to Billy is already apparent in this episode, though in a mild and nonpathological form. As we showed in our discussion of resentment, Claggart experiences Billy's successful exhibitionism as a personal slight, as Jackson, according to Redburn, reacts to his. Similarly, Tommo resents the way that Marnoo "engrossed the attention of every one" (137), and is, indeed, slighted by an actual snub, when Marnoo pretends indifference to Tommo and ignores his greeting: "Had the belle of the season, in the pride of her beauty and power, been cut in a place of public resort by some supercilious exquisite, she could not have felt greater indignation that I did at this unexpected slight" (136). The same image of the invidious competition between beauties at court turns up in *Billy Budd*: "As the handsome Sailor, Billy Budd's position aboard the seventy-four was something analogous to that of a rustic beauty transplanted from the provinces and brought into competition with the high born dames of the court" (*BB*, 50–51).

It is in the opening section of *Billy Budd* that the wish to be the fascinating center of attention, to be the impressive object of an admiring gaze, finds its most spectacular manifestation. We have already touched on this passage in terms of visual merger or union through looking, but it is equally interpretable from the perspective of a merger through expression or self-display. The figure of the handsome sailor moves among the flanking sailors "like Aldebarean among the lesser lights of his constellation"; he is a "signal object," a "cynosure," and the recipient of "the spontaneous homage of his shipmates," of "spontaneous tribute," "the tribute of a pause and stare, and less frequent an exclamation—the motley retinue showed that they took that sort of pride in the evoker of it which the Assyrian priests doubtless showed for their grand sculptured Bull when the faithful prostrated themselves" (43–44). Billy is the supreme example of this type of male beauty, and his adoption of the role with such careless ease suggests the fantasy of a wildly successful exhibitionism. In receiving the admiration that is lavished on him, he evinces a complete absence of self-consciousness: he doesn't have to say, in so many different ways, "Look at me": people cannot help but do it. Even Captain Vere will find his attention captured by the prepossessing Billy; even before his attention is drawn to the handsome sailor by Claggart, he has already been making plans of having Billy transferred closer to him, so that he might have the pleasure of gazing on him at his leisure:

> Now the Handsome Sailor as a signal figure among the crew had naturally enough attracted the captain's attention from the first. . . . the new recruit's qualities as "a sailor-man" seemed to be such that he had thought of recommending him to the executive officer for promotion to a place that would more frequently bring him under his own observation, namely, the captaincy of the mizzentop, replacing there in the starboard watch a man not so young whom partly for that reason he deemed less fitted for the post. (95)

The crew's final merger with Billy at the moment of his execution represents the culmination of this exhibitionistic wish. When we look at the figure of Billy as drawing on both the myth of the innocent Christ child ("he lay as in a trance, that adolescent expression previously noted as his taking on something akin to the look of a slumbering child in the cradle" [119]) and that of the sacrificial Lamb ("the vapory fleece hanging low in the East was shot through with a soft glory as of the fleece of the Lamb of God seen in mystical vision" [124]), we may conclude at first that such imagery is an expression of the deep yearning for merger with an idealized object. As Kohut observes of Christianity, however, this merger with the omnipotent figure of Christ serves primarily to defend against ambitious assertions of the grandiose self (1978, 619). In his discussion of Nietzsche and shame, Schneider points out Nietzsche's disdain for such shameless idealization; Nietzsche believed that, at least in Christian myth, it masked its opposite: that in the merger of the communicant with Christ "the paroxysm of Paul was at its height, and so was the obtrusiveness of his soul; with the thought of the oneness [with Christ] all shame, all subjection, all barriers were taken from it, and the unruly will of ambition revealed itself as an anticipatory revelling in Divine glories" (quoted in Schneider 1977, 12). It would appear that, in a similar way, in Melville's work fascination with the idealized selfobject serves primarily to curb and defend against, the wish—most explicitly presented in the figure of Billy Budd—to indulge in the most unbridled and gratifying form of self-display.

It is the shamelessness of such grandiosity that Nietzsche found particularly distasteful. In this connection, one symptom of the strong exhibitionistic tendency in Melville's work is, in fact, the presence of that which, in reaction, inhibits or discourages such open self-display. One of Christopher Ricks's observations about Keats applies perhaps just as well to Melville: "Nor is it true that there is nothing which adolescents are particularly good at; they are particularly good at blushing. What they know about, and can help us to know about is embarrassability" (1974, 51). Ricks quotes Darwin on "The Nature of the Mental States which induce Blushing," which "consist of shyness, shame, and modesty; the essential element in all being self attention. . . . It is not the simple act of reflection on our own appearance, but the thinking what others think of us, which excites a blush" (345). This self-attention is, as we have seen, a particular feature of Redburn's character, who also shows a proneness to blushing. The chief mate's pun on his rather distinctive name—"A pretty handle to a man, that; scorch you to take hold of it, haven't you got any other?" (*R*, 28)—suggests the heat and blushing that accompany both blushing and the anger that is a frequent reaction to shame.

We touch here once again on the interrelatedness of ambition, anger, and shame. As we have noted, one can burn with all of these. Ambition, which often has a raging quality about it, is clearly related to the need to overcome feelings of shame and to bask once again in the exhibitionistic warmth sparked by the gleam in the (m)other's eye. "There is a tendency," as Nathanson puts it, "for people to attempt to reduce chronic shame by initiating behaviour which may produce pride, just as they may engage in activities that require bravery in order to reduce chronic fear" (1987a, 191). In a similar vein, Kohut speaks of the "variant of narcissistic rage wherein the dominant propelling emotion is less the revenge motif and more the wish to increase self-esteem" (1977, 194). When Redburn speaks of his disappointed ambitions at the beginning of the novel, of the shattered grandiose plans he has had for his life, it is this wish that seems to be involved.

Rage proper—shame-anger or humiliated fury—is a response to those "searing" forms of shame that strike deepest, like the narcissistic mortification that Redburn feels at the grievous loss of his father. Interestingly, Redburn himself makes reference to this underlying bedrock of shame-anger or narcissistic rage that he shares with so many of Melville's protagonists: "I was naturally of an easy and forbearing disposition; though when such a disposition is temporarily roused, it is perhaps worse than a cannibal's" (R, 58). The "red" in Redburn is reflected again in the novel in the coloring of Max the Dutchman, and resurfaces, years later, in the Red Whiskers of Billy Budd; in both these cases redness goes with a combustible disposition. As Alan Lebowitz observes, Max "appears as a full-grown Redburn, providing . . . a possible prophetic image of what Redburn will become" (1970, 115). Max is described as follows: "His hair, whiskers, and cheeks were of a fiery red; and as he wore a red shirt, he was altogether the most combustible-looking man I ever saw" (R, 79). In spite of being "perhaps the best natured man among the crew," his appearance did not "belie him; for his temper was very inflammable" and "[h]e was "a great scold, and fault-finder, and often took me to task about my short-comings" (79). A minor character in Billy Budd, Red Pepper, is similarly described as "an irascible old fellow of brick-colored visage and hair" (BB, 83).

But Redburn's name connotes, perhaps above all, the blushing that fits with the character's self-consciousness and susceptibility to feeling shame in the presence of others. Blushing, as Tomkins observes, is "a reaction to heightened self-consciousness" (1963, 121); it paradoxically increases "facial communication, even though the response is instigated by the feeling of shame and the wish to reduce facial visibility" (120). There is a good example in Typee when Tommo finds himself the embarrassed object of the curious gazes of the natives as he bathes himself: "Somewhat embarrassed by the presence of the female portion of the company, and feeling my cheeks burning with bashful timidity, I formed a primitive basin by joining my hands together, and cooled my blushes in the water it contained . . ." (89). In Redburn, the protagonist, feeling uncomfortable and particularly self-conscious in the sumptuous house of pleasure to which Harry Bolton takes him in London, observes "one of the waiters eyeing me a little impertinently" and experiences a prototypical instance of shame and embarrassment: "I felt my face burning with embarrassment, and for the time, I must have looked very guilty of something. But spite of this, I kept looking boldly out of my eyes, and straight through my blushes . . ." (229). He defiantly refuses to lower his eyes in shame and stares back in an attempt to counter his feeling of passive exposure. In contrast to this experience of shame, the healthy ruddiness of Billy Budd, an expression of what Claggart resentfully perceives as his "frank enjoyment" (BB, 78) of life, suggests the suffusion of the body with what Kohut calls "a warm glow of approved and echoed exhibitionistic libido" (1963, 655).

The relation of blushing to the exhibitionistic drive is illustrated by the episode in chapter 5 in which Redburn, having just bought "a red woolen shirt," tries it on in front of the mirror to see what it looks like:

> After dinner I went into my room, locked the door carefully, and hung a towel over the knob, so that no one could peep through the keyhole, and then went to trying on my red woolen shirt before the glass, to see what sort of looking sailor I was going to make. As soon as I got into the shirt I began to feel a sort of warm and red about the face, which I found was owing to the reflection of the dyed wool upon my skin. (*R*, 24)

The exhibitionistic wish is fulfilled in the form of a gratifying narcissistic viewing of oneself (the cooperative object here is imaginary), and thus Redburn finds himself "warm and red about the face," flushing with warm, exhibitionistic pleasure, instead of blushing and burning with shame. That he ascribes the heat to the shirt is a transparent displacement of the cause; the shirt is red, and Redburn fantastically ascribes its intense heat to its reflection in the mirror. The fear in exhibitionism is apparent here as well. Significantly, when Lacan makes the distinction between the eye and the gaze, he focuses on the experience of shame and cites the passage from *Being and Nothingness* in which Sartre

> refers to the sound of rustling leaves, suddenly heard while out hunting, to a footstep heard in a corridor. And when are these sounds heard? At the moment when he has presented himself in the action of looking through a keyhole. A gaze surprises him in the function of voyeur, disturbs him, overwhelms him and reduces him to a feeling of shame. . . . Is it not clear that the gaze intervenes here only in as much as it is not the annihilating subject, correlative of the world of objectivity, who feels himself surprised, but the subject sustaining himself in a function of desire? (1978, 85)

"The gaze I encounter," Lacan asserts, "is not a seen gaze, but a gaze imagined by me in the field of the Other" (84). It is quite precisely such an imagined gaze and the consequent fear of passive exposure that lead Redburn—the exhibitionist, in this case, and not Sartre's voyeur—to take the defensive precaution of hanging "a towel over the knob, so that no one could peep through the keyhole." The action is clearly in self-conscious anticipation of being (voyeuristically) spied on and surprised in his function of desire, of exhibitionistic self-display—of being surprised, disturbed, overwhelmed, and reduced to a feeling of shame.[4]

III

The fear of exposure—the passive mode of *delophilia*, in Wurmser's scheme, in which the subject "dreads being stared at, being overcome and devoured by the looks of others" (1981, 162)—culminates in Redburn's encounter with Jackson, but it is already foreshadowed in Redburn's reaction to his social environment earlier in the novel. In his initial foray into the greater world, instead of an indulgent environment, it is "evil eyes and cold suspicious glances" (*R*, 12) that surround him, and he reacts in the same resentful way as he does to his overwhelming sense of shame in the presence of Jackson: "They were certainly a cheerless set, and to me they all looked stony-eyed and heartless. I could not help it, I almost hated them; and to avoid them, went on deck, but a storm of sleet drove me below" (12). As he later feels like an Ishmael, an unwanted outcast, so now he feels rejected by the passengers on deck; his rejection, however, is brought on, at least in part, by the reciprocal nature of his responses: "[T]here might have been something ugly in my eye" (12). His painful self-consciousness—the feeling that he is being devoured by the eyes of others, scrutinized by aggressive and shaming gazes—and the way that his own feelings of shame are projected onto others represent the passive and phobic counterpart to his wish to fascinate.

The "specific punishment for the exhibitionist," according to Fenichel, is that "the eye which looks at him will bite off part of him or devour him whole. One often meets with ideas of this sort when analyzing an exaggerated sense of shame" (quoted in Wurmser 1981, 156). Jackson is a dramatic embodiment of such a terrifying, devouring gaze. But it is not only Jackson's stare but the "fantastically overpowering and intruding effect" (Wurmser 1981, 162) of his shameless exhibition of himself that is so intimidating.

The shame-ridden Jackson, as we have seen, exemplifies the turning of the passive into the active: the one who has himself been subjected to shameful exposure, as Wurmser observes of this mechanism, changes into the "shameless exhibitor, one who fears to be seen as weak into one who is seen and feared as strong" (306). Looking plays an important part here, as the spellbound and fascinated victim now puts on the face of the fascinator, "this *falsum visagium* that casts its evil eye and glowering grimace on the spectator" (306).

> [O]ne glance of his squinting eye, was as good as a knock-down, for it was the most deep, subtle, infernal looking eye, that I ever saw lodged in a human head. I believe, that by good rights, it must have belonged to a wolf, or starved tiger; at any rate, I would defy any oculist, to turn out a glass eye, half so cold, and snaky, and deadly. It was a horrible thing; and I would give much to forget that I have ever seen it; for it haunts me to this day. (*R*, 57)

As Tomkins notes in his synopsis of Edward S. Gifford Jr.'s survey of the folkloric belief in the malignancy of "looking askance," signs of the evil eye may include "[a]ny drooping of one or both eyelids, a missing eye, an inflammation of the eyes or a squint" (1963, 166). As Melville depicts it, the evil eye may be a jealous or envious look, or a disdainful, contemptuous look, or a combination of these, but its effect on its object is ultimately the same: searing shame or mortification. In *Mardi* there is the following description of the evil eye cast by a mysterious "incognito" who haunts Yillah and the narrator:

> Upon the third day, however, there was noticed a mysterious figure, like the inscrutable incognitos sometimes encountered, crossing the tower-shadowed Plaza of Assignations at Lima. It was enveloped in a dark robe of tappa, so drawn and plaited about the limbs; and with one hand, so wimpled about the face, as only to expose a solitary eye. But that eye was a world. Now it was fixed upon Yillah with a sinister glance, and now upon me, but with a different expression. However great the crowd, however tumultuous, that fathomless eye gazed on; till at last it seemed no eye, but

a spirit, forever prying into my soul. Often I strove to approach it, but it would evade me, soon reappearing. (186)

The description here captures perfectly the idea of the sinister and intrusive nature of such a look, "forever prying into my soul," invading the inmost area of the self. It is an intrusive or devouring look that shame, in its role as what Wurmser calls "the guardian of inner reality," protects against (1981, 64–65). Sartre describes the feeling of shame as "an immediate shudder which runs through me from head to foot without any discursive preparation" (1956, 198), and this a perfect description of the feeling that runs through Redburn when he finds himself invaded by Jackson's unsettling cold and snaky gaze.

And indeed, unless it was so, how could I account to myself, for the shudder that would run through me, when I caught this man gazing at me, as I often did; for he was apt to be dumb at times, and would sit with his eyes fixed, and his teeth set, like a man in the moody madness.

I well remember the first time I saw him, and how I was startled at his eye, which was even then fixed upon me. (58)

Jackson's eye is the same baring and fascinatory weapon we later find in Claggart's accusatory and mesmerizing glance. Indeed, the power of such a gaze lies in its ability both to expose and to fascinate—*oculus fascinus* was the term for the evil eye in ancient Rome, the eye being considered the privileged weapon of the fascinator (Tomkins 1963, 162)—so that escape from it seems impossible, fight as one may to ward it off: "But though I kept thus quiet, and had very little to say, and well knew that my best plan was to get along peaceably with every body, and indeed endure a good deal before showing fight, yet I could not avoid Jackson's evil eye, nor escape his bitter enmity" (*R*, 62). In his domination of the group, the power of Jackson's eye is combined with the shameless exhibition or self-exposure of his frightening body and face: "But he had such an overawing way with him; such a deal of brass and impudence, such an unflinching face, and withal was such a hideous looking mortal, that Satan himself would have run from him" (57).

Ahab's power over the crew of the *Pequod* is not dissimilar. Like Jackson, he exemplifies the ability to overawe others through a sort of shameless and often hideous self-exposure. Indeed, he seems to be able to exercise this intimidating power, which breaks down all resistance, even in his sleep. In chapter 123 ("The Musket"), with the loaded musket in his hand and Ahab asleep in his hammock, Starbuck plots his captain's death. At the last moment, however, his courage fails him.

> I can't withstand thee, then, old man. Not reasoning; not remonstrance; not entreaty wilt thou hearken to; all this thou scornest. Flat obedience to thy own flat commands, this is all thou breathest. Aye, and say'st the men have vow'd thy vow; say'st all of us are Ahabs. Great God forbid! . . . What! hope to wrest this old man's living power from his own living hands? Only a fool would try it. Say he were pinioned even; knotted all over with ropes and hawsers; chained down to ring-bolts on this cabin floor; he would be more hideous than a caged tiger, then, I could not endure the sight; could not possibly fly his howlings; all comfort, sleep itself, inestimable reason would leave me on the long intolerable voyage. (MD, 515)

As already discussed, Ahab is a classic example of the charismatic personality; such figures, as Kohut depicts them, "demand full control over the other person, whom they need as regulator of their self-esteem, without regard for his rights as an independent person" (1978, 831). This wish for control is, more precisely, an expression of *delophilia* or archaic magic exhibitionism, which involves the wish to "impose one's power or love" on the object. "In its extreme form the object becomes a puppet, a mechanized thing" (Wurmser 1981, 165). Ahab's ability to fascinate the crew is manifested largely through the demagogic style of his speech, as most dramatically represented in the riveting oratorical performance in "The Quarter-Deck" chapter. With his first words Ahab notes "the hearty animation into which his unexpected question had so magnetically thrown [the crew]" (MD, 161), who themselves "began to gaze curiously at each other, as if marvelling how it was that they themselves became so excited at such seemingly purposeless questions."[5] The merger that consolidates Ahab's mesmeric control is emphasized when he touches the axis of the crossed lances of the three mates:

It seemed as though, by some nameless, interior volition, he would fain have shocked into them the same fiery emotion accumulated within the Leyden jar of his own magnetic life. The three mates quailed before his strong, sustained, and mystic aspect. Stubb and Flask looked sideways from him; the honest eye of Starbuck fell downright. (165)

The signs of shame at being overawed are explicit: the mates' averting of their gaze and Starbuck's "downcast eyes" (165). Ahab's explanation for their looking away points to the energy of his personal magnetism, the electric force of his personality: "For did ye three but once take the full-forced shock, then mine own electric thing, *that* had perhaps expired from out me. Perchance, too, it would have dropped ye dead. Perchance ye need it not" (166). The magnetization of the crew is completed when, like a magician waving a wand, Ahab imperiously dissolves the scene: "[W]aving his free hand to them, they all dispersed" (166). In chapter 130 ("The Hat"), the puppeteer-like control that Ahab imposes on the crew is dramatically underscored in the following passage:

As the unsetting polar star, which through the livelong, arctic, six months' night *sustains its piercing, steady, central gaze*; so Ahab's purpose now *fixedly gleamed down upon the constant midnight of the gloomy crew. It domineered above them so*, that all their bodings, doubts, misgivings, fears, were fain to hide beneath their souls, and not sprout forth a single spear of leaf.

. . . Alike, joy and sorrow, hope and fear, seemed ground to finest dust, and powdered, for the time, in the clamped mortar of Ahab's iron soul. *Like machines, they dumbly moved about the deck, ever conscious that the old man's despot eye was on them.* (536; emphasis added)

As Ahab, in the soliloquy of chapter 37 ("Sunset"), describes his power over the crew: "'Twas not so hard a task. I thought to find one stubborn, at the least; but my own cogged circle fits into all their various wheels, and they revolve" (167). Starbuck shamefully confesses: "My soul is more than matched; she's overmanned. . . . Will I, nill I, the ineffable thing has tied me to him; tows me with a cable I have no knife to cut" (169). Being the object of this kind of control, being treated as a means, is, as Wurmser observes, "the deepest shame," entailing as it does "the complete disregard of oneself as a person in one's own right, a form of contempt" (1987, 80).

The expression of narcissistic rage through the cold and contemptuous exercise of control over others finds one of its most disturbing forms in the vindictive character of Goneril in *The Confidence-Man*. Goneril is a perfect example of a *shamer*, a fascinator with an evil touch, which she wields, in the most deliberate and sadistic fashion, to ostracize her husband. Like Jackson, she goes about "corrupting and searing every heart that beat near [her]" (*R*, 104). The sense of visual exposure that often overwhelms the victim of shame turns up in the detail of Goneril's unsettling habit of staring: "During the interval she did little but look, and keep looking out of her large, metallic eyes, which her enemies called cold as a cuttle-fish's, but which by her were esteemed gazelle-like; for Goneril was not without vanity" (*CM*, 61). Like Claggart, she has the evil eye of the fascinator—staring, cold, fish-like eyes—and like him, she is vain and full of self-love. Such vanity or narcissism is a dense antishame structure in the personality and represents a rigid disavowal of intense feelings of shame, envy, and jealousy. Her husband is eventually forced to leave home with his daughter to protect her from the violent feelings of *jealousy* emanating from her own mother. Violent jealousy and envy, however, are themselves a manifestation of even more painful feelings of shame and unlovability. Goneril is a perfect example of someone who, filled with resentment, turns the tables on others, denying and alleviating her own feelings of shame by aggressively inspiring shame in others, often by her mere mesmerizing presence and gaze. She is reported contemptuously to "fling people's imputed faults into their faces. . . . Like an icicle-dagger, Goneril at once stabbed and froze; so at least they said; and when she saw frankness and innocence tyrannized into sad nervousness under her spell, according to the same authority, idly she chewed her blue clay, and you could mark that she chuckled" (61). This description of her petrifying effect on her victims is similar in its details to the description of the spell that Claggart casts over Billy with his hypnotizing gaze: stabbing, freezing one's victim, tyrannizing "frankness and innocence" into "sad nervousness."

As Tomkins observes, in folkloric belief the means of fascinating victims "might include speaking and touching" (1963, 162), and indeed the

evil eye, which all Melville's shamers wield in one form or another, assumes
in Goneril the additional form of an "evil touch":

> In company she had a strange way of touching, as by accident, the
> arm or hand of comely young men, and seemed to reap a secret
> delight from it, but whether from the human satisfaction of hav-
> ing given the evil-touch, as it is called, or whether it was some-
> thing else in her, not equally wonderful, but quite as deplorable,
> remained an enigma. (61)

The effect of such an operation is akin to that of a touching phobia or taboo, and its result is exactly the same as the optical counterpart that we
find, for example, in Jackson and Claggart. It produces deep shame and
confusion in Goneril's husband; we are told

> the unfortunate man *could never endure so much as to look upon* the
> touched young gentleman afterwards, *fearful of the mortification* of
> meeting in his countenance some kind of more or less quizzingly-
> knowing expression. He would *shudderingly shun* the gentleman.
> So, that here, to the husband, Goneril's touch had the dread opera-
> tion of the heathen taboo. (62; emphasis added)

The imagery and language of shame are quite explicit here: gaze aversion,
the fear of mortification, a shuddering feeling, and the act of shunning or
avoiding others. Like a taboo, Goneril's evil touch contaminates those she
comes in contact with and cuts off her husband from any further affiliation
with the victims. The husband feels in their mere presence actual *mortification*, and the ultimate effect of his wife's peculiar operations is to drive him
away and ostracize him from society.

In *Pierre*, the evil eye that causes shame appears in the depiction of
Plotinus Plinlimmon, a character who induces in Pierre feelings of shame
and mortification akin to those provoked in her husband by Goneril. Indeed,
this figure's appearance in the novel only makes sense when we recognize
that his relationship to Pierre externalizes the shame and self-contempt
that is directed at the latter from within. Pierre happens to pass by this
figure in the vicinity of his apartment on the morning he learns that his

mother has died. The news is both a grievous and a most humiliating blow, for in her "equally immense pride and grief" and "mortally-wounded love for her only and best-beloved Pierre" she has left the family estate of Saddle Meadows to his—in his mind, treacherous—rival Glen Stanly. "As Pierre conjured up this phantom of Glen transformed into the seeming semblance of himself; as he figured it advancing toward Lucy and raising her hand in devotion; an infinite quenchless rage and malice possessed him" (289). Pierre's narcissistic rage is triggered by an archaic sense of betrayal and entitlement: that he is being robbed of what is most proper, most essential to himself—his very identity; it is a feeling "strangely akin," as the narrator puts it, "to that indefinable detestation which one feels for any imposter who has dared to assume one's own name and aspect in any equivocal or dishonorable affair" (289). The theme of the twin or double, which is often closely linked to aggressive rivalry and to feelings of jealousy and envy, is underscored here, as Glen, by a "freak of nature," is "almost the personal duplicate of the man whose identity he assumes" (289). It is at this critical moment, having just read his mother's letter, that he bumps into Plinlimmon:

> Now, as this person deliberately passed by Pierre, he lifted his hat, gracefully bowed, smiled gently, and passed on. But Pierre was all confusion; he flushed, looked askance, stammered with his hand at his hat to return the courtesy of the other; he seemed thoroughly upset by the mere sight of this hat-lifting, gracefully-bowing, gently-smiling, and most miraculously self-possessed, non-benevolent man. (290)

Pierre finds himself frozen by the encounter and in a distressing state of nervousness and confusion. His reaction recalls the way in which "frankness and innocence" are "tyrannized into sad nervousness" under Goneril's mysterious spell: "[T]he man himself—the inscrutable Plotinus Plinlimmon himself—did visibly brush by him in the brick corridor, and all the trepidation he had ever before felt at the mild-mystic aspect in the tower window, now redoubled upon him, so that, as before said, he flushed, looked askance, and stammered with his saluting hand to his hat" (293). At this point, he is suddenly filled with the burning desire to find the pamphlet authored by Plinlimmon that he has misplaced. This outline of the Grand Master's chronometrical theory is an ingenious system that discourages idealists from striving to be, in Mapple's terms, their morally inexorable selves. It encourages them to accept the shameful disparity between the values and ideals embodied in their ego ideal and the insurmountable limitations of their true capacities. The core of Plinlimmon's theory is inspired, in fact, by poisonous feelings of shame, invidiousness, and *ressentiment*.

Pierre, of course, is already acquainted with Plinlimmon. Before passing him outside his apartment, he has suffered for days at his closet window under the man's inscrutable "tower face," the "steady observant blue-eyed countenance at one of the loftiest windows of the old gray tower." This vaguely sinister figure emits an "inscrutable atmosphere," and "One would almost have said, his very face, the apparently natural glance of his very eye, disguised this man" (290). When Pierre encounters him for the first time in person, he sees him *through glass*, two panes of glass in fact, as he glimpses, through his own window, Plinlimmon staring at him out of the window of the tower adjoining his apartment. What is suggested here is the impossibility of knowing such a man, of engaging in any intimacy with him; thus, his all-enveloping "non-Benevolence" ("it was neither Malice nor Ill-will; but something passive") and "Inscrutableness" ("the inscrutable atmosphere eddied and eddied roundabout this Plotinus Plinlimmon") (290, 291). Mindful of his simple and good-hearted friend, Charlie Millthorpe, who has fallen under Plinlimmon's influence, Pierre "could not help thinking, that though in all human probability Plotinus well understood Millthorpe, yet Millthorpe could hardly yet have wound himself into Plotinus;—though indeed Plotinus . . . might . . . have tacitly pretended to Millthorpe, that he (Millthorpe) had thoroughly wriggled himself into his (Plotinus') innermost soul" (291–92).

This section of *Pierre* bears comparison with chapters 17 and 18 of Hawthorne's *Blithedale Romance*, which recount how Coverdale, who has taken up an apartment in town, spends his days staring through an adjacent window and observing the comings and goings of Priscilla, Zenobia, and Westervelt. Zenobia appears at the window and glares at him; she then scornfully rebukes him by closing the curtains. Similarly, Pierre tries to block out Plinlimmon's face by placing some muslin over his closet window; the image of the face now curtained like a portrait but still haunting him recalls, significantly, Pierre's fascination with the ambiguous portrait of his father, a father by whom his son feels, when he has uncovered the truth, so deeply disappointed and cruelly betrayed. The connection with Hawthorne—who for Melville, it seems, was both a potential lover and a surrogate father—is further hinted at in the image of "the gay youth Apollo . . . enshrined in that eye" and "paternal old Saturn [sitting] cross-legged on that ivory brow" (293).[6] The obscurantist and mystifying strategy that Plotinus takes concerning any straightforward revelation of his "innermost soul" recalls other possible depictions of Hawthorne in Melville's work: the insensitive and egotistical Orchis in the China Aster story in *The Confidence-Man,* or the coy and shadowy Vine in *Clarel,* who can be communed with only through "the wicket." What Hawthorne has to say about his own guardedness and reserve surrounding his "inmost Me" at the beginning of *The Scarlet Letter* epitomizes this impulse to veil the self and protect oneself from any unduly frank exposure. This excessive protectiveness, this exaggerated guarding of the self, proves to be both a defense against shame and the basis of an aggressive posture that is capable of inducing shame in others; ultimately, it gives its subject the power to turn the tables and relocate shame in others, while remaining withdrawn and hidden himself. This is the insidious, aggressive tactic, of course, of a number of Hawthorne's characters, and it appears to be Plinlimmon's as well, if it is not in part a projection on the part of Pierre and his own crushing feelings of self-contempt.

As Murray puts it in the very language of shame and exposure: "Strip Plinlimmon of the disguising title of Grand Master . . . and snatch off his false beard, and you have a striking physical and psychological likeness of Hawthorne, the inscrutable Paul Pry of the guilty human heart" (1962, lxxviii). Even Plinlimmon's prying stare, Murray speculates, may indeed have been modeled on Hawthorne's "silent steady gaze," which, like Melville's but perhaps for different reasons, seems to have been "embarrassing or distressing to some people" (lxxviii). "Wonderful, wonderful eyes," one observer commented. "They give, but receive not" (Frederika Bremer, quoted in E. H. Miller 1975, 240)—an observation that, however enthusiastic in its admiration, might suggest that his look, while not very lavish of itself, could put others on the defensive. An intrusive, prying eye is associated with the crime, thematized throughout Hawthorne's work, of intruding and violating the core of another's private and protected self. The eye, "the organ of shame par excellence," as Wurmser puts it, is a potent shaming weapon, and this shaming power of the eye is related in both Melville's and Hawthorne's writings to the magic belief in the evil eye, to the idea that "the eye of an evil one will injure wherever its gaze happens to fall" (Tomkins 1963, 159). In *The House of the Seven Gables*, for example, the evil eye is associated with the uncanny magical powers that belong to members of the Maule family: "There was a great deal of talk among the neighbours, particularly the petticoated ones, about what they called the witchcraft of Maule's eye. Some said that he could look into people's minds; others, that, by the marvellous power of this eye, he could draw people into his own mind, or send them, if he pleased, to do errands to his grandfather, in the spiritual world; others, again, that it was what is termed an Evil Eye, and possessed the valuable faculty of blighting corn, and drying children into mummies with the heartburn" (Hawthorne 1965, 189–90).[7]

In Plinlimmon the aggressivity of the evil eye—so glowering and ostentatious in Jackson and Claggart—is disguised in a strange kind of passivity. The paralyzing effect of his mild countenance is produced by a kind of nonaffirmation. It is, as noted, a kind of nonbenevolence that he exudes; he is not malicious, but perhaps something worse and even more humiliating for those who would seek an affective response—there is "something passive," nonempathic, nonresponsive about him. This passivity suggests a densely narcissistic defense against shame and hints at the presence of deeply concealed feelings of envy and resentment toward others, which express themselves in this very effective countershaming attitude. The passage culminates with Pierre's acute consciousness of being observed by Plinlimmon and feeling ashamed, as though the latter were telepathically controlling his self-estimation, transmitting the thoughts: "Vain! vain! vain! said the face to him. Fool! fool! fool! said the face to him. Quit! quit! quit! said the face to him" (*P*, 293). In the end, Pierre is overwhelmed and crushed by the humiliating feeling of intense exposure, of being known and judged in his most secret self as someone worthy of only scorn and contempt, of not being able to escape this judging and shaming gaze that, as an internal or "*subjective* sort of leer," penetrates even when its victim tries to block it out by covering the window.

> Though this face in the tower was so clear and so mild . . . it at last wore a sort of malicious leer to him. But the Kantists might say, that this was a *subjective* sort of leer in Pierre. Anyway, this face seemed to leer upon Pierre. And now it said to him—Ass! ass! ass! This expression was insufferable. He produced some muslin for his

closet-window; and the face became curtained like any portrait. But this did not mend the leer. Pierre knew that still the face leered behind the muslin. What was most terrible was the idea that by some magical means or other the face had got hold of his secret. (293)

In the end, it becomes clear that this sinister, prying figure is at the same time a projection, that "this was a *subjective* sort of leer in Pierre"; the paranoid nature of Pierre's emotional state here is evident in his terrible feeling "that by some magical means or other the face had got hold of his secret." What is suggested is the wounding, deeply mortifying experience of being crushed by the relentless judgment of the superego, against which no defense seems viable and from which no escape offers itself. It is this experience of himself as a contemptible and hated object that is described earlier in the novel, when Pierre, in a fit of self-directed narcissistic rage, succumbs to an overwhelming wave of self-contempt and self-disgust: "The cheeks of his soul collapsed in him: he dashed himself in blind fury and swift madness against the wall, and fell dabbling in the vomit of his loathed identity" (171).

Wurmser speaks of the petrified petrifier, or the shamed shamer. The one who has been overpowered by shame becomes the "shameless exhibitor" and the "one who fears to be seen as weak" becomes the "one who is seen and feared as strong" (1981, 306). This exertion of a shaming and fascinatory power over others can be seen in the use of magically threatening gestures. In his discussion of the gaze, Lacan points to the relation between the gesture and what he calls the moment of seeing, a relation that is extremely important in the scenes of confrontation in Melville.

What is a gesture? A threatening gesture, for example? It is not a blow that is interrupted. It is certainly something that is done in order to be arrested and suspended. . . .
    What is very remarkable in the Peking Opera . . . is the way fighting is depicted. One fights as one has always fought since time immemorial, much more with gestures than with blows. Of course, the spectacle itself is content with an absolute dominance of ges-

tures. In these ballets, no two people ever touch one another, they move in different spaces in which are spread out whole series of gestures, which, in traditional combat, nevertheless have the value of weapons, in the sense that they may well be effective as instruments of intimidation. Everyone knows that primitive peoples go into battle with grimacing, horrible masks and terrifying gestures. You mustn't imagine that this is over and done with! When fighting the Japanese, the American marines were taught to make as many grimaces as they. Our more recent weapons might also be rewarded as gestures. Let us hope that they will remain such. (1978, 116–17)

The need for "grimacing, horrible masks and terrifying gestures" is certainly not over and done with in Melville's work. Characters in Melville often fight with the eye and by fascinating the other with the face or threatening gestures. Jackson looked into a man's mouth to count his teeth and "probed a little with his jack-knife, like a baboon peering into a junk-bottle. I trembled for the poor fellow, just as if I had seen him under the hands of a crazy barber, making signs to cut his throat. . . . For I watched Jackson's eye and saw it snapping, and a sort of going in and out, very quick, as if it were something like a forked tongue" (*R*, 60). The power of terrifying gestures is combined here with the fascinatory power of Jackson's serpentine gaze. The image of the crazy barber, interestingly enough, recurs in "Benito Cereno" in the form of a sort of macabre masquerade, with the unwitting Delano looking on trustingly. Making a show of shaving his master, Babo selects and sharpens a razor, and

> then made a gesture as if to begin, but midway stood suspended for an instant, one hand elevating the razor, the other professionally dabbling among the bubbling suds on the Spaniard's lank neck. Not unaffected by the close sight of the gleaming steel, Don Benito nervously shuddered. . . . Altogether the scene was somewhat peculiar, at least to Captain Delano, nor, as he saw the two thus postured, could he resist the vagary, that in the black he saw a headsman, and in the white a man at the block. But this was one of those antic conceits, appearing and vanishing in a breath, from which, perhaps, the best regulated mind is not always free. (*PT*, 85)

A certain theatricality of the intimidating gesture is also important in Steelkilt's face-to-face confrontation with Radney, another shamer wielding a "malignant eye." The question of the taboo on interocular intimacy, however, is also important here. Tomkins regards the evil eye as a classic expression of the "universal taboo on looking," which is "most severe when two individuals . . . look directly into each other's eyes at the same time." (1963, 157). The nature of this taboo is twofold: "it is a taboo on intimacy," which is maximized by "mutual looking," and it expresses the constraints found in all cultures on the direct expression of affects (157), the face and eyes being the site of such expression. In Melville the expression of affect through the eyes seems never to involve intimacy. It involves, rather, the glare of contempt and hatred. In such a case, according to Tomkins, "affective contagion . . . readily leads to escalation" and the "control of affect is seriously undermined" (158). This is a perfect description of what takes place in the face-to-face confrontation between Steelkilt and Radney where the former's attempts to control affective contagion are for naught. Steelkilt, peering into the eyes of his enemy, "perceived the stacks of powder-casks heaped up in him and the slow-match silently burning along towards them" (*MD*, 247). As it does elsewhere in Melville, this imagery of combustion indicates explosive narcissistic rage or shame-anger. Radney, having conceived "an unconquerable dislike and bitterness" against his rival, sets out to "pull down and pulverise that subaltern's tower, and make a little heap of dust of it" (246). We touch here again on the tower or "erection" imagery that in Melville is consistently associated with what Nathanson calls the shame-pride axis, and specifically with the ability to stand erect. Ahab, who identifies with "the proud tower" in "The Doubloon" chapter in *Moby-Dick*, is defeated and dis-masted by his rival, the white whale, and becomes obsessed with turning the tables; Radney, feeling reduced by what he perceives to be his rival's sense of superiority, becomes obsessed with pulling down the proud Steelkilt's "tower."

As Steelkilt stares into Radney's eyes and watches "the slow-match silently burning along," he reacts first of all with "that strange forbearance and unwillingness to stir up the deeper passionateness in any already ireful being," which the narrator notes is a mark of "really valiant men even when aggrieved" (247). In other words, Steelkilt does what he can, given the taboo on direct expression of affect, to neutralize the situation, to "defuse," as it were, the fuse in Radney's eye. He thus answers "in his ordinary tone." Radney then escalates the tension, replying with an oath and "in a most domineering and outrageous manner unconditionally reiterating his command" and threatening him with "an uplifted cooper's club hammer" (247). Steelkilt, again, "Heated and irritated as he was," still manages to smother "the conflagration within him," but remains "doggedly rooted to his seat, till at last the incensed Radney shook the hammer within a few inches of his face, furiously commanding him to do his bidding" (247–48). Steelkilt then retreats, "steadily followed by the mate with his menacing hammer," and to warn off "the foolish and infatuated man," he makes "an awful and unspeakable intimation with his twisted hand but it was to no purpose. And in this way the two went once slowly round the windlass" (248). Finally Steelkilt takes his stand to fight, "resolved at last no longer to retreat," and advises his superior: "Mr Radney, I will not obey you. Take that hammer away, or look to yourself." At this point, Radney finds himself in the threatening pose, weapon in hand, that we have seen assumed by both Jackson and Babo in their confrontations with a rival or victim:

> But the predestinated mate coming still closer to him, where the Lakeman stood fixed, now shook the heavy hammer within an inch of his teeth; meanwhile repeating a string of insufferable maledictions. Steelkilt, clenching his right hand behind him and creepingly drawing it back, told his persecutor that if the hammer but grazed his cheek he (Steelkilt) would murder him. Immediately the hammer touched the cheek; the next instant the lower jaw of the mate was stove in his head; he fell on the hatch spouting blood like a whale. (248)

IV

It is the same paradigm of confrontation that is apparent in the encounter between Claggart and Billy Budd. Here, however, Claggart's means of attack are covert and indirect. Slander—"the envious 'I,'" according to Berke, "is penetrating, provocative, controlling, and poisonous" and "inserts slander just as the shaming eye inserts disgrace" (1987, 330)—is the weapon of choice.

The theme is emphasized by the allusion to Ananias who plots against Paul (as Claggart plots against Billy) and falsely accuses him of being an agitator among the Jews in Damascus; struck on the mouth by Ananias's men, Paul prophesies: "God shall strike you, you whitewashed wall!" (Acts 23:3). Vere points to the body of Claggart, and exclaims to the surgeon: "It is the divine judgment on Ananias!," and after a pause: "Struck dead by an angel of God! Yet the angel must hang!" (*BB*, 101).[8] In Melville the envious eye is thus combined with the shaming eye, as Claggart's slander aims specifically at bringing disgrace on Billy as a traitor and mutineer, at having him ostracized (which in the circumstances means executed as well). By the same token, Billy's central concern throughout the trial is not to save his life but to defend his honor and the truth of his word: "I have eaten the King's Bread and I am true to the King" (106). Claggart's deep-seated envy is rooted in his own feelings of defectiveness, and his decision to slander Billy is a perfect illustration of countershaming, of turning the tables on the one in whose presence one feels crushed and defeated by shame. Thus he attempts to destroy Billy, the envied object, by exposing him and overwhelming him with disgrace in the presence of the captain.

But Claggart's plot backfires, and he finds that he is the one, in the presence of Vere, who is suddenly threatened with exposure. It is at this point that he tries to turn the tables and fixes his gaze on Billy, who under its relentless scrutiny falls into a state of confusion and paralysis that can be described only as an intense state of mortification—he is, like Sartre's voyeur, overwhelmed and reduced, to a point of complete incapacity and powerlessness, to a feeling of shame:

> With the measured step and calm collected air of an asylum physician approaching in the public hall some patient beginning to show indications of a coming paroxysm, Claggart deliberately advanced within short range of Billy and, mesmerically looking him in the eye, briefly recapitulated the accusation.
>
> Not at first did Billy take it in. When he did, the rose-tan of his cheek looked struck as by white leprosy. He stood like one impaled and gagged. Meanwhile the accuser's eyes, removing not as yet from the blue dilated ones, underwent a phenomenal change, their wonted rich violet blurring into a muddly purple. Those lights of

human intelligence, losing human expression, were gelidly protruding like the alien eyes of certain uncatalogued creatures of the deep. The first mesmeristic glance was one of serpent fascination; the last was the paralysing lurch of the torpedo fish. (*BB*, 98)

Emphasized here, through the elaborate and rather lurid description of Claggart's inhuman gaze, is Billy's overwhelming sense of horrifying exposure. Overawed by the shameful accusation made against him, he is then helplessly subjected to the mesmeric power of Claggart's look, whose hypnotic and crippling power is particularly underlined ("mesmerically looking"; "mesmeristic glance . . . of serpent fascination"; "paralysing lurch"). We are reminded of Lacan's description of the evil eye: "The evil eye is the *fascinum*, it is that which has the effect of arresting movement and, literally, of killing life. At the moment the subject stops, suspending his gesture, he is mortified. The anti-life, anti-movement function of this terminal point is the *fascinum*, and it is precisely one of the dimensions in which the power of the gaze is exercised directly" (1978, 118). The "rose-tan" of Billy's cheek is "struck as by white leprosy," the flow of blood drained from his face. Billy is frozen in terror and mortification, powerless to ward off the hypnotic spell of Claggart's devouring look.

In Billy's encounter with the conspirator planted by Claggart, his response is first confusion and then resentment. His strong emotion makes him stutter—"in his resentful eagerness to deliver himself his vocal infirmity somewhat intruded" (*BB*, 82)—and he then feels angry. He undergoes, in other words, a series of responses to mounting shame. The next time he sees the fellow, he finds himself once again at a loss when the man offers "a flying word of good-fellowship, as it were, which by its unexpectedness, and equivocalness under the circumstances, so embarrassed Billy that he knew not how to respond to it" (84). In the confrontation with Claggart, these precise reactions are repeated, but in a dramatically intensified and magnified form. Billy is once again surprised and made to feel painfully self-conscious and at a loss; but this time he is in the passive position of an accused person under a deliberately shaming gaze, and in the presence of the one person (Vere) he has the most reason to seek to please. He is too overwhelmed to speak and thus the appeal from Vere for him to speak backfires, causing but a strange dumb gesturing and gurgling in Billy; amazement at such an accusation so suddenly sprung on inexperienced nonage; this, and it may be, the horror of the accuser's eyes, serving to bring out his lurking defect and in this instance for the time intensifying it into a convulsed tongue-tie; while the intent head and entire form straining forward in an agony of ineffectual eagerness to obey the injunction to speak and defend himself, gave an expression to the face like that of a condemned vestal priestess in the moment of being buried alive, and in the first struggle against suffocation. (98–99)

This passage recalls Darwin's description of people in the most helpless and distressful embarrassment: "Most persons, whilst blushing, have their mental powers confused. . . . Persons in this condition lose their presence of mind, and utter singularly inappropriate remarks. They are often much distressed, stammer, and make awkward movements or strange grimaces" (1901, 341–42). Billy's gurgling, stammering, and dumb gesturing, his confusion and incapacity, are the unmistakable signs of a suddenly heightened and extremely agonizing self-consciousness in someone who until now, in his frank and innocent enjoyment of life, has been depicted as supremely unselfconscious, singularly unaware of himself. For Billy, the confrontation with Claggart is a traumatic moment of birth into objective self-awareness in the most negative form imaginable; Billy's sole wish is to disappear, or, failing that, to make the other disappear.

Vere quickly judges that part of Billy's problem is his desire to please and perform well in his presence, and he thinks of the analogy of an old classmate with a similar "vocal impediment" whom "he had once seen struck by much the same startling impotence in the act of eagerly rising in the class to be the foremost in response by a testing question put to it by the master" (*BB*, 99). The analogy here of the student rising in class, eager to answer and shine in the teacher's eyes, is, of course, a classic example of a situation fraught with the risk of embarrassment and humiliation. As Fenichel, who draws the connection between stuttering and ambition, observes: "In cases where only public speaking evokes the symptom, obviously an inhibition of an exhibitionistic tendency is at work. . . . An actor, struck by stagefright, might not only forget his lines but actually begin to stutter" (1945, 316). In Billy's case, the eager seeking of approval—"the intent head and entire form straining forward in an agony of ineffectual eagerness to obey the injunction to speak and defend himself" (*BB*, 98–99)—occurs in a situation where speech is absolutely imperative and yet where shame and the most painful self-consciousness have made speech impossible. Billy's "vocal embarrassment" (106), his "emotional difficulty of utterance" (196), is both a common symptom of the fear of shame that accompanies acute self-awareness and a perceived defect, the sensitivity to which exacerbates, against the person's most intense wishes, the feeling of humiliation. The ordeal of being exposed and transfixed by his shamer, and of being unable to speak or to take flight results in a crushing feeling of entrapment and enclosure. The expression on the face of the "transfixed one" (98) is "like that of a condemned vestal priestess in the moment of being buried alive, and in the first struggle against suffocation" (99). The imagery of being suffocated and buried alive perfectly captures this fear of being trapped, overpowered and closed in by the mortifying presence of the other. Unable to overcome his paralysis, Billy thus finds himself in the situation of Steelkilt who, cornered by Radney, can no longer retreat but must stand and fight.

> Going close up to the young sailor, and laying a soothing hand on his shoulder, [Vere] said: "There is no hurry, my boy. Take your time, take your time." Contrary to the effect intended, these words so fatherly in tone, doubtless touching Billy's heart to the quick, prompted yet more violent efforts at utterance—efforts soon ending for the time in confirming the paralysis, and bringing to his face an expression which was a crucifixion to behold. (99)

Unable to defend himself verbally because of the stammer that is both induced and aggravated by his intense embarrassment and self-consciousness, and unable any longer to withstand the pain of exposure and the horrifying feeling of claustrophobia, Billy, exasperated, strikes out violently against his provoker. The blow is almost a reflex, an immediate and direct expression of explosive rage triggered by the unbearable feeling of searing shame. "The next instant, quick as the flame from a discharged cannon at night, his right arm shot out, and Claggart dropped to the deck" (99).

"That Truth Should Be Silent
I Had Almost Forgot"

And as he thus made his defense, Festus said with a loud voice, "Paul, you are mad; your great learning is turning you mad." But Paul said, "I am not mad, most excellent Festus, but I am speaking the sober truth. For the King knows about these things, and to him I speak freely; for I am persuaded that none of these things has escaped his notice, for this was not done in a corner."
—Acts 26:24–26

For in this world of lies, Truth is forced to fly like a scared white doe in the woodlands; and only by cunning glimpses will she reveal herself, as in Shakespeare and other masters of the great Art of Telling the Truth,—even though it be covertly, and by snatches.
—Melville, "Hawthorne and His Mosses"

The ultimate fear at the heart of Melville's work is the fear of paralyzing, petrifying shame, the fear of being struck dumb and powerless by humiliating exposure. The downfall of Billy Budd—"the frank one," as the narrator calls him with reference to his "impulsive aboveboard manner" (*BB*, 106) when he is testifying later before the court—is that he is made helpless and unable to speak and defend himself against a lie, against the disgrace brought on by slander: "Could I have used my tongue I would not have struck him. But he foully lied to my face in presence of my captain, and I had to say something, and I could only say it with a blow" (106). Even when Vere tenderly exhorts him, he is unable to overcome his paralysis and can only stutter and stammer in distress. Shame makes speech difficult, even impossible. It conspires against the speaking of the truth because it robs the individual of the intimacy and trust that would make the fullest expression and perception possible.

Thus throughout his work and correspondence Melville emphasizes the importance of *frankness*, of speaking freely, without inhibition or fear of offense. "The sailor is frankness," the narrator comments at the beginning of *Billy Budd*, "the landsman is finesse. Life is not a game with the sailor, demanding the long head—no intricate game of chess where few moves are made in straightforwardness and ends are attained by indirection, an oblique, tedious, barren game hardly worth that poor candle burnt out in playing it" (86-87). This value given to frank and open speaking explains Vere's impatience and frustration with the insinuating indirections of Claggart ("Be direct, man; say *impressed men*"), as "something even in the official's self-possessed and somewhat ostentatious manner in making his specifications strangely reminded him of a bandsman, a perjurious witness in a capital case" (94). The effect of Claggart's "foggy" (95) tale is, contrary to his intent, to leave Vere with "strong suspicion clogged by strange dubieties" (96) concerning the accuser himself, not the accused. As a slanderer and as someone whose hiding and concealments relate as much to himself as to others, Claggart is, of course, as far in every way from truth-telling, as an ideal that Melville dreamed of, as can be imagined. Thus the urgency in Vere's insistence that Billy be forthcoming: "Speak, man! . . . Speak! Defend yourself!"

Melville's concern for seeing and speaking the truth is perhaps at its most intense during what seems to have been the most creative period of his life, the period during and immediately surrounding the composition of *Moby-Dick*. Given his hopes of an audience equal to his own creative ambitions, he must have taken the unenthusiastic and censorious treatment of his work as a cruel betrayal by the literary establishment. Duyckinck's unfriendly and moralizing review of *Moby-Dick*—for which Hawthorne, to his credit, chastised the editor—with its pious criticisms of Ishmael's role in the novel must have been particularly painful: "This piratical running down of creeds and opinions . . . is out of place and uncomfortable. We do not like to see what, under any view, must be to the world the most sacred associations of life violated and defaced" (quoted in Branch et al. 1984, 266, 265). The accusation here is that the author is being shameless, when it was clearly the false shame and modesty of his moralizing audience that Melville meant to ridicule and expose in the name of a more complete perception of reality. As we have seen, the relationship that Schneider has explored between "shame, exposure, and privacy" was something to which Melville was acutely sensitive; in the passage in *Moby-Dick* concerning Starbuck's ruined valor, for example, it is "the most sacred associations of life," as Duyckinck puts it—the sacred quality of those areas of privacy touching the self—that are held up as an essential value. But the other side of this very positive and protective sense of shame is the angry assault on the hypocrisies and false concealments that try to inhibit the perception and expression of human reality as it is.[1] Not surprisingly, the scandalized response that *Pierre* elicited from even the most literate readers was even more violent than that provoked by *Moby-Dick*, and reveals very clearly a countershaming posture on the part of a public that felt "attacked": "The reviewers were almost unanimously shocked by its style and themes, and some, as if personally insulted, directed rage against the author himself, charging Melville with moral depravity and even insanity" (Hayford et al. 1982, 178).[2] To the sense of shame, resentment, insult, and rage that Melville expresses in the book, his audience responded in fashion. Given such surveillance by the public, and doubtless feeling upon him at all times the anxious eyes of "the ever watchful Melville-Shaw-Gansevoort clans" (178), it is not surprising that the advocacy of unflinching perception and expression should be almost obsessive in his letters to Hawthorne, whose artistic ability to "tell the truth" he deeply admired. In the course of praising Hawthorne for *The House of the Seven Gables*, for example, he writes to his friend in the most idealistic terms, with respect to the latter's work:

> We think that into no recorded mind has the intense feeling of the visable truth ever entered more deeply than into this man's. By visable truth, we mean the apprehension of the absolute condition of present things as they strike the eye of the man who fears them not, though they do their worst to him,—the man who, like Russia or the British Empire, declares himself a sovereign nature (in himself) amid the powers of heaven, hell, and earth. He may perish; but so long as he exists he insists upon treating with all Powers upon an equal basis. If any of those other Powers choose to withhold certain secrets, let them; that does not impair my sovereignty in myself; that does not make me tributary. And perhaps, after all, there is *no* secret. We incline to think that the Problem of the Universe is like the Freemason's mighty secret, so terrible to all children. It turns out, at last, to consist in a triangle, a mallet, and an apron—nothing more! (*Corr.*, 186; [16 April?] 1851)

This impulse to frankness and truth, opposed in the passage above to the countervalues of secrecy and concealment, doubtless was spurred on by

Melville's personal experience of and involvement in the strategies of cloaking and hiding adopted by a family burdened with secrets and narcissistically obsessed with reputation, false honor, and the family name.

It was an involvement from which, in the end, he was unable to disentangle himself. His early flights from home and adventures at sea occupied a good four years of his life, and on his return his life as a writer promised its own kind of freedom. This promise was never fulfilled. Renker has rightly debunked the legend of Melville as someone who, as "the only man in a household composed of women and children" (1994, 136), became swallowed up by a controlling and shrouding female environment that destroyed his independence and creativity. What seems closer to the truth is that he chose unconsciously to become dependent on an indulgent domestic environment that freed him to escape with compulsiveness into his writing, and he himself attempted to control that environment through fear and secrecy. Like his mother, Melville seems to have expected indulgence, and was strangely dependent on his immediate family; it is striking, for example, that it was his brothers—Gansevoort and then Allan, and not Herman himself—who would undertake, on his behalf, negotiations with publishers. This dependency and the expectation of indulgence, as we have suggested, point to a conflict laden with shame—the wish for independence and self-assertion and the conflicting fear of being left alone. Since Melville must have felt anger at himself and self-contempt for being unable to achieve the independence and recognition he sought for in the competitive male world of adventure and literature, he would have experienced resentment toward those who reminded him of his dependence and tried to escape self-directed shame and hostility by redirecting it at those closest to him.

In their analysis of the pressures of his family background, Cohen and Yannella have addressed to what extent Melville was unable to break free of his family entanglements.

> For the sake of the family he collaborated in the common response to the mistakes and misfortunes of his father, uncle, and brother— the smoothing over and the things left unsaid. His more personal response was reticence, to reveal as little as possible of his thoughts and to withdraw into himself. What had been a family strategy become for him a personal tactic. . . . The pathos of this introversion, whether as artist or as anguished son, father, brother, or hus-

band, whether as individual or as a member of a cohesive, demanding tribe, is that Melville cherished congeniality and openness and as a writer he was outgoing. The structure and substance of his first books support this. Until *Pierre* he wrote open-ended, personal narratives that emerged from an expansive ego. *Pierre*, with its movement away from the autobiographical or obvious display, suggests Melville's deepening distrust of his experienced universe. (1992, 75)

It was, we would argue, the strength of his wish to transcend strategies of withdrawal, concealment, and secrecy and to speak as freely and openly as possible that seems to have made Melville, for a period, so astonishingly productive. Inversely, painful feelings of shame and the deep-rooted fear of being acutely disappointed and wounded by rejection are implied by this movement away from "obvious display," this introspective withdrawal and, as Cohen and Yannella put it, "deepening distrust of his experienced universe." We return to the most primary effects of shame, as so well described by Lynd: "Sudden experience of a violation of expectation, of incongruity between expectation and outcome, results in a shattering of trust in oneself, even in one's body and skill and identity, and in the trusted boundaries or framework of the society and the world one has known" (1958, 46). When Melville met with a noncooperative public, his despair over the possibility of expressing himself truthfully may inevitably have led to the receding of his most expansive impulses and a gradual "progress into silence," as Alan Lebowitz has dubbed the tragic shrinking of his creativity.

In the famous letter to Hawthorne of [17?] November 1851, written in response to the latter's praise of *Moby-Dick*, Melville gives voice to the heightened sense of self that his friend's "joy-giving and exultation-breeding letter" gives him, and his deep gratitude and sense of appreciation at being understood: "for not one man in five cycles, who is wise, will expect appreciative recognition from his fellows, or any one of them. Appreciation! Recognition! Is Jove appreciated?" (*Corr.*, 212) Hawthorne, he says, has given him "the crown of India." The intense excitement and joy at being appreciated by the author of *The Scarlet Letter* would have represented a distinct contrast with the acute disappointment at the other reviews of his work at the time, and there is in the letter a somewhat desperate sense of the singularity of the event, and of the fragility of this momentary communion and sense of merger with Hawthorne; behind it lies the anticipation of the defeat to be expected in any attempt at self-expression and communication with others, of the impediments and betrayals that inevitably leave one in a state of failure and shame ("we pygmies must be content to have our paper allegories but ill comprehended"). Hawthorne's gift is his "glorious gratuity." The postscript to the letter—the only existing letter signed "Herman," outside of those addressed to members of his family—in which Melville speaks of writing an endless letter to Hawthorne, recalls the opening of a letter to Richard Dana (1 May 1850) in which he speaks in similar terms of the intense feeling of reciprocal understanding and recognition that exists between the two:

> And I am specially delighted at the thought, that those strange, congenial feelings, with which after my first voyage, I for the first time read "Two Years Before the Mast," and while so engaged was, as it were, tied & wedded to you by a sort of Siamese link of affectionate sympathy—that these feelings should be reciprocated by you, in your turn, and be called out by any White Jackets or Redburns of mine—this is indeed delightful to me. (*Corr.*, 160)

The image of being "tied & wedded to you by a sort of Siamese link of affectionate sympathy" is the same imagery used to describe the unitedness of Ishmael and Queequeg, those bosom friends, in "The Monkey-rope" chapter: "So that for better or for worse, we two, for the time, were wedded"; "an elongated Siamese ligature united us" (320). There, as we noted, this motif of a fraternal joining is the converse of the struggling brothers theme. So "affectionate sympathy" is the antithesis of the invidious malice and hatred that, as the narrator observes in *Billy Budd*, "may spring conjoined like Chang and Eng in one birth" (77). Thus, to understand and recognize another, and be in turn recognized and understood, to be able to exercise one's expression and perception in such a reciprocal and fully confident manner, without fear of hurt, envy, jealousy, slight, or misunderstanding, without fear of disappointment or shame, this was, for Melville, the ultimate meaning of friendship—a friendship that, ultimately, and perhaps unfortunately, he seemed only to conceive of as possible between men. In a letter to his brother Thomas (25 May 1862), then a ship's captain, he jocularly evokes the advantages of having a particularly sleepy crew under one's command, a situation that affords just such a noninvidious state of congeniality. Freedom from quarrel and misunderstanding can truly be found only beyond the grave: "Think of those sensible & sociable millions of fellows all taking a good long friendly snooze together, under the sod—*no quarrels, no imaginary grievances, no envies, heart-burnings, & thinking how much better the other chap is off*—none of this: but all equally free-&-easy, they sleep away & reel off their nine knots an hour, in perfect amity" (*Corr.*, 377; emphasis added). The thought expressed here, a decade after the failure of *Moby-Dick* and *Pierre*, may by tinged with bitter irony. But the idea of "perfect amity" was, nonetheless, a genuine ideal for Melville, who envisioned friendship as a consummate situation of frankness in which trust is so taken for granted that all fear of impediment is gone. It is no accident that among the passages that Melville marked in his reading of Balzac in his later years was the letter Balzac wrote to Stendhal (6 April 1839) praising *La Chartreuse de Parme;* it reads: "Sir,—One must never put off giving pleasure to those who have given us pleasure. 'La Chartruse' is a great and splendid book. I say this without flattery, without envy. And I should be incapable of writing it" (see W. Cowan 1987, 1:110). The letter Hawthorne wrote to Melville in praise of *Moby-Dick* must have come to mind, as well as his own praise of Hawthorne in his review of *Mosses:* "For, at bottom, great excellence is praise enough to itself; but the feeling of a sincere and appreciative love and admiration towards it, this is relieved by utterance; and warm, honest praise ever leaves a pleasant flavor in the mouth; and it is an honorable thing to confess to what is honorable in others" (*PT*, 249).

Interestingly enough, in a letter to Sophia Hawthorne, in thanking her for her and her husband's praise of *Moby-Dick*, Melville speaks precisely of the affective impediments to communication that are an inevitable part of human existence. Melville, having been praised himself, feels unable to praise Hawthorne's *A Wonder-Book*, fearing that whatever he says will be taken as something he was obliged to say.

Now, Madam, had you not said anything about Moby Dick, & had Mr Hawthorne been equally silent, then had I said perhaps, something to both of you about another wonder-full Book. But as it is I must be silent. *How is it, that while all of us human beings are so entirely disembarrassed in censuring a person; that so soon as we would*

praise, then we begin to feel awkward? I never blush after denouncing a
man: but I grow scarlet, after eulogizing him. And yet this is all wrong;
and yet we can't help it; and so we see how true was that musical
sentence of the poet when he sang—
> "We can't help ourselves"

For tho' we know what we ought to be; & what it would be
very sweet & beautiful to be; yet we can't be it. (*Corr.,* 219; emphasis added)

Censuring or denouncing another person, as we have seen, is often a means
of averting attention and shame from oneself, of—as Melville puts it—
disembarrassing ourselves. On the other hand, the sense of shame as discre-
tion or tact that Melville speaks of here—the taboo against praising someone to the face ("praise to the face is disgrace")—would seem to exist because
such praise is open to misinterpretation. The one praised may see it as an
intrusion and consequently feel embarrassed and self-conscious. Melville
laments this paralyzing obstacle to the expression of genuine and heartfelt
admiration for others, but sees no way around the psychological mechanism that lands one in this involuntary condition. He deems it something
that we cannot help: "For tho' we know what we ought to be; & what it
would be very sweet & beautiful to be; yet we can't be it." The recognition
of our helplessness in such matters—that "we can't help ourselves"—recalls
the comic acceptance of shame that we find in characters such as Stubb and
Captain Boomer, in sharp contrast to the unforgiving reaction to mortification in Ahab.

Melville's observations about the embarrassment of praise, and his painful sense of the unavoidable limitations placed on human communication,
reveal, however casually, a wistfulness on Melville's part—a dream of complete fulfillment in the area of expression and perception, showing and
seeing, in a world gloriously unimpeded by unnecessary or toxic forms of
negative affect. It is this desire for an unobstructed communion on Melville's
part that, we may speculate, clashed in the end with Hawthorne's profound
reticence and reclusiveness, with the latter's apparent inability (outside his
marriage) to express his feelings fully enough or respond adequately to those
of others. William Dean Howells once described Hawthorne as being cor-
dial enough for a man so shy, but "there was a great deal of silence in it all,
and, at times, in spite of his shadowy kindness, I felt my spirits sink" (quoted

in E. H. Miller 1975, 172). Frustration with Hawthorne's shyness, and with his own unsuccessful efforts to draw his friend out of it, must have—to use that most Melvillian of words again—exasperated Melville at times, as is evident in his comment to Evert Duyckinck that there was "something lacking—a good deal lacking—to the plump sphericity of the man. What is that? —He doesn't patronize the butcher—he needs roast-beef, done rare.—" (*Corr.*, 181; 12 February 1851). His letters to Hawthorne reveal, as we have seen, a certain self-consciousness, almost aggressively stressed at times, about the possibility that his own frank and direct manner might cause his friend, who had a more refined and aristocratic style, to withdraw. "It is but nature," he writes in the same letter in which he speaks of the ability to apprehend "visable" or visible truth, "to be shy of a mortal who boldly declares that a thief in jail is as honorable a personage as Gen. George Washington" (190–91; [1 June? 1851]). Melville liked to adopt this posture of the ruthless democrat, the man for whom genuine frankness and truth were only possible in a truly egalitarian situation. But since such situations are hard to come by, he had to keep reminding himself of the significance of Enobarbus's statement, which he emphatically marked with double check marks in his copy of *Antony and Cleopatra*: "That truth should be silent I had almost forgot" (see W. Cowan 1987, 2:440). He then goes on in the same letter:

> But Truth is the silliest thing under the sun. Try to get a living by the Truth—and go to the Soup Societies. Heavens! Let any clergyman try to preach the Truth from its very stronghold, the pulpit, and they would ride him out of his church on his own pulpit bannister. It can hardly be doubted that all Reformers are bottomed upon the truth more or less; and to the world at large are not reformers almost universally laughing-stocks? Why so? Truth is ridiculous to men. (*Corr.*, 191)

Characteristically, Melville then checks himself, out of fear that he has allowed himself to talk too much and made a fool of himself, in ironic confirmation of the very point he is making: the speaking of truth makes one ridiculous, and therefore the fear of being ridiculous in speech with another, which makes us awkward and unnatural—that is, fearful of shame or embarrassment—may well be the clearest sign that we are in the vicinity of the true. "Truth uncompromisingly told," says the narrator in *Billy Budd*, "will always have its ragged edges" (128)). As with expression, so with perception. He says in a letter to Duyckinck (3 March 1849) of Emerson and his ilk:

> And, frankly, for the sake of the argument, let us call him a fool;— then had I rather be a fool than a wise man.—I love all men who *dive*. Any fish can swim near the surface, but it takes a great whale to go down stairs five miles or more; & if he dont attain the bottom, why, all the lead in Galena can't fashion the plummet that will. I'm not talking of Mr Emerson now—but of the whole corps of thought-divers, that have been diving & coming up again with bloodshot eyes since the world began. (*Corr.*, 121)

In another letter to Duyckinck Melville bemoans the poor reception of *Mardi:* "What a madness & anguish it is, that an author can never—under no conceivable circumstances—be at all frank with his readers.—Could I, for one, be frank with them—how would they cease their railing—those at least who have railed" (*Corr.*, 149; 14 December 1849). Murray comments that Melville here is "predicting that if conventions permitted him to be as honest as he wished," his readers would, like Hawthorne, embrace his soul and overlook "the imperfect body" (1962, xxiii). In other words, shame and the fear that one is unlovable would overcome the fear of displaying oneself and one would be recognized at last, in the form one likes to be seen. Murray concludes that it was in the writing of *Pierre* that "Melville was impelled . . . to a more explicit confession of his soul's career, even to an exposure, before the flower fell to the mould, of the heart of his mystery, the positive Truth, left out of his preceding works" (xxiv). It is worth noting that this same image of diving for ever-elusive truth comes up in that novel, where, significantly, the tone is that of an embittered idealist whose most fundamental trust, and faith in the truth, has suffered some deep and inalterable disappointment: "For the more and the more that he wrote, and the deeper and the deeper that he dived, Pierre saw the everlasting elusiveness of Truth . . ." (*P*, 339).

In his very acute analysis of the obsession with truth in Melville, Murray distinguishes three types of meaning that Melville gives to truth-saying, and each bears on shame in a different way. There is the "veritable compulsion," most pronounced in *Pierre*, "to cast forth his inmost self and in so doing to disclose certain secrets that were dreadfully real to him" (1962, xxviii). Nineteenth-century taboos "prevented him from completely fulfilling his mission," though, in the final account, "much is laid bare for the appreciation of a cunning, pliant reader whose perceptions are not blocked at the literal level" (xxviii). Secondly there are the great psychological insights, the sort of things that spring from the mouths of Shakespeare's characters and that, as Melville writes in "Hawthorne and His Mosses," "we feel to be so terrifically true, that it were all but madness for any good man, in his own proper character, to utter, or even to hint of them. Tormented into desperation, Lear the frantic King tears off the mask, and speaks the sane madness of vital truth" (*PT*, 244). Finally, truth for Melville is a "statement of value which he strongly endorses," which may be "either positive or negative. A positive truth, for Melville, is always some expression of love for an estimable object (often an object that has been neglected, depreciated, or condemned by his culture); and out of love for this thing (which may be the self) flows negative truth, the expression of hatred (or contempt) for that which opposes it" (Murray 1962, xxix). Melville's ideal, as Murray concludes, was "positive truth," the truth of Shakespeare and Christ. It was Melville's greatest ambition, as he writes to Evert Duyckinck, to equal "Shakespeare and other masters of the great Art of Telling the Truth,—even though it be covertly and by snatches." He expresses the wish that "Shakespeare had lived later, & promenaded in Broadway . . . that the muzzle which all men wore on their souls in the Elizabethan day, might not have intercepted Shakespeare's full articulations. For I hold it a verity, that even Shakespeare, was not a frank man to the uttermost. And, indeed, who in this intolerant Universe is, or can be?" (*Corr.*, 122; 3 March 1849). He then insists: "But the Declaration of Independence makes a difference." It did not, it would seem, make the difference he had counted on.

In contrasting Keats with Shelley, Christopher Ricks cites a passage in which the latter speaks defensively and apologetically of "describing the deepest effects of abstract love"; unable to "avoid the danger of exciting some ideas connected with this mode of expression," he has thus "exposed himself to the danger of awakening ludicrous or unauthorized images" (1974, 60). Shelley here is contrasted with Keats, who

would never have been betrayed into the total defensiveness of
this (as if the possibility of the ludicrous were simply an unfortunate side-effect rather than a true concomitant of the true). . . .

Shelley was chary; Keats's greatness was that though subtly
considerate and alert he was unchary. His muse was, in his own
words, "the unchariest muse"—the least chary of muses. (60)

What Ricks has to say about Keats's uncanny ability "to deal intelligently
and sensitively with the possibilities of embarrassment" (62) applies, to some
extent, to the operation of Melville's creative genius as well. In a letter to
Hawthorne (29 June 1851), for example, Melville indicates his awareness of
the perceived inappropriateness, the potential embarrassment, of his own
expressive self-display:

I am sure you will pardon this speaking all about myself,—for if I
say so much on that head, be sure all the rest of the world are
thinking about themselves ten times as much. Let us speak, though
we show all our faults and weakness,—for it is a sign of strength to
be weak, to know it, and out with it,—not in [a] set way and osten-
tatiously, though, but incidentally and without premeditation.
(*Corr.*, 195–96)

Indeed, it can be said of Melville, as Ricks says of Keats, that he is one of the
very few writers who "come at embarrassment from a different angle of
necessity: from the wish to pass directly through—not to bypass (however
principled and perceptive the bypassing)—the hotly disconcerting, the potentially ludicrous, distasteful, or blush-inducing" (Ricks 1974, 68). For both
writers, the way to "the true" is through shame and "the blushful," and art
or literature is the medium by which shame is transcended, providing as it
does that unimaginable state of intimacy where embarrassment or shame
help to guide us toward, rather than away from, the true. "I have written a
wicked book," Melville writes to Hawthorne, "and feel spotless as a lamb.
Ineffable socialities are in me" (*Corr.*, 212; [17?] November 1851). Expressed
here is Melville's unbelieving astonishment that he has managed the miracle
of communicating the truth free from the impediment of personal, paralyzing inhibitions or taboos. This is perhaps, as Ricks claims, what literature is
capable of offering us: "It is a crucial fact about the genuine mutuality and

reciprocity, and indeed intimacy, of our relation to books that there is no mutuality or reciprocity of embarrassment" (1974, 189).

In the same vein, Wurmser speaks of the desire to transcend shame as one of the greatest incentives to creativity. Such creativity involves an intense experience of merger, "this bursting through boundaries on so many levels, this glowing, warm fusion experience [that] stands against the dark foil of destruction" (Wurmser 1981, 293). It produces "A heightened sense of being alive, of attaining the best within, the ultimate meaning of oneself" and "is accompanied by a reaching out to others: the primary audience to whom the creative work is directed" (293). Such creativity is "a form of love with strong narcissistic aspects." Shame, on the other hand, "is the defeat of such love—the dark side of night compared with the shining brilliance of this 'greatest and most creative power,' as Plato called Eros in the *Symposium*, the 'best friend of man, the helper and the healer'" (166).

For a brief but blessed time, and then in sporadic moments throughout his life, Melville seems to have known this creative power, in both its fusing and its aggressive power, the bright, glowing warmth and the "dark foil of destruction." With it came the somewhat manic exhilaration in knowing that he was possessed of it. In the letters to Hawthorne the excitement is often palpable. In the letter of 17 November 1851, in particular, he refers to the apparent madness of an unimpeded expression of his feelings and thoughts, and evokes a powerful image of merger, the violent but creative fusion of colliding fraternal hearts: "But, believe, I am not mad, most noble Festus! But truth is ever incoherent, and when the big hearts strike together, the concussion is a little stunning" (*Corr.*, 213). A similar image, an expression of the same intense wish for love and communion occurs in the exhortation to the poor sub-sub-librarian in the "Extracts" of *Moby-Dick:* "Here ye strike but splintered hearts together—there, ye shall strike unsplinterable glasses!" (xviii). This festive image of the most frank and open communication appears in his letters to Hawthorne whenever the subject is communion with his friend. Indeed, the imagery of sociability and congeniality in the letter of 1 June 1851 recalls the same humorous upside-down world, with its imagery of Rabelaisian dialogue, drinking, and comic drubbing:

> Would the Gin were here! If ever, my dear Hawthorne, in the eternal times that are to come, you and I shall sit down in Paradise, in some little shady corner by ourselves; and if we shall by any means

be able to smuggle a basket of champagne there (I won't believe in
a Temperance Heaven), and if we shall then cross our celestial legs
in the celestial grass that is forever tropical, and strike our glasses
and our heads together, till both musically ring in concert,—then,
my dear fellow-mortal, how shall we pleasantly discourse of all the
things manifold which now so distress us,—when all the earth shall
be but a reminiscence; yea, its final dissolution in antiquity. Then
shall songs be composed as when wars are over; humorous, comic
songs,—"Oh, when I lived in that queer little hole called the world,"
or, "Oh, when I toiled and sweated below," or, "Oh, when I knocked
and was knocked in the fight"—yes, let us look forward to such
things. (191–92)

In the letter of 29 June 1851, he anticipates a future visit to Hawthorne:
"When I am quite free of my present engagements, I am going to treat myself to a ride and visit to you. I have ready a bottle of brandy, because I
always feel like drinking that heroic drink when we talk ontological heroics
together" (196). "In a sense," Wurmser writes, "love at its peak means being
as fully accepted as is humanly possible in the wish for enriching self-
expression and in the desire to be gloriously and abidingly fascinated and
impressed—and to have reciprocity in this on uncounted levels of communication and attentiveness" (1981, 166). This would seem to be what Melville
sought in his friendship with Hawthorne. It is most certainly what he sought
in his writing. In his most ambitious expectations, in both his personal and
in his creative life, he met, it seems, with disappointment and defeat. But
the work remains. Through it he continues to speak. And we continue to
listen—with the greatest possible attentiveness.

Introduction: Melville and Shame

1. For a summary of Kohut's ideas, see also Bacal (1990, 225–73) and, in the context of literary criticism, Layton (1986, 1–27), Bouson (1989, 11–24), Berman (1990, 20–34), and Sussman (1993, 63–81).

2. Harold Beaver's note in the Penguin edition is a good example: "'Caper,' for Ishmael, always carries a hint of the caprine, and so of sex. . . . cf. Young Ishmael's attempt 'to crawl up' his stepmother's 'chimney'; and the dead grasp of that 'supernatural hand'" (1986, 715). Or as Edwin Haviland Miller notes: "The dream deals symbolically, as Leslie Fiedler points out, with the boy's desire for intercourse with the stepmother and with the punishment he accords himself for his violation of the universal taboo" (1975, 79).

3. The first two volumes of Tomkins's work were published in 1962 and 1963, and the last volumes appeared in 1991 and 1992. For a good introduction to Tomkins's work, see Nathanson 1992, 35–149.

4. For Wurmser's summary of Freud's views, see Wurmser 1981, 147.

5. For a psychoanalytic treatment of tragedy and the tragic character, see, for example, Wurmser 1978, 324–34 and 1989, 41–127. Also, see the discussion of tragic versus guilty man in Kohut 1978, 757–61 and his examination of the tragic character in Kohut 1990, 166–76.

6. The relationship between shame and laughter has been discussed by Nathanson 1992, 378–95; by Kohut in relation to empathy and wisdom (1971, 324–28); and by Retzinger (1987).

7. Renker's argument in "Herman Melville, Wife Beating, and the Written Page" "intends both to call specific and corrective attention, as a biographical and historical issue, to the wife beating that scholars have either silenced or failed to confront and to explore the implications of such a revelation for our understanding of Herman's writings" (1994, 123).

See also Clare Spark's lively analysis of the scholarly cover-ups. In one of her letters to Paul Metcalf, she comments that, as an investigative journalist expert "on institutional censorship of artists & writers," she has "never seen anything so amazing as the repression of Herman Melville's writing by the very people who believe they are his champions" (quoted in Metcalf 1991, 26–27). In her dissertation she cites the example of the suppression by a number of scholars (Olson, Leyda, Murray) of the letter (from Thomas Melville Jr. to Lemuel Shaw) suggesting "that Allan Melvill had fathered a natural child; that the abandoned mother and daughter, claimants upon Allan's estate, had visited Thomas' mother and his sister Helen after Allan's death in 1832 and had been paid $200 by Thomas Melville Jr" (quoted in Metcalf 1991, 70). See also chapter 1, "History of a Secret Sister," in Young 1993, 9–26.

8. Melville's Uncle Thomas, interestingly enough, similarly "overextended himself and was involved in questionable financial manoeuvres. He borrowed heavily from his father and Judge Shaw and at one point was confined to a debtor's prison" (Cohen and Yannella 1992, 70). Later, in Galena, Illinois, where "he lived the life of a local aristocrat, successful businessman, and civic leader," and where Herman visited him in 1840, he "disgraced himself by embezzling from his friend and business partner" (70). Melville's attitude to his uncle, a man who possessed the aura (at least in his nephew's eyes) of a romantic adventurer, was, typically, "sympathetic and defensive. Uncle Thomas was another father who betrays son Herman" (70).

9. Tolchin has examined conflicted mourning as a source of psychological turmoil that Melville attempted to resolve in his creative life. He explains the explosive burst of creativity in Melville's career, which began with *Typee* and culminated in *Moby-Dick* and *Pierre*, as, in part, a delayed response to the traumatic effects of his father's death and the disturbed process of grief that followed it.

10. See, for example, Cohen and Yannella 1992, 146–51.

11. Allan Melvill composed "a laudatory biography of Major Melvill to be sent to President Andrew Jackson," and made strenuous efforts "to publish biographical memoirs of his father-in-law, General Peter Gansevoort, the 'Hero of Fort Stanwix.'" Herman himself contributed "a life of his Uncle Thomas Melville for inclusion in a history of Pittsfield" (Cohen and Yannella 1992, 32).

12. "Recently discovered correspondence describing views in 1867 of

Elizabeth and others of Melville's alleged insanity makes clear that life with Herman was at times almost impossible. The family minister and Sam Shaw, who were privy to Elizabeth's upset over Melville's behaviour, sought a way to get her to Boston without arousing his suspicions. Elizabeth seriously considered taking some action, but fortunately for Melville she never did. Only a few months later in September, the oldest child, Malcolm, eighteen years old, died of a gunshot wound. The death devastated Elizabeth and deeply affected Herman, who likely kept his grief to himself" (McCarthy 1990, 124). See also Paul Metcalf, who mentions in one of his letters to Clare Spark a story told him by Charles Olson, who was in touch with Henry Murray "about Herman beating on Lizzie, about Herman coming home one night drunk and throwing her down the back stairs" (1991, 14–15).

13. Clare Spark has imaginatively reconstructed the family dynamic, characterized by social snobbery, concealment, and "explosive resentments," as it may have formed around the powerful and intimidating figure of Maria Gansevoort Melville (see, in particular, Metcalf 1991, 57–59).

14. The groundbreaking work of Alice Miller, with its focus on childhood trauma caused by parental abuse and authoritarian child-rearing practices, has had a significant influence on current biographical writing. Miller believes "that childhood is the key to understanding a person's entire later life. By becoming sensitive to childhood suffering, I gained emotional insight into the predicament of the totally dependent child, who must repress his trauma if there is no sympathetic and supportive person he can talk to. On the other hand, I became increasingly aware of the power adults wield over children, a power sanctioned or concealed in most societies but one that has become more and more apparent in recent decades as a result of psychohistorical studies, therapy involving psychotics, children, and families, and above all psychoanalytic treatment of patients. . . . I came to the conclusion that not only destructiveness (i.e., the pathological form taken by healthy aggression) but also sexual and other disturbances, especially of a narcissistic nature, can be more easily understood if the reactive character of their origins is given more attention" (1986, 6).

15. Melville, with the publication of *Typee*, became fixed "in the public mind as a writer of South Sea romances. It was not, he came increasingly to feel, the sort of success he wanted. When, some ten years and nine books later, he closed his career as a professional writer, he did so in large part out of anger at this label and at the expectations that went with it" (Bowen 1960, 1).

16. As Elizabeth Foster writes: "During the next few years *Mardi* was remembered occasionally in the British press, with less amusement, and was confirmed in the place it was to hold into the twentieth century as the first of the series of books (with *Moby-Dick*, *Pierre*, and *The Confidence-Man*) fatal to Melville's popularity, in which, as his contemporaries thought, he obstinately turned away from his true direction and lost himself in the fogs of dark philosophy and obscure meanings and, except in *The Confidence-Man*, extravagant, half-insane writing" (1970, 666).

Chapter One: How to Make a Misanthrope

1. Much of the initial inspiration for this chapter derives from the work of Ruth Benedict and her intriguing descriptions, in *The Chrysanthemum and the Sword*, of shame, ostracism, and the fear of abandonment as social regulators in Japanese society. (I am aware, of course, of the controversial context of Benedict's work—the book was commissioned as part of the American war effort—and the extent to which, since then, Benedict's cultural biases have been thrown into question, but it seems to me that her essential insights remain valid.) The Japanese psychoanalyst Takeo Doi, in his ground-breaking work *The Anatomy of Dependence*, written over twenty years ago, attempted to find a psychoanalytic model suitable to the nature of Japanese society, and in so doing came to conclusions that are quite consistent with much of what Benedict has to say.

2. The story may also be based on the disgrace of his Uncle Thomas as well. See note 8 to the introduction. As Cohen and Yannella observe: "Melville recalled the pathos of [his uncle's] faded gentility in the magazine sketch 'Jimmy Rose' (1855), named for a character he pities and defends against imputations of dishonesty, and included a wry reflection of his disastrous business career in Chapter 40 of *The Confidence-Man*, 'the story of China Aster'" (1992, 70).

3. "But Allan damaged the family name and fortune as significantly as had his brother. He borrowed heavily from Major Melvill to start and sustain his business. He then entered a 'confidential' relationship to rescue it. The son so proud of his family name supplied family capital to his partners, but kept his own involvement secret. He gave the firm the backing of his reputation and endorsed its notes, as if he were not financially involved.

The arrangement failed, and plunged Melville into bankruptcy" (Rogin 1983, 29). Rogin sees these events, which had such an enormous impact on Melville's personal history, as the "real" story behind *The Confidence-Man*. See his full account at Rogin 1983, 249–54.

4. See Watson 1988, 186–87.

5. As Bainard Cowan observes: "Ishmael's narrative is, as we have said, retrospective; there are always two Ishmaels, as scholars have seen 'two Dantes' in the *Commedia*" (1982, 75). In other words, "a difference in knowledge and understanding separates the two Ishmaels—the prior one is characterized by his ignorance" (75).

6. Bainard Cowan observes that "the central procedure of this paragraph, as of much of the first chapters, is de-flation" (1982, 74). Cowan makes good use of Bakhtin's theory of the carnivalesque in his reading of *Moby-Dick*. Compare his analysis of Melville's use of the parable of Lazarus and Dives at p. 72.

7. According to Nathanson, rue and contrition involve three affects: "*shame* triggered by awareness (both the nature of one's actions and the nature of the self who committed them); *fear* of punishment for what one has done; and *distress* produced by the constancy of one's shame" (1992, 327).

8. Pip's desertion by his companions is about as close as one can get to the starkness of the child's terror at abandonment. In his study of narcissism in literature, Berman quotes the following passage from Bettelheim's *Uses of Enchantment*: "There is no greater threat in life than that we will be deserted, left all alone. Psychoanalysis has named this—man's greatest fear—separation anxiety; and the younger we are, the more excruciating is our anxiety when we feel deserted, for the young child actually perishes when not adequately protected and taken care of. Therefore the ultimate consolation is that we shall never be deserted" (Bettelheim 1977, 145; quoted in Berman 1990, 53).

9. Arwin, for example: "Doubtless she preferred the more brilliantly promising boy Gansevoort to this less taking younger brother. . . . In the long run the ambitious and commanding side of Maria Melville's nature was to gain the upper hand, and to wreak injury on the emotional career of her 'meek' second son" (1957, 18).

10. Miller structures his biography of Melville according to this myth, with chapters entitled "Abraham—Allan Melvill," "Sarah—Maria Gansevoort Melvill," "Isaac—Gansevoort Melville," "Ishmael—Herman Melville."

11. There may be an echo here of *Oedipus the King*—a play that is of special interest in terms of the themes and imagery of traumatic shame. In an exchange between Creon and Oedipus, the former asks: "What if you're wholly wrong?" To which Oedipus replies: "No matter—I must rule" (ll. 701–2).

Chapter Two: Mortifying Inter-Indebtedness

1. In *Moby-Dick* whales in the heat of the chase—here (and elsewhere) I am indebted to Eugene F. Irey's *A Concordance to Herman Melville's "Moby-Dick"*—are often "exasperated." I find four such infuriated creatures in the novel. Beyond that, as we have already seen, the word is remarkably insistent in Melville's work. Ahab, not surprisingly, is associated with the word three times, and each time in the context of his narcissistic rage. The word occurs twice in this chapter of *Moby-Dick*, along with three occurrences of the word "rage," and one of "fury."

2. As we have already suggested with reference to Ishmael's splenetic depression at the beginning of the novel, undischarged shame-anger that remains directed at the self, and not guilt, would seem to be the most likely basis of depression in Melville. Similarly, Grunberger explains depression in terms of a "want of narcissistic confirmation," which reopens the child's "narcissistic wound. He is reminded of his paradise lost, and, in contrast to this earlier narcissistic omnipotence, he has a searing sense of his inadequacy and insignificance, a feeling that can be compared to shame, *shame that the ego feels before its ego ideal*" (1979, 225). Depression is "the psychic expression of a lack . . . of [the self's] confirmation by the ego ideal," which gives "rise to a feeling in the ego of shameful weakness, a mixture of mental dejection, despondency, disgrace, and disgust" (225).

3. The adverb "abjectly" in this passage has a very precise weight. It occurs in another passage: in chapter 34 ("The Cabin-Table"), where Ahab's sultanic lordliness is the theme. The crew has already been introduced in the preceding chapters in such as way as to emphasize the trenchantly hierarchical nature of the divisions of rank aboard ship. Flask, before he enters the cabin, "pauses, ships a new face altogether, and, then, independent, hilarious little Flask enters King Ahab's presence, in the character of Abjectus, or the Slave" (*MD*, 150). Nathanson notes that *abject*, as its etymology sug-

gests, "is a synonym for *downcast*, and of nearly identical origin. Both words describe the physical actions associated with shame affect" (1992, 254).

4. As has been noted by a number of critics, leg injury is an insistent theme in Melville's work. For Chase, the impaired leg imagery is part of the theme of "the maimed man in the glen," an expression of the hero's "fear of castration" (1949, 12). For alternative interpretations, see, for example, Tolchin 1988, 40 and Rogin 1983, 44. My feeling is that the idea of castration here, quite valid in itself, is clarified by the shame-related issues of dependency and independence. Besides Ahab's ivory leg, there is, most obviously, Tommo's leg injury in *Typee*, which carries connotations of a prolonged and dangerous state of infantile dependency—or "castration"—a situation caused by, and itself a source of, feelings of shame. Another example is Redburn—a case we shall look at in some detail—who wishes to be able to *walk on his own*, as it were, but whose fear of abandonment and consequent psychological dependency on surrogate parental figures prevents him from experiencing pride in his own independence.

5. The pioneering work on humor and the comic spirit in Melville is Edward Rosenberry's *Melville and the Comic Spirit*. Jane Mushabac's *Melville's Humor: A Critical Study* is also of great interest. The latter study looks at the idea of frontier humor in Melville within a Bakhtinian framework of the grotesque. This comic spirit is inevitably linked in Melville to his deepest democratic and communal impulses. As Mushabac proposes: "I suggest Melville found a tradition of prose humor which, beginning in the Renaissance with the opening of the New World frontier, celebrated a new man, a man of infinite potentials. Singing this new man's praises as well as continually undercutting his glory, these works gave Melville a tone. . . . . Melville's humor releases the tension of man's predicament in an ideal, democratic society" (1981, 2, 4).

6. Kohut bestows on humor a similar power to heal what he calls narcissistic personality disorders: "All of a sudden, as if the sun were unexpectedly breaking through the clouds, the analyst will witness, to his great pleasure, how a genuine sense of humor expressed by the patient testifies to the fact that the ego can now see in realistic proportions the greatness aspirations of the infantile grandiose self or the former demands for the unlimited perfection and power of the idealized parent imago, and that the ego can now contemplate these old configurations with the amusement that is an expression of its freedom" (1971, 325).

7. Narcissistic mortification, it seems to me, is the psychological explanation for this anxiety focused on the body-self that Sharon Cameron has treated from a philosophical perspective in her study of corporeal imagery in Melville (see, for example, 1991, 47–48, 60–65).

8. The preceding discussion has, I am sure, made apparent by now another aspect of this theme of inter-indebtedness. Carolyn Porter has contrasted the dialogical capacity of Ishmael's voice with Ahab's terrible monologism, "doomed to hear nothing but his own voice, since he is deaf to the voices of others" (1986, 103). It is not surprising that Ahab resents, among other obligations, the fact that he owes "for the flesh in the tongue I brag with" (*MD,* 472). Porter rightly speaks of his dream of "discursive isolation," of "discourse purified by amnesia of any 'mortal inter-indebtedness' to others" (1986, 104). The contrast between Ahab's narcissistic isolation and Ishmael's celebration of a universal anatomy of dependence thus finds its rhetorical counterpart.

9. Compare the following passage from *Mardi:* "Yet not I, but another: God is my Lord; and though many satellites revolve around me, I and all mine revolve around the great central Truth, sun-like, fixed and luminous forever in the foundationless firmament" (368). Or a similar passage in *Redburn:* "Then was I first conscious of a wonderful thing in me, that responded to all the wild commotion of the outer world; and went reeling on and on with the planets in their orbits, and was lost in one delirious throb at the center of the All" (66).

Chapter Three: The Inexorable Self

1. This judging, all-seeing, invasive God is the God that Nietzsche did his utmost to kill. An extreme expression of the dread of shameful exposure, as Carl Schneider points out, is Nietzsche's horror at "the divine violation of the human" (1977, 130). For Nietzsche, the "shamelessness of God, his all-knowing, all-invading eyes" is "an image of rape, in which man is denuded of all protective covering, and his most private space penetrated without leave." Similarly, Wurmser speaks of Nietzsche's "killing of God" as a way of eliminating "the eye that saw everything; the 'ugliest man' commits the deed of murdering God because the man who obeys the 'you ought' does not want to command himself." He then quotes Nietzsche: "He—*had*

s passage, and passages like it in Melville, such as the exaltation
n *Billy Budd*, bears comparison with the lengthy passage from a
er Gansevoort in which are clearly displayed Allan Melvill's "level
actual hero worship, and awe of institutions" (quoted in Cohen
lla 1992, 150).

lville's interest in the Christian faith, and in the figure of Christ,
is fascination with this idealizing pole. Starbuck's worldview, as
ted, is associated with Christian idealism, the faith in lofty ideals
n experience so tragically falls short of. There is, for example, in
speech, a possible allusion to the hymn *Sonne der Gerechtigkeit:*

of righteousness, shine forth
. . . .
us to behold afar
his age thy glory's star,
, in what small strength we own,
ghtly virtue may be shown.

tural allusion is to Mal. 4:2: "But for you who fear my name, the
hteousness, shall rise, with healing in its wings."
ohut, it appears, cites the same passage from the Talmud: "He who
le the face of his companion in public [i.e., embarrasses his com-
it is as if he had spilled his blood" (Kohut 1978, 655).
Wurmser emphasizes this "area of inwardness and interior value,"
ngement of which causes "shame and often violent rage" (1981,

mplicit in Melville's assimilation of *Hamlet* is the acute perception
kespeare's tragedy touches on similar matters of paralysis caused by
shame-laden conflict. It is worth comparing Pierre's psychological
with Kohut's description of Hamlet's dilemma in Kohut 1971, 235–
1990, 173ff.
Ivan Morris's *Nobility of Failure: Tragic Heroes in the History of Japan* is
about the tendency in Japanese society to idealize heroic losers: "In
minantly conformist society, whose members are overawed by au-
and precedent, rash, defiant, emotionally honest men like Yoshitsune
amori have a particular appeal. The submissive majority, while bear-
discontents in safe silence, can find vicarious satisfaction in identify-
f emotionally with these individuals who waged their forlorn struggle

to die. He looked with eyes which saw *eve*
reasons, all his concealed disgrace and ugl
he crawled into my dirtiest corners. Tl
overpitiful one had to die. He was always
venge on such a witness—or to cease livin
also Man: this God had to die! Man does i
lives" (quoted in Wurmser 1992, 32–33).

2. As Tomkins depicts the posture: "B
his head and sometimes the whole upper
calls a halt to looking at another person, par
and to the other person's looking at him, par

3. In a recent study, Hershel Parker has
about almost any aspect of Billy Budd withou
Text are pretty much wasting their time, or a
their time" (1990, 100).

4. Bowen was writing over thirty years a
nature of divisions over the story has not e
difference is that, in a period of literary criticis
ideological concerns, the prosecution of Vere
chal authority has most definitely gained the

5. Unlike the biblical story, of course, tl
tragic, not comic. *Billy Budd* also bears com
Euripides' *Iphigenia*, in which the threatened ti
biblical story, avoided by a last minute rescue.

6. Bowen's *Long Encounter*, a study of self a
work, represents a valuable contribution to ur
the development and realization of the self: "T
one's sense of self (as distinguished from mere bl
tism), the keener the awareness of one's separat
the basic hostility or indifference of the universe
will come the problem of the choice—or of the a
life-attitude, a policy or course of action, in the fol
man realizes himself and his destiny. In all of Melv
in most of his minor ones, we find ourselves loo
some sense, of the single individual against the ui
ter, understood as a problem both of perception a
the center of all of Melville's work" (1960, 3).

7. Thi
of Nelson i
letter to Pet
of idealism
and Yanne

8. Me
is part of h
we have nc
that huma
Starbuck's

Sun
. .
Hel
in t
tha
kni

The scrip
sun of rig

9. K
makes pa
panion],

10. V
the infri
62).

11.
that Sha
a severe
conflict
37 and

12.
a book
a predo
thority
and Ta
ing its
ing itse

against overwhelming odds; and the fact that all their efforts are crowned with failure lends them a pathos which characterizes the general vanity of human endeavour and makes them the most loved and evocative of heroes" (1975, xxii). This is, to some extent, a good way of describing "rash, defiant, emotionally honest" characters such as Kleist's Michael Kohlhaas and Melville's Pierre and Ahab.

Chapter Four: Motiveless Malignity

1. See Merlin Bowen's perceptive discussion of the stance of defiance, titanism, and tragic heroism in Melville in Bowen 1960, 128–97.

2. See Murray's account of the reading that went into *Moby-Dick* and *Pierre*, and particularly in terms of the titanic theme and Melville's fascination with "a cluster of embattled figures of the same substance with the indomitable Captain Ahab—Titan, Prometheus, Satan, Lear, Timon, Cain, and Manfred. . . . At the center of this circle . . . stands Byron in person, prototype of the Romantic genius, as celebrated by his biographer Thomas Moore" (1962, lxxxvi). According to Moore, "[A]mong the infallible symptoms of greatness are: an easily wounded heart, transitoriness of all joys, quick dissatisfaction with every human relationship, acute aversion to marriage, a bottomless well of grief (proof of wisdom), towering disdain of the world, interminable religious conflict" (lxxxvi).

3. It is true that the Christian name "Peter" was honored in the Gansevoort family, but the use of the French form, besides evoking a world of romantic travel and illicit experience associated in both *Pierre* and *Redburn* with the father's buried and shameful past, makes it clear that Melville intended the "stoniness" of the name to be marked. In other words, to use the psychoanalytic term, the name is overdetermined.

4. That Keats's "Fall of Hyperion" may be an intertext here is worth pondering, especially in light of the English poet's own shame-proneness, which Christopher Ricks has explored in intriguing ways. In the following description, for example, the same imagery of paralysis and petrification is at work:

> Long, long, those two were postured motionless,
> Like sculpture builded up upon the grave
> Of their own power. A long awful time

I look'd upon them; still they were the same;
The frozen God still bending to the earth,
And the sad Goddess weeping at his feet.

(ll. 382–87)

5. See the analysis of a similar psychological type in the chapter, "Narcissistic Vulnerability and Rage in Dostoevsky's *Notes from the Underground*," in Bouson 1989, 33–50.

6. See Parker 1990, 122–23 and Hayford and Sealts 1962, 165.

7. Another possible intertextual echo of *Othello* can be detected in the passage in *Billy Budd* concerning the dig in the ribs that the Red Whiskers gives Billy: "[T]he Red Whiskers in presence of the others, under pretense of showing Billy just whence a sirloin steak was cut—for the fellow had once been a butcher—insultingly gave him a dig under the ribs" (47). The passage from *Othello* is Iago's vain boast to his master regarding Brabantio: "Nine or ten times / I had thought t'have yerk'd him here under the ribs" (1.2.4–5).

8. See also Bouson's chapter, "Insect Transformation as a Narcissistic Metaphor in Kafka's *Metamorphosis*" (1989, 51–63), an illuminating reading of narcissistic rage in Kafka's "Metamorphosis."

9. See Hayford and Sealts 1962, 164–65.

10. See Henry Sussman's reading of Othello (1993, 7–26). In his words: "For all his personal repulsiveness, however, there is the 'touch of an artist' about Iago. His scheming and use of others are nothing if not artful. We cannot assess his character without according full credit to the fact that in terms of artistry and dramatic direction, Iago is Shakespeare's 'man in the text,' the character coming closest to an internal playwright and director in the play" (25). Sussman describes Iago's personality as "characterized by weak identity, a persistent bubbling jealousy and rage, callous manipulative relationships, and a joy in destructive polarization for its own sake." As he points out, with reference to Otto Kernberg's conception of narcissistic personality disorder: "Many of the traits making Iago most memorable have configured themselves around the personality disorder axis of the diagnostic manual" (23). "Iago, the real central character in Shakespeare's *Othello*, is a creature of the object-relations model of subjectivity. Always different from him'self,' always manipulating the other characters in the play to act out his own ongoing bubbling, Kernberg would say primitive rage, Iago is also

the most esthetically interesting surrogate in the play, and his schemes amount to Shakespeare's internalized dramas in the text" (188).

11. The precursor of Claggart in Melville's work is the similarly respectable Bland of *White-Jacket*. Publicly harangued by the captain to suppress the traffic of smuggled goods, he touches "his cap in obsequious homage, as he solemnly assured the Captain that he would still continue to do his best; as, indeed, he said, he had always done. He concluded with a pious ejaculation, expressive of his personal abhorrence of smuggling and drunkenness, and his fixed resolution, so help him Heaven, to spend his last wink in setting up by night, to spy out all deeds of darkness" (*WJ*, 185). The same possible sexual connotations are also hinted at here: the same word, "ejaculation," is used in association with the potentially lurid image of spying "out all deeds of darkness."

12. Wurmser makes this connection between the mask, shamelessness, hiding, and putting down others (1981, 302).

13. Henry Sussman has emphasized this particular device of shaming used by the impostors in the novel, who shame their victims for having no shame in order to extort money from them. "Thus the Methodist minister . . . assumes the characteristic pose of the operators. First he shames, then he forces the cynical customs house official into charity" (1988, 97). The "array of ploys at the operator's disposal" range "from the bluntest acts of appeal and shaming to highly intricate performances" (97).

14. See Bowen's section "In the Cave of Man" (1960, 33–39), a valuable analysis of the motifs of secret motive, the labyrinth, and a hidden self in Melville.

Chapter Five: Turning the Tables

1. As Bowen puts it: "[W]hatever the meaning Ahab finally gives to him, what is certain is that he has found in Moby Dick a bodily target for the pent-up and compounded angers of a lifetime. In one form or another, that malicious and 'inscrutable thing' that had sought him out and maimed him was already known to him. The shock of the encounter came to him not as a sudden awakening from illusion . . . but as the crowning indignity of a long course of outrage and humiliation suffered both in his own person and on behalf of man" (1960, 146–47).

2. Sussman has explored the significance of the representation of grandiosity and borderline personalities in contemporary American cinema (1993, 157–83). He offers an intriguing analysis of Jonathan Demme's *Silence of the Lambs* and mentions Scorsese's *Cape Fear* as an example of the same phenomenon.

3. It is worth comparing the ending of *Le Rouge et le Noir* with the ending of *Pierre*. In both cases the hero reads a letter denouncing him, signed by someone with whom he has had close ties in the past; in both cases the hero enters into a kind of trancelike rage, seeks out the signatory, and shoots him/her down.

4. *Random House Unabridged Dictionary*, 2d ed., s.v. "gloat."

5. See Hayford and Sealts 1962, 174–75.

6. Compare the chapters (145–47) concerning King Bello in *Mardi*, where we are offered a brilliant comic resolution to the parody-quarrel that threatens between Bello and Media. King Bello sends a dwarf as negotiator to Media, the neighboring potentate, who resents the gesture as an affront and an insult, and sends the envoy packing. Bello perceives the rejection of his negotiator as a terrible slight and threatens hostilities. Media, however, comes up with "an honorable expedient to ward off an event for which he was then unprepared. With all haste he dispatched to the hump-backed king a little dwarf of his own; who voyaging over to Dominora in a canoe, sorry and solitary as that of Bello's plenipo, in like manner, received the same insults. The effect whereof, was, to strike a balance of affronts; upon the principle, that blow given, heals one received" (466).

7. We find a similar phenomenon in Tommo's companion Toby in *Typee:* "He was a strange wayward being, moody, fitful, and melancholy—at times almost morose. He had a quick and fiery temper too, which, when thoroughly roused, transported him into a state bordering on delirium.
It is strange the power that a mind of deep passion has over feebler natures. I have seen a brawny fellow, with no lack of ordinary courage, fairly quail before this slender stripling, when in one of his curious fits" (32).

8. Contempt, in Iago, clearly reveals its affective basis in disgust. In alerting Brabantio of the elopement at the beginning of the play, Iago focuses luridly on the act of cuckoldry and copulation in the most disgusting and bestial terms: "an old black ram / Is tupping your white ewe" (*Othello* 1.1.88–89); "the devil will make a grandsire of you" (1.1.91); "You'll have your daughter covered with a Barbary horse; you'll have your nephews neigh

to you; you'll have coursers for cousins and gennets for germans" (1.1.110–13). Hazlitt rightly focuses on the lasciviousness of Iago's imagery, such as the famous image of "making the beast with two backs" (1.1.116–17). It is the deeply contemptuous (and ultimately self-contemptuous) attitude behind such disgusting images that is significant here, and Coleridge is responding precisely to this psychological element when he exclaims on the subject of Iago's "motive-hunting," with disgust himself of course, "how awful!" and "this Shakespeare has attempted—executed—without disgust, without scandal!" (1969, 190). Melville expresses his surprise at a similar lack of disgust at himself when he writes to Hawthorne, unashamedly: "I have written a wicked book, and feel as spotless as the lamb" (*Corr.*, 212).

9. Anyone who has seen Martin Scorsese's film *Good Fellas* may be reminded in reading this passage of the memorable episode in which the protagonist of the story (Henry Hill) is similarly manipulated by his rage-prone friend Tommy. The latter is entertaining the crowd at the table with a hilarious story, and as they laugh uproariously Henry admiringly comments, "You're funny Tommy." His friend suddenly turns deadly serious, acting insulted and outraged, as if he were being treated with derision. He starts demanding in the most threatening manner: "You think I'm funny, you think I'm a clown." He prolongs the threat to the very last moment, when his friend nervously starts laughing again; but though the tension is defused by the apparent return of Tommy's good humor, lurking just beneath the surface is the archaic rage just waiting to explode—of which we get an ample display in the rest of the film—while the demonstration of his power to intimidate and manipulate the group reveals his underlying contempt.

Chapter Six: Dangerous Mergers

1. We cited the passage earlier in which the same paternalistic (and in this case racist) attitude is ascribed to Delano, a man prone himself to dangerously exaggerated idealizations, as he ponders what he takes to be the solicitous Babo hanging on every word and gesture of his master: "In fact, like most men of a good, blithe heart, Captain Delano took to negroes, not philanthropically, but genially, just as other men to Newfoundland dogs" (*PT*, 84).

2. This fear is the passive mode of scopophilia. See the account of Alfred J. Siegman's analysis of fantasies concerning states of fascination at Wurmser 1981, 152.

3. In Ovid, the possibility of a suicidal plunge, though not actualized, is certainly hinted at in passing:

> Stretched on the grass, in shadow,
> He watches, all unsatisfied, that image
> Vain and illusive, and he almost drowns
> In his own watching eyes. . . .
> (*Metamorphoses* 3.439–42)

4. *Webster's 3d New International Dictionary of the English Language,* 1976 ed., s.v. "charisma."

5. For a fuller discussion, though not in psychoanalytic terms, of the implications of "madness" in Melville, see McCarthy 1990.

6. Lewis observes that shame is akin to awe and to "the feeling-state to which one is more susceptible when one has fallen in love. The 'other' is a prominent and powerful force in the experience of shame" (1971, 41).

7. Caleb Crain has argued, on the basis of many of the same passages as I have quoted here, that "In nearly every one of Melville's novels, cannibalism and homosexuality seemed to be tangled up with each other" (1994, 49), an argument that is certainly not inconsistent with the reading we are offering here. "Melville mixed the language of love between men with the language of cannibalism. . . . In his late works, the mixing is deeply pessimistic: homosexual love has become cannibalism, a love that devours and destroys. But in *Moby-Dick* there is a brief and happy quirk in the imagery. Instead of a homosexual love that is cannibalistic, there is a cannibal love that is homosexual: Queequeg" (45).

8. It is interesting that we find the same fantasy in Stendhal's fiction: that of the naive young man—Julien Sorel or Fabrice del Dongo, for example—who is adopted by powerful and admiring protectors. The father figure is split as well: the natural father hates the child, while the protectors, such as the Marquis de la Mole and Count Mosca, are in oedipal rivalry with the young aspirant. The difference is that in Stendhal the fantasy is richly and indulgently fulfilled before the pathos of the tragic conclusion.

9. As Rogin observes, "[T]he pleasure on Typee is passive and oral rather

than aggressive or genital. Tommo (as the natives call the narrator) has a swollen leg on Typee. Thanks to the leg, he is attended to physically. The swollen leg signifies the stimulation of Tommo's desire, and prevents him from satisfying it. He pays for his pleasure with his leg's incapacity. Tommo experiences Typee as neither patriarchy nor matriarchy but as child-centred paradise. But the paradise, which is also a prison, depends on his helplessness. To get pleasure, Tommo gives up power" (1983, 44).

Chapter Seven: The Evil Eye

1. Both Melville's father and mother, of course, were highly conscious of belonging to illustrious or eminent families: Major Melvill, Alan Melvill's father, played an important part in the American Revolution, though in his later days he became somewhat of a ridiculous figure and the butt of the local satirists in Boston; Maria Melvill was the proud daughter of a well-known Albany family, whose patriarch was General Peter Gansevoort, the hero of Fort Stanwix.

2. See the analysis of this use of garments as an "attention-getting device" in E. H. Miller 1975, 152–53.

3. In his discussion, in *The Hidden Dimension*, of the way that "shame prevents the other from infringing upon the private sphere of ourselves" (1978, 260), Wurmser cites Hawthorne's "words: it 'keeps the inmost Me behind its veil'" (260).

4. Christopher Ricks observes that "the link between blushing and seeing is preserved in a wrinkle of the language. To blush is 'to cast a glance' (O.E.D. vb. 2), and a blush is a glance (O.E.D. sb. 2 and 3)" (1974, 87). In making "the connection between blushing and voyeurism or scopophilia" (88) in Keats, he quotes Edmund Bergler, who claims that "traces of the original voyeur wishes themselves are included in the final symptom [of blushing]. In the first place, according to Freud, every exhibitionist identifies himself with the voyeur, and by this detour enjoys voyeur pleasure. In the second place, the erythrophobe projects his own wishes to peep upon his surroundings. As virtually all analytic observers stress, these patients have pseudoparanoid ideas of being watched and observed. Thus peeping pleasure finds surreptitious satisfaction along the projective by-path of identification with an onlooker, buttressed by the moral alibi, 'Others, not I, are

looking.' The erythrophobe makes use of others as a mirror in order to look at himself with a clear conscience" (quoted in Ricks 1974, 88).

5. According to Wurmser, the wish to fascinate is often manifested "as an enigmatic, mystifying way of talking, as if every word should have a spellbinding, charming, overwhelming, and paralysing quality" (1981, 162).

6. For a convincing analysis of this connection, see Murray (1962, lxxviii).

7. For an intriguing study of the "look" in Hawthorne, see Dolis 1993.

8. There is, of course, another Ananias in Acts (there are, as far as I can tell, three individuals by this name in this book of the Bible) who is struck down, along with his wife, for lying in the presence of the Holy Spirit, and Melville may have in fact linked the liar and the slandering conspirator. The fact that Ananias of Damascus is a leader of a malicious conspiracy against Paul, however, links him more closely with the series of figures associated with Claggart: Guy Fawkes, Titus Oakes, and Henri de Guise.

Epilogue: "That Truth Should be Silent I Had Almost Forgot"

1. There is evidence, for example, "that all of [his] publishers except the Harpers at times exercised some restraints on his free expression of religious unorthodoxies" (Branch et al. 1984, 271).

2. Melville transgressed by "freely using autobiographical material, some of it harmless enough but other elements all too horrifyingly indiscreet for his immediate family. Moreover, he was going much too far for any possible reviewers and lady readers in treating 'stirring passions' that conduced to illegitimacy and incest. He was also, apparently, not pillorying the perpetrators of such behavior but satirizing the unchristian behavior of professed Christians and expressing irreverent authorial 'opinions and religious views'" (Branch et al. 1984, 269–70).

Arwin, Newton. 1957. *Herman Melville*. New York: Viking.

Augustine, Saint. 1961. *The Confessions*. Translated by R. S. Pine-Coffin. Harmondsworth, England: Penguin.

Bacal, Howard, and Kenneth M. Newman. 1990. *Theories of Object Relatiolns: Bridges to Self Psychology*. New York: Columbia University Press.

Basch, Michael Franz. 1989. "A Comparison of Freud and Kohut: Apostasy or Synergy?" In Detrick 1989, 3–22.

Beaver, Harold. 1986. "Commentary." In *Moby-Dick, or the Whale*, by Herman Melville, 689–987. Harmondsworth, England: Penguin.

Bellis, Peter J. 1990. *No Mysteries Out of Ourselves: Identity and Textual Form in the Novels of Herman Melville*. Philadelphia: University of Pennsylvania Press.

Benedict, Ruth. 1946. *The Chrysanthemum and the Sword: Patterns of Japanese Culture*. Boston: Houghton Mifflin.

Berke, Joseph H. 1987. "Shame and Envy." In Nathanson 1987c, 318–34.

Berman, Jeffrey. 1990. *Narcissism and the Novel*. New York: New York University Press.

Bettelheim, Bruno.1977. *The Uses of Enchantment*. New York: Vintage.

Bouson, J. Brooks. 1989. *The Empathic Reader: A Study of the Narcissistic Character and the Drama of the Self*. Amherst: The University of Massachusetts Press.

Bowen, Merlin. 1960. *The Long Encounter: Self and Experience in the Writings of Herman Melville*. Chicago: The University of Chicago Press.

Branch, Watson, Hershel Parker, and Harrison Hayford, with Alma A. MacDougall. 1984. Historical Note to *The Confidence-Man*, by Herman Melville, 255–357. Evanston, Ill.: Northwestern University Press; Chicago: The Newberry Library.

Brodhead, Richard H., ed. 1986. *New Essays on Moby-Dick or, The Whale*. Cambridge: Cambridge University Press.

Browne, Thomas. 1977. *The Major Works*. Edited by C. A. Patrides. Harmondsworth, England: Penguin.

Buell, Lawrence. 1986. "Moby-Dick as Sacred Text." In Brodhead 1986, 53–72.

Burton, Robert. 1977. *The Anatomy of Melancholy*. Edited by Holbrook Jackson. New York: Vintage.

Cameron, Sharon. 1991. *The Corporeal Self: Allegories of the Body in Melville and Hawthorne*. New York: Columbia University Press. Originally published in 1981.

Chase, Richard. 1949. *Herman Melville: A Critical Study*. New York: Macmillan.

Cohen, Hennig, and Donald Yannella. 1992. *Herman Melville's Malcolm Letter: "Man's Final Lore."* New York: Fordham University Press and The New York Public Library.

Coleridge, Samuel Taylor. 1969. *Coleridge on Shakespeare*. Edited by Terence Hawkes. Harmondsworth, England: Penguin.

Cowan, Bainard. 1982. *Exiled Waters: Moby-Dick and the Crisis of Allegory*. Baton Rouge: Louisiana State University Press.

Cowan, Walker. 1987. *Melville's Marginalia*. 2 vols. New York: Garland.

Crain, Caleb. 1994. "Lovers of Human Flesh: Homosexuality and Cannibalism in Melville's Novels." *American Literature* 66:25–53.

Darwin, Charles. 1901. *The Expression of the Emotions in Man and Animals*. London: John Murray.

Detrick, W. Douglas, and Susan P. Detrick. 1989. *Self-Psychology: Comparison and Contrasts*. Hillsdale, N.J.: The Analytic Press.

Doi, Takeo. 1973. *Anatomy of Dependence*. Tokyo: Kodansha.

Dolis, John. 1993. *The Style of Hawthorne's Gaze: Regarding Subjectivity*. Tuscaloosa: The University of Alabama Press.

Dostoevsky, Fyodor. 1989. *Crime and Punishment*. Translated by Jessie Coulson. Oxford: Oxford University Press.

Durand, Régis. 1981. "'The Captive King': The Absent Father in Melville's Text." In *The Fictional Father: Lacanian Readings of the Text*, edited by Robert Con. Davis. Amherst: The University of Massachusetts Press.

Emerson, Ralph Waldo. 1957. *Selections from Ralph Waldo Emerson*. Edited by Stephen E. Wicher. Cambridge, Mass: Riverside.

Erikson, Erik H. 1958. *Young Man Luther: A Study in Psychoanalysis and History*. New York: Norton.

———. 1968. *Identity: Youth and Crisis*. New York: Norton.

Fenichel, Otto. 1945. *The Psychoanalytic Theory of Neurosis*. New York: Norton.

Foster, Elizabeth S. 1970. Historical Note to *Mardi (and A Voyage Thither)*, by Herman Melville, 657–81. Evanston, Ill.: Northwestern University Press; Chicago: The Newberry Library.

Freud, Sigmund. 1955. *Group Psychology and the Analysis of the Ego*. In *The Standard Edition of the Complete Psychological Works*. Vol. 18. London: The Hogarth Press.

Frye, Northrop. 1957. *Anatomy of Criticism*. Princeton: Princeton University Press.

————. 1981. *The Great Code: The Bible and Literature*. Toronto: Academic Press.

————. 1993. *The Eternal Act of Creation: Essays, 1979–1990*. Edited by Robert D. Denham. Bloomington: Indiana University Press.

Grunberger, Béla. 1979. *Narcissism: Psychoanalytic Essays*. Translated by Joyce S. Diamanti. New York: International Universities Press.

Hawthorne, Nathaniel. 1962. *The Scarlet Letter*. Columbus: Ohio State University Press.

————. 1965. *The House of the Seven Gables*. Columbus: Ohio State University Press.

Hayford, Harrison, and Merton M. Sealts Jr. 1962. Notes and Commentary to *Billy Budd, Sailor (An Inside Narrative)*, by Herman Melville. Chicago: University of Chicago Press.

Hayford, Harrison, Hershel Parker, and G. Thomas Tanselle. 1982. Historical Note to *Israel Potter: His Fifty Years of Exile*, by Herman Melville, 173–235. Evanston, Ill.: Northwestern University Press; Chicago: The Newberry Library.

Hazlitt, William. 1948. *Liber Amoris* and *Dramatic Criticism*. London: Peter Nevill.

Hirsch, Gordon. 1992. "Shame, Pride and Prejudice: Jane Austen's Psychological Sophistication." *Mosaic* 25, no. 1:63–78.

Hobbes, Thomas. 1937. *Leviathan*. London: J. M. Dent.

Kafka, Franz. 1984. *The Trial*. Translated by Willa Muir and Edwin Muir. New York: Schocken.

Keats, John. 1978. *The Poems of John Keats*. Edited by Jack Stillinger. Cambridge: Belknap Press of Harvard University Press.

Kelly, Wyn. 1983. "Melville's Cain." *American Literature* 55:24–40.

Kierkegaard, Søren. 1973. *The Concept of Dread*. Translated by Walter Lowrie. Princeton: Princeton University Press.

Kohut, Heinz. 1971. *The Analysis of the Self: A Systematic Approach to the Psychoanalytic Treatment of Narcissistic Personality Disorders*. Madison, Conn: International Universities Press.

———. 1977. *The Restoration of the Self*. New York: International Universities Press.

———. 1978. *The Search for the Self*. Vol. 2. Madison, Conn: International Universities Press.

———. 1990. *The Search for the Self*. Vol. 3. Madison, Conn: International Universities Press, 1990.

Lacan, Jacques. 1977. *Ecrits: A Selection*. Translated by Alan Sheridan. New York: Norton.

———. 1978. *The Four Fundamental Concepts of Psycho-Analysis*. Edited by Jacques-Alain Miller. Translated by Alan Sheridan. New York: Norton.

Layton, Lynne, and Barbara Ann Schapiro, eds. 1986. *Narcissism and the Text: Studies in Literature and the Psychology of Self*. New York: New York University Press.

Lebowitz, Alan. 1970. *Progress into Silence: A Study of Melville's Heroes*. Bloomington: Indiana University Press.

Lesser, Simon. 1957. *Fiction and the Unconscious*. Boston: Beacon Press.

Lewis, Helen Block. 1971. *Shame and Guilt in Neurosis*. New York: International Universities Press.

———. 1987a. "The Role of Shame in Depression Over the Life Span." In Lewis 1987c: 29–50.

——— 1987b. "Shame and the Narcissistic Personality." In Nathanson 1987c, 93–132.

———, ed. 1987c. *The Role of Shame in Symptom Formation*. Hillsdale, N.J.: Lawrence Erlbaum.

Lynd, Helen Merrell. 1958. *On Shame and the Search for Identity*. New York: Harcourt Brace.

Martin, Robert K. 1986. *Hero, Captain, and Stranger. Male Friendship, Social Critique, and Literary Form in the Sea Novels of Herman Melville*. Chapel Hill and London: The University of North Carolina Press.

Marvell, Andrew. 1967. *Selected Poetry*. Edited by Frank Kermode. New York: Signet.

Mason, Marilyn J. 1993. "Shame: Reservoir for Family Secrets." In *Secrets in Families and Family Therapy*, edited by Evan Imber-Black, 29–43. New York: Norton.

McCarthy, Paul. 1990. *"The Twisted Mind": Madness in Herman Melville's Fiction*. Iowa City: University of Iowa Press.

Melville, Herman. 1962. *Billy Budd, Sailor (An Inside Narrative)*. Edited by Harrison Hayford and Merton M. Sealts Jr. Chicago: University of Chicago Press.

———. 1991. *Clarel: A Poem and Pilgrimage in the Holy Land*. Evanston, Ill.: Northwestern University Press; Chicago: The Newberry Library.

———. 1984. *The Confidence-Man: His Masquerade*. Evanston, Ill.: Northwestern University Press; Chicago: The Newberry Library.

———. 1993. *Correspondence*. Edited by Lynn Horth. Evanston, Ill.: Northwestern University Press; Chicago: The Newberry Library.

———. 1982. *Israel Potter: His Fifty Years of Exile*. Evanston, Ill.: Northwestern University Press; Chicago: The Newberry Library.

———. 1970. *Mardi (and A Voyage Thither)*. Evanston, Ill.: Northwestern University Press; Chicago: The Newberry Library.

———. 1988. *Moby-Dick, or the Whale*. Evanston, Ill.: Northwestern University Press; Chicago: The Newberry Library.

———. 1987. *The Piazza Tales (and Other Prose Pieces), 1839–1860*. Evanston, Ill.: Northwestern University Press; Chicago: The Newberry Library.

———. 1971. *Pierre, or the Ambiguities*. Evanston, Ill.: Northwestern University Press; Chicago: The Newberry Library.

———. 1963. *Poems*. New York: Russell & Russell.

———. 1969. *Redburn: His First Voyage*. Evanston, Ill.: Northwestern University Press; Chicago: The Newberry Library.

———. 1968. *Typee*. Evanston, Ill.: Northwestern University Press; Chicago: The Newberry Library.

———. 1970. *White-Jacket (or The World in a Man-of-War)*. Evanston, Ill.: Northwestern University Press; Chicago: The Newberry Library.

Metcalf, Paul, ed. 1991. *Enter Isabel: The Herman Melville Correspondence of Clare Spark and Paul Metcalf*. Albuquerque: University of New Mexico Press.

Miller, Alice. 1981. *The Drama of the Gifted Child*. Translated by Ruth Ward. New York: Basic Books, 1981.

———. 1986. *Thou Shalt Not Be Aware: Society's Betrayal of the Child*. Translated by Hildegarde and Hunter Hannum. New York: Meridian.

———. 1990. *The Untouched Key: Tracing Childhood Trauma in Creativity and Destructiveness*. Translated by Hildegarde and Hunter Hannum. New York: Doubleday.

Miller, Edwin Haviland. 1975. *Melville*. New York: George Braziller.

Milton, John. 1957. *Complete Poems and Major Prose*. Indianapolis, Ind.: Odyssey.

Morris, Ivan. 1975. *The Nobility of Failure: Tragic Heroes in the History of Japan*. London: Secker & Warburg.

Morrison, Andrew. 1989. *Shame: The Underside of Narcissism*. Hillsdale, N.J.: The Analytic Press.

Moss, Sidney. "Hawthorne and Melville: An Inquiry into Their Art and the Mystery of Their Friendship." In Wilson 1991, 150–91.

Murray, Henry. 1962. Introduction to *Pierre or, The Ambiguities*, by Herman Melville, xii–ciii. New York: Hendricks House.

Mushabac, Jane. 1981. *Melville's Humor: A Critical Study*. Hamden, Conn: Archon.

Nathanson, Donald L. 1987a. "Shame/Pride Axis." In Lewis 1987c, 183–205.

———. 1987b. "A Timetable for Shame." In Nathanson 1987c, 1–63.

———. 1992. *Shame and Pride: Affect, Sex, and the Birth of the Self*. New York: Norton.

———, ed. 1987c. *The Many Faces of Shame*. New York: The Guilford Press.

The New Oxford Annotated Bible. 1973. Revised Standard Version. Edited by Herbert G. May and Bruce M. Metzger. New York: Oxford University Press.

Olson, Charles. 1947. *Call me Ishmael*. New York: Reynal & Hitchcock.

Ovid. *Metamorphoses*. 1955. Translated by Rolfe Humphries. Bloomington: Indiana University Press.

Parker, Hershel. 1990. *Reading Billy Budd*. Evanston, Ill: Northwestern University Press.

Piers, Gerhardt, and Milton B. Singer. 1971. *Shame and Guilt: A Psychoanalytic and a Cultural Study.* New York: Norton.

Plato. *The Last Days of Socrates.* 1969. Translated by Hugh Tredennick. Harmondsworth, England: Penguin.

Porter, Carolyn. 1986. "Call Me Ishmael, or How to Make Double-Talk Speak." In Brodhead 1986, 73–108.

Rabelais, François. 1970. *Five Books of the Lives, Heroic Deeds and Sayings of Gargantua and his son Pantagruel.* Translated by Sir Thomas Urquhart of Cromarty and Peter Antony Motteux. London: The Fraser Press.

Renker, Elizabeth. 1994. "Herman Melville, Wife Beating, and the Written Page." *American Literature* 66:123–50.

Retzinger, Suzanne R. 1987. "Resentment and Laughter: Video Studies of the Shame-Rage Spiral." In Lewis 1987c, 151–81.

Ricks, Christopher. 1974. *Keats and Embarrassment.* London: Oxford University Press.

Riviere, Joan. 1964. "Hate, Greed and Aggression." In *Love, Hate and Reparation,* edited by Melanie Klein and Joan Riviere, 3–53. New York: Norton.

Rogin, Michael Paul. 1983. *Subversive Genealogy: The Politics and Art of Herman Melville.* New York: Knopf.

Rosenberry, Edward. 1969. *Melville and the Comic Spirit.* New York: Farrar. Originally published in 1955.

Sartre, Jean-Paul. 1956. *Being and Nothingness: An Essay in Phenomenological Ontology.* Translated by Hazel Barnes. Secaucus, N.J.: The Citadel Press.

Schapiro, Barbara A. 1983. *The Romantic Mother: Narcissistic Patterns in Romantic Poetry.* Baltimore: The Johns Hopkins University Press.

Scheff, Thomas J. 1987. "The Shame-Rage Spiral: A Case Study of an Interminable Quarrel." In Lewis 1987c, 109–49.

Scheler, Max. 1961. *Ressentiment.* New York: Free Press of Glencoe.

Schiffer, Irvine. 1973. *Charisma: A Psychoanalytic Look at Mass Society.* Toronto: University of Toronto Press.

Schneider, Carl D. 1977. *Shame, Exposure and Privacy.* Boston: Beacon.

Schwartz-Salant, Nathan. 1982. *Narcissism and Character Transformation: The Psychology of Character Disorders.* Toronto: Inner City Books.

Sedgwick, Eve Kosofsky, and Adam Frank, eds. *Shame and its Sisters: A Silvan Tomkins Reader.* Durham, N.C., and London: Duke University Press, 1995.

Shakespeare, William. 1947a.*The Tragedy of Hamlet, Prince of Denmark*. Edited by Tucker Brooke and Lawrence Mason. New Haven: Yale University Press.

———. 1947b. *The Tragedy of Othello, The Moor of Venice*. Edited by Tucker Brooke and Lawrence Mason. New Haven: Yale University Press.

Slotkin, Richard. 1973. *Regeneration Through Violence: The Mythology of the American Frontier, 1600–1860*. Middletown, Conn: Wesleyan University Press.

Sophocles. 1982. *The Three Theban Plays: Antigone, Oedipus the King, Oedipus at Colonus*. Translated by Robert Fagles. New York: Viking.

Spenser, Edmund. 1968. *Edmund Spenser's Poetry*. Edited by Hugh Maclean. New York: Norton.

Sussman, Henry. 1988. *High Resolution*. Baltimore: Johns Hopkins University Press.

———. 1993. *Psyche and Text: The Sublime and the Grandiose in Literature, Psychopathology, and Culture*. Albany: State University of New York Press.

Thompson, Lawrance. 1952. *Melville's Quarrel with God*. Princeton: Princeton University Press.

Tolchin, Neal L. 1988. *Mourning, Gender, and Creativity in the Art of Herman Melville*. New Haven: Yale University Press.

Tomkins, Silvan. 1962. *Affect, Imagery, Consciousness*. Vol. 1, *The Positive Affects*. London: Springer, 1962.

———. 1963. *Affect, Imagery, Consciousness*. Vol. 2, *The Negative Affects*. London: Springer, 1963.

———. 1987. "Shame." In Nathanson 1987c, 133–61.

Tripp, Edward. 1970. *The Meridian Handbook of Classical Mythology*. New York: Meridian.

Watson, Charles N., Jr. 1988. "Melville and the Theme of Timonism: From *Pierre* to *The Confidence-Man*." Reprinted in *On Melville: The Best from American Literature*, edited by Louis J. Budd and Edwin H. Cady. Durham, N.C., and London: Duke University Press. Originally published in 1972.

Wilson, James C., ed. 1991. *The Hawthorne and Melville Friendship: An Annotated Bibliography, Biographical and Critical Essays, and Correspondence between the Two*. Jefferson, N.C.: McFarland.

Winnicott, D. W. 1974. *Playing and Reality*. Harmondsworth, England: Penguin.

Wurmser, Léon. 1978. *The Hidden Dimension: Psychodynamics in Compulsive Drug Use*. New York: Jason Aronson, 1978.

———. 1981. *The Mask of Shame*. Baltimore: Johns Hopkins University Press, 1981.

———. 1987. "Shame: The Veiled Companion of Narcissism." In Nathanson 1987c, 64–92.

———. 1989. *Die Zerbrochene Wirklichkeit: Psychoanalyse als das Studium von Konflikt und Komplementarität*. Berlin: Springer-Verlag.

———. 1992. "'Man of the most dangerous curiosity'—Nietzsche's 'Fruitful and Frightful Vision' and his War against Shame." Unpublished paper.

———. 1995. "'Correct comprehension and misunderstanding of the same don't exclude each other': Comments on Kafka's 'Trial.'" Unpublished paper.

Young, Philip. 1993. *The Private Melville*. University Park: The Pennsylvania State University Press.